Accounting and Finance
——a firm foundation

ALAN PIZZEY
Principal Lecturer in Accounting, Trent Polytechnic

Holt, Rinehart and Winston

London · New York · Sydney · Toronto

Holt, Rinehart and Winston Ltd: 1 St Anne's Road,
Eastbourne, East Sussex BN21 3UN

Typeset in India by The Macmillan Company of India Ltd, Bangalore 1

Printed in Great Britain by Cambridge University Press

ISBN 0–03–910275–0

Last digit is print number: 9 8 7 6 5 4 3 2 1

Contents

Preface

The purpose of this book is to help students who are commencing their studies in accounting, by ensuring that the basic techniques are mastered and principal ideas understood at an early stage. Once a firm foundation is laid the young accountant can proceed to more complex matters without the disadvantage of misconceptions which might hamper his or her progress.

The book sets out to introduce the techniques of financial accounting, to discover why one method is preferred to others, and to demonstrate how to use the accounting statements which are produced. A discussion of the elements of finance follows naturally from chapters which consider the work of the financial accountant, and also acts as a prelude to the interpretation of accounting statements. In a practical subject such as accounting, the techniques are important for the student, but they must not be allowed to dominate a course or a book to the exclusion of other matters. Concepts are important to underpin the choice of technique, and to provide a basis of comprehension on which the interpretation and use of accounting statements can rest. In this book I have attempted to blend theory with practice by mixing methodology with explanation, in the hope that students will not only learn how to account, but also develop an ability to discuss their work. To this end the text includes comment of a theoretical nature alongside explanation of accounting methods. Most chapters have suggestions for discussion topics, as well as accounting exercises (with solutions) which will provide practice in applying techniques. A workbook is to be published to accompany this volume which will provide the student with further opportunities to practice the techniques discussed here.

This book has developed from the first year undergraduate course taught at Trent Polytechnic, and represents the lecture notes, seminar problems and tutorial discussion topics built up by a team of accounting teachers over the last seven years.

I am indebted to my colleagues for their helpful suggestions, and to past students whose requirements have encouraged me in the preparation of this work. In my view tutorial discussion is an important element in an accounting course, enabling students to marshal their ideas, present them in logical form in discussion, develop the ability to make constructive criticism and use judgement to decide the relative strengths of conflicting views. Resources are scarce, however, and it is not always possible to teach in small groups where a meaningful discussion can take place. However, teachers can still inject an element of critical appraisal into a course by including some discussions in the accounting exercises. For this reason many of the exercises in the book contain discussion questions. Solutions are provided to enable students to check the mechanics of their answers, but in general suggested answers to discussion questions have not been provided, in order to encourage students to think out their own solutions.

At the present time accounting must be seen against a background of unstable economic conditions, which have promoted much discussion and not a few changes to the subject. This atmosphere of argument and development, although stimulating to the academic, is bewildering to students just starting their accounting career. I have therefore tried to explain some of the current discussions in as simple a way as possible in the hope that students will begin to appreciate the efforts made by our profession to solve the problems with which it is faced. For this reason Accounting Standards are mentioned where they fit into the text, but this is considered too early a stage for a detailed study of the standards. Ideally we need to train young people to enter the accounting profession with open minds, a capacity for independent thought and the ability to test doctrinaire views before accepting them.

One difficulty encountered in the production of an introductory textbook on accounting is that the student has little or no practical experience of the subject, and therefore terms have to be explained as they are introduced. I have tried in this book to set the subject in context with other disciplines such as law and economics, and on the practical side to introduce the systems which are necessary to provide the basic data which the accountant uses. No doubt some introductory accounting courses will include matters which I have omitted, while some teachers may not consider all the items I have covered as appropriate for their courses. Although auditing and taxation are separate subjects, in my view they need to be introduced at this early stage to familiarize students with them and to demonstrate how they stem from the more general work of the financial accountant.

The workbook which accompanies this text is designed to reinforce and extend the coverage of accounting techniques for students who need the practice, and for those whose course is aimed at a syllabus which contains a greater proportion of practical work.

I would like to thank B. D. Coleman, D. Hewitt and Ian A. Wright, whose comments were very useful. Also sincere thanks to Tom Perlmutter, whose encouragement and advice have proved most helpful.

ALAN PIZZEY

To Barbara, Jonathan and Joscelin

WITHOUT WHOSE FORBEARANCE AND ENCOURAGEMENT
THIS BOOK WOULD NEVER HAVE BEEN COMPLETED

'*Complacency is the enemy of study.*'

MAO TSE TUNG.

'*They should have . . . a supercilious knowledge of accounts.*'

MRS MALAPROP.

'*Receive before thou wryte, and wryte before thou paye;*
Thus wilst thou well assured be, thy counte will never decay.'

FROM THE TOMB OF AN OLD BURGHER IN CHESTER
CATHEDRAL.

PART
ONE

Basic Principles and Techniques

1 | Accounting: The Provision of Financial Information and Its Use

THE WORK OF THE ACCOUNTANT

The work of the accountant is diverse in its nature, but basically it deals with the recording, planning and control of financial transactions, whether income or expenditure. In every organization money will be spent on administration, and thus there will be a need for an accountant. Broadly speaking, accountants can be divided into two classes: those in professional practice and executive accountants who work for organizations.

Accountants in practice have a number of clients for whom they provide a service. This service takes the form of auditing, accounting, taxation work, and general financial advice. Auditing involves checking that the accounts of a business, which have been prepared by accountants within the business, show a true and fair view. The auditor must ensure that the accounts have been properly drawn up, that legal requirements concerning limited companies have been complied with, that no fraud has taken place, and that the system of accounting operated by the business is such that fraud is discouraged. A second task often undertaken by the accountant in practice is to prepare a taxation computation to translate the accounting profit into a taxable profit by applying the rules embodied in the tax laws. Some companies are large enough to employ a permanent tax specialist, but in most cases the practising accountant with special taxation expertise will undertake this work. The practitioner may find himself involved with tax planning, advising his clients, both companies and individuals, on how best to reduce the burden of taxation. He might also act as a liquidator when a company ceases trading and is wound up. Incomplete records work is important in practice, since it involves producing accounts for small firms where proper books of account have not been maintained and the basic records may be difficult to assemble.

The type of work done by executive accountants who work for a company or some other organization, e.g. local authority, hospital board or a charity, can be further subdivided. First, there are financial accountants, whose main job is to record transactions. They are responsible for maintaining accurate records of what their company owns (its assets), and what it owes (its liabilities). They are concerned with the system of book-keeping used to record sales and purchases, the payment and receipt of cash, and keeping an accurate account of stocks, debts, and fixed or long-term assets of the company. Financial accountants act as stewards, showing the financial effect of the actions of the owners and managers of the business. One way this effect is revealed is through accounting statements such as the balance sheet and the profit and loss account.

The financial accountant produces the accounts which are later checked by the auditor. Other duties of a financial accountant may be company secretarial work dealing with insurance, pension funds, share transfers and statutory meetings, or the general management of office procedures, business systems and mechanized or electronic methods of recording transactions. Some companies have an internal audit section which liaises with the external auditors, checks systems and protects the assets of the business.

The second type of executive accountant is the management accountant, whose job it is to use his expertise in any way he can to help the management of the company in the administration of the organization and the formulation of decisions. He does this by preparing financial reports and statements which give information about the subject of a decision or show up what has happened in the recent past. In this way managers are better able to plan the future operations of the business and allocate scarce resources between alternatives, and are made more aware of the financial effect of transactions which have taken place so that they can act quickly to control a situation where, for example, losses are being incurred. Cost analysis and budgetary control are important tools for the management accountant.

THE HISTORICAL DEVELOPMENT OF ACCOUNTING

Merchants and others have kept records of their transactions from very early times. However, it was not until an Italian monk, Luca Pacioli, wrote a book in 1494 that the system of accounting which had evolved among the merchants of Italy was formulated. Pacioli's description of the 'Italian method' is a simple one, and probably more sophisticated systems than that outlined by Pacioli existed in larger firms of merchants and manufacturers of the time. The rudiments of double entry book-keeping had developed, as had the practice of showing a position statement for the business rather than for the individuals who owned it and the practice of accounting at regular intervals so that the profits could be computed and divided among the owners of the business. The idea of accounting once a year had not yet been adopted, since in those days businessmen tended to account for each venture as an entity, irrespective of how long it took to complete.

After Pacioli came a steady development of accounting, with the emergence of a need to account in a common monetary unit and for a set period of time, and to enable the credit-worthiness of a firm to be established. Estate owners, merchant bankers and manufacturers began to operate standardized systems to reduce fraud within their large enterprises. In 1605 a Dutchman, Simon Stevin, advocated that the profit and loss account should be produced at yearly intervals, and by 1655 Jaques Savary was suggesting that the balance sheet should be drawn up at certain stated intervals. In 1673 the Code of Commerce produced in France recommended that all businesses produce a balance sheet at least every two years.

The industrial revolution increased the scale of businesses and the intricacy of their transactions. The organization of finance on a large scale, the separation of loan and venture capital, the principle of limited liability, and the emergence of joint stock banks created a demand for more sophisticated methods of accounting.

The emergence of a profession of accountants with a code of ethics and standards of performance was followed by the formation of professional accounting bodies. In 1854 a Royal Charter was granted to a society of accountants in Scotland, in 1880 the Institute of Chartered Accountants in England and Wales was formed and in 1887 the Association of Public Accountants was launched in the USA.

Even at this time, however, the accounts kept by many businesses consisted of little more than the recording of cash movements in and out. Dividends were often paid before the existence of a profit had been established, and fixed assets were bought and used without providing for depreciation. As the scale of industrialization increased, however, there was a gradual divorce of management and ownership, and it became obvious that management needed accounting information of a different type from that required by shareholders and lenders. The accounting profession therefore enlarged its scope to cater for this need, and over the last forty years the provision of information to management has become the most important function of the accountant, who has in fact become a member of the management team.

THE PROFESSIONAL ACCOUNTING BODIES IN GREAT BRITAIN AND IRELAND

At present there are in the UK and Ireland six separate organizations for accountants, each of which gives a professional qualification with its own designatory letters. The first three are the Institutes of Chartered Accountants in England and Wales, Scotland and Ireland. These are quite separate from one another, each one having its own membership, rules, governing council, examination syllabus, and student members. The one rule which unites them is that all student members must serve a fixed period under a training contract with a member of the Institute, so that they gain the appropriate experience before they qualify. Chartered accountants dominate the practising side of accounting, although many who have qualified and have gained experience with a practising accountant then leave the practice to work in industry and commerce.

The fourth body of accountants is the Association of Certified Accountants, whose members are found mainly in industry and commerce, although there are a significant number in practice. Members of the Association, as well as members of the Institutes, are recognized by the Department of Trade and can act as auditors to public companies. The students of the Association must undergo a period of training to gain experience before they qualify, but this period may be spent either as a clerk to a practising accountant or in an accounting office in industry, nationalized industry or local authority.

The fifth body of accountants is the Institute of Cost and Management Accountants. As the name implies, the members of this body are found almost exclusively in industry, and students of this Institute must gain their experience, prior to qualifying, by working in an accounting office within industry.

The sixth and last body of accountants is the Chartered Institute of Public Finance Accountancy. Members of this body work for local authorities and Government agencies, and it is in this type of organization that the student members of this Institute gain their experience.

THE PURPOSE OF ACCOUNTING

Accounting has four main purposes. First, an accountant is needed to identify, measure and record transactions. These records show the relationship of the organization with other bodies, e.g. what is owed to and by the business. Such information summarizes for managers the transactions they have initiated and gives an element of control.

Second, accounting acts as a language for business, since the commercial world communicates in accounting terms, e.g. what should be paid to a supplier or by a customer, the price for a product or a service, or the value of an asset.

Third, the accountant acts as a steward, using his records to report to the owners of the company, i.e. the shareholders, on transactions made during a period and the effect these transactions have had on their investment. For this purpose the balance sheet, which analyses the position of the business, and the profit and loss account, which measures the success or failure of its operations, are both important statements.

Fourth, the accountant helps management to operate the business. His figures are important in planning future operations via the budget, in making decisions between alternatives, in allocating scarce resources, and in controlling the business by reporting on events soon after they have taken place and comparing them with the budget or plan.

We can now see that the task of the accountant is to look back at the past, to record, analyse and report as a steward, and also to look into the future and assist management with decision-making and control. Both aspects of this task require figures to be assembled in statements that are easily assimilated, interpreted and used in the evaluation of performance by both accountants and non-accountants.

THE MAIN FINANCIAL STATEMENTS

A significant part of the task of an accountant is to explain and interpret the figures which have been produced to those who are going to use them. There are four main financial statements commonly used by accountants to produce an extract from the figures in the books so that others may use this information for their own purposes.

The more important two are the balance sheet and the profit and loss account. The balance sheet shows the position of the business at a particular moment in time and sets the assets of the business against the liabilities or sources from which funds have been raised to finance those assets. The profit and loss account is a summary of transactions for a stated period, e.g. a year. This sets the costs of the period against the revenue from the period, thus showing the profit or loss made during that period. These are the two most important accounting statements, but there are two others which are widely used.

The funds flow statement attempts to analyse the sources from which funds have been raised and the ways in which those funds have been spent during a period between two balance sheet dates. It is now considered as part of the published financial statements of a company, since under Standard Accounting Practice 10, a funds flow statement must be appended to the published balance sheet and profit and loss account.

Another statement is the budget of a business, which sets out, in detailed financial terms, a plan for the future operations of that business. All aspects of the business are covered by the budget, e.g. sales, purchases, expenses, so that it is possible to forecast what the balance sheet and the profit and loss account might be at a future stated date.

THE USERS OF ACCOUNTING INFORMATION

Many different types of people use accounting information, each type requiring slightly different information from the basic financial data produced by the accountant. The accountant must therefore design his reports in such a way that the appropriate information is visible and understandable.

Management are the most important users of accounting information. An analysis of revenues and expenses will provide information which is useful when plans are formulated and decisions made. Once the budget for a business is complete, the accountant can produce figures for what actually happens as the budget period unfolds, so that they can be compared with the budget to measure achievement. Management will need to know, in great detail and soon after the event, the cost consequences of a particular course of action, so that steps can be taken to control the situation if things go wrong. Speed and the ability to communicate and interpret are needed here.

Shareholders and Potential Shareholders are another important group of users of accounting information. This group includes the investing public at large and the stockbrokers and commentators who advise them. The shareholders should be informed of the manner in which management has used their funds which have been invested in the business. They are interested in the profitability and safety of their investment, which helps them to appraise the efficiency of the management. This is simply a matter of reporting on past events. However, both shareholders and potential shareholders are also interested in the future performance of the business, and use past figures as a guide to the future if they have to vote on proposals or decide whether to disinvest. Financial analysts advising investors such as insurance companies, pension funds, unit trusts and investment trusts are among the most sophisticated users of accounting information, and the company contemplating a takeover bid is yet another type of potential shareholder. The accountant has an obligation to all those in this category to provide information on which they can depend when making their decisions, but the fact that some members of the group are more financially sophisticated than others causes difficulties, since the volume of information required by the financial analyst may confuse the ordinary shareholder.

Employees and their Trade Union Representatives also use accounting information to assess the potential of the business. This information is relevant to the employee, who wishes to discover whether the company can offer him safe employment and promotion through growth over a period of years, and to the trade unionist, who uses past profits and potential profits in his calculations and claims for higher wages or better conditions. The viability of different divisions of a company are of interest to this group.

Those who have lent Money to the Business. This group includes some who have financed the business over a long period, by lending money which is to be repaid at the end of a number of years, as well as short-term creditors such as a bank which allows a company to overdraw its bank account for a number of months, and suppliers of raw materials, who permit a company to buy goods from them and pay in, say, six to twelve weeks' time. Lenders are interested in the security of their loan, so they will look at an accounting statement to ensure that the company will be able to repay on the due date or meet the interest requirements before that date. The amount of cash available and the value of assets which form a security for the debt are of importance to this group. Credit rating agencies are interested in accounts for similar reasons.

Government Agencies also use accounting information, either when collecting statistical information to reveal trends within the economy as a whole, or, in the case of the Inland Revenue, to assess the profit on which the company's tax liability is to be computed.

Customers of a business may use accounting data to assess the viability of a company if a long-term contract is soon to be placed. Competitors will also use the accounts for purposes of comparison.

TUTORIAL DISCUSSION TOPICS

1.1. Define accounting, with reference to the various operations undertaken by accountants.

1.2. Classify the users of accounting information. Discuss their different requirements.

1.3. What kind of information, other than that based on past events, can accountants provide?

1.4. Name the four major accounting statements and discuss the purpose of each one.

1.5. It is said that accounting is the language of business. Why does accounting occupy this important position and what problems limit its usefulness as the language of business?

2 | The Theoretical Framework of Accounting

If asked to point out one major weakness in the knowledge of accounting students many teachers of the subject would say that students do not understand the framework of ideas which surrounds the practice of accounting and which is basic to its proper appreciation. The principles which concern us are the rules and conventions which govern accounting. Different authorities refer to them in different ways: some use the terms 'postulate', 'concept' and 'principle', although what is a concept for one is sometimes a principle for another. Some authorities hold that postulates are assumptions on which the principles of accounting are based, that concepts are ideas basic to a proper understanding of accounting, and that principles are rules which govern existing practice and underlie the preparation of accounting statements, the valuation of assets and the measurement of income. Students should ignore these academic differences in terminology at this stage, and make sure they understand the basis of their subject. The classifications in this chapter are simply an attempt to summarize.

These rules are general and have been adopted as a guide or basis of conduct by those practising accounting. Detailed practice must of course be tailored to fit the circumstances or company concerned, but should be within these basic guidelines. It is necessary to know the basis used in order to find the precise meaning of figures in an accounting report. For example, when an accountant says that stocks of material are valued at cost, does he mean cost when they were bought, or what it would cost to replace them at the balance sheet date, or some other measure of their cost?

It is important to realize that the principles of accounting are man-made and have evolved as the best way to solve problems which arise in accounting, and have been adopted by general consent because they work. As time passes and conditions change, however, a principle which was previously accepted may be criticized because it no longer functions usefully, and may eventually be dropped. For example, fixed assets are shown in the balance sheet at historic cost, but some accountants are criticizing this practice because it seems to them that it does not work well during a period of inflation.

POSTULATES

Monetary Measurement

Accounting statements are expressed in monetary terms, since money acts as a common denominator to express the many different facets of an organization, e.g. costs, sales, the value of stocks, machinery, debts and investments. If all the items covered by an accounting statement are stated as an amount of money, then the relative cost or value of these items can be seen and their aggregate cost or value determined. The disadvantage of monetary measurement is of course that the value of money may not remain stable, especially in a period of inflation. Not only does this hinder comparison of statements computed at different times, but it also creates difficulties when the costs of assets bought at different times are added together in the same statement. Suppose a company bought a machine two years ago for £5000, and another exactly the same last week for £8000. Would it be correct to add these two amounts together to express the two machines in a position statement? Liabilities are payable according to the law, as an agreed amount of money, so it seems correct to record them in money terms.

Accountants are now beginning to realize, however, that some elements of a business, such as morale of employees and strength of competition, cannot be measured in money terms, even though they must be classed as assets since profit derives from them. A good labour relations record in a company means that there will be little disruption of production through strikes, and thus profits will increase, but it is hard to work out exactly the profit that would have been made had labour relations in the business been less harmonious. Other assets which are difficult to quantify are 'know-how', the possession of a good management team, and goodwill. This last asset often appears in balance sheets of companies, though its existence and valuation may not be agreed upon by all accountants. Fixed assets can be quantified, but the figure shown makes no comment about their state of repair, or their suitability for the tasks which they undertake.

Going Concern

Unless there is evidence to the contrary, it is assumed when accounting statements are compiled that the firm which is the subject of these statements is going to continue in operation for an indefinite period. Without this postulate, year-end accounts would have to be worked out on a 'winding-up' basis, that is, on what the business is likely to be worth if sold piecemeal at the accounting date. This value is often different from its value if the present owners intend to carry on the business. Fixed assets, for example, are shown at cost less depreciation to date, rather than at their current value in the second-hand market, because they are held by the firm not for immediate resale, but to be used by the business until their working life is over. This is clearly an assumption on which the balance sheet is based, but some accountants feel that it is more a matter of common sense than something which needs to be sanctified as a postulate. Professor D. Solomons has written 'we do not need a concept to tell us that depending on whether we are accounting for a continuing concern or for one which is expected to terminate in the foreseeable future, our accounting methods should be chosen appropriately'.

Before he certifies the accounts as showing a true and fair view, the auditor must satisfy himself that the company is a going concern and that it will continue to function successfully in the future. The criteria to be used in this appraisal will depend on the circumstances, but some general rules are as follows:

a. The market: Is there a steady demand for the company's product which has a reasonable chance of being sustained in the future?
b. Finance: Does the company possess sufficient liquid (cash) resources to meet all known liabilities in the future? A profitable business may be brought to a halt if its creditors no longer give it financial support and it is unable to pay its way.
c. Sound capital structure: Are there sufficient long-term funds in the business to give enough strength to overcome inflation, high interest rates, a credit squeeze, increases in taxation or any other hazard of the business world?
d. What is the company's competitive condition? Here one must consider the efficiency of the company compared with that of its rivals, and its ability to aquire sufficient raw materials and labour and to replace worn-out plant and equipment.

Thus the profit measurement calculation is insulated from fluctuations in the value of fixed assets, and the spread of the capital cost of an asset over the years of its useful life, by depreciation, is supported by this postulate.

Example

Jack owns a steam roundabout which he operates at fairgrounds. The machine attracts many customers, and fares collected for the rides total £10 000 per annum. Jack would not sell his roundabout if he were to be offered £50 000 for it, but if tastes change and Jack's customers prefer a newly invented ride, his takings will fall and he will not be able to sell the machine at all, since its potential has evaporated. It will no longer be a going concern and must be accounted for at the price obtainable if sold to a museum or for scrap.

This example shows that the value of an asset is dependent on its ability to earn a profit, but cost rather than value is recorded by the accountant, since the figure for cost is an objectively determined amount. Jack can show his roundabout in the accounts at cost less depreciation to date so long as he intends to continue operating it, but this amount cannot be shown if the machine is no longer to be used, since it is now judged on what it can fetch on the scrap market.

Realization

This postulate is significant in the calculation of sales revenue and profit, since it determines the point at which the accountant feels that a transaction is certain enough for the profit made on it to be calculated and taken to the profit and loss account, and if necessary distributed to the shareholders. Realization is when a sale is made to a customer. The basic rule is that revenue is created at the moment a sale is made, and not when the price is later paid in cash. Profit can be taken to the profit and loss account on sales made, even although the money has not been collected. The firm has acquired a debt, and provision must be made in the profit statement for debts not likely to be collected. The sale is deemed to be made when the goods are delivered, and thus profit cannot be taken to the profit and loss account on orders received and not yet filled. Goods manufactured but not yet delivered are not deemed sold, so no element of profit can enter into the value of stocks of such goods at the accounting date. There are some exceptions to this basic rule, e.g. contract accounting, which involves payments on account before completion of the work, and these will be fully discussed in a later chapter.

Realization implies that no increase in the value of an asset can be recognized as a profit unless it is realized. Assets are recorded at the historic cost at which they were purchased (the objectively determined amount which was paid out for them) and it is considered prudent to keep them in the books at this amount even if there is reliable information that they are worth more.

In the example of Jack the showman, the steam roundabout would not be written up in the books to £50 000 in case this apparent increase in value could not be maintained. The profit element can be shown as such only if it is realized through the sale of the machine, or considered on reliable expert advice to stem from a permanent increase in the value of the asset.

CONCEPTS

The Business Entity

This concept separates the individuals behind a business from the business itself, and records transactions in the accounting statements as they affect the business, and not its various owners. In a large company this concept emphasizes the division between owners and managers. The accountant prepares reports to the shareholders on how the managers have used the funds entrusted to them by the owners. This aspect of accounting is sometimes called reporting on stewardship, as opposed to management accounting, where reports are prepared to assist management in their job of controlling the business and deciding on future courses of action.

In a small business run by partners or a sole trader, this concept avoids confusion between business transactions and those of private life. The accountant is trying to measure the profit made by an individual in his business, and thus a loss made when the family washing machine is scrapped and money is withdrawn from the bank account to replace it is not a business transaction. A man running a sweet shop will want to know what profit he is making, and that profit will be incorrect unless goods taken from the shop for his own consumption are accounted for as sales. Goods taken for the owner's use are part of the profit withdrawn by the man from his business. There must also be a reasonable apportionment of the costs incurred partly for the family and partly for business reasons, e.g. rent and rates of a shop or office with a flat for the proprietor above it.

The law does not recognize this distinction between owner and business, since if a business cannot pay its debts the creditors can take the possessions of the owner or partners to satisfy their claims. In the case of a company, however, the shareholders are the owners, and their liability for the debts of the business is limited to the extent of their investment in the business. The business entity concept ensures that the amount invested by the owners in the business is defined (capital) and allows a return on capital employed to be computed to show whether the investment is worth while. Some owners may have investments in more than one business, and in any case will be interested in the results of their business activities unencumbered by the financial details of their private lives. This concept is sometimes confused with a less important idea, that of the accounting unit, which seeks to define the area of business activity to be encompassed by a set of accounts. Often the entire business is accounted for within one set of books, but more often nowadays business operations are fragmented, and the accounting unit is found at the level of subsidiary companies, divisions, or factories, which have their own accounting systems.

Objectivity

This concept holds that an accounting statement should not be influenced by personal bias on the part of the accountant who compiles it. Of course, there are times when an accountant has to use judgement when drawing up a set of accounts, but he must use his own expertise to ensure a correct result. For example, a change in value of an asset should be recognized when it can be measured in objective terms. Estimates sometimes have to be made in accounting and are permissible if they are made with care and within reasonable tolerances and accuracy, e.g. provision for doubtful debts. Another example of an objective figure is the amount actually paid out by the company when it acquires an asset. This figure is real and can be proved by documentation recording the transaction. Unfortunately, such a figure for an asset purchased many years ago is not indicative of current value.

Figures built into accounting statements should rely as little as possible on estimates or subjective decisions. Historic cost represents an amount actually paid out for an asset, which can be proved by means of a voucher and verified as the market cost of the asset. This amount, it is argued, is to be preferred to a subjective valuation of an asset based on estimates of its future profitability.

Fairness

This concept follows naturally from that of objectivity, and holds that in drawing up his statement the accountant must serve all groups interested in the statement fairly and equitably. The shareholders, the creditors and long-term lenders to the business must be able to rely on an accounting statement as showing the unbiased truth. The auditor certifies the accounts as showing a true and fair view, and this is thus a protection against bias in the figures. A current trend is to preserve the independence of the auditor by urging him to sell any shareholdings he possesses in client companies, and to give up any consultancy posts he holds with them.

Consistency

The methods used to treat certain items in the accounts may differ from one company to another, although remaining within the bounds of good accounting practice. When a company chooses to treat certain transactions in a particular way in the accounts it should go on using that method year after year. If accounting procedures are consistent from period to period, a useful comparison of results over time can be made. Methods should be changed only when the income or year-end position will be shown with greater clarity as a result of the change. A note of the change must be appended to the statement concerned, since the calculation of profits may be affected during the period of change.

Example

Suppose a company calculated depreciation at 15 per cent per annum, and applied this rate to all new plant for the year in which it was purchased. An annual investment of £60 000 in new plant would mean a charge of £9000 to the profit and loss account. Suppose also that the investment is made in the last quarter of the year, and the company decides to change its system and to calculate depreciation at 15 per cent, but pro rata to time in the first year. This means that only a quarter of £9000 will not be charged to the profit and loss account, so profits in that year will be improved by £6750 at a stroke.

It would be quite unfair to use the procedure which gave the best profit each year, since the accounts would then show the best possible position rather than the true and fair position, and comparison of one year with another would be impossible.

Consistency may give a comparison over time for the same company, but it cannot offer a comparison between companies unless the same basis is consistently used in each of them. Unfortunately the idea of consistency is used as a weapon to resist change, since any new method suffers from the disadvantage that it is inconsistent with what has gone before. The answer to this dilemma is to change bases as little as possible, but when a change is made, to inform users of accounts, by means of a note to the statement, of exactly what the change is, why it has been made, and the impact it has had on the profit and loss account and balance sheet.

Disclosure

Accounting statements must be formulated in such a way as to lay out information in a useful form, so that it can be assimilated with ease. An accounting statement should not be misleading and should be furnished with adequate footnotes to explain its contents. Where there is a departure from the concept of consistency, a note to the accounts will show the impact of the change so that comparability is maintained. The accounting requirements of the Companies Acts 1948 and 1967 provide examples of matters which must be disclosed in company accounts.

Statement of Standard Accounting Practice 2 (SSAP2) is concerned with the disclosures of accounting policies. The standard states that there should be four basic assumptions underlying all accounting statements, namely 'going concern', 'accruals', 'consistency' and 'prudence'. Accounting bases and policies are the methods used to comply with the basic assumptions, and since these can vary from company to company they should be disclosed in a note to the accounts. Thus this standard improves on the legal minimum of information as specified in the Companies Acts, but still leaves the form of disclosure at the discretion of the accountant. Too much detail can render a statement meaningless to an untrained reader, and too many notes may mean that the trained reader has to spend much time and energy in tracking down the information he needs.

Materiality

Accounting statements should concern themselves with matters which are significant because of their size, and should not consider trivial matters. Analysis is expensive and the presentation of too much detail can be confusing, so insignificant items in accounting statements are merged with others, and not reported separately, since they are considered to be immaterial. The difficulty lies in setting a dividing line between what is material and what is immaterial. Individual opinions differ on this point, but perhaps the cost of collecting accounting information can be used here as a decision criterion, together with the relative importance of the item in the picture revealed by the statement as a whole. What is material in a small business may prove to be immaterial in a large business. In a recent case concerning an international group, the collapse of a foreign subsidiary with losses in the region of £5 million to the group was not clearly shown in the consolidated accounts. There was some criticism of the accounting treatment of these losses, and the answer made by those responsible for the accounts was that in their view the amount of £5 million was not material in such a large company when the overall position of the group profit and loss account had to be considered.

Conservatism or Prudence

This concept has resulted in accountants being thought of by businessmen as pessimists. Whenever there are alternative procedures or values, the accountant selects the one which results in a lower asset value or profit and a higher liability. The concept can be summarized by the phrase 'anticipate no profit and provide for all possible losses', and stems from the accountants' fear that if they approach the compilation of accounting statements with too much optimism they may overstate profits and cause dividends to be paid out of capital. If an unrealized profit is distributed to shareholders as dividend, the danger exists that the funds will be paid out, yet the profit may never be realized, and may even melt away. In the absence of certainty it is best to be prudent. It is considered preferable to understate profit where doubt arises, since mistakes in this direction can be corrected later when the situation is clarified.

PRINCIPLES

Matching

This is sometimes called the accruals principle. When a profit statement is compiled the cost of the goods sold should be set against the revenue from their sale. Expense and revenue must be matched up so that they concern the same goods and time period, if a true profit is to be computed. Costs concerning a future period must be carried forward as a prepayment of that period, and not charged in the current profit and loss account. Expenses of the current period not yet entered in the books must be estimated and inserted as accruals. There has been much argument among accountants about whether overhead expenses should be charged against the period in which they are incurred or carried forward to the period in which the goods made when these costs were incurred are eventually sold.

Cost

Fixed assets are shown in the accounts at the price paid to acquire them, i.e. their historic cost less depreciation written off to date. They are acquired by a company to be used, and it is argued that their historic cost should be spread over the years of their useful life. However, inflation or obsolescence may change the value of a long-lived asset. The concepts of consistency, objectivity and conservatism are used to support the use of historic cost in accounting for such assets. The opponents of the cost principle use the concepts of disclosure and materiality to support their arguments.

Accountants avoid the idea of value, since a value is often a matter of personal bias and may change according to the method of valuation used. Under the going concern postulate we account for assets at their value in use, which we interpret as the original historic cost of the asset net of depreciation to date. If this amount is out of line with the true value, then the asset should be revalued by an expert.

In the example of Jack the showman and his roundabout, if Jack's grandfather had purchased the machine eighty years ago for £500, this would be its historic cost as recorded in the books, but of course there is a great difference between what £500 could buy at that time and what it can buy now. Thus historic cost does not show the real capital employed in an asset or any fluctuations in the value of the asset that have taken place since it was bought. If depreciation written off the machine during its working life amounts to £450, then the net book value would be £50, and this amount might not be at all representative of the true value of the asset, as calculated on the basis of what it can earn if it can still attract customers at fairgrounds, or what it would fetch if sold for scrap or to a museum, or to another showman. An accountant might argue that the use of historic cost is consistent, objective, since it is based on a transaction which actually took place rather than an estimate of value, and conservative, since it does not overstate the value of the asset.

The Dual Aspect

This principle is the basis of double-entry book-keeping, and stems from the fact that every transaction has a double effect on the position of a business as recorded in the accounts. When an asset is acquired, either another asset (cash) is reduced, or a liability (promise to pay) is acquired, at the same time. When a sale is made stock (an asset) is reduced, while either cash or debtors (assets) are increased. If the business borrows money, a liability to the lender is created, and at the same time an asset (cash) is increased. It follows that the assets of the business are equalled by claims on the business, either by creditors or owners, for the funds they have invested in the business and which have been translated into assets for use by the business. The balance sheet which summarizes assets and claims (liabilities) must therefore balance.

When Jack's grandfather bought the roundabout he acquired an asset, by reducing his cash, another asset, and when Jack buys coal on credit terms for the machine he acquires an asset (stock of raw material) and at the same time a liability to the coal merchant. When the liability is discharged cash, an asset, is reduced. Thus assets equal liabilities at all times.

TUTORIAL DISCUSSION TOPICS

2.1. Is the difference between a concept, a postulate, and a principle in accounting more than a matter of terminology?

2.2. Discuss the limitations of money measurement as a postulate on which to base accounting statements.

2.3. Explain how the concepts of consistency and conservatism support the principle of historic cost, while the opponents of this principle use the concepts of disclosure and materiality in their arguments.

2.4. Is the alternative to the going concern postulate a viable one?

2.5. Why should a businessman separate the transactions of his business from those of his private life? After all, in private life the transactions concerned are mainly to spend the profits made in his business life, and thus the one is an extension of the other.

3 | Double Entry

THE PRINCIPLES OF DOUBLE ENTRY

The principle of duality underlies the double entry system. Every transaction has a dual effect on the business, and therefore should be recorded twice to reveal this effect. The books are divided into accounts or pages in the ledger, an account being opened not for each transaction but to summarize transactions of a similar nature on the same page, e.g. a page for repair costs, another for factory wages, another for sales revenue, and another for rent and rates. If there are many transactions of one type, then a separate book or ledger will be opened, e.g. the cash book to record the cash part of transactions, payments or receipts, and the debtors ledger to maintain a detailed record of amounts owed to the business by customers who have bought goods on credit. In this case each debtor will have an account or page of his own in the debtors ledger.

Each page acts as a T account, having two sides, one for debits and one for credits. The debits are always on the left-hand side and the credits on the right-hand side. When the two sides are added up, if the entries on the debit side are more than those on the credit side then the account is said to have a debit balance, and vice versa.

Example

Dr.	Vehicles Account		Cr.		Dr.	Cash		Cr.
	£		£			£		£
1 Two cars purchased for cash	4000	**2** One car sold to Brown	2000				**1** Paid for vehicles	4000
		3 Balance c/f	2000					
	£4000		£4000					
3 Balance c/f	2000							

Dr.	Brown		Cr.
	£		£
2 Owing for vehicles purchased	2000	**4** Balance c/f	2000
	£2000		£2000
Balance b/d	2000		

A company buys two cars for £4000 and pays for them in cash. The company then sells one of the cars to Brown for £2000 on credit terms.

In this example the vehicle account has been debited with the purchase price of the assets (the corresponding credit will occur in the cash book) and credited with the sale. Follow the numbered sequence through to check debit against credit. At the end of the accounting period, when the account is closed the debit side is heavier than the credit side, and to balance the account to the total of the heavier side the difference between the two sides must be added to the lighter side. Thus the account has been credited with its balance, and a corresponding debit is required. This is supplied by carrying the balance down below the line to start the next accounting period on the opposite side. (See entries 3 and 4 above.) Thus the preponderance of debit over credit of this account is shown in the balance brought down. The asset cash has been reduced by £4000 and the £2000 owed by Brown is shown as an asset balance. Total debits equal total credits.

   Note that the amount for vehicles sold has not been taken away from the debit side, but has been posted to the credit side. This has the same effect, since it reduces the amount of the debit balance carried forward, but also allows the duality of transactions to be recorded via the double entry system. This system has four basic rules.

1. Every debit must have a credit and every credit must have a debit. Each transaction is recorded twice, once on each side of separate accounts in the books, with debits traditionally on the left-hand side.
2. As in the quadrant shown in a later chapter, the assets and expenses are debit balances and the liabilities and sales revenue are credit balances. The purchase of every asset by a business is financed by funds invested in or lent to the business by owners or creditors (lenders), who then have a claim against the company for the return of their funds. Thus claims equal assets in the balance sheet, and when in the income statement sales exceed costs and a profit is made, this profit is added to the balance sheet claims on the credit side to balance the increase in assets represented by the profit.
3. When an asset or cost account is to be increased the entry is on the debit side and when a liability or sales revenue account is to be increased the account is credited. When, however, an account is to be decreased, the amount is not deducted from the side on which the balance is shown, but is instead posted to the opposite side, so that the balance is reduced in this way. For example, an asset or cost account is decreased by crediting the account and a liability or sales revenue account is decreased by debiting the account.
4. The giving account is credited while the receiving account is debited. For example, when wages are paid, the wages account receives and is debited, while cash is given out so this account is credited, and when a debtor pays what he owes, cash receives and is debited, while the debtor gives and his account is credited (thus reducing his debit balance). This is a rather rough and ready rule which does not have a logical application in all cases.

RECORDING TRANSACTIONS

Before entries can be made in the books transactions must be recorded and evidenced on working documents from which the books themselves are written up. Some of these 'prime documents' are listed below:

a. invoices or bills to evidence the cost, date and exact description of items purchased or expenses incurred;
b. credit notes, which are used when an invoice is cancelled or when the amount of the bill is reduced for some reason, e.g. goods are returned;
c. cheque book stubs to record cash paid out and remittance advices to show in detail what was paid for;
d. petty cash vouchers to show what has been bought for cash;
e. the paying-in book to record cash received from sales, debtors etc and which has been paid into the bank;
f. the clock cards and wages sheets to analyse the amount paid out for labour;
g. sales invoices to record sales made, whether for cash or credit;
h. goods received notes to evidence the receipt of goods for which an invoice can be expected in the near future;
i. journal vouchers for internal transactions and transfers between accounts.

There are, of course, other prime documents, but these are the major ones.

BOOKS OF PRIME ENTRY

When there is a large volume of transactions the prime documents have to be summarized and analysed before they are posted into the books of account. Originally the daybook for sales or purchases was the device used for this purpose. It used to be written up daily, with a total column and sub-columns for analysis. At the end of the month the daybook would be closed, the columns cast, and the analysis column totals cross-cast to reconcile with the total of the major column. The analysis column totals were then entered into the appropriate ledger accounts and the individual items posted to the personal account of the customer or supplier. Daybooks were maintained for purchases, sales, internal transactions and transfers (the journal), and cash. Some systems had a daybook for returns inwards (goods sold sent back by the customer) and for returns outwards (purchases returned to suppliers). The cash book acted as both a book of prime entry from which items were posted to other accounts, and also as a ledger account, to record the balance of the asset cash. In the case of the purchases daybook the analysis columns would be debited to the various expense accounts to show the costs incurred, while the individual amounts in the major column would be credited to the personal accounts of suppliers in the creditors ledger. The sales daybook analysed sales to product or area (a credit entry) and allowed each sale in the major column to be debited to the customer's (debtor's) personal account.

As business became more sophisticated and the number of transactions to be accounted for increased, so the old handwritten system of keeping the books became inadequate to deal with the new volume of work. The daybook was replaced by a machine list or computer list of transactions, and analysis is now undertaken by mechanical or computer systems which sort and total entries. The ledgers produced by book-keeping machines show additions and deductions in the form of black and red entries in one total column. In some cases the account itself is little more than a set of pulses on a computer tape which can be printed out on demand. Some systems of ledgerless book-keeping avoid the maintenance of personal ledgers by filing all invoices owed to one supplier or by one customer in the same filing pocket, adding new invoices as they arrive and extracting invoices when they are settled. Basically, however, prime documents are still summarized and analysed, and recorded both as a debit and a credit in the accounts of the business no matter what form those accounts take.

THE JOURNAL

In some systems the journal for recording internal transactions and alterations is the only book still entered by hand. If by mistake the wrong account has been debited with an expense or an asset acquired, the mistake must be put right by crediting the account entered in error and debiting the correct account. A journal entry will record the appropriate account to be debited and credited with a narration as to the reason for the alteration. In some systems even this book has been replaced by a file of journal vouchers which evidence the debit and credit entries made in the mechanized or computer system. Some internal transactions, however, are extremely important and must be evidenced by an extract from the minutes of the board meeting at which the decision concerning the transaction was made. The payment of dividends, transfers to reserve accounts, and changes in the share capital of the business are all examples of the type of transaction which enters the books of account through the journal.

The form of the journal is that it is ruled in four columns, with the second column wider than the others.

Date	Narration	Debit £	Credit £
1 April	Mr J. Bloggs	500	
	Mr R. Goodfellow		500
	Being goods purchased by Bloggs, charged to Goodfellow in error.		

The narration column names the accounts to be debited or credited, and gives a short description of the reason for the entry. In the example above Bloggs' account is debited, since he owes £500 for goods not yet paid for and Goodfellow's account is credited to nullify the debit of £500 entered on his account in error.

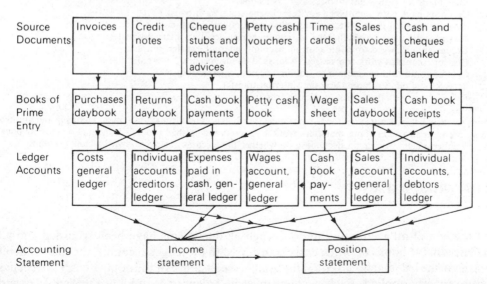

Figure 1. The Accounting System, from the prime document via books of prime entry and the ledger to the accounting statement. The cash book is both a book of prime entry and a ledger account. The journal is used as a book of prime entry to transfer items between ledger accounts or to record internal transactions.

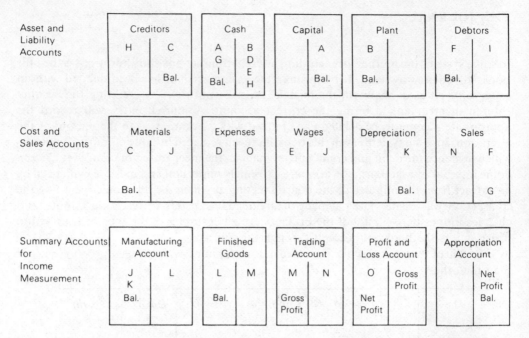

Figure 2. The Accounting System, showing the debit and credit entries for transactions in the ledger accounts and the computation of the accounting statements.

The transactions are listed below, with a note about the source document and book of prime entry involved.

Transactions. Debits on the left-hand side and credits on the right-hand side. The entries for each transaction are shown by the following designatory letters.

A. Shareholders apply for shares in cash, journal entry.
B. Plant purchased for cash, invoice and cash book.
C. Materials bought on credit, invoice and purchases daybook.
D. Expenses paid in cash, bill and cash book.
E. Wages paid in cash, wage sheet.
F. Sales made on credit terms, sales invoices and daybook.
G. Sales made for cash, sales invoices and cash book.
H. Creditors paid, copy remittance advices, cheque stubs, cash book.
I. Payment received from debtors, bank paying-in book and cash book.
J. Materials used and wages charged to manufacturing account, internal transfer journal.
K. Depreciation charged to manufacturing account, internal transfer journal.
L. Cost of completed work transferred to finished goods accounts, internal transfer.
M. Cost of goods sold transferred to trading account, internal transfer.
N. Sales 'closed off' to trading account, internal transfer.
O. Expenses 'closed off' to profit and loss account.

Items marked 'bal.' will appear in the balance sheet. The balances on the materials, manufacturing and finished goods accounts are stocks of raw materials, work in progress and finished goods. The balance on the cash book can be either a debit or a credit depending on whether the business has overdrawn its bank account.

THE TRIAL BALANCE

At the end of an accounting period, when all documents have been recorded and all balances in the books of prime entry transferred to the ledger accounts, the total of debit entries in the ledgers should equal the total of credit entries if the double-entry system has been properly applied. Each account must be balanced by adding the two sides and finding whether a debit or a credit balance is brought down. The accounts in the ledger

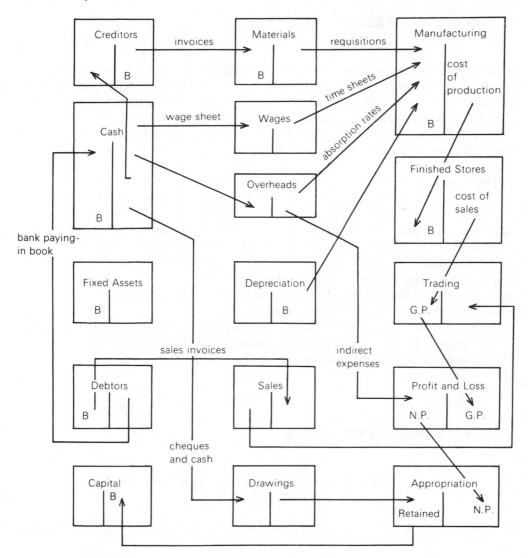

Figure 3. Simple Chart of Accounts for a Manufacturing Company. B denotes a balance remaining at the year end after the income measurement entries have been extracted, which will appear on the balance sheet. The source documents are shown on the arrows which indicate the debit and credit entries.

are then listed on a separate sheet with the balance of the account shown in a debit or a credit column. If the total of debit balances equals the total of credit balances then prima facie each transaction has been recorded as a debit and a credit. This is a valuable check on the accuracy of the book-keeping, but it does not reveal the situation where an item has been debited to the wrong account, omitted entirely, or analysed incorrectly, or where compensating errors have been made. The trial balance is a summary of the balances recorded in the ledger accounts, and can thus be used as a basis from which the income and position statements can be computed. The transactions recorded in the ledgers have to be adjusted for accruals and prepayments by extending the trial balance to include these items.

THE PETTY CASH BOOK

Small disbursements for expenses made on a day-to-day basis by local purchase are recorded in this book and analysed in a number of columns. The totals of these columns are cast and cross-cast to the main total, and the amounts are then posted as from a daybook to the appropriate account in the general ledger. These amounts are debited to various expenses, with a total credit to the petty cash account. When cash is drawn from the bank to reimburse the petty cashier the cash book is credited and the petty cash book debited.

The imprest system is commonly used to operate a petty cash book. The system allows the petty cashier to draw a cash float (a fixed amount of money) to cover the petty cash expenses for a stated period. The expenses are totalled at the end of the month or week, and the petty cashier then draws exactly the amount that he has spent during the period from the main cash book. This amount will make up the petty cash in the till to the pre-ordained amount of the float. So that control over the system is maintained, the cashier is required to retain vouchers for expenditure for audit purposes. A further measure of control is that at any time the petty cash box or till must contain cash and/or vouchers which add up to the amount of the imprest float.

An example of the operation for the double-entry system, with reference to T-accounts, is contained in Question 2 in the seminar exercises below. Students should work through the example, noting the interplay of debit and credit in the solution.

TUTORIAL DISCUSSION TOPICS

3.1. How does the imprest system for the control of petty cash operate?

3.2. What is a trial balance and what are the major objects of preparing a trial balance?

SEMINAR EXERCISES 1

1. Explain how the double-entry system works and attempt to formalize the basic rules which apply in double-entry book-keeping. Illustrate your answer with a short, simple example, with specific reference to the way in which an account is balanced.

2. Brian Grange starts to trade as a wholesale dealer on 1 September at a warehouse which he owns himself and which is valued at £24 000. Grange has provided fixtures and fittings which cost £17 000, and has brought into the business his car, worth £2800, and a van valued at £900. He opens a business bank account by paying £8500 into it. He has already bought goods on credit from the following firms, and these goods comprise his opening stock: Collie and Co, £471; Lot and Mee, £360; and Edmunds, £615.

(a) Calculate Grange's capital and enter the balances shown in the appropriate books. These opening entries could be made direct to T accounts or through an opening journal entry.

(b) Record the undermentioned transactions in suitable subsidiary accounts and the cash book. Post to the ledger and prove your work by extracting a trial balance.

1 September	Bought on credit terms from Apple Ltd two typewriters at £180 each.
	Bought office stationery, £174, paid by cheque.
	Drew £250 from bank to cover petty cash expenses.
2 September	Sold goods to T. Veron for £627 and K. Jones for £460.
	Paid cash for cartons, £61, and cleaning materials, £16.
3 September	Cash sales to date, £165, banked.
4 September	Paid wages in cash, £83.
5 September	Bought goods from J. Lewin, £190, less 10 per cent trade discount.
	Paid cheques as follows: Collie and Co. £300 on account; Edmunds Ltd £600 in full settlement after deducting £15 as a cash discount.
6 September	Goods returned from T. Veron, £127.
7 September	Paid rates on premises, cheque for £181.
	Exchanged van at book value at Car Sales Ltd for a new van, costing £2800, and accepted liability for the balance.
	Returned goods costing £20 to J. Lewin.
	Sold goods on credit terms to H. Same Ltd, £430.
8 September	Withdrew goods from stock for own use, £53.
	Paid wages in cash, £76.
	Banked cash sales, £431.
	Paid office expenses in cash, £18.
9 September	Paid insurance premium by cheque, £160.
	Bought goods on credit terms from Edmunds Ltd, £280.
	Received cheque from T. Veron in settlement of his account net of 5 per cent cash discount.
10 September	Paid Lot and Mee £200 on account by cheque.
	Sold goods on credit terms to H. Same Ltd, £165.
	Drew £5 from cash to pay for Grange's lunch.
11 September	Paid carriage charge, £29, and telephone bill, £23, by cheque.
	Banked all office petty cash except a float of £50.

4 | The Position Statement or Balance Sheet

This accounting statement shows the status of a firm at any given moment. It is always stated 'as at' a certain date, and is a statement of the affairs of a business on that date. The balance sheet shows the items owned by the business, which are termed assets, and sets against them a list of claims on those assets by those who have provided the funds with which the assets have been purchased; these are termed liabilities, or what the business owes. Thus when shareholders put money into a business or when a lender makes funds available to a business, a claim to the return of the funds is acquired. The funds are then invested by the business in assets which it buys and uses in its chosen trade. Thus everything owned by a business must have been financed, and the finance must have been provided by those who have claims on the business, so liabilities or claims must equal assets.

Some authorities see the balance sheet as a list of the sources of funds used in the business set against a list of the ways in which the funds have been laid out by the management. The term 'balance sheet' may give an erroneous view of this statement, since it implies that it is correct if it is able to balance assets against liabilities. Basically the statement is made up as a list of balances taken from the books of the business, and the balance of asset against liability is derived from the principle of double entry, under which every transaction has a double effect on the accounts of the business. An American term which is now being used in the United Kingdom is 'position statement', since it implies that the balance sheet should correctly reflect the position of a business rather than merely summarize the balances in its books.

The balance sheet is like a photograph in that it shows the position of a business at one point in time but does not show how that position was arrived at. It also suffers from the disadvantages of the monetary measurement postulate, in that assets which cannot be measured objectively in money terms are left out of the statement, and assets included at historic cost are shown at an unrepresentative amount after inflation.

THE FORM OF THE BALANCE SHEET

First we will deal with the assets of a business. These are not simply listed, but are grouped to show a sub-total for (a) fixed or long-term assets, (b) current or short-term assets, and (c) other assets. Among the fixed assets are land and buildings, both freehold and leasehold, plant and machinery, vehicles, and investments which are held for strategic or long-term reasons. Fixed assets are not held for resale but are to be used in the business in the long term. A fixed asset for one company may be a current asset for another. For example, a car is a fixed asset if it is to be driven by a salesman for the next two years, but a current asset if it is held as stock for sale by a car sales company. The business entity concept is followed in that only assets belonging to the company or partnership, or business assets of a sole trader, are included in the balance sheet. The cost principle is adhered to in that assets are shown at historic cost, i.e. the funds laid out when they were purchased less depreciation written off to date, leaving the net unexpired capital cost to affect the balance sheet total. The going concern postulate assumes that the business will continue, so that the historic cost net of depreciation can be used for fixed assets rather than the lower and more conservative scrap value of those assets if they were sold immediately in the second-hand market. By tradition the assets on a balance sheet are always shown in reverse order of liquidity, i.e. the least liquid, land and buildings held more or less permanently, come at the top.

Another category of assets, termed intangible assets, is also shown on the balance sheet, sometimes above the fixed assets and sometimes below. These assets are items which, although they are not visible and cannot be physically touched, make a contribution to the profits of the business. For example, the possession of a patent or trade mark often improves profits and therefore the patent or trade mark is an asset. Often this asset has been purchased, so its cost can be objectively valued and recorded in the balance sheet as one of the items which the business owns. Another intangible asset is goodwill, which is discussed in a later chapter.

The current assets of the business, also listed in reverse order of liquidity, are stocks, debts, short-term investments and cash. Stocks may be in the form of raw materials, work in progress (semi-finished items in the factory), or finished goods awaiting sale. These are always shown at cost or net realizable value, whichever is the lower, to adhere to the concept of conservatism and ensure that no element of profit is taken before stocks are sold, but that any loss made because stocks are held is taken into account at once. Debts are sums owed to the business, usually by customers who have bought goods on credit terms. It is expected that these debts will be turned back into cash in the near future when the debts are paid. Short-term investments are held to provide a safe repository for idle funds so that they can earn some return while at the same time they can be quickly liquidated if they are required for use elsewhere in the business. The term 'cash' covers the money in the bank account and also money held at other points in the business, such as the tills of the shops or the petty cash box in the office safe. All current assets are expected to work their way through the business cycle, i.e. purchase, storage, manufacture, sale, payment, and turn themselves back into cash within a short period, usually the accounting year. For this reason they are sometimes referred to as the circulating capital of the business.

The liabilities are also stated in reverse order of liquidity, the claims which have to be repaid soonest coming at the bottom. At the top is the capital which represents the original amount invested in the business by the owner. In a company, capital takes the form of shares owned by the various shareholders. As they are the last to be repaid in the event of the business being discontinued, they are deemed to take the biggest risk. Share capital is sometimes for this reason called venture capital. Next come the reserves of the business. They also belong to the owners or shareholders, but represent profits made by the business in the past and not distributed. When a profit is made it is appropriated or divided up, some being paid to the Inland Revenue as taxation, some being paid to the shareholders in the form of a dividend or to the proprietor as drawings, and the remainder being retained in the business as a source of finance. Thus reserves or profits ploughed back into the business represent a further investment by the shareholders made out of past profits. When added together, share capital and reserves total the owner's interest in the business, being the funds provided initially and out of past profits by the legal owners of the business. Sometimes this amount is termed the equity interest, since all ordinary shareholders have an equal right to participate pro rata to their holding of shares, if these funds are repaid.

The remaining liabilities of the business are divided according to the period for which they are lent. The long-term liabilities include loans made for periods of more than one year, and often for such long periods as to be viewed as part of the long-term capital employed in the business. These loans are sometimes termed mortgages or debentures, and are often secured on the assets of the business. This means that if the company fails to pay the annual interest on a loan or goes into liquidation before the period of the loan is ended, the lender may take possession of some assets of the business and sell them in order to recoup the funds he has lent.

Current liabilities are amounts lent to the business for a period of less than one year. They include trade creditors who have supplied goods and services and are awaiting payment, short-term loans from the bank, usually in the form of an overdraft, the Inland Revenue awaiting payment of tax on the due date, and the shareholders themselves awaiting payment of a dividend from the previous year's profits.

Contingent liabilities are amounts which might become liabilities of the firm, depending upon circumstances which may arise after the balance sheet date, e.g. damages in a court action where judgement is pending at the balance sheet date. Because of the concept of conservatism these items are shown as a note under the balance sheet and do not form part of the liabilities which are added to equal the total of the assets.

In the United Kingdom the balance sheet can take two forms. A slightly outdated form shows the assets listed on the right-hand side and the capital and liabilities on the left-hand side. This is often called a T account. A form of balance sheet which is more easily assimilated is the vertical form, which sets out the capital and long-term liabilities first and then shows the assets which represent these funds employed underneath. Alternatively, the assets can be listed above the liabilities. Both types are shown below.

Balance Sheet of XYZ Co. Ltd as at 31 December 19..

	£	£		£	£	£
Capital:			Intangible assets:			
Ordinary shares	75 000		Goodwill			40 000
General reserves	25 768		Fixed assets:	Cost	Depn	
Equity interest		100 768	Land and buildings	70 000	–	70 000
			Plant	47 000	23 000	24 000
Long-term liabilities:			Vehicles	10 412	6 208	4 204
Long-term loan at 10 per				127 412	29 208	98 204
cent interest		60 000				
Current liabilities:			Current assets:			
Trade creditors	6310		Stock		18 640	
Bank overdraft	9618		Debtors		15 325	
Inland Revenue	4134		Investments		10 000	
Dividend payable	3750	23 812	Cash		2 411	46 376
		£184 580				£184 580

T   Account. This form is slightly outdated.

Balance Sheet of XYZ Co. Ltd as at 31 December 19..

	£	£	£
Capital:			
Ordinary shares			75 000
General reserves			25 768
Equity interest			100 768
Long-term liabilities:			
Long-term loan at 10 per cent interest			60 000
Net capital employed			160 768

	Cost	Depreciation	
Represented by:			
Fixed assets:			
Land and buildings	70 000	–	70 000
Plant	47 000	23 000	24 000
Vehicles	10 412	6 208	4 204
	£ 127 412	£ 29 208	98 204
Intangible assets:			
Goodwill			40 000
			138 204
Current assets:			
Stock		18 640	
Debtors		15 325	
Investments		10 000	
Cash		2 411	
		46 376	
Less current liabilities:			
Trade creditors	6 310		
Bank overdraft	9 618		
Inland Revenue	4 134		
Dividend payable	3 750	23 812	
Working capital			22 564
Net assets			£ 160 768

Balance Sheet in Vertical Form. The amounts involved are the same as those in the T account, but this form sets off current liabilities against current assets to reveal the working capital.

ASSETS

Any item which belongs to a business is an asset of the business so long as it has a value, that value can be objectively measured, and the ownership of the asset can be proved. Assets are usually recorded in the books at their cost or the amount paid out when they were acquired. Some assets, however, are excluded from the balance sheet because it is too difficult to obtain a precise value for them or because they could evaporate very quickly. For example, the possession of a skilled workforce and an established trade connection are both assets which improve the profitability of the business, but whose original cost and current value are difficult to determine.

Traditionally accountants record assets at their historic cost and not at their estimated current market value. Thus the cost of drilling an oil well is entered in the balance sheet, although this amount may not be related in any way to the value of the oil to be exploited from the well. In some cases, however, the historic cost of the asset gets out of line with the current value of the asset, and when this is so a professional valuer is asked to revalue the assets and make the balance sheet reflect current conditions more accurately.

It is very difficult to assess the value of a trade mark or the development costs of a new project carried forward, so these items are shown in the balance sheet at cost rather than at value. An economist might wish to value an asset by determining the current value of the future stream of income to be derived from the asset. In practice, however, it is very difficult to compute a value in this way.

A balance sheet using historic costs as recorded in the books for assets with long lives will show an unreal position for their value after a period of inflation. The balance sheet is not a valuation device, but accountants do have assets revalued so that the position shown by the balance sheet is made more realistic.

Example

Suppose a football club bought a left winger for £200 000, while at the same time its right winger, who is as good as his counterpart and thus as valuable, has been with the club for some time and cost them only the £10 signing-on fee. Here are two assets of the same value which might be recorded very differently in the books, if the principle of historic cost is observed too rigidly.

The fixed assets of the business are held for a long period. They are termed long-lived assets, and it is said that capital has been 'sunk' in them. Usually a large proportion of the fixed assets are factory buildings and machinery, which make the goods which are sold for a profit. Consequently accountants take the view that profit stems from, or is earned by, the fixed assets of the business. The current assets, however, are held for a short period. These assets are said to oil the wheels of the business so that the fixed assets can make a profit more easily; e.g. it is difficult to manufacture without the current asset of raw materials stock to back you up, and difficult to sell your product without working capital available to provide trade credit to your debtors.

THE ACCOUNTING EQUATION

One way in which the balance sheet and its relationship to the profit and loss account can sometimes be explained is in the form of an algebraic formula or model. If symbols are allotted to the components of the balance sheet a formula will emerge which can express the interrelationship of basic ideas such as equity, liabilities, assets, revenue, and expenses. The formula can be built up in steps as follows. The amounts are taken from the balance sheet of XYZ Co. Ltd, already shown.

a.   Assets = claims, A = C, £184 580 = £184 580.
     This demonstrates the basic financial position of the business as shown by the balance sheet, in that the funds invested in the business equal the assets owned by the business at any one time. The funds invested have been provided by owners and lenders, and

thus these persons have claims on the assets of the business.

b. Assets = ownership interest + loans, $A = OI + L$, $£184\,580 = £100\,768 + £83\,812$.
The formula now analyses the claims to differentiate between the funds invested by the owners in the business and the funds used in the business which have been provided by others. This relationship can also be expressed as $A - L = OI$, to reveal the extent of the investment by the legal owners in the firm.

c. Assets = ownership interest + long-term liabilities + current liabilities,
$A = OI + LTL + CL$,
$£184\,580 = £100\,768 + £60\,000 + £23\,812$.
Here long-term loans are separated from short-term liabilities to demonstrate the idea that all funds lent to the business, whether short or long term or invested permanently by the owners, are represented by the assets.

d. Total assets = fixed assets + current assets + intangible assets,
$A = FA + CA + IA$,
$£184\,580 = £98\,204 + £46\,376 + £40\,000$.
This analysis of the assets side of the balance sheet shows the various types of possession which a business can buy with the funds at its disposal. Since cash is a liquid asset and can flow into any other form of asset which the firm decides to buy, there is no way of identifying particular assets with certain funds used to buy them. However, it is wise to have a fund of permanent capital at least equal to the fixed assets, since if the loan capital, long or short term, needs to be repaid, there will be sufficient current assets which can be exchanged for cash to meet the repayment.

e. Assets = loans + share capital + retained earnings,
$A = L + SC + RE$,
$£184\,580 = £83\,812 + £75\,000 + £25\,768$.
This development of the model divides the ownership interest into its two constituent parts: the original share capital contributed by the shareholders at the commencement of the business, and the profits belonging to the shareholders which have not been distributed to them in the past, but have been retained in the business since the commencement date.

f. Assets = loans + share capital + retained earnings at the start of the year
+ (profit − tax and dividend),
$A = L + SC + RE_{t-1} + [P - (T + D)]$, where t = this year.
In this case the formula explains the derivation of retained earnings, showing them to be that part of the profit figure not appropriated to pay taxes or dividends. This is a significant development of the model, since at this point the connection between the balance sheet and the profit and loss account begins to emerge, i.e. any amount of profit not appropriated for payment of tax or dividend is added to the capital of the business, since it is part of the owners' interest in the business.

g. The connection between the balance sheet and the profit and loss account is underlined by the next development of the formula.
Assets = loans + share capital + retained earnings at the start of the year + [(sales − costs) − tax and dividend],
$A = L + SC + RE_{t-1} + [(S - C) - (T + D)]$, where t = this year.
The increase in retained earnings can be expressed as a separate formula,
$RE = RE_{t-1} + [(S - C) - (T + D)]$.
There is one notable flaw in this argument, which is that retained earnings or reserves can be affected by certain transactions which do not go through the profit and loss account. For example, the revaluation of fixed assets results in an increase in the asset value with a corresponding increase in the reserves which make up part of the ownership interest.

The full extent of the balance sheet model can be seen by combining the formula in (d) with the formula in (g):

$$FA + CA + IA = LTL + CL + SC + RE_{t-1} + [(S - C) - (T + D)]$$

TUTORIAL DISCUSSION TOPICS

4.1. Are there any assets of a business which do not appear on the balance sheet? If so, why are they excluded and how can it be said that the assets which are shown equal the claims on the business by those who have financed the assets?

4.2. The following statement is made by a shareholder: 'The equity interest on the balance sheet shows me what my shares are worth'. Discuss the balance sheet as a statement of 'net worth'.

4.3. Define an asset for balance sheet purposes. Differentiate between current assets and fixed assets.

4.4. How, if at all, would you record the following events in the books of a business?

(a) Oil is discovered under the company's car park.
(b) The sales director leaves to work for a rival company.
(c) Political changes cause the company to be expelled from a country in which it owned mineral rights.
(d) A fire destroys the accounting department's building and all the records stored in it.
(e) The company suffers its first strike in ten years.

4.5. Many companies rely on bank overdraft as a source of funds. How is this reliance compatible with the inclusion of bank overdraft among the current or short-term liabilities on the balance sheet?

SEMINAR EXERCISES 2

1. Prepare a position statement from the following information presented to you on 31 December. Your answer should be in good form.

Company A	£
Creditors	43 614
Cash in hand	1 270
Bank balance	8 186
Stock	29 941
Freehold land	60 000

Long-term loan owed	20 000
Wages payable	1 102
Nottingham Corporation bonds	8 000
Debtors	19 487
Buildings	35 000
Expenses paid in advance	904
Share capital	50 000
Vehicles	8 000
Plant at cost	25 000
Depreciation on plant	6 000
Shares of company X	7 000
Taxation owed	13 000
Depreciation on buildings	10 000

2. Show how each of the following transactions changes the balance sheet which you produced in answer to Question 1.

   (a) Shareholders invest a further £20 000 in the company.
   (b) The wages payable are paid.
   (c) The company buys raw material for cash, £1200.
   (d) The company buys raw material for credit, £4000.
   (e) The company sells its property at book value.
   (f) The company pays £5000 to its creditors.
   (g) The Nottingham bonds are realized for cash, £8000.
   (h) £10 000 is paid to the Inland Revenue.

3. Company B has been in business for a number of years. Recently there has been a fire at the head office, in which the accounting records of the business have been destroyed. The company's accountant has left and the directors have asked you to reconstruct, as far as possible, the records. You take stock, visit the bank, inform customers, and investigate the ownership of buildings, machinery and other assets. You discover the following information:

	Balance or Market Value (£)
Cash in safe	8 000
Bank balance	36 000
Stock of raw material and finished goods	74 000
Debtors	52 000
Shares of other companies	18 000
Land and buildings	156 000
Machinery and vehicles	64 000

After a check of invoices received from creditors and statements of account received you compute that £80 000 is owed to such creditors and a further £40 000 is owed to the Inland Revenue. The land and buildings are mortgaged in the sum of £70 000. The share register is at the office of the company's solicitor, and shows that 100 000 ordinary shares of £1 each have been issued.

   (a) Draw up a balance sheet for Company B.
   (b) How has the accounting equation helped you to find an answer?

4. On 1 January Mr See set up business as a shopkeeper. He withdrew his life savings of
   £5894 from a building society and used them to open a business bank account. He
   borrowed a further £13 000 from a friend, and used the money to buy the freehold of a
   shop with storage space at the rear. It cost Mr See £2714 to fit out the shop with
   counter, till, window displays and display cabinets, but he has paid only £2000 of this
   bill to the shopfitter so far. One supplier who sold stock to Mr See at a cost of £930
   demanded payment in cash, but another who sold Mr See stock for £1831 is willing to
   wait until the end of the month for payment. Mr See uses his car, bought recently for
   £2150, entirely for business purposes. He has spent £285 from the bank account to
   purchase a freezer for Mrs See, and has lent £500 from the same account to a
   business aquaintance, Mr Exe. There are no other transactions during the month of
   January. Draw up a balance sheet for Mr See as at 31 January.

5. (a) William Durr is the proprietor of a small building contracting firm. He does not
       understand the term 'balance sheet' and asks you to explain to him whether the
       following items should be on his balance sheet. Indicate the nature of the items, e.g.
       current asset, long-term liability, not applicable etc.

        (i) stock of sand and cement;
       (ii) air compressor purchased for cash;
      (iii) air compressor purchased on credit terms;
       (iv) air compressor hired for three weeks;
        (v) wages paid to labourer;
       (vi) lorry used for transporting vehicles;
      (vii) diesel fuel in lorry fuel tank;
     (viii) washing machine bought for Mrs Durr;
       (ix) bank overdraft;
        (x) £250 owing from a customer for work done;
       (xi) road fund licence for lorry;
      (xii) stock of paper and envelopes, value 90 pence;
     (xiii) petty cash in hand;
      (xiv) £2500 owing to Aunt Joan, who says William need not repay her until four
            years have elapsed.

   (b) In respect of any of the assets in (a) above which you consider to be fixed, would it
       be possible for the same asset to be current in another type of business? Explain.
   (c) What other items would you need in order to construct a balance sheet for William
       Durr?

5 | The Income Statement

This statement is designed to measure the results of transactions which have taken place between two balance sheet dates. Since it shows the result of operations for a period of time it is not a statement 'as at' but a statement 'for the year ended'. It is a summary of all transactions which have taken place during a period, not a statement to show the position at one moment in time.

Sometimes it is called the revenue account and sometimes the income statement, but in the United Kingdom the term 'profit and loss account' is usually used. This term, however, is a misnomer, since the income statement is often divided into four parts, one of which itself is called the profit and loss account. The first part is called the manufacturing account, and it reveals the cost of production and in some cases a factory profit. This part is produced only for a manufacturing company and is sometimes called the work in progress account. The second part is the trading account, in which the cost of goods sold is set against sales revenue to show a gross profit. The third part is the profit and loss account, in which the general expenses of the business are set against gross profit to reduce it to net profit. The fourth part is the appropriation account, which shows how the net profit is divided up according to the various ways in which it is used; e.g. part is set aside for taxation, part is used to cover dividends paid to shareholders or drawings by a sole trader, and the remainder is retained in the business as part of its reserves. The manufacturing and trading accounts are produced for internal management purposes, while under the Companies Acts the shareholders and investors at large are entitled to see only certain figures on the profit and loss account and the appropriation account. Companies treat the income statement as a confidential document, since a rival business might gain a significant advantage if the full details were disclosed. Examples of the various accounts are shown below.

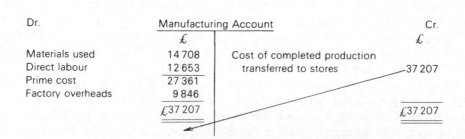

Dr.	Manufacturing Account		Cr.
	£		£
Materials used	14 708	Cost of completed production	
Direct labour	12 653	transferred to stores	37 207
Prime cost	27 361		
Factory overheads	9 846		
	£37 207		£37 207

35

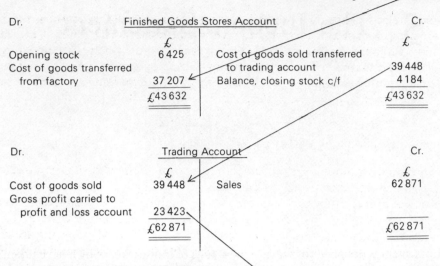

Dr.   Finished Goods Stores Account   Cr.

	£		£
Opening stock	6 425	Cost of goods sold transferred	
Cost of goods transferred		to trading account	39 448
from factory	37 207	Balance, closing stock c/f	4 184
	£43 632		£43 632

Dr.   Trading Account   Cr.

	£		£
Cost of goods sold	39 448	Sales	62 871
Gross profit carried to			
profit and loss account	23 423		
	£62 871		£62 871

Note: The calculation of opening stock plus purchases less closing stock to show the cost of goods sold is sometimes undertaken in the trading account.

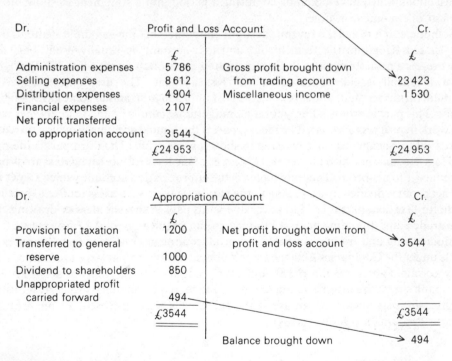

Dr.   Profit and Loss Account   Cr.

	£		£
Administration expenses	5 786	Gross profit brought down	
Selling expenses	8 612	from trading account	23 423
Distribution expenses	4 904	Miscellaneous income	1 530
Financial expenses	2 107		
Net profit transferred			
to appropriation account	3 544		
	£24 953		£24 953

Dr.   Appropriation Account   Cr.

	£		£
Provision for taxation	1200	Net profit brought down from	
Transferred to general		profit and loss account	3 544
reserve	1000		
Dividend to shareholders	850		
Unappropriated profit			
carried forward	494		
	£3544		£3544
		Balance brought down	494

This balance appears in the balance sheet as unappropriated profits, and is part of the owners' interest in the business.

Note that in the profit and loss section the expenses have been grouped under certain convenient headings. The statements could also be presented in columnar form, as will be shown in a later chapter.

A disadvantage of the balance sheet is that it shows the position at one moment in time only, but this is to some extent remedied by the income statement, which shows in part how that position has been attained. The result of the statement, the profit or loss figure, can be set against the capital employed in the business, as revealed by the balance sheet, to show as a percentage the profitability of the operation and the return earned by the management on the funds entrusted to them by the owners. This return is satisfactory only if it is sufficient to compensate for the risk taken by the owners when investing their capital in the enterprise. The return on capital employed percentage can be used to compare the performance of one company with that of another similar company, or with its own performance in previous years.

$$\frac{\text{Net Profit}}{\text{Capital Employed}} \times \frac{100}{1} = \frac{£50\,000}{£250\,000} \times \frac{100}{1} = 20\,\%$$

Care must be taken, however, to ensure the comparison of like with like, or a misleading conclusion may be drawn from the figures.

The choice of accounting period is important in the measurement of income. Business transactions go on from day to day, and there is never any one time at which all business transactions cease and then start again on the next day. Thus whatever the accounting date chosen there will always be some transactions which transcend the end of the period. The idea of an accounting period is thus an artificial one, but it would be equally false to go on recording transactions without attempting to measure their profitability. Pacioli recognized this when he wrote that frequent accounting in a partnership makes for long friendship.

The choice of accounting period depends upon the person for whom the income statement is to be prepared. Most companies publish accounts annually to show their shareholders how the business has performed during the year, and many companies also produce an interim set of accounts half-way through the year to provide investors with extra information on which to base their decisions. For management purposes accounts are usually produced monthly, and in much greater detail.

The choice of accounting period is an arbitrary one, and is determined for reasons of convenience. Some companies organize their year to run from 1 April until 31 March so that it is the same as the fiscal year of the Inland Revenue Authorities. Others, however, prefer the calendar year, and their accounts are for the period 1 January to 31 December. Companies in a seasonal industry usually arrange for their year end to come after the end of the season, while others plan their year end to fall in the slack season for audit staff. Obviously, if many companies had a year end date at 31 December there would be a heavy demand for the services of audit clerks during the months of January, February and March.

THE ACCRUALS PRINCIPLE

The accruals, or matching principle, is the device adopted by the accountant to isolate the transactions of any one accounting period from those of the next period. If a true profit is to be computed sales for the period must be set against the cost of goods sold during that period. This means that the cost of the products sold this year must be charged in the revenue account this year, even though those products were made last year. It also means that there is a difference between expense and expenditure, since money may be paid out for costs incurred in one accounting period, but those costs cannot be charged against sales as an expense until the next accounting period, when the goods are sold. (See figure 4.)

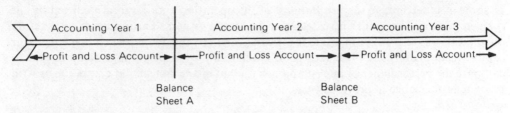

Figure 4

A cost is the amount paid out for a service or benefit received, or a sacrifice made in order to achieve a stated end. The cost is entered in the books of account when it is paid for, or when a liability for such payment is recognized. At this point the cost has been incurred to acquire an asset, and this asset can be charged to the profit and loss account as a cost when it is consumed or used up, but not when the cash changes hands. A cost incurred in one period will often be carried forward in the balance sheet as an asset and written off to the profit and loss account in the next period, since it is then that the goods made when the cost was incurred are sold. Cost properly chargeable to the income statement in a particular period includes the cost of products sold this year, even though they were made in a previous year, the wages earned by employees who made and sold these products, even though these wages were earned and paid in a previous year, and in some cases a share of the overhead expenses of the business for the year of manufacture rather than the year of sale. The stock of finished goods made in Year 1 but not sold by the end of that year appears in balance sheet A as an asset, at an amount equal to the costs incurred in Year 1 to make the goods.

Four separate cases emerge.

a.   A cost this year which is paid for this year: An example of such a cost is the payment of wages for labour used to make products which have been sold during the year.

b.   A cost this year which was paid for last year: This means that an asset acquired last year, and shown in the balance sheet at the end of that year, becomes a cost in the profit and loss account this year. For example, raw materials purchased last year and kept in stock are charged to the income statement this year, when they are consumed in the production process.

c.   The cost of a future period which is paid for this year: For example, raw materials bought during the year but not used, which appear in the closing balance sheet as an asset, stock.

d.   The cost of this year which will be paid for in a future period: For example, raw materials delivered and used up during the year for which a bill has not been received and payment has not yet been made.

PREPAYMENTS AND ACCRUALS

The amounts recorded in the books of the business have to be adjusted for the four cases shown above, so that the true cost is entered in the income statement. A prepayment, or payment in advance, is such an adjustment. Suppose that rent is paid on business premises for a year in advance on 30 June. If the accounting year of the business runs from 1 January until 31 December, at the end of the year half of the rent paid on 30 June will be a cost properly chargeable for the year to 31 December, and the other half will represent the cost of the next accounting period, paid in advance. This prepayment is an asset at 31 December, since the business possesses the right to use the premises for the next six months. Technically the landlord owes the business six months' rent, or six months' use, at 31 December, and this is shown in the balance sheet as a debtor. In the next accounting period this asset will be converted to a cost and charged to the income statement. Other expenses which can be paid in advance include insurance premiums, rates for a year, rentals on leased plant and vehicles, and the annual road fund licence for a vehicle. Two examples of case (c) are shown below.

Dr.		Rent Account		Cr.
	£			£
Year 1: 30 June cash paid	1 200	31 December charge to profit and loss		600
		31 December balance carried forward		600
	£1 200			£1 200
Year 2: 1 January balance brought down	600	31 December charge to profit and loss		1 300
30 June cash paid	1 400	31 December balance carried forward		700
	£2 000			£2 000
Year 3: 1 January balance brought down	700			

Rent Paid in Advance. Note that the rent has increased in the second year. It is paid annually in advance.

Dr.		Materials		Cr.
	£			£
1 Jan purchased for cash	439	31 Dec charge to manufacturing account		14 387
15 May purchased on credit from J. Brown	5 617	31 Dec balance of stock carried forward		1 304
25 Sept purchased on credit from A. Smith	9 635			
	£15 691			£15 691
1 Jan balance brought down	1 304			

Raw Materials Purchased but not Consumed. Stock and purchases are recorded in the same account in this example. Sometimes stock is shown in a stock account which has only the opening balance on the account until that balance is transferred to the manufacturing account or trading account at the year end and replaced by the closing stock, which is the opening stock for the next year.

An accrued expense is a cost for the current year which has been incurred but not yet paid for or even invoiced. In this case the accountant must use his expertise to estimate what the expense is likely to be when the bill is eventually presented, and to charge this amount in the income statement so that a true profit is shown. According to the principle of duality, if a cost is entered on one side of the ledger a liability to meet the cost must be shown on the other side.

The cost of electricity provides a good example of an accrued expense. Electricity will have been used by the office and factory right up to the accounting date, but the most recent bill for electricity will show only the cost up to the date on which the meter was read, which could be a month or more before the year end. The accountant must estimate the liability for electricity for the period between the meter reading and the year end and charge it in the income statement. The balance sheet will show a liability for this amount, and when the electricity bill is presented at some date in the next year, that part of it which concerns this year will already have been charged to the profit and loss account and thus will not distort next year's costs.

Dr.		Electricity		Cr.
	£			£
		Profit and loss account		
Year 1: 10 April electricity bill	514	charge for the year		2326
14 July electricity bill	632			
9 October electricity bill	580			
31 December accrued				
balance carried forward	600			
	£2326			£2326
Year 2: 20 Jan electricity bill	612	1 Jan balance brought		
		down		600

Electricity Consumed but no Bill Received – an Accrual. The accountant has estimated the missing bill for electricity consumed in the last three months of the year as £600. This has been charged to Year 1 and carried forward to Year 2 so that when the bill eventually appears it is offset by the credit balance waiting for it. Thus a Year 1 expense is not allowed to interfere with profit measurement in Year 2, except in so far as the accountant has incorrectly estimated the amount of the bill.

Fixed assets of a business are acquired for use in more than one accounting period. Thus the cost of a machine with a ten-year life should be charged out to the ten accounting periods covered by that life. The term used for spreading the cost of a fixed asset over several accounting periods is depreciation. A charge for depreciation is made in the income statement each year and gradually the asset is turned into an expense and written off against sales in the years in which it makes a contribution to those sales.

Deferred revenue expenditure is a term given to costs which provide a benefit in more than one accounting period and which are spread across those periods for this reason. An advertising campaign to establish a new product may give benefit by generating sales over the next two or even three years. Accordingly it is fair to charge out this cost to the accounting periods which benefit from it, so that at the end of the first year the cost of advertising not yet charged out will appear in the balance sheet as an asset.

Development expenditure on a product or project yet to be marketed is sometimes carried forward as an asset until such time as there is sales revenue from that product against which the development costs can be written off. An accountant, however, will defer such revenue expenditure only if he is certain that sales will follow, since it is contrary to the concept of conservatism to carry forward the cost if there is a chance that revenue will not ensue.

The accruals principle also applies to revenue from sales. Cash received is not synonymous with sales. Goods may be sold on credit, and even though the payment has not been received the sales can be counted in the income computation. Once again the concept of conservatism ensures that provision for doubtful debts is made in this case.

Cash received in one year may not concern sales of that year, since it may represent payments made by debtors for sales made in a previous period. In this case one asset, a debt, has been exchanged for another, cash, with no impact on the income statement.

Some authorities hold that a true profit for the accounting period can be shown only if extraordinary or non-recurring items such as the impact of a fire or strike are separated from the main profit computation. Some entries in the income statement which correct mistakes in adjustments made in previous years will also blur the true profit for the current year. When an accountant makes adjustments such as those discussed above he must use a degree of care and professional skill, yet at the same time he must apply the concept of materiality in that where a truer estimate could be made after detailed analysis of a position, the cost of the analysis may be more than the benefit to be derived from the extra accuracy it provides.

CAPITAL AND REVENUE EXPENDITURE

The division of expenditure between capital expenditure and revenue expenditure has a significant impact on the computation of business income, since revenue expenditure is chargeable to the income statement, while capital expenditure concerns the acquisition of an asset which is to be carried forward in the balance sheet. Any expenditure for acquiring, extending or improving assets of a permanent nature which are to be used to carry on the business or to increase the earning capacity of the business is termed capital expenditure. A revenue expenditure item is one made to carry on the normal course of the business and to maintain the capital assets in a state of efficiency, e.g. repairs and renewals.

There are no hard and fast rules to delineate capital and revenue. The guidelines used when an accountant arrives at his opinion of how to treat a certain expenditure are as follows. Capital expenditure will improve the earning power of the business or reduce running costs. It is usually laid out to create or acquire a long-lived asset, but it need not concern a tangible asset. In cases where the labour force of the business is used in the construction of capital assets, there must be a transfer out of the costs for the year into the asset account, which will be carried forward in the balance sheet. Revenue expenditure is outlay to maintain the earning capacity of the business and keep the fixed assets in a fully efficient state. Since the border line between capital and revenue expenditure is not clearly defined, individual cases are dealt with on their merits. An asset classed as a capital or fixed asset for one company may be a current asset for another company. For example, a vehicle is usually a fixed asset, since the company intends to use it over a period of years, but it could be classed as stock in trade if it is used for resale.

RESERVES AND PROVISIONS

A provision is an amount charged against profit for depreciation, or to provide for any known cost the exact amount of which cannot be accurately determined, such as bad debts. An accrual is a provision, since it is the charge made against profits for a cost which has been incurred but cannot be determined accurately at the accounting date. Thus provisions are charges against the profit figure before the profit is struck.

A reserve is an amount set aside for other purposes. It is an appropriation of profit and represents that part of the year's profit which is to be retained in the business for various reasons. On the balance sheet the reserves show the total of past profits retained in the business. Although these 'ploughed-back' profits represent a further investment in the business by the shareholders, the legal position is that reserves are available for distribution as dividend unless it is stated on the balance sheet that they are not available for distribution.

THE QUADRANT AND THE SEXTANT

The quadrant is a device which helps to explain the duality of accounting transactions so far as they affect the income statement and the balance sheet. The balance sheet sets assets against liabilities, while the income statement sets costs against sales. Therefore if a diagram with four boxes is drawn, showing assets and costs on the left (the debit side) and liabilities and sales revenue on the right (the credit side), the interplay of transactions on these four basic items can be demonstrated, and the rudiments of the double-entry system revealed.

Dr.	Cr.	
Assets	Liabilities + Capital	Position Statement
Costs	Revenue	Income Statement

The principle of duality states that every transaction has a double effect on the position of a business as recorded in the accounts, and thus the double-entry book-keeping system records transactions twice, once on the debit side and once on the credit side. A transaction which increases the assets or costs of the business, and thus increases the debits recorded in the books, must also either increase the liabilities or revenue on the credit side, or reduce some other asset on the debit side, so that the overall balance of debits against credits is maintained. When this device is extended to a sextant, by adding a line to analyse movements in the cash book, the impact of transactions on one single but important asset, cash, is shown.

Dr.	Cr.	
Assets	Liabilities + Capital	Position Statement
Costs	Revenue	Income Statement
Receipts	Payments	Cash Book

Example

The following transactions recorded in the ledgers of a business would have the following dual impact.

a. Share capital subscribed, £20 000: A liability is recorded on the credit side and a receipt of cash on the debit side.
b. Plant purchased for cash, £10 000: Assets have increased on the debit side and payments in the cash book on the credit side.
c. Stock purchased on credit terms, £5000: Assets have increased again but are balanced by an increased liability on the credit side.
d. Part of the stock payed for, £4000: The payment of cash is recorded on the credit side and is balanced by a decrease of the liability, also on the credit side.
e. Some of the stock is used in production, £3000: An asset has decreased but it is balanced by an increase in cost, also on the debit side. If accounting statements were prepared at this moment part of the stock would be charged as a cost and the remainder carried forward as an asset in the balance sheet.
f. Wages paid, £2000: Costs have increased on the debit side and are balanced by a payment of cash on the credit side.
g. Payment of insurance premium, £600: An increase in cost balanced by a payment of cash.
h. Part of the insurance premium concerns the next accounting period and is thus a prepayment in the sum of £200: Costs must be decreased on the debit side and balanced by an increase in assets when the provision for payment in advance is made and recorded in the balance sheet.
i. Plant depreciated by £1000: Costs have increased and are balanced by a decrease in assets.
j. An accrual is made for electricity costs, £100: Costs have increased on the debit side and are balanced by an increased liability when the estimated amount is recorded as a creditor in the balance sheet.
k. Goods are sold on credit terms, £12 000: The sales revenue is recorded on the credit side and is balanced by the creation of an asset, debtors, on the debit side.
l. Some debtors pay, £6000: The decrease in the asset is balanced by the receipt of cash, both on the debit side. The books can now be balanced at the end of the year.
m. Closing: In the cash book any surplus of receipts over payments will be recorded as an asset, cash, in the balance sheet. The income statement can then be completed so that the surplus of sales over costs can be added to the owner's interest on the liabilities side of the balance sheet. The other balances outstanding in the accounts in the ledger are recorded in the balance sheet, which must also balance.
n. The board decide to pay a dividend of 10 per cent: Thus £2000 is to be appropriated out of the profit and paid to the shareholders. This will increase the debit side of the costs (though a dividend is not really a cost) and, since the dividend is not yet paid, it must appear in the balance sheet as a liability. Alternatively, the provision of a dividend can be seen as a reduction in the owner's interest, since profits retained are reduced.

If the above transactions are correctly entered on both sides of a sextant, a set of accounts such as those below can be produced.

Income Statement . . . Period

	£		£
Costs:		Sales	12 000
Materials	3 000		
Wages	2 000		
Insurance	400		
Depreciation	1 000		
Electricity	100		
Net Profit	5 500		
	£12 000		£12 000

Balance Sheet as at . . .

	£	£	Fixed Assets:	£	£
Capital		20 000	Plant at cost		10 000
Add net profit		5 500	Less depreciation		1 000
		25 500			9 000
Current Liabilities:			Current Assets:		
Creditors	1000		Stock	2000	
Accruals	100		Debtors	6000	
		1 100	Prepayments	200	
		£26 600	Cash	9400	
					17 600
					£26 600

TUTORIAL DISCUSSION TOPICS

5.1. What is the difference between capital expenditure and revenue expenditure? Why is this difference important?

5.2. Differentiate between payments made in an accounting period and costs incurred in that period. Why is this difference important?

5.3. What effect will profit have on the amount of an owner's interest in the business? Are the drawings of the proprietor an expense of the business?

5.4. The terms 'revenue' and 'income' are often used interchangeably. Are they synonymous?

5.5. Differentiate between a reserve and a provision. What do the reserves represent in the balance sheet and how are they linked to the income statement?

SEMINAR EXERCISES 3

1. (a) Indicate the extent to which each of the following items is an expense of the year ended 31 December, and show the total expenses for the year.

   (i) goods received and paid for during the year, £37 712, of which items costing a total of £2430 were still in stock at the year end;
   (ii) goods received during the year but not yet paid for, £3840, of which items costing a total of £360 were still in stock at the year end;
   (iii) goods in stock at the beginning of the year, £800, and all sold during the year;
   (iv) payments during the year (additional to the above) to suppliers for goods received last year, £937;
   (v) wages paid during the year and all earned during the year, £230;
   (vi) insurance policy taken out on 30 June, one year's premium of £360, being paid in advance;
   (vii) other expenses relating to the year and all paid for in that year, £1790;
   (viii) equipment purchased in earlier years, having a value at the beginning of the year of £4000 and expected to be used for a further three years;
   (ix) You estimate electricity used but unpaid for at 31 December to be £380.

   (b) Complete the following calculation of profit (or loss) for the year:

	£
Revenue for the year from sales	45 000
Less total expenses as in (a) above	
Profit (or loss) for the year	£

   (c) Complete the balance sheet as it would have appeared at the beginning of the year:

	£		£
Owner's capital		Equipment	
Trade creditors		Stock	
		Creditors	2100
		Cash	450
	£		£

   (d) Write up the summary of the cash book to compute the balance at the beginning of the year:

	£		£
Balance at beginning		Payments for:	
Receipt for sale of goods		Goods	
(all goods sold were		Wages	
paid for during the year)		Insurance	
		Expenses	
		Balance at end	
	£		£

(e) Draw up the balance sheet as it would appear at the end of the year:

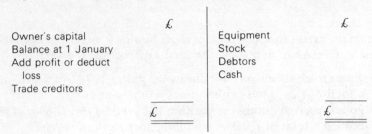

	£		£
Owner's capital		Equipment	
Balance at 1 January		Stock	
Add profit or deduct		Debtors	
loss		Cash	
Trade creditors			
	£		£

(f) What assumptions have you made in producing these figures?

2. John Ash runs a tobacconist's shop. On 1 January his assets consisted of a stock of pipes and tobacco which had cost £10 800, a bank account containing £910, and his shop premises, which were worth £15 000. He owed suppliers £3200. On 31 December, after one year's trading, his assets were: pipes and tobacco, £7700; debtors, £2300; cash, £1237; and his premises as above. During the year he had taken £20 per week out of the till to be used as housekeeping money. Creditors at the year end were owed £1460.
   What profit has John Ash made during the year?

3. M. A. Tellow started to trade as an agent for the sale of canal cruisers on 1 January. During his first month of trading he sold boats for £53 000, comprising £10 800 for cash and the remainder on credit terms. He introduced £20 000 of his own money into the business at its inception, and an aunt lent him a further £10 000. He rented premises on 1 January and paid £500 as two months' rent in advance on that day. The costs of running his premises, including the wages of an assistant, were paid in cash on the last day of the month in the sum of £980. He was unable to pay his electricity bill as the meter had not been read, but estimated the cost for the month as £50. An insurance premium for a year's cover was paid on 1 January. It cost £1200. During the month boats were purchased for £47 000, and so far £7000 has been paid to the suppliers. Boats remaining unsold on 31 January had cost £15 000.

   (a) Compute the bank balance of M. A. Tellow as at 31 January.
   (b) Calculate the profit he made during January.

4. Jack Purser is a trader in leather goods who conducts his business in a London street market. He trades on both cash and credit terms. At the start of a week he had a stock which cost £1200, £400 in his bank account and debts owed to him by past customers totalling £1120. He had no assets other than his barrow (worth £800) and no liabilities. During the week he sells goods for cash at £2520 and makes credit sales of £2400. His purchases of stock amount to £2300 and he pays for them in cash. At the end of the week he still has his barrow, and a stock of goods which cost him £1360. His bank balance stands at £880, and the amount owed to him by credit customers has risen to £3040.

   (a) Work out a profit figure for Jack's trading for the week and draw up his balance sheet at the end of the week.
   (b) What assumptions have you made in computing the figures in (a) above?

5. The following information refers to rent, rates and insurance account for the year to 30 June. Rent is paid quarterly in advance on the last day of March, June, September and December. Rates are paid half yearly in advance, in March and September. Insurance is an annual premium paid on 1 January.

> Opening balances:
>> Payment in advance   Insurance £600
>> Accrued   Rent £400
>>   Rates £200
>
> Payments:
>> Rent   30 September £400
>>   31 December £400
>>   31 March £400
>>   30 June £400
>> Insurance   1 January £1200
>> Rates   10 July £400
>>   30 September £500

Note: It seems as though the local authority were slow in sending out their rate bills in March of last year.

Write up the rent, rates and insurance account for the year.

6 | Depreciation

A popular definition of depreciation among accountants is that it is the diminution in value of a fixed asset due to use and/or the passage of time. SSAP 12 defines it as the measure of the wearing out, consumption or other loss of value of a fixed asset, whether arising from use, passing of time or obsolescence through technology and market changes.

Economists have noted the fact that the fixed assets of a business lose their value, and have given several reasons for this loss. First, assets become worth less merely because they are second-hand, even though they are as useful as a new asset. Second, assets suffer a fall in value because their earning capacity is reduced. The asset may be just as efficient as it was on the day that it was purchased, but because improved technology has produced more efficient machines to compete with it, or because demand for the products of the asset has fallen, the asset may no longer be capable of profitable operation. This is often termed 'obsolescence'. Third, physical deterioration or wear and tear is a reason for a fixed asset losing its value during its working life. The asset is worth less simply because it is less efficient and its performance has deteriorated.

Fourth, the passage of time reduces the value of an asset which has a definite limit to its life, such as a lease or patent right granted for a number of years. It is the task of the accountant to attempt to account for the fall in value of an asset noted by the economist, but the accountant approaches this task as a matter of allocation rather than valuation.

The financial accountant will attempt to spread the capital cost of an asset, less its terminal scrap value, over the years of its estimated useful life, gradually translating an asset into an expense. He sees depreciation as a product of time, not a measure of the fall in value or physical deterioration of the asset to be charged to an accounting period. Unfortunately, the choice of method used for depreciation is often made arbitrarily, and the charge does not reflect the real fall in value, whether from obsolescence or wear and tear (allocation rather than valuation). A cost accountant views depreciation as a means of charging for the use of an asset during the period in which it has been used. He seeks to match cost against revenue produced by the asset.

Thus there are two different approaches to the same problem. However, depreciation means that a charge is being made to the income statement to set aside out of revenue something to make up for that part of a past investment which has been used up during the accounting period. If this is not done then capital depletion will occur. A business which fails to take depreciation into account finds, at the end of the life of a particular asset, that it has used up the asset over a period of years without setting aside out of the profits of those years amounts with which to replace the capital of the company which was invested in the asset many years previously. A provision for depreciation reduces profit by an amount which might otherwise have been seen as available for distribution as a dividend. Without depreciation the fixed asset is used up, profits are overstated since no charge for the use of the asset has been made, and if those profits are all distributed in the form of a dividend, the funds invested in the business will have been run down during the life of the asset. When this asset is worthless, the store of assets representing the shareholders' funds invested in the business will have been depleted, unless the annual provision for depreciation (reinvested in the business and not distributed) maintains the general stock of assets, and thus the amount of shareholders' capital employed.

Many students make a connection between depreciation and replacement, saying that the amount calculated for depreciation is set aside to provide a fund with which to replace the asset. However, this is not so. The amounts set aside for depreciation reduce the profit available for distribution and are reinvested in the business. At the end of the life of the asset these amounts are tied up in the general assets of the business and can be released by the sale of those assets to provide liquid funds (cash). These funds can be used to buy another similar asset, but need not be so used. They are available to be used in whatever way the directors of the company wish. They can be withdrawn from the business, they can be used to finance a new venture, they can be used to buy more machinery, or they can stay where they are as finance supporting the general assets of the business. It is unlikely that they will be used to buy exactly the same type of machine, since as technology is improved more sophisticated machines replace the old ones which are being retired. Depreciation is not a saving scheme to provide funds for replacement, unless of course it is linked to a 'sinking fund' whereby cash is set aside each year and invested outside the company to mature at the end of the life of the asset. The annual investment of an amount of cash, equal to the provision for depreciation, outside the business is a separate operation, and is not part of accounting for depreciation as such. Very few companies now use this sinking fund technique, since they take the view that the best use of the depreciation amount is to reinvest it in their own company and avoid an outflow of cash.

The role of estimates in depreciation must be recognized. The length of the useful life of an asset is uncertain and can be shortened by unforeseen obsolescence, while the scrap value to be received for what is left of the asset at the end of its life must also often be estimated.

Example

Jack Spratt starts up in the demolition business and uses all his funds to buy a bulldozer for £10 000. He expects the machine to last for four years before it is worn out. Each year he receives £50 000 for work he has done and pays out £40 000 for the costs of the work. Thus his cash book will show a balance of £10 000 at the end of his first year of trading.

An accountant advises him that he has not made a profit of £10 000, and warns him that he must spread the cost of the bulldozer over the years of its useful life. His real profit is £7500, and this is the amount he draws out of the business that year.

Opening Balance Sheet of Jack Spratt

	£		£
Capital	10 000	Cash	10 000

Balance Sheet of Jack Spratt at end of Year 1

	£		£
Capital	10 000	Bulldozer	10 000
		Less	
		depreciation	2 500
			7 500
		Cash	2 500
	£10 000		£10 000

At the end of four years his balance sheet would appear as follows:

Balance Sheet of Jack Spratt

	£		£
Capital	10 000	Bulldozer	10 000
		Less	
		depreciation	10 000
			Nil
		Cash	10 000
	£10 000		£10 000

Thus he is back in the same position as at the start of the life of the asset, with a capital of £10 000 represented by cash. The bulldozer is shown at no value, and this is a true statement of the situation. If he had failed to provide for depreciation he would have had a profit of £10 000 each year, and if he had drawn that amount his capital would have been depleted, and would have been completely consumed by the end of year four. As it is, he now has funds in liquid form again, and it is for him to decide what he now wishes to do with them. He may buy another bulldozer, he may retire and buy a country cottage, or he may decide to invest his funds in stock exchange securities and live off the income from them. Unfortunately, in a period of inflation, depreciation puts back out of the profits only the money amount of the original investment used up, and this may not be sufficient to buy the same amount of goods and services as the original funds could buy. In a more sophisticated example the £10 000 of cash in the balance sheet of year four would instead be held in the form of general assets such as stock or debtors.

THE METHODS USED

The methods used to account for depreciation are arbitrary and reflect the uncertainty in the estimates made by the accountant and his colleagues. It is only with the revaluation method that depreciation each year is the same as the real fall in value experienced by the asset. SSAP 12 does not recommend any one method as being better than others.

The Straight Line Method

The cost of an asset less its scrap value is divided by the years of its useful life to compute the charge per annum. Thus this method gives an equal charge per annum over the assumed life of the asset, it is simple to compute, and it spreads the cost in a fair way over the years of the life of the asset. The obsolescence factor can be built into the estimate of the useful life in the formula.

However, this method does not take into account use, since the same charge is made to the profit and loss account each year although the asset may not work as hard in one year as in another. Some accountants argue that even though a machine does not work it is still losing value, and that this loss is the cost of holding the asset for the year even though it is not used. Others take the view that if there is no revenue for the use of an asset during the year then the cost of holding the asset has not been matched with the revenue produced by the asset, and that it is wrong to have the same charge each year, since it is unlikely that the asset will depreciate evenly over the years of its life. They further argue that the cost of repairs for a machine is likely to be heavier in the later years of its life, while its performance will be least effective at this time, and therefore a lighter depreciation charge is needed to compensate for this situation.

In spite of this argument the straight line method remains the most widely used method of depreciation in this country. The formula for the method is:

$$\frac{\text{Cost} - \text{Scrap}}{\text{Life}} = \text{Annual Charge}$$

The Reducing Balance Method

This method writes off a constant proportion of a continually reducing balance each year and has the merit of making a high charge in the early years of the asset's life and a low one later, when repair bills may be heavy. It is argued in favour of this method that this will provide a uniform expense throughout the life of the asset. Also, if the obsolescence factor of the asset is high then more is written off in the early years, so that a smaller amount is left in the later years to form a capital loss if the asset should prove worthless before the end of its estimated life. Some accountants, however, argue that it is not right to charge a different amount of depreciation for the use of the same machine in successive years, and that the fact that repair bills are high in the later years only reflects the facts which should influence what appears in the accounting statements.

This method is nevertheless widely used, but the percentage to be written off the reducing balance each year is often decided arbitrarily. Those who wish to be more scientific in the calculation of the rate can use the formula

$$r = \left(1 - \sqrt[n]{\frac{s}{c}}\right) \times 100\%$$

where r = the rate, s = the scrap value, c = the cost, and n = the number of years.

Example

A machine costing £20 000 is deemed to have a six-year life and a scrap value of £5240 at the end of its working life. By application of the formula a rate is found which can be applied to the reducing balance:

$$\text{Rate} = \left(1 - \sqrt[6]{\frac{5240}{20\,000}}\right) \times 100\%$$

$$= \left(1 - \sqrt[6]{\cdot 262}\right) \times 100\%$$

$$= (1 - \cdot 8) \times 100\%$$

$$= 20\%$$

The depreciation computation is as follows:

	£
Cost	20 000
Depreciation Year 1 (20% ×£20 000)	4 000
Written down value	16 000
Depreciation Year 2 (20% ×£16 000)	3 200
Written down value	12 800
Depreciation Year 3 (20% ×£12 800)	2 560
Written down value	10 240
Depreciation Year 4 (20% ×£10 240)	2 048
Written down value	8 192
Depreciation Year 5 (20% × £8192)	1 638
Written down value	6 554
Depreciation Year 6 (20% ×£6554)	1 310
Written down value when sold	£5 244

The difference of £4 is due to rounding in the calculation.

If the machine makes 4000 articles each year, is it fair to charge for depreciation £1 to the cost of each article made by the machine in Year 1, and only 33 pence to each of 4000 articles made in Year 6? The difference represents no cost saving or efficiency, but is a result of the method of depreciation selected. Unless the situation is suitable to this method, the calculation may give a rate which distorts the cost and profit shown. For example, a machine costing £20 000, with a four-year life and a scrap value of £512, produces a rate of 60 per cent, which, when applied, writes off £12 000 as depreciation in the first year.

A similar method which also concentrates the bulk of the depreciation charge in the early years is the sum of the digits method. In this case the years are treated as digits and are added together. Thus the total digits for a machine with a three-year life would equal $1 + 2 + 3 = 6$. The annual depreciation charge is computed by dividing the total of the digits into the digit for a particular year to give that proportion of the total cost to be charged in that year. Thus depreciation in the first year would be 3/6 times the cost, in the second year 2/6 times the cost, and so on.

The Revaluation Method

This method takes the view that the charge for depreciation, or the cost of holding the asset during the year, is the amount by which the asset has fallen in value during the year. Thus the asset is revalued at the end of each year and the amount of depreciation is computed. This method is advantageous where the amount of deterioration of the asset is uncertain, because objective valuation can be used to provide the amount. Items such as contractors' plant, loose tools, livestock, etc. are all examples of assets which can be depreciated in this way. However, much depends upon the efficiency of the valuer, since bias can intrude into the valuation process. If this method is to be used correctly the same valuer should be employed each year. Arguments against this method are that valuation takes time, is expensive, and is after all only an estimate. It is also difficult to separate the increase in the value of an asset caused by inflation from the decrease in the value of an asset caused by wear and tear. In certain cases special conditions could result in a negative charge for depreciation. This is the only method in which the depreciation noted by the economist equals the amount written off by the accountant.

The Production Unit Method

This method attempts to relate depreciation to the use of the asset. The cost of the asset net of the scrap value is divided by the number of units the asset is expected to produce during its useful life. Thus a rate is computed which can be applied each year to the number of units actually produced to calculate the depreciation charge. The production unit method can be operated successfully if all units produced by the asset are the same and have the same work value. It is sometimes used to depreciate the cost of a mine where one can forecast the amount of ore to be produced before the mine is worked out, or of a press which should perform a certain number of operations before it is worn out. However, the depreciation charge is made only when the machine is used, so obsolescence during an idle period cannot be accounted for. Attempts are sometimes made to build an obsolescence factor into the calculation of the units in the life of the asset, but this amount is often an estimate of doubtful validity. The formula for this method is

$$\frac{\text{Cost} - \text{Scrap}}{\text{Expected Units}} = \text{Unit Rate}.$$

The Production Hour Method

This is a variation of the production unit method; it provides a rate per hour for depreciation rather than a rate per unit produced. To compute the rate to be used the cost of the asset less the scrap value is divided by the working hours in the life of the asset. The advantage of this method is that it can be applied to a machine which produces different items and takes different amounts of time to produce them. A machine such as a lathe can be employed on many different operations, and since time is the common denominator depreciation can be linked directly to the product cost. Once again depreciation is related to use, and there is the disadvantage that no charge is made if the asset is not used. The formula is

$$\frac{\text{Cost} - \text{Scrap}}{\text{Hours}} = \text{Rate}.$$

THE ACCOUNTING ENTRIES

The accounting entries to record depreciation have a dual purpose. They show the charge to be made in the profit and loss account for the use of the asset during the year, and in the balance sheet they show the cumulative amount of expired cost which has been provided against the original investment in the asset. In the balance sheet the fixed assets are always shown at cost less total depreciation to date = net. Although there is no section in the

Companies Acts which says that a company must depreciate its fixed assets, if it does depreciate, the amount of depreciation must be shown, and additional charges for renewal must be noted, as must provisions for replacement of fixed assets other than by depreciation charge, or the fact that no provision has been made.

An interesting position arises when assets are used after they have been fully depreciated. This means that their actual life is longer than that estimated when they were first purchased, and therefore the depreciation charge in past profit and loss accounts has been too high, so profit has been understated. There are three courses of action open to the accountant in this event.

First, he can charge nothing for depreciation of this asset, since it has already been fully written off. This, however, is taken to be unrealistic, since the machine is being used, and on the grounds that a profit figure computed on this basis is unreal for comparison purposes with the results of previous years.

A second course is to charge the same amount of depreciation as before. Having debited the profit and loss account, one is left with the problem of what to do with the corresponding credit. Some say that it should be set off against the overheads of the business, while others prefer to enter it into a reserve for obsolescence account which can be used in cases where other assets are prematurely retired and capital losses are made.

A third alternative is to revalue the machine, debiting the asset and crediting a capital reserve account, and then to write off the new asset value over what is considered to be the remaining life of the asset. It is of course preferable to discover that the depreciation charge is too much well before the end of the life of the asset, so that the annual charge for the remaining years can be revised.

Premature Retirement

Where assets are retired prematurely, i.e. their actual life is shorter than estimated, there may be a loss, since they may not be written down to their estimated realizable value at the time of their retirement. In this case past depreciation has been too small and thus profit has been overstated. For these reasons some accountants argue that the capital loss should be written off at once, although they can see that it is unfair to charge any of this loss to a particular product or department of the business. In this situation, however, the accountant often meets pressure from management to spread the burden of the capital loss over more than one accounting period.

Example

Depreciation in the ledger accounts: A company aquires a machine for £2100. It decides to depreciate it over a five-year life, and assumes that its scrap value at the end of five years will be £100.

$$\frac{\text{Cost} - \text{Scrap}}{\text{Life}} = \frac{£2100 - £100}{5} = £400 \text{ p.a. as depreciation.}$$

The machine is sold at the end of four years for £300 cash.
Steps in the accounting procedure are:

1. Record the acquisition of an asset, a machine, for cash, as the reduction of another asset.

2. Record the depreciation as a cost in the income statement each year and show the year-end position, i.e. cost less depreciation to date gives the unexpired capital cost at the end of Year 4 immediately before the sale.
3. Record the disposal of the asset for cash at the end of Year 4 and the transfer of any profit or loss on the deal to the income statement for that year.

Note: Under the principle of duality every debit must have a credit.

Dr.	Machine Account		Cr.
	£		£
Year 1: Cash paid for asset	2100	Year 4: Transfer to disposal account	2100

Dr.	Cash Book		Cr.
	£		£
		Year 1: Asset bought	2100
Year 4: Asset sold	300		

Dr.	Profit and Loss Account		Cr.
	£		
Year 1: Depreciation	400		
Year 2: Depreciation	400		
Year 3: Depreciation	400		
Year 4: Depreciation	400		
Loss on sale	200		

Dr.	Depreciation Provision Account		Cr.
	£		£
		Year 1: Charge to profit and loss account	400
		Year 2: Charge to profit and loss account	400
		Year 3: Charge to profit and loss account	400
Year 4: Transfer to disposal account	1600	Year 4: Charge to profit and loss account	400
	£1600		£1600

Dr.	Disposal Account		Cr.
	£		£
Year 4: Cost of machine	2100	Year 4: Depreciation to date	1600
		Cash	300
		Loss to profit and loss account	200
	£2100		£2100

Excerpt from balance sheet as at end of Year 4 but before sale of machine:

Fixed assets	Cost	Depreciation	Net
	£	£	£
Plant and machinery	2100	1600	500

In the last example the balance sheet at the end of Year 4 showed as net figure the written-down value at that time. The balances in the machinery account and the depreciation account for this asset were transferred to the disposal account, thus ensuring that they no longer appeared in the balances of those two accounts shown in the balance sheet after the sale of the machine. The term used for these entries is 'writing off' to the disposal account. The cash received from the sale of the asset was set against the written-down value of the asset in the disposal account, to reveal whether a profit or a loss had been made on the sale. A loss at this point means that depreciation to date set off against profits in previous years has not been sufficient to keep pace with the declining value of the asset, and as such shows that past profit has been overstated. The loss is transferred at once to the debit side of the profit and loss account, so that it is set off against profits in the year of its discovery. If the price received for the asset had exceeded the written-down value, then a profit on the sale would have been made. This profit would have appeared as a debit balance in the disposal account, and would have been credited to the profit and loss account. In this way over- or under-depreciation over a period of years will distort the profit shown in the year of sale of the asset, and should strictly speaking be shown as an extraordinary item so that a true profit figure for trading operations appears separately.

In the case of an asset retired prematurely, the cost and depreciation to date can be written off to a retirement account, so that entries for the retired asset are deleted from figures which appear in the balance sheet. When an asset is retired before reaching the end of what was considered to be its useful life, there is a surplus of cost over depreciation, i.e. a debit balance on the retirement account, which is written off to the profit and loss account to charge the loss made on the scrapped asset against profits for the year. Any cash received from the sale of the asset is debited to the cash book and credited to the retirement account, thus reducing the loss on retirement.

Example

Taking the figures in the ledger entries example above, suppose that at the end of Year 3 the machine is found to be obsolete, as the process for which it is used is no longer required. The machine is promptly written off and sold to a scrap dealer for £50.

Dr.	Machine Account		Cr.
	£		£
Year 3: Balance	2100	Year 3: Transfer to disposal account	2100·

Dr.	Depreciation Provision Account		Cr.
	£		£
Year 3: Transfer to disposal account	1200	Year 3: Balance	1200

Dr.   Retirement Account   Cr.

	£		£
Year 3: Transfer from asset account	2100	Year 3: Depreciation to date	1200
		Cash	50
		Loss on machine profit and loss	
		account	850
	£2100		£2100

Dr.   Cash Book   Cr.

	£		£
Year 3: Sale of machine for scrap	50		

In effect the loss of £850 charged against profit in Year 3 is to catch up as soon as possible with the fact that profits in Years 1 and 2 have been overstated, because of a mistake made when the life of the machine was originally estimated for the depreciation calculation.

SSAP 12 states that where the cost of an asset is not likely to be recouped from revenue generated by that asset, the book value of the asset must be reduced accordingly as soon as possible.

Extension of Useful Life

Suppose that the machine had instead worked on until the end of its calculated life, and had then been found to have several more years of useful working life left in it. The management estimate the extra life to be three years, and the value of the machine at the beginning of those three years to be £700. The eventual scrap value is still £100. The accounting entries to record these circumstances are as follows.

The balances on the machinery account and the depreciation account are closed off to a revaluation account. This means that the original cost and depreciation to date are summarized in this account as the written-down value of £100. Next the increase in the value of the asset, as disclosed by the valuer, is debited to the revaluation account and credited to a capital reserve account. The revaluation account is closed off by a credit entry of £700, which is reflected as a debit to the machinery account. Thus the new value of the machine is disclosed by this account and depreciation can go ahead normally in the forthcoming years.

Dr.   Machinery Account   Cr.

	£		£
Year 1: Purchase	2100	Year 5: Transfer to revaluation account	2100
Year 5: Revaluation of machine	700		

Dr.		Depreciation Provision Account		Cr.
	£			£
Year 5: Transfer balance to revaluation account	2000	Year 5: Accumulated depreciation		2000
		Year 6: Profit and loss account		200

Dr.		Revaluation Account		Cr.
	£			£
Year 5: Original cost	2100	Year 5: Depreciation to date		2000
Increase in value transferred		New value recorded in		
to reserve	600	machine account		700
	£2700			£2700

Dr.		Capital Reserve Account		Cr.
	£			£
		Year 5: Revaluation of machine		600

Note: The revaluation has not been realized in cash. It is a book entry, and as such cannot be distributed as a dividend.

SSAP 12 states that whenever an asset is revalued, or its estimated life changed, or a different method used to calculate the depreciation charge on the grounds that the new method will give a fairer presentation, the unamortized cost should be charged over the remaining useful life and the effect of the change must be noted in the accounts. If assets are written up to recognize an increase in value, the depreciation charge must be increased accordingly, and the fact that an asset is considered to be worth more at the end of a year than at the beginning is not an excuse for failing to depreciate it.

SSAP 12 ACCOUNTING FOR DEPRECIATION

This standard is in agreement with the International Accounting Standard No. 4. It is a short document, and most of its recommendations have already been mentioned.

The standard gives as the objective of depreciation the allocation of the cost of an asset to accounting periods so as to charge a fair proportion to each period during the life of the asset. It seems obvious that the Accounting Standards Committee wished to avoid a discussion of the nature of depreciation and the respective merits of the techniques used, when the Standard was compiled. Unlike stock valuation in SSAP 9, no method has been outlawed, but a set of general principles are set out. The standard urges accountants to disclose in accounting statements the depreciation method used, the lives or rates for various classes of assets, total depreciation for the period, and the gross amount of depreciable assets and cumulative depreciation on them, so that users of accounting statements get a better view of the accounting policies which form the basis of the statements.

There has, however, been some argument about the section of the standard concerning the depreciation of buildings. Property companies and other owners of freehold land and buildings, such as brewers, are of the opinion that the suggestion that buildings should be depreciated is wrong. The standard clearly states that freehold land will not normally require a provision for depreciation, unless considerations such as the desirability of its location reduce its value. It also states, however, that buildings have a limited life and should be depreciated as in the case of other fixed assets. The property companies argue that:

a. it is impossible to separate the value of a building from the value of the site on which it is built;
b. buildings have very long lives and should therefore be accorded a special accounting treatment;
c. buildings tend to increase in value year by year, so depreciation should not be charged.

The fact remains, however, that buildings wear out, so perhaps a refurbishment fund built up over twenty years, rather than an annual depreciation charge, would be more appropriate.

TUTORIAL DISCUSSION TOPICS

6.1. 'Depreciation writes down the plant to its true value' – managing director. 'Depreciation allocates the cost of plant to the years in which it is used' – accountant. Who is right?

6.2. Albert Jones is in business as a builder. He started business with equipment which cost £5800 and which he thinks will last five years before it is worn out. He has consulted an accountant, who suggests that he should depreciate his plant. What will be the result if he ignores this advice?

6.3. State the objectives of depreciating equipment by one of the decreasing charge (reducing balance) methods. Under what circumstances is this type of method particularly suitable? Are there any disadvantages in the use of this type of depreciation technique?

6.4. Distinguish between deterioration and obsolescence as factors causing an asset to lose its value. In what ways may obsolescence arise?

6.5. Albert Kerr qualified as a dentist five years ago, and borrowed £8000 from a relation to buy the surgery equipment which he needed in order to set himself up in practice. The loan was for five years, at the end of which time the full sum was to be repaid. Mr Kerr consulted an accountant and was advised to write off one fifth of the cost of the equipment each year. 'In that way,' said the accountant, 'you will set aside out of profits an amount equal to the proportion of your original investment which has been used up during the year.' Acting on this advice Albert drew out of the practice all the profits each year for his personal use. At the end of the five-year period his balance sheet showed that there was just enough cash in the practice bank account to repay the loan. Albert Kerr then found that his equipment was worn out and that he would have to buy new equipment. The replacement cost of similar equipment was £11 000, but there was no more cash in the bank and he faced the prospect of having to borrow even more money if he wished to continue his practice. Puzzled and not a little annoyed at the situation, he went to see his accountant. 'The business should have been able to finance the purchase of new equipment after five years' operation. You depreciated the old equipment and I withdrew only the net profits each year. Therefore the depreciation should have created a reserve for replacement,' he said. Explain the situation to A. Kerr.

SEMINAR EXERCISES 4

1. (a) The production manager of the company of which you are accountant has recently attended a one-day seminar on accounting for managers. On his return he asks you, 'Why is it necessary for accountants to depreciate the fixed assets of a business? The capital investment is sunk and gone, come what may, and even the taxation authorities allow plant to be written off in the year of acquisition, with capital allowances at 100 per cent.'
   Write a brief answer to his question.
   (b) In June, Year 2, the company purchased plant for a new process at a cost of £330 000. The process was expected to operate until 31 March, Year 10, when the estimated scrap value of the plant would be £10 000. The company has adopted the straight line method of depreciation. In June, Year 5, further plant was purchased for £200 000, to be used specifically on this process. This plant was expected to be worn out and valueless by 31 March, Year 10. In March, Year 7, the process was found to be obsolete. It ceased production and the original plant bought in Year 2 was sold for £106 000.
   Record the above transactions in the ledger and show how the remaining plant would appear in the balance sheet as at 31 March, Year 7.
   (c) What extra information would you require to treat the remaining plant correctly in the accounts?

2. Manor Ltd recently purchased a new machine at a basic catalogue price of £30 000. The machine is expected to have a useful life of twelve years and a scrap value of £1000 at the end of that period. Repairs and maintenance costs are expected to be £200 in the first year and to increase thereafter by linear progression each year (that is, £200 in the first year, £400 in the second, £600 in the third etc.). Installation costs amounted to £2000. There is considerable argument within the company's accounting department about the most appropriate method of depreciation. Furthermore, the company secretary maintains that the actual method of depreciation is immaterial, and that the main advantage to be derived from the depreciation provisions accumulated over the life of the asset is that they can be used to purchase a replacement.

(a) Using the information given above to illustrate your answer, discuss the arguments for and against adopting one of the reducing balance methods of depreciation.

(b) What is the purpose of depreciation? In the light of your answer discuss the arguments put forward by the company secretary of Manor Ltd.

3. Bulford Dozers Ltd own and hire out heavy plant to the civil engineering industry. On 31 March last year the company purchased an articulated plant transporter for use in the business, at a cost of £86 000. Because equipment on building sites is usually treated roughly it is expected that the transporter will have a useful life of only five years, at the end of which its scrap value will be £1000. During its life the vehicle will travel 100 000 miles, but it is unlikely that the mileage will be the same each year, since the vehicle may stand idle for long periods.

(a) Discuss three methods of depreciation which could be applied to the transporter, recommending one of them.

(b) Show how the transporter would appear in the balance sheet of the company as at 30 September next year if depreciation was provided by the method you have chosen in (a) above.

(c) Explain the interrelationship of the provision for depreciation and the replacement of fixed assets.

7 | The Accounting Treatment of Current Assets

The current assets which are usually found in a balance sheet are stocks, debtors, short-term investments and cash. They are shown in reverse order of liquidity, that is, with stocks first and cash last.

INTERNATIONAL EXPOSURE DRAFT 14: CURRENT ASSETS AND LIABILITIES

This draft has recently been issued by the International Accounting Standards Committee in the expectation that it will eventually be developed into an International Accounting Standard. The draft sets out two alternative views of current assets and liabilities. One view sees them as a measure of the ability of an enterprise to carry on its activities day by day, indicating its ability to pay its way from liquid resources. In this case the criterion used to identify a current asset or current liability is whether it will be liquidated in the near future. The alternative view is that the classification specifies resources and obligations which are circulating in the business, and the criterion used in this case to identify current assets or liabilities is whether the items will be consumed in the production of revenue or settled during the term of a normal operating cycle. A compromise is to use a year or the operating cycle, whichever is the longer, as the realization period, to determine whether or not an item should be treated as current.

This treatment is in accordance with the view of the balance sheet as showing the financial position of an enterprise, where the segregation of current assets and current liabilities discloses the short-term financial position. An interesting suggestion is that slow-moving stocks which are likely to be in store for more than a year should be excluded from current assets, or that a note should draw attention to them. A similar treatment is proposed for trade credit or bank loans due for payment in more than a year, since current liabilities are normally understood to be obligations payable on demand or for settlement within one year. Bank balances which cannot be used because of restrictions, e.g. exchange control, should not be considered as current assets.

STOCKS

A quotation from the explanatory note to the Statement of Standard Accounting Practice 9 (SSAP 9) reads as follows: 'No area of accounting has produced wider differences in practice than the computation of the amount at which stocks and work in progress are stated in financial accounts'.

The stocks of a business may be in any of five categories:

a. goods etc. purchased for resale, e.g. stock in a shop;
b. consumable stores, e.g. a stock of fuel oil or stationery;
c. raw materials and components to be used in production;
d. finished goods awaiting sale;
e. work in progress, or products and services in an intermediate stage of completion.

The accounting treatment accorded to stocks is significant, since it will affect both income measurement and the position statement. Opening stock plus purchases less closing stock equals the cost of goods sold, and this figure, when subtracted from sales, produces the gross profit. Thus the basis used to find the cost of stocks will affect the profit and the stock figure in the balance sheet.

The measurement of income implies that costs will be matched with related revenues, and that stocks of unused items will be carried forward to a later period when their sale produces revenue to affect their consumption. The principle of matching, however, must be subordinated to the concept of conservatism in so far as that, if there is no reasonable expectation that revenue in the future will be sufficient to cover the costs incurred and a loss is likely to be made, it is prudent to provide for that loss as soon as possible. For this reason stocks and work in progress are shown in the accounts as at the lower of cost or net realizable value. If they are worth less than their cost the loss is recognized, but if they are worth more than their cost no element of profit is taken until it is realized when a sale is made.

The Standard states that the comparison of cost and net realizable value should be made for each item of stock, or at least for groups of similar items. If the total net realizable value is set against the total cost, a situation could arise where foreseeable losses are set off against unrealized profits.

The definition of 'cost' for stock purposes covers all expenditure incurred in the normal course of business to bring the product or service to its present location and condition. This includes the purchase price plus any import duties payable, as well as transport and handling costs. Trade discounts negotiated with a supplier will of course be deducted when the purchase price is computed. The cost attributable to work in progress is, however, a less straightforward matter. It is not argued that the cost of work-in-progress stocks should not include the prime cost (direct labour and material) expended on them to date, but not all accountants agree with SSAP 9, which states that a share of production overheads, e.g. depreciation and other overhead expenses attributable to that stock, must be added. Overhead costs such as rent, rates, salaries and depreciation are considered by some accountants to accrue over time, i.e. they are incurred on an annual basis, and as such should be matched with the revenue of the year rather than carried forward in the cost of work in progress stock to be matched with revenue arising when the stock is eventually completed and sold. Companies which fail to follow the rules of SSAP 9 run the risk of their auditors qualifying the accounts.

Net realizable value is defined as the actual or estimated selling price of the stock net of any trade discount, from which is deducted any cost incurred to put the stock into a saleable condition, and all cost to be incurred in marketing, selling and distribution of the stock. Those who argue that it is not prudent to carry forward overhead expenses from one year to another are answered by the point that an element of prudence can best be injected into the situation through the calculation of net realizable value.

Events occurring between the balance sheet date and the date of completion of the accounts must be considered when the net realizable value is determined. If prices fall after the year end, then current stocks may not be sold at more than their cost in the future. In a famous case concerning a publishing company, the stocks of unsold magazines were carried forward at cost over a period of several years, until reporting accountants decided that a net realizable value based on their sale as scrap paper was more appropriate, and the subsequent stock write-down had a devastating impact on profits that year. Net realizable value is likely to fall below cost when selling prices fall, stocks deteriorate physically, products requiring those stocks become obsolete, a product is sold as a 'loss leader', or when mistakes in production or purchasing have been made. The length of time which stocks spend in the stores before being used or sold is called the stock turnover period. A long turnover period creates an increased risk of obsolescence, deterioration or adverse price movements, and must therefore be considered when assessing the net realizable value.

The rule that stock should be valued at the lower of cost or net realizable value has been criticized by some accountants on the grounds of inconsistency. A conservative approach to profit measurement can, it is argued, lead to an understatement of profit in one year, and an overstatement in the next year. If you recognize a decrease in value which occurs before sale, but ignore an increase in value before sale, then the full amount of the increase is taken as profit in the year of realization. Academic accountants ask why, if net realizable value is better than cost when it is less than cost, it is not to be preferred for the same reasons of objectivity, certainty, verifiability etc. when it exceeds cost. No academic answer has been made to this question, but accountants continue to use the lower of cost or market rule because they consider that the advantages of conservatism outweigh the disadvantages. The same argument applies to the provision for doubtful debts.

THE FLOW OF COSTS

The activities of a trader are to buy, store and sell, whereas a manufacturer buys raw materials, combines them with machinery and labour and converts them into manufactured goods which are then sold. Therefore costs flowing through a trading organization will follow a different pattern from the costs flowing through a manufacturing business. The flow of costs can be seen from the interrelationship of the ledger accounts used to record, accumulate and summarize the figures. Assumptions made about the flow of costs will have an impact on the profit figure eventually computed.

There is some argument as to whether factory overheads should be charged in full to the accounting period in which they are incurred, or whether part of them should be allocated to the stock of work in progress and carried forward in the cost of that stock to the next accounting period, when the work in progress is completed and perhaps sold. Some accountants see factory overheads as period costs and wish to relate them to time, since they concern such items as rent, insurance, and factory manager's salary all for the year. Other accountants prefer to match the cost of goods sold with the revenue from their sale and argue that the overhead expenses of one period must be carried forward in the cost of work in progress to set the full cost of these items against the revenue from their eventual sale, if a true profit is to be shown. They argue that this expenditure is incurred to bring the stock to its present condition and location.

This argument has never been settled and different firms adopt different practices. In a leading case some years ago the Inland Revenue authorities took the Duple Motor Body Company Ltd to the House of Lords in an attempt to define whether overhead expenses should be written off or carried forward. The answer they got was that either system is acceptable so long as it is followed consistently. Thus the cost flow assumption as to the treatment of factory overhead expenses can have an impact on the profit calculation.

STOCK VALUATION METHODS

The four main methods of valuing stocks of raw materials for inclusion in the balance sheet or operating statement are the first in first out method (FIFO), the last in first out method (LIFO), the weighted average method (AVCO), and the standard cost method. The assumption as to the flow of raw materials through the stores will have an effect on the amounts charged from the stores into the manufacturing account for materials used, and also on the balance sheet, since it affects the cost of closing stocks.

The bases on which raw materials are valued, both for charging to the manufacturing account and for inclusion in the balance sheet, may vary. Different methods will suit firms in different industries and situations, but it must be stressed that, once a firm has chosen to use one method, then it should act consistently and not change from one method to another without very good reason. Different methods of stock valuation can, as we shall see, cause a different profit to be disclosed, and it is often tempting for a company with disappointing results to suggest a change of stock valuation method in order to show a better profit.

Some firms will assume a first in first out (FIFO) pattern, i.e. the first batches of raw materials to be bought and stored are the first to be transferred to the manufacturing processes and used up. It follows that those raw materials remaining at the end of the period under this assumption are from the most recently purchased batches. Materials used will be charged to production at cost and closing stocks will also be shown in the balance sheet at cost. If the price of raw materials fluctuates during the year so that early batches are bought at one price and later batches bought at a higher price, this assumption will ensure that the manufacturing account is charged with the lower-priced materials while the higher-priced batches are shown in the balance sheet as stocks. Thus the cost flow assumption will influence the profit figure and the balance sheet.

An alternative to FIFO is last in first out (LIFO), which assumes that the most recent batches bought and stored are the first to be used up. Thus, using LIFO, in a period of inflation the manufacturing process will be charged with materials at the later or higher price, while the balance sheet will show stocks at a lower or historic cost.

It is of course impossible to substantiate, with many raw materials, that those which have been in stock longest will be used first. If, for example, there is a large bin containing 10 000 bolts, or a pile of sand, or a vat of paint, there is no way of telling from which delivery batch the units used up in production have been drawn.

During a period of inflation the FIFO cost flow assumption shows stocks in the balance sheet at an accurate current cost, while charging raw materials to the manufacturing process at an outdated cost. Therefore it can be said that under this assumption profits are overstated, since the replacement cost of the raw materials used is not charged in measuring the profit. Conversely, the LIFO cost flow assumption will charge current cost to the manufacturing process and thus compute a truer profit, while the balance sheet figure for closing stocks will be shown at an outdated cost. If the volume of stock falls under LIFO it might seem that these old stocks are used up, and outdated costs will be set against current revenues when profit is measured. There has been some pressure from accountants in the United Kingdom to persuade the Inland Revenue to accept accounts produced on a LIFO basis, since under the FIFO system, which is approved by the Inland Revenue, profits are overstated, and it can be argued that taxation is levied on a book profit caused by inflation rather than a manufacturing profit from transactions.

While SSAP 9 does not approve of LIFO, since it states that LIFO does not bear a reasonable relationship to actual cost, it does not substantiate this view. However, International Accounting Standard 11 states that both the LIFO and base stock methods may be used, even though they are specifically rejected by SSAP 9. This international standard is otherwise in broad agreement with the UK standard, especially on the point that a proportion of production overheads used up to bring the stock to its present location and condition should be included in the cost of the stock. IAS 11 recommends the FIFO and weighted average methods, and suggests that stocks maintained for specific purposes should be segregated and accounted for at their own prices.

The base stock method of stock valuation assumes that the same quantity and value of stock is in store or process at the end of the year as at the beginning. Thus the cost of all material movements are written off to the manufacturing account each year. This method is now rarely used, since it requires conditions in which a similar volume is in process at the beginning and the end of the year.

Standard costing values opening and closing stocks at a standard cost per unit computed in advance of the accounting period. Any difference between actual cost and standard is written off to the profit and loss account as a 'variance' from standard.

Example

This example demonstrates the impact on profit of the various stock valuation bases. A trading company buys the following quantity of raw materials during the first six months of the year.

	Tonnes	Price (£)	Cost (£)
3 January	40	228	9 120
15 February	60	240	14 400
21 March	50	210	10 500
19 April	80	252	20 160
15 May	30	258	7 740
25 June	20	264	5 280
Total tonnes	280	Total cost	£67 200

On 28 June the company sold 200 tonnes of material at £260 per tonne.

Under the FIFO assumption the 80 tonnes of stock remaining will comprise the most recent purchases:

		£
	20 tonnes at £264	5 280
	30 tonnes at £258	7 740
Purchased	30 tonnes at £252	7 560
19 April	80	£20 580

Under the LIFO assumption the 80 tonnes of stock remaining will comprise the earliest purchases made in the period:

		£
	40 tonnes at £228	9120
Purchased	40 tonnes at £240	9600
15 February	80	£18720

In the trading account opening stock plus purchases less closing stock determines the cost of sales, which in its turn influences the profit. Under FIFO the closing stock will be £1860 more than under LIFO, so the cost of sales will be correspondingly less and the profit correspondingly more.

If stock had been carried forward at the beginning of the period, it would have been assumed to form part of the closing stock under LIFO. In this way a batch of material can form part of the stock for several years under this system, and the balance sheet figure can become very outdated.

By the AVCO (average cost) method the 280 tonnes purchased are divided into the cost of £67 200 to give a weighted average of £240, and this figure is applied to the closing stock to calculate an amount of £19 200.

A simple average cost could be found by adding the different prices paid during the period and dividing by the number thereof, but this method would obscure the fact that far more material was bought at £252 than at £264 and therefore greater weight or significance must be given to the former price than the latter. The average calculation must be weighted for quantities purchased at different prices. In formula terms this is

$$\frac{\text{aggregate of price} \times \text{weight}}{\text{total weights (tonnes)}} = \frac{67\,200}{280} = £240$$

The profit on the transaction is measured at different amounts according to the method used.

	FIFO	LIFO	AVCO
	£	£	£
Purchases	67 200	67 200	67 200
Less closing stock	20 580	18 720	19 200
Cost of sales	46 620	48 480	48 000
Sales	52 000	52 000	52 000
Profit	£5 380	£3 520	£4 000

Note that FIFO shows the largest profit, which is more likely to be overstated during an inflationary period when historic costs lag behind current selling prices. The AVCO result is a compromise between the other two methods, and while it is true to say in criticism that the average used, £240, was the real price paid for only one batch and is thus not a realistic figure to use in accounts, the fact remains that this method, unlike LIFO, is acceptable to the Inland Revenue in the UK.

STOCK RECORDS

Accounting for movements of stock in the stores, both receipts and issues, needs care and a measure of internal control. Many companies operate a bin card system whereby when stock is withdrawn from a bin the card is entered and a new running total calculated to show the quantity which remains in the bin. When the re-order point is reached the buyers are automatically warned to order more stock. The re-order point is calculated with reference to the lead time. The buying department will order materials and there may be a lead time of, say, three weeks before they are delivered, during which period the factory will still be using materials. There will also be a safety margin below which, as a matter of policy, stocks are not allowed to fall. The amount of the safety margin plus the quantity which will be used during the lead time sets the re-order point. The management accountant, together with the buyers, will have computed the economic order quantity as the optimum amount to be purchased so that the advantages and disadvantages of buying and holding large quantities are finely balanced. The economic order quantity plus the amount in store at the safety margin will determine the maximum amount of storage space required for each material or component stored.

A stock record card will be maintained for each material to record receipts and issues to production. The cost at which materials are issued to the factory will depend on whether a FIFO, LIFO or AVCO system is in operation.

Example

Material XD 131 has the following receipts and issues:

Date	Receipts	Issues
1 January	1000 at 50p	
2 January		500
20 January	800 at 60p	
25 January		500
1 February		500
4 February	700 at 80p	
20 February		500

Write up a stock record card for FIFO, LIFO and AVCO for the months of January and February.

FIFO Stock Record Card, Material XD 131

Date	Receipts			Issues			Balance	
	Invoice		£	Requisition		£		£
1 January	800	1000 at 50p	500				1000 at 50p	500
2 January				B481	500 at 50p	250	500 at 50p	250
20 January	962	800 at 60p	480				500 at 50p} 800 at 60p}	730
25 January				B508	500 at 50p	250	800 at 60p	480
1 February				B512	500 at 60p	300	300 at 60p	180
4 February	980	700 at 80p	560				300 at 60p} 700 at 80p}	740
20 February				B521	300 at 60p	180		
					200 at 80p	160	500 at 80p	400
				Charge to production		£1140		Closing stock

Note that lines across the issues and receipts columns help to show when each batch is used up.

LIFO Stock Record Card Material XD 131

Date	Receipts			Issues			Balance	
	Invoice		£	Requisition		£		£
1 January	803	1000 at 50p	500				1000 at 50p	500
2 January				B481	500 at 50p	250	500 at 50p	250
20 January	962	800 at 60p	480				500 at 50p ⎫ 800 at 60p ⎭	730
				B508	500 at 60p	300	500 at 50p ⎫ 300 at 60p ⎭	430
1 February				B512	300 at 60p	180		
					200 at 50p	100	300 at 50p	150
4 February	980	700 at 80p	560				300 at 50p ⎫ 700 at 80p ⎭	710
20 February				B521	500 at 80p	400	300 at 50p ⎫ 200 at 80p ⎭	310
				Charge to production		£1230		Closing stock

Note the greater charge to production than under FIFO and that some material in stock on 1 January is assumed to be still there on 28 February.

AVCO Stock Record Card, Material XD 131

Date	Receipts			Issues			Balance	
	Invoice		£	Requisition		£		£
1 January	800	1000 at 50p	500				1000 at 50p	500
2 January				B481	500 at 50p	250	500 at 50p	250
20 January	962	800 at 60p	480				1300 at 56p	728
25 January				B508	500 at 56p	280	800 at 56p	448
1 February				B512	500 at 56p	280	300 at 56p	168
4 February	980	700 at 80p	560				1000 at 73p	730
20 February				B521	500 at 73p	365	500 at 73p	365
				Charge to production		£1175		Closing stock

Note that a fresh weighted average is calculated after each receipt. Alternative methods of calculation may be used.

Workings

	£		£
500 at 50p	250	300 at 56p	168
800 at 60p	480	700 at 80p	560
1300	£730	1000	£728

$$\frac{£730}{1300} = \text{say } 56p \qquad \frac{£728}{1000} = \text{say } 73p$$

LONG-TERM WORK IN PROGRESS

Some contracts in the building or engineering industry may extend over more than one accounting year. It is argued, therefore, that to take profit at the end of the job will distort the profit calculation both in that year and in the years when the job was in production. Thus at the year end the stock of work in progress on such jobs should be calculated on the basis of prime cost plus a share of overheads, plus a proportion of the profit on each job which reflects the amount of work completed and inequalities of profitability in various stages of the contract. Losses likely to be made must be provided for in full. The amount of work-in-progress stocks computed by this method should be shown net of any cash received from the customer as a progress payment. This rule, expressed in SSAP 9, does not, however, meet with wholehearted acceptance from accountants and others.

The opponents of this method argue that it is more conservative to take no profit until the job is completed, unless the management are confident that profits which appear to be made at an intermediate stage will not be diminished by losses sustained before completion. A new international standard (IAS 11) expresses the view that contract work in progress can be valued by including profits on the percentage of completion method or by the completed contract method, and sets constraints on the use of the percentage method. As such it is at odds with the UK standard, SSAP 9.

DEBTORS

The accounting treatment of debtors ensures that all balances owed to the company are recorded, and cancelled when payment is received. Difficulties arise if payment is not made and a bad debt occurs. In this case the debt must be written off to the profit and loss account via the bad debts account. The procedure is to credit the debtor's personal account and debit the bad debts account when the debt goes bad, and to credit the bad debts account and debit the profit and loss account with the total at the end of the year. The significance of a bad debt is shown by the following example. A company sells goods to Mr A for £100. The mark-up on the goods is 25 per cent on cost, so the profit made is £20. If Mr A fails to pay for the goods then four times the volume of goods sold to him must be sold to make a profit equal to the cost of the goods he has received. Thus it is important to ensure that goods are sold on credit terms only to customers who are likely to pay for them.

A further difficulty with bad debts concerns the matching principle. If debts go bad during the year when the goods are sold they are written off against profit in that year, but if a debt carried forward at the year end in the balance sheet is subsequently found to be bad, it will be written off against profit in the year after the sale was made. This distortion overstates profit in the first year, understates profit in the second year, and overvalues the asset in the balance sheet between those two years. At the end of an accounting year the debtor balances must be carefully reviewed to identify 'doubtful' debts which may go bad in a subsequent period, so that a provision can be made out of profits for the first year, thus matching cost with revenue and calculating profit on a conservative basis. The provision will appear in the books as a credit balance (debit profit and loss account) and in the next year bad debts can be debited against it, and thus have no impact on profit measurement in the second year. Some companies adopt a routine policy for the calculation of the provision for doubtful debts, but it must be stressed that such a provision requires the accountant to exercise judgement to recognize the loss as soon as it arises, and before it has been confirmed.

Those companies which use a formula for doubtful debt provision are not exercising judgement unless the percentage applied to debts or to credit sales is based on past experience and reviewed at frequent intervals. An accountant or credit controller should scrutinize all debtor balances, taking into account their age and what he knows about the credit worthiness of the customer, when the provision is computed.

Examples

The accounting entries are as follows:

(A) Bad Debt Written off to the Profit and Loss Account. In this example only one bad debt is experienced. In reality the bad debts account acts as a collecting point for bad debts before they are charged as one figure to the profit and loss account.

Kester Jon owes Jos Ltd £500, but is unable to pay. In the books of Jos Ltd:

Dr.	Kester Jon		Cr.	Dr.	Bad Debts		Cr.
	£		£		£		£
Debtor balance	500	Balance written off to bad debts	500	Kester Jon	500	Bad debts for the year written off to profit and loss account	500

Dr.	Profit and Loss		Cr.
	£		£
Bad debts	500		

(B) Provision for Doubtful Debts which Later Go Bad. Kester Jon owes Jos Ltd £500 at the year end, 31 December, and says that he is unable to pay on 30 June of the next year. Jos Ltd provides for the debt at 31 December.

Dr.	Kester Jon		Cr.	Dr.	Provision for Doubtful Debts		Cr.
	£		£		£		£
31 Dec. Debtor balance	500	31 Dec. Balance c/f	500	31 Dec. Balance c/f	500	31 Dec. Charge to profit and loss account	500
1 Jan. Balance b/d	500	30 June Bad debt written off to provision	500	30 June Kester Jon	500	1 Jan. Balance b d	500

Note that the bad debt has not affected profit measurement in the second year, but the provision reduces profit in the first year.

(C) Bad Debt Written Off, Is Later Collected and must be Written Back. Suppose Kester Jon pays the £500 he owes on 31 March of the third year.

Dr.	Cash	Cr.		Dr.	Kester Jon	Cr.
	£	£			£	£
31 March Kester Jon	500			31 March Bad debt written back	500	31 March Cash	500

Dr.	Bad Debts	Cr.
	£	£
31 Dec. Other bad debts	2500	31 March Kester Jon	500
		31 Dec. Balance to profit and loss	2000
	£2500	£2500

Thus the amount written back has reduced the cost of bad debts to be written off to profit and loss in year three.

(D) Overestimate of Provision for Doubtful Debts. Jos Ltd provided £1000 for doubtful debts last year, but only £500 of bad debts occur this year.

Dr.	Provision for Doubtful Debts	Cr.		Dr.	Bad Debts Account	Cr.
	£	£			£	£
31 Dec. Bad debts written off	500	1 Jan. Opening balance	1000	31 Dec. Bad debts of the year from personal accounts	500	31 Dec. Bad debts written off to provision	500
Balance to profit and loss account	500					
	1000		1000			

Dr.	Profit and Loss	Cr.
	£	£
		31 Dec. Doubtful debts overprovided in a previous year	500

The underutilized balance on the provision account is written back to the profit and loss account as soon as it is decided that it is not required. Profit last year was understated as the result of an excess of caution, but this is no reason why the position should not be corrected as soon as objective information is available. In practice the underutilized balance reduces the charge to the income statement for the provision next year.

Note. In these four examples every debit has a credit, and vice versa.

Debtors are shown in the balance sheet under current assets with the amount of provision for doubtful debts shown as a deduction from the total of debtor balances in the personal ledger.

INVESTMENTS

Investments made by a company can be treated as either long-term or short-term investments. The purchase of shares in another company or the loan of funds for a long period is often undertaken for strategic purposes, e.g. some commercial advantage gained by the possession of a share stake in a supplier of raw materials or chain of retail outlets. Investments of this nature are shown separately in the balance sheet, usually not as part of the fixed assets, but above the current assets. This indicates that the investment has been made for a long-term reason, and is not for resale or a short-term repository of idle funds which cannot be gainfully employed in the business in the near future. Short-term investments such as deposits with local authorities or commercial banks, as well as investments in shares intended for resale within a year, are current assets.

The basic rule for accounting for investments is to show them in the balance sheet at cost. Long-term investments can be revalued from time to time, but this is wise only if the change in value is permanent and not a short-term fluctuation. It is considered prudent to recognize a rise in the value of an investment only when it is realized. Although investments are shown at historic cost, their correct worth ought to be communicated to shareholders and others. For this reason the Companies Act 1967 requires that investments should be classified as 'quoted', i.e. those that can be traded on a recognized stock exchange, and 'unquoted'. A note to the accounts must show the market value of the quoted investments and the directors' valuation of unquoted investments, together with the amount of capital gains tax that would be payable if the investments were realized at these values.

TUTORIAL DISCUSSION TOPICS

7.1. Discuss the impact of the matching and conservatism concepts on the accounting treatment of stocks.

7.2. What is meant by FIFO and LIFO cost flow assumptions?

7.3. What is the significance of a FIFO or LIFO assumption for income measurement and the position statement?

7.4. Why should an enterprise provide for doubtful debts?

7.5. Discuss the accounting treatment of investments in the balance sheet.

SEMINAR EXERCISES 5

1. General Accounting Machines Ltd is a business which sells accounting machines entirely on credit terms to a wide range of customers. The following balances were extracted from its ledgers at 30 November.

	£	£
Sales		538112
Creditors, balance at 30 November last year		36118
Debtors, balance at 30 November last year	61803	
Purchases of components	275480	
Discounts allowed	4762	
Discounts received		6184
Cash received from debtors	519267	
Cash paid to creditors		247981
Returns inwards	26916	
Carriage outwards	2794	
Overdraft interest	8106	
Provision for doubtful debts, balance at 30 November last year		4300

A cheque for £1015 from J. Smith, a customer, has been returned from the bank marked 'refer to drawer'. Bad debts totalling £4328 are to be written off, and the provision for doubtful debts is to be raised to 10 per cent of the debtor balances at 30 November this year.

Produce for the period ended 30 November this year:
(a) a total figure for debtors;
(b) the bad and doubtful debts account;
(c) the balance sheet entry for debtors as at that date.

2. Trentvend Ltd are wholesalers for a packaged article in the grocery business. The data below summarizes their transactions during the first three months of this year.

Period		Purchases			Sales	
	Units	Price	Total	Units	Price	Total
		£	£		£	£
January	1000	5	5000	–	–	–
	600	8	4800	900	9	8100
February	600	9	5400	–	–	–
	400	10	4000	1100	10	11000
March	1200	11	13200	600	12	7200

(a) Compare the effect on profit for the quarter, and the closing balance sheet if stocks are valued using the FIFO, LIFO and weighted average methods.
(b) Explain the different impacts of the FIFO and LIFO systems upon the profit and loss account and balance sheet.

3. A shop near the Houses of Parliament has recently been buying from the Wedgwood Pottery Co. Ltd replicas of 'Big Ben', affectionately known as 'Wedgwood Bens', for sale to American souvenir hunters. The shop started off on 1 January with 10 'Bens' in stock, which had cost them £30 each in December. From 1 January to the end of May they bought 20 'Bens' per month, but each month the cost per 'Ben' had risen by £1 on the previous month. During the same period 80 'Bens' were sold to customers.

(a) Calculate, on on the the basis of FIFO and LIFO, the stock valuation as at 31 May, and the impact on profit of a change from FIFO to LIFO.
(b) Discuss the impact of inflation on stocks in a business. State, with reasons, why a business may be better or worse off as a result of inflation on stocks.

8 | The Production of Accounts from a Trial Balance

The purpose of this chapter is to show how a list of balances is converted into a trial balance, to make the adjustments necessary at the year end, and to produce detailed accounts in vertical form.

The following balances have been extracted from the books of Columnar Ltd at 31 December last, by the inexperienced book-keeper who is employed by the company as an office manager. Mr Doric, the Managing Director and majority shareholder, has asked you to act as the company's accountant, and to prepare a manufacturing account, trading account, profit and loss account and appropriation account, for the year ended 31 December last, and a balance sheet as at that date. He says that the accounts should be presented in vertical form to facilitate their assimilation by the managers of the business.

Balances on the Books of Columnar Ltd at 31 December Last

	£
Advertising	920
Bad debts	711
Bank account, overdrawn	1 064
Bank charges	230
Cash in hand	409
Creditors	3 290
Debtors	11 680
Depreciation on plant at 1 January	2 000
Dividend paid	9 000
Discount received	641
Doubtful debts, provision	1 200
Factory power	4 729
Fixtures and fittings, office	2 000
General expenses	687
Insurance	1 146
Interest on loan stock	500
Investment in Ionic Industries Ltd	24 337
Light and heat	595
Loan stock, 10 per cent interest rate	10 000
Plant and machinery	18 000
Purchases of raw material	36 219
Packaging expenses	964
Profit and loss account (unappropriated profit b/d)	7 809
Repairs and renewals to plant	853
Rent and rates	1 571

Returns outwards	58
Salaries	8 690
Sales	103 662
Share capital	45 000
Stocks, 1 January: finished goods	8 438
raw material	6 118
work in progress	2 147
Transport expenses	1 204
Wages	30 715
Warehouse expenses	2 861
	£349 448

An investigation of the ledger accounts and some conversations with Mr Doric produce the following significant factors which will necessitate the adjustment of the book figures before the accounts are prepared.

1. The following liabilities are to be provided for: factory power £625, rent and rates £429, light and heat £125.
2. Mr Doric says that in his view 80 per cent of the expense for rent, rates, light, heat and insurance should be allocated to the factory, the balance being an administrative cost. The general expenses are to be apportioned one third as an administration expense and the balance to the factory.
3. The following payments have been made in advance: insurance £196, road fund licences (included in transport expenses) £210.
4. Depreciation is to be provided on the straight line basis at 10 per cent per annum on machinery (pro rata to time) and at 5 per cent per annum on furniture. Mr Doric informs you that plant costing £3000 was purchased on 30 June and has been included in the balance in the books.
5. Stock is taken on 31 December and the stock sheets reveal that closing stocks are: raw material £4683, work in progress £1274, finished goods £7926 and packing materials £217. Work in progress stocks contain no overhead expense allocation.
6. Mr Doric has examined the debtors ledger and decides that the provision for doubtful debts should be increased by a further £300.
7. Interest on the loan stock has been paid only up to 30 June last.
8. An analysis of the salaries account shows it to include £5000 paid to the factory manager. Analysis of the wages account shows it to include £6000 paid to the warehousemen and £2800 paid to drivers.
9. Mr Doric says he would like to know whether the factory operation has made a profit separate from the profitability of the trading operation. He has maintained a careful check on the quantity of finished goods transferred from the factory to the finished goods store and estimates its value on the wholesale market to be £80 000. Mr Doric also intends to pay his factory manager a commission of 10 per cent of the factory profit.
10. You decide to provide £5000 for tax on the profit made which is payable in the future.

PROCEDURE

To produce the set of accounts first convert the list of balances to a trial balance in order to check that the book-keeping is accurate. If the credit balances are separated from the main list and then added together, they should total half the total of the whole list. Credit balances are liabilities, capital, accumulated depreciation, sales, and other miscellaneous income. Thus the items remaining in the debit or left-hand column are balances representing assets or costs. It should be remembered that provisions are deducted from assets on the face of the balance sheet and are thus represented in the ledger accounts by credit balances. Armed with this information it is a fairly simple task to compute a trial balance which totals £174 724 on each side.

Trial Balance at 31 December

	Debits *(Assets + Expenses)*	Credits *(Liabilities + Sales +* *Provisions + Capital)*
	£	£
Advertising	920	
Bad debts	711	
Bank account, overdrawn		1 064
Bank charges	230	
Cash in hand	409	
Debtors and creditors	11 680	3 290
Depreciation on plant at 1 January		2 000
Dividend paid	9 000	
Discount received		641
Doubtful debts, provision		1 200
Factory power	4 729	
Fixtures and fittings, office	2 000	
General expenses	687	
Insurance	1 146	
Interest on loan stock	500	
Shares in Ionic Industries Ltd	24 337	
Light and heat	595	
Loan stock (10 per cent interest rate)		10 000
Plant and machinery	18 000	
Purchases of raw material	36 219	
Packaging expenses	964	
Profit and loss (unappropriated)		7 809
Repairs and renewals	853	
Rent and rates	1 571	
Returns outwards		58
Salaries	8 690	
Sales		103 662
Share capital		45 000
Stocks 1 January: finished goods	8 438	
raw material	6 118	
work in progress	2 147	
Transport expenses	1 204	
Wages	30 715	
Warehouse expenses	2 861	
	£174 724	£174 724

The next step is to adjust the balances in the ledgers by the amounts in the notes, so that the amounts to be entered in the accounts will be computed.

Note 1. Liabilities to be provided for are accruals. The accounts for factory power, rent and rates, and light and heat will be debited with £625, £429 and £125 respectively, while accrued charges or creditors will be increased in the balance sheet by £1179 to complete the double entry. The costs for the year will therefore be: factory power £5354, transferred to the manufacturing account; rent and rates £2000; apportioned £1600 to the manufacturing account and £400 to the profit and loss account; and light and heat £720 apportioned £576 to the manufacturing account and £144 to the profit and loss account. The ledger account for light and heat would appear as follows:

Dr.		Light and Heat		Cr.
	£			£
31 Dec.		31 Dec.		
Balance (costs recorded)	595	Charge to manufacturing account		576
Accrual c/f	125	Charge to profit and loss account		144
	£720			£720
	(x)	1 Jan. balance b/d		(y) 125

Thus when the bill is received in the next accounting period and debited to the account (x), the credit balance of £125 (y) will automatically reduce the impact of that bill on the costs of that period.

Note 2. This is a simple apportionment. The adjusted amounts for rent and rates, light and heat, and insurance are divided by five, and four-fifths are allocated to the manufacturing account. The remainder will be debited to the profit and loss account. General expenses are treated similarly, but divided by three. Thus the general expenses account is credited with £687 while the manufacturing account and profit and loss account are debited with £458 and £229 respectively.

Dr.		Rent and Rates		Cr.
	£			£
Balance b/d	1571	Charge to manufacturing account		1600
Accrual c/f	429	Charge to profit and loss account		400
	£2000			£2000
		Balance b/d		429

Note 3. Payments in advance must be deducted from the recorded costs, since they concern the next accounting period. They should not be debited to the current profit and loss account. An amount of £210 will be carried forward as a debit balance on the transport expenses account (appearing in the balance sheet as a debtor or prepaid expense), while £994 will be debited to the profit and loss account.

In the insurance account, the balance of £1146 will be reduced to £950 as the cost for the year, to be apportioned £760 to the manufacturing account and £190 to the profit and loss account. The debit balance carried forward will be a cost chargeable to the next accounting period. The ledger account will appear as follows:

Dr.		Insurance	Cr.
	£		£
31 Dec.		31 Dec.	
Balance (costs recorded)	1146	Charge to manufacturing account	760
		Charge to profit and loss account	190
		Payment c/f	196
	£1146		£1146
1 Jan. Balance b/d	196		

Note 4. Depreciation on plant, to be charged to the manufacturing account as a factory expense, is to be computed at a rate of 10 per cent per annum on cost. Plant costing £3000 was purchased on 30 June, and will bear depreciation for only a half year, i.e. £150, while depreciation on the other plant, which cost £15 000, will be £1500 for the year. The manufacturing account is debited and the accumulated depreciation account is credited with £1650, the balance of depreciation to date (£3650) being deducted from the cost of the asset on the face of the balance sheet.

Dr.		Depreciation on Plant	Cr.
	£		£
Balance c/f	3650	Balance b/d	2000
		Charge to profit and loss account	1650
	£3650		£3650
		Balance b/d	3650

Depreciation on fixtures and fittings will be provided in the sum of £100 (5 per cent of £2000), resulting in entries similar to those above except that the profit and loss account will be charged (debited). The fixtures may be new, since they have not been depreciated in previous years.

Dr.		Depreciation on Fixtures and Fittings	Cr.
	£		£
Balance c/f	100	Charge to profit and loss account	100
		Balance b/d	100

Note 5. The closing stock figures are derived from a physical check of the stock quantities as recorded and priced on the stock sheets. The usage of raw material, or the cost of goods sold, is computed by adding opening stock to purchases (or production) and deducting closing stock. This sum is worked out in the manufacturing and trading accounts and means that opening stocks are debited to those accounts (credit the stock account, thus closing it) while closing stocks are credited to the manufacturing account or trading account (debit the stock account, thus re-opening it and leaving a debit balance on the account to be recorded as an asset in the balance sheet). The closing stock is often credited to the manufacturing account by deducting it from the debit side. With a columnar

approach it is a deduction. This set of postings is often called a 'stock adjustment'. Such an adjustment is needed in the manufacturing account to convert the figure for factory cost incurred during the period to the cost of production completed during the period. The opening stock of work in progress (partly completed work in the factory) is added to factory cost during the period, and the closing stock figure for work in progress is deducted, so that the cost of work completed during the period is isolated, for transfer to the finished goods account or direct to the trading account on the debit side.

Note 6. The provision for bad and doubtful debts is made to charge the profit and loss account in one period with the cost of debts of that period, which might go bad in a subsequent period. It is yet another example of matching cost with revenue. The profit and loss account is debited, and the provision is credited and carried forward as a credit balance which is shown. in the balance sheet as a deduction from the current asset, debtors. When in the next accounting period bad debts are incurred, they are written off to the provision account (credit the debtor and debit the provision), where the balance carried forward on the credit side is waiting to neutralize their effect on the current profit and loss account. The amount of the provision made is a matter for estimate. If the estimate is wrong, an over or under provision will arise which will distort the current profit figure.

Dr.		Provision for Doubtful Debts		Cr.
31 Dec.	£	1 Jan.		£
Bad debts written off	711	Balance b/d (old provision)		1200
		31 Dec.		
Increased provision c/f	1500	Charge to profit and loss account		1011
	£2211			£2211
		1 Jan.		
		Balance b/d		1500

The charge to the profit and loss account is this year's provision of £1500 less last year's provision no longer required, £489 (£1200−711).

Alternatively, bad debts could be debited direct to the profit and loss account so that the increased provision of £300 could be credited to the provision account and debited to profit and loss as a separate item.

Note 7. The annual interest on the loan stock is £1000, but only £500 has been paid. Thus £500 of unpaid interest should be charged to the profit and loss account (a debit) and credited to the creditors or accrued charges, which will show up in the balance sheet as a current liability.

Note 8. The factory manager's salary of £5000 should be charged to the factory overhead expenses in the manufacturing account, while the balance of salaries are debited to administration expenses in the profit and loss account. Warehouse wages and drivers' wages are charged to selling and distribution expenses, and the balance on the wages account is debited to the manufacturing account.

Note 9. As Mr Doric can supply a wholesale price for the finished goods transferred from the factory to the stores, it is possible to set the cost of finished production against this figure to compute a notional profit for the factory. The profit is a debit item in the manufacturing account, and is credited to the profit and loss account along with the trading profit and other miscellaneous income. The factory manager's commission has not yet been paid, so must appear in the balance sheet among the creditors, as well as being debited to the manufacturing account. The amount of 10 per cent on the profit will equal one-ninth of the profit remaining after charging the commission.

$$£3365 \div 10 = £337$$
$$£3028 \div 9 = £337.$$

Note 10. Tax is an appropriation of profit, so the amount set aside to meet future tax will be debited to the appropriation account and credited to a provision for future tax account, the balance of which appears on the balance sheet with the current liabilities until it is paid.

Once the adjustments have been made to the figures in the ledgers, the accounts can be produced.

An alternative method is to enter the adjustments in the appropriate column of an 'extended trial balance' and produce the income statement and balance sheet therefrom.

Trial Balance as at 31 December

	1	2	3	4
	Balances		Provisions	
	Debit	Credit	Prepaid	Accruals
Advertising	920			
Bad debts	711			
Commission owed	—	—		
Doubtful debts, provision		1 200		
Bank account, overdrawn		1 064		
Bank charges	230			
Cash in hand	409			
Debtors	11 680			
Creditors		3 290		
Depreciation, plant		2 000		
Dividend paid	9 000			
Discount received		641		
Factory power	4 729			625
Fixtures and fittings, office,	2 000			
Fixtures and fittings, office, depreciation	—	—		
General expenses	687			
Insurance	1 146		196	
Interest on loan stock	500			
Shares in Ionic Industries Ltd	24 337			
Light and heat	595			125
Loan stock		10 000		
Plant	18 000			
Purchases of raw material	36 219			
Packaging expenses	964			
Profit and loss (unappropriated)		7 809		
Repairs and renewals	853			
Rent and rates	1 571			429
Returns outwards		58		
Taxation provided	—	—		
Salaries	8 690			
Sales		103 662		
Share capital		45 000		
Stocks, 1 January: finished goods	8 438			
raw material	6 118			
work in progress	2 147			
Transport expenses	1 204		210	
Wages	30 715			
Warehouse expenses	2 861			
	£174 724	£174 724	406	1179

5	6	7	8
Income Statement		*Balance Sheet*	
Expense	Income	Asset	Liability
920			
711			
337			337
300			1 500
			1 064
230			
		409	
		11 680	
			3 290
1 650			3 650
9 000			
	641		
5 354			
		2 000	
100			100
687			
950			
1 000			500
		24 337	
720			
			10 000
		18 000	
36 219			
747		217	
			7 809
853			
2 000			
	58		
5 000			5 000
8 690			
	103 662		
			45 000
8 438	7 926	7 926	
6 118	4 683	4 683	
2 147	1 274	1 274	
994			
30 715			
2 861			
126 741	118 244	70 526	78 250

Note 1. Entries in columns 3–8 cross cast on each line to equal the entries in columns 1 and 2.

Note 2. The income statement columns carry all the entries for manufacturing, trading, profit and loss and appropriation accounts.

Note 3. The difference between the income and expense is profit retained. In this case a negative figure, since capital is depleted. Drawings exceed profit for the year.

Note 4. Closing stocks are credited to the income statement and debited to the balance sheet.

Note 5. Provisions for commission, taxation and interest are entered in the balance sheet liability columns, to balance the income statement entry.

Note 6.

£	
126 741	Expenses, assets and prepayments are equal to income, liabilities and accruals. This proves that the adjustments have been correctly made and that debits still equal credits, so the financial statements can now be written out.
70 526	
406	
£197 673	
118 244	
78 250	
1 179	
£197 673	

*Columnar Ltd. Manufacturing, Trading and Profit and Loss Accounts
for the Year ended 31 December*

		£	£
Manufacturing Account	Raw material opening stock	6 118	
	Add purchases less returns	36 161	
		42 279	
	Less closing stock	4 683	
	Cost of material used	37 596	
	Labour	21 915	
	Prime cost		59 511
	Add opening stock of work in progress	2 147	
	Less closing stock of work in progress	1 274	873
	Prime cost of completed production		60 384
	Factory overhead expenses		
	Power	5 354	
	Rent and rates	1 600	
	Insurance	760	
	Light and heat	576	
	Plant repairs	853	
	Plant depreciation	1 650	
	General expenses	458	
	Factory manager's salary	5 000	
	Factory manager's commission	337	16 588
	Cost of production		76 972
	Factory profit carried to profit and loss account		3 028
	Value of completed production on wholesale market		£ 80 000
Trading Account	Sales		103 662
	Opening stock of finished goods	8 438	
	Add completed production transferred to stores	80 000	
		88 438	
	Less closing stock of finished goods	7 926	
	Cost of goods sold		80 512
	Gross profit		£ 23 150

Note: Usually the cost of goods produced is transferred to the finished goods stock account, and from there to the trading account as the cost of goods sold. In this example the market value of completed production has been introduced to enable a factory profit to be computed.

		£	£	£
Profit and	Gross profit			23 150
Loss	Factory profit			3 028
Account	Discount received			641
				26 819
	Total revenue			
	Less administration expenses:			
	Salaries	3 690		
	Rent and rates	400		
	Light and heat	144		
	Insurance	190		
	General expenses	229		
	Depreciation on fixtures	100	4 753	
	Less selling and distribution expenses:			
	Advertising	920		
	Packing net of closing stock	747		
	Transport expenses	3 794		
	Warehouse expenses	8 861	14 322	
	Less financial expenses:			
	Bank charges	230		
	Bad and doubtful debts	1 011		
	Loan interest	1 000	2 241	21 316
	Net profit			5 503
Appropriation	Undistributed profits b/d			7 809
Account	(from previous year)			13 312
	Provision for taxation		5 000	
	Dividend paid		9 000	14 000
	Unappropriated loss c/f			(£688)

Columnar Ltd Balance Sheet as at 31 December

	£	£	£
Capital:			
45 000 ordinary shares of £1 each, authorized, issued and fully paid			45 000
Unappropriated profit			(688)
Equity interest			44 312
Long-term liabilities:			
10 per cent loan stock			10 000
Net Capital Employed			£54 312

	Cost	Accumulated Depreciation to date	Net
Represented by:			
Fixed assets:			
Plant and machinery	18 000	3 650	14 350
Fixtures and fittings	2 000	100	1 900
	20 000	3 750	16 250
Investment in Ionic Industries Ltd			24 337
			40 587

Columnar Ltd Balance Sheet as at 31 December (Continued)

	£	£	£
Current assets:			
Stock (see note 5 below)		14 100	
Debtors	11 680		
Less provision	1 500	10 180	
Prepayments		406	
Cash in hand		409	
		25 095	
Less current liabilities:			
Creditors	3 290		
Interest outstanding	500		
Commission owed	337		
Accrued expenses	1 179		
Taxation due	5 000		
Bank overdraft	1 064	11 370	
Working capital			13 725
Net assets			£54 312

A careful survey of the accounts of Columnar Ltd will bring to light some interesting points.

1. A dividend has been paid on the ordinary shares at a rate of 20 per cent, or 20 pence per share, while profit for the year after tax is insufficient to cover this dividend, and consequently the equity interest in the business has been depleted.
2. There is a large investment in another company, Ionic Industries Ltd, but there appears to be no income from this investment during the year. It follows that the market value of an apparently unprofitable investment may have fallen below its book value, so the balance sheet may give a false impression of this asset.
3. Although there are transport expenses, including drivers' wages and road fund licences, in the profit and loss account, there are no vehicles shown as assets in the balance sheet. Perhaps it will be discovered on further investigation that the vehicles are hired, and thus have no place as assets in the balance sheet.
4. The ratio of gross profit to sales is $£23\,150 \div £103\,662 \times \dfrac{100}{1}$, which is calculated at 22 per cent. This ratio reflects the profit margin on sales, and if it is different from the mark-up used to compute prices, it points to an error in the accounts such as a wrong stock figure or some sales made but not recorded. The significance of this ratio will be developed in a later chapter. For example, a 25 per cent mark-up added to cost as a profit margin will show up as a 20 per cent gross profit on sales.
5. Finished goods are transferred from the factory after a factory profit has been added to them. If the closing stock of finished goods is shown at a figure which includes this profit element, a provision must be made. No profit can be taken until it is earned.

SEMINAR EXERCISES 6

1. The trial balance of John Doe, a baker, at 31 December was:

	£	£
Drawings	7 650	
Sales		140 500
Investment and loan interest		2 380
Purchases of raw materials	34 630	
Manufacturing wages	39 720	
Repairs and renewals	1 580	
Rates	2 600	
Heat and light	3 574	
Power	8 600	
Office expenses	2 140	
Telephone	662	
Supervisory wages	8 656	
Office salaries	5 460	
Selling and distribution expenses	10 400	
Land, at cost	8 500	
Factory etc. buildings, at cost	25 000	
Depreciation on buildings		8 000
Plant and machinery, at cost	54 000	
Depreciation on plant and machinery		22 000
Investments at cost	8 000	
Opening stocks 1 January:		
Raw materials	7 800	
Finished goods	21 600	29 400
Debtors	19 600	
Loans	5 000	
Creditors		27 970
Capital account		68 400
Provision for doubtful debts		750
Insurances	1 460	
Bank overdraft		6 632
	£276 632	£276 632

Notes

(a) Closing stocks (at cost) were:

	£
Raw materials	8 240
Finished goods	23 420

(b) Rates for the year to 31 March next year had been paid, £2 040.

(c) The following accruals were estimated:

	£
Heat and light	140
Power	430
Telephone	31

(d) Insurance had been paid:

2 Jan. half year	340
24 June half year	642

(e) Office repairs were analysed at £83.

(f) The factory occupies four-fifths of the buildings, and this fraction is applied to insurances, as well as to rates and to heat and light to apportion these costs.

(g) Bad debt provision is to be adjusted to 5 per cent of debtors.

(h) Depreciation on cost is 5 per cent on buildings and 10 per cent on plant and machinery, using the straight line method.

Prepare a manufacturing, trading and profit and loss account for the year ended and balance sheet as at 31 December.

2. Paul Over carries on business in the knitting industry. Being a firm believer in the delegation of authority he has organized his business into two parts, manufacturing and selling. Each part is under the authority of a manager, who receives a bonus of $12\frac{1}{2}$ per cent of the profits after charging the bonus of his department. Finished goods are transferred from the factory, run by Mr Smith, to the sales department, run by Mr Jones, at cost (exclusive of manager's bonus) plus 20 per cent. The trial balance of the firm as at 30 April is as follows:

	£	£
Capital account, Paul Over		95 000
Freehold factory at cost (including land £27 000)	75 000	
Plant and machinery at cost	18 600	
Salesmen's cars	9 900	
Provision for depreciation b/d, factory		7 820
Provision for depreciation b/d, plant		6 900
Provision for depreciation b/d, cars		5 650
Stocks as at 1 May last year		
Raw material at cost	24 200	
Finished goods at transfer price	7 800	
Finished goods stock provision		1 300
Trade debtors and creditors	14 200	15 600
Provision for doubtful debts		1 120
Raw materials purchased	125 600	
Cash discount received		600
Wages and salaries	71 200	
Rates and insurance	4 210	
Postage and stationery	1 120	
Factory power	1 808	
Sundry expenses	7 320	
Maintenance of machinery	615	
Motor expenses	1 206	
Sales		255 000
Bank	26 211	
	£388 990	£388 990

The following information is relevant:

(a) Stocks at 30 April were: raw material at cost, £28 000; finished goods at transfer value, £8400.
(b) Analysis of the wages and salaries account shows that salaries paid to Smith and Jones were £4500 and £4200 respectively, that Paul's drawings of £6600 had been debited to the account and that sales department wages and salaries were £7100.
(c) Depreciation is computed on the factory building, plant and cars at 2 per cent, 10 per cent and 25 per cent on cost, respectively.
(d) Expenses common to the factory and the sales department are to be apportioned in the ratio 8:2.
(e) An invoice for £490 for fuel oil delivered to the factory has not been entered in the books, and rates paid in advance are £600.
(f) Bad debts totalling £298 are to be written off. These debts concern a previous

accounting period and provision has already been made for them. The provision for doubtful debts is to stand at 0.5 per cent of sales.

(a) Prepare a revenue account for Paul Over for the year ended 30 April showing prime and factory cost, and the profit made by each department.
(b) Prepare a balance sheet as at that date.
(c) State one serious flaw in the system for paying bonus to the factory manager.

Note: Calculations to the nearest £1.

3. Andy Pinder is in business manufacturing and selling light fittings, and operates from a small factory on the outskirts of a large town. A trial balance extracted from his books on 31 May was as follows:

	£	£
Capital account, Andy Pinder		57 112
Drawings account, Andy Pinder	4 220	
Cash at bank and in hand	4 384	
Sundry trade debtors and creditors	17 732	5 866
Land and buildings at cost	25 000	
Plant and machinery at cost	20 000	
Plant and machinery depreciation		10 000
Motor vehicles at cost	2 604	
Motor vehicles depreciation		1 500
Fixtures and fittings at cost	3 438	
Fixtures and fittings depreciation		1 470
Stock 1 June last year: raw materials	17 456	
work in progress	15 900	
finished goods	18 700	
Provision for doubtful debts		356
Bad debts	181	
Rates and insurance	1 432	
Wages	17 020	
Factory power	4 511	
Light and heat	4 120	
Maintenance	3 114	
Salaries	15 200	
Returns inwards and outwards	263	518
Advertising	1 400	
Transport expenses	1 670	
Bank charges	415	
Sundry expenses	800	
Purchases, sales	52 880	123 788
10 per cent loan account, Lite Finance Ltd		30 000
Discounts received		1 830
	£232 440	£232 440

The following notes are relevant:

(a) Provision for doubtful debts is to be adjusted to a figure equal to 10 per cent of debtors (to nearest £1).
(b) Depreciation is to be provided, using the reducing balance method and applying rates of 15 per cent on plant, 25 per cent on vehicles and 10 per cent on fixtures and fittings.

(c) At 31 May:

    Electricity accrued was   £52

    Insurance prepaid was   £21

    Rates prepaid were   £86

    Stocks were valued at: raw material   £18 760

                       work in progress   £14 900

                       finished goods   £19 100

(d) Light and heat, insurance, rates and sundry expenses were to be apportioned in the ratio 3:1 between the factory and administrative overheads. An amount of £2200 posted to the salaries account concerns the factory manager.

(e) Included in the sales are goods which cost £338 and which have been charged out with a profit margin of £78 added. It has been agreed that these goods will be accepted back from the customer without charge.

(f) Loan interest has not yet been paid this year.

Prepare, in good vertical form, manufacturing, trading and profit and loss accounts for the year ended 31 May, and a balance sheet as at that date.

The Work of the Financial Accountant

9 | Miscellaneous Practical Matters

ACCOUNTS FROM INCOMPLETE RECORDS

It is not every business that maintains a complete double-entry accounting system; indeed, in many firms the records fall short of a complete system. In some cases the reason for this shortfall is neglect, the absence of good systems analysis when the accounting system was first designed, or the piecemeal growth of the accounting system over a number of years without the direction of a firm organizing hand. In other cases the lack of a complete set of records, or indeed of any records at all, is caused by their loss, for example in a fire or a burglary.

Some systems will be more complete than others, and the procedure adopted by an accountant to produce sensible statements will depend on the records and documents he discovers when he begins the job. Sometimes there will be what is called a single-entry system where one side of each transaction has been recorded in the cash book, for example, so that all that is needed to complete the system is to post the single entries to the appropriate accounts in order to produce a set of double-entry records. The bank statement is a very useful document in this respect, since all movements in and out of the bank account of the firm will be shown here, even though some of the items on the bank statement are not shown in the cash book. In more primitive systems the accountant will have to build up the figures by drawing conclusions from the answers to enquiries he makes, and by deduction from other scraps of information which he can glean from the business.

The starting point for the production of accounts from incomplete records is the computation of an opening statement of affairs. This is a list of assets and a list of liabilities, so that when liabilities are deducted from assets the capital invested in the business at the beginning of the period will be found.

It is often difficult to set a value on the assets of the business as they stood at the beginning of the accounting period, and some accountants prefer to use for such assets the figure of original cost less an amount to represent accumulated depreciation up to the opening date of the accounting period. The figures for stock, debts and liabilities have to be estimated, but the bank balance can be determined with some accuracy from the bank statement. If an account is opened for each of the fixed and current assets and the liabilities and capital amount, then the foundation of the double-entry system has been laid.

The next step is usually to analyse the bank statement, on which will be found the receipts and payments of cash during the period. Receipts are generated by cash takings paid into the bank and money received from debtors. Other receipts include miscellaneous income, amounts of fresh capital introduced into the business, and liquid funds generated by the sale of assets. The payments shown on the bank statement can be analysed into separate columns for expenses paid in cash, amounts paid to creditors, wages paid, petty cash expenses paid, cash drawn out by the proprietor or expenses paid for the proprietor through the business bank account, and assets purchased. The bank statement may not show a complete picture of all monies received, since some amounts received from cash takings may not have been paid into the bank because they were used to pay the running expenses of the business, or because they were used by the proprietor for personal expenditure. Enquiries must be instigated to determine such amounts so that sales and costs or drawings can be increased by the appropriate amount. Further enquiries should determine the amounts of stock drawn from the business for the personal use of the proprietor or his family. The appropriate entry in this case is to debit drawings and reduce the cost of goods sold. The opening cash float should be included in the statement of affairs, and this float will have an impact on the cash takings figure.

Once this analysis has been made the totals of the analysis columns can be posted to the relevant accounts, and a set of double-entry accounts emerges. Journal entries will be needed to introduce into the system the amounts of takings used to pay cash expenses or withdrawn by the proprietors. Estimates must be made in the normal way of amounts prepaid and accrued expenses.

From records produced so far it is now possible to compute the sales and purchases figures by deduction. Purchases can be computed from the creditors figures by taking the amount paid to creditors during the year, subtracting the amount owed to creditors at the beginning of the year, and adding on the amount owed to creditors at the end of the year. One disadvantage of this technique is that it produces a figure for credit purchases only, so the amount of cash purchases must be added on if the correct total is to be obtained. In the same way the figure for sales can be computed from the debtors figures by taking the amount paid by debtors during the period, subtracting from it the amount owed by debtors at the start of the period, and adding on the amount owed by debtors at the end of the period. Once again this formula provides a figure for credit sales only and any cash sales must be added to this amount if the correct total is to be found. Cash sales are not always the same as cash takings banked, since this amount must be increased to cover those cash takings which have been spent in cash to pay the running expenses of the business.

Sometimes the use of the mark up or gross profit percentage is helpful as a check on the accuracy of figures. The application of the mark up to the cost of goods sold will show a figure for sales, and likewise if the gross profit percentage is applied to sales an amount for costs can be worked out. For example, if the cost of goods sold is £1000 and the mark up on cost is 20 per cent, then the figure for sales must equal £1200. Likewise sales minus a gross profit margin of 20 per cent on cost will show the cost figure, so £1200 minus one sixth of £1200 equals £1000, the cost of goods sold.

Note: A mark up of one fifth on cost means that one sixth must be subtracted from the sales figure to get back to the cost figure. Five fifths plus one fifth equals six fifths, and this figure must be divided by six to get back to one fifth of cost.

Example

The incomplete records technique is similar to using a child's building bricks to compute the figure needed from the evidence available.

	£
Cash paid to creditors during period	5000
Less opening creditors	2000
	3000
Plus closing creditors	1000
Purchases on credit terms	£4000

Add cash purchases, if any, to find total purchases. Ensure that all cash paid to creditors is for revenue rather than capital items. By a simple rearrangement you can deduce the missing cash figure if the purchases and opening and closing creditors are known.

	£
Opening creditors	2000
Plus purchases	4000
	6000
Less closing creditors	1000
Cash paid	£5000

The same logic can be applied to the credit sales figure by using cash received and the opening and closing debtors. The computation of the overall sales figure does, however, require more information.

	£
Cheques received from debtors	14 000
Less opening debtors	4 000
	10 000
Plus closing debtors	5 000
Credit sales	15 000
Plus cash takings banked	8 000
Plus cash takings spent on expenses	3 000
Plus increase in cash float	500
Plus cash drawn from till by proprietor	1 000
Total sales	£27 500

If any debts have been written off during the year they must be added back in the computation to show the true sales figure.

The gross profit percentage or mark-up can often be used to compute the sales figure. If the cost of goods sold can be found, then by applying the gross profit percentage, the figure can be 'grossed up' to sales. The sales figure can also be used to work back to cost of sales.

Sales of £440 000 at a mark up on cost of 10 per cent means a deduction of 1/11 from sales to get back to cost, £400 000. Once the cost of sales is determined, then by using the opening and closing stocks, the purchases figure can be worked out. Then, if the opening and closing creditors are known the cash paid to creditors can be found, or, if cash paid and opening creditors are known, the closing creditors figure can be computed.

Example

Peter Bean commenced business on 1 January as a wholesaler of frozen vegetables. The accounting system used in the business is rudimentary, and you have been asked to produce accounts for the year ended 31 December.

The following is a summary of the bank statements for the year:

Receipts. Cash introduced as capital on 1 January, £22 000; banked from cash received from customers, £50 800.

Payments. Motor van £4000; freezer equipment £10 000; office furniture £1500; factory rent £1500; wages £7088; commission to sales manager £4800; goods purchased for resale £39 600; rates £800; repairs £250; insurance £220; van expenses £746.

Note: The following cash payments were made before banking the balance of the takings: motor expenses £516; wages £592; sundry expenses £100; drawings by Peter Bean £54 per week.

The following information is also relevant:

1. Discounts allowed to customers during the year were £490, while discounts received totalled £220. Goods sold to Rooster during the year amounted to £800, but he has now disappeared without paying for them. Peter Bean has taken goods for his own use which could have been sold for £500.
2. On 31 December £3000 was owed to suppliers and £6200 was owed by customers. The prepayment of rates was £100 and insurance £20. Stock at cost amounted to £4820. The factory had been occupied since 1 January at an annual rent of £2000.
3. Peter Bean tells you that in his view the van will have a useful life of four years, and the office and freezer equipment will last ten years.
4. On 31 December there was £10 in the petty cash box.

Do not forget that depreciation should be provided on the van at 25 per cent of cost, and on the freezer and office equipment at 10 per cent of cost. In the absence of a scrap value it is best to act conservatively and assume that the assets will be worthless when worn out.

The first step is to write up the petty cash account to determine as the balancing figure the amount of sales receipts raised to pay expenses. Do not forget the £10 closing balance, especially in the balance sheet.

Dr.		Petty Cash Account	Cr.
	£		£
Sales receipts	4026	Motor expenses	516
		Wages	592
		Sundries	100
		Drawings	2808
		Balance c/f	10
	£4026		£4026
Balance b/d	10		

The next step is to write up the cash book to find the closing bank balance. If the bank balance is found from the bank statement the figure for cash received from customers can be computed.

Dr.	Cash Book		Cr.
	£		£
Capital	22 000	Motor van	4 000
Received from		Freezer equipment	10 000
customers	50 800	Office furniture	1 500
		Rent	1 500
		Wages	7 088
		Sales commission	4 800
		Purchases paid for	39 600
		Rates	800
		Repairs	250
		Insurance	220
		Van expenses	746
		Balance c/f	2 296
	£72 800		£72 800
Balance b/d	2296		

In practice it would be possible to start a set of double-entry accounts by recording the other side of these cash transactions. Do not forget, however, that there is a difference between cash recorded and the profit and loss account amount. Some cash items will need to be capitalized.

The next step is to write up accounts for creditors and debtors, to find the amounts needed for the trading account, purchases and sales. There are no opening balances because the business only commenced on 1 January.

Dr.	Creditors Account		Cr.
	£		£
Bank, payments	39 600	Trading account	42 820
Discounts received	220	(balancing figure)	
Creditor on 31			
December c/f	3 000		
	£42 820		£42 820
		Balance of creditors b/d	3 000

Dr.	Debtors Account		Cr.
	£		£
Trading account	62 816	Petty cash	4 026
(balancing figure)		Bank	50 800
		Drawings in kind	500
		Discounts allowed	490
		Bad debts, Rooster	800
		Debtors on 31	
		December c/f	6 200
	£62 816		£62 816
Balance of debtors			
b/d	6 200		

The trading and profit and loss accounts can now be prepared, together with a balance sheet.

Trading and Profit and Loss Account for the Year Ended 31 December

	£	£
Sales		62 816
Purchases	42 820	
Less closing stock	4 820	38 000
Gross Profit		24 816
Add discounts received		220
		25 036
Expenses:		
Wages, £(592 + 7088)	7 680	
Rent, £(1500 cash + 500 accrued)	2 000	
Rates, £(800 cash − 100 prepaid)	700	
Insurance, £(220 cash − 20 prepaid)	200	
Sales commission	4 800	
Motor expenses, £(516 + 746)	1 262	
Bad debt, Rooster	800	
Discounts allowed	490	
Repairs	250	
Sundries	100	
Depreciation:		
Van	1 000	
Freezer equipment	1 000	
Office furniture	150	20 432
Net Profit		£4 604

Peter Bean, Balance Sheet as at 31 December

	£ Cost	£ Depreciation	£
Fixed assets:			
Freezer equipment	10 000	1 000	9 000
Office equipment	1 500	150	1 350
Vehicle	4 000	1 000	3 000
	15 500	2 150	13 350
Current assets:			
Stock		4 820	
Debtors (including prepayments)		6 320	
Bank		2 296	
Cash		10	
		13 446	
Less current liabilities:			
Trade creditors	3 000		
Accruals	500	3 500	
Working capital			9 946
Net assets			£23 296
Financed by:			
Peter Bean capital			22 000
Add net profit		4 604	
Less drawings, £ (500 + 2808)		3 308	1 296
Net capital employed			£23 296

RECEIPTS AND PAYMENTS ACCOUNTS, AND INCOME AND EXPENDITURE ACCOUNTS

When the transactions of a club or a non-trading organization are recorded the double-entry system is not often used, so the production of accounting statements for such organizations presents the accountant with a single-entry or incomplete records problem.

Bills are received and paid through the bank account operated by the organization or from its cash resources, and monies are received by the organization for various reasons. The majority of transactions are therefore on a cash basis and thus it is easy to prepare from the vouchers of the organization a receipts and payments account. This account, as its name implies, shows on one side the monies received and on the other side the payments made by the organization. It is a summary of the cash book and combines movements through the bank account with cash transactions. The account is operated on debit and credit lines, beginning with a balance which represents the cash and bank account resources of the organization on the first day of the accounting period. It is debited with funds received and credited with payments made so that its closing balance represents the cash and bank account resources of the organization on the last day of the accounting period. It must be stressed that the receipts and payments account is merely a cash account; there is no attempt to distinguish capital transactions from revenue ones, or to bring into the account accruals or prepayments, so any balance shown cannot be described as a surplus or profit revealed by the account.

The income and expenditure account represents the profit and loss account of a club or non-trading organization. In this account the expenses of a period are set against the revenue of that period so that a profit, or excess of revenue over expense, can be revealed for the period and added to the accumulated fund, which is the term used for the capital account in the balance sheet of clubs and societies etc.

Thus the major differences between these two accounts are that the receipts and payments account deals only with cash transactions, includes capital items as well as revenue ones, and shows as its balance the total of funds held in cash or in the bank account of the organization, while the income and expenditure account includes expenses and revenues which have not been the subject of movement of cash, i.e. accruals and prepayments, excludes capital transactions and shows as its balance the surplus or deficit (profit or loss) made by the organization during the period.

It is often the lot of an accountant to prepare an income and expenditure account from a receipts and payments account, since as a member of the society he has been persuaded by the committee to do so. His first step is to analyse the receipts and payments account so that the costs of various activities are grouped together, and receipts from such activities are separated, and then to post the items to the income and expenditure account. This account will be credited with such items as subscriptions, fees, grants received and other items of miscellaneous income, all of which will have appeared on the debit side of the receipts and payments account. The costs of the organization shown on the credit or payments side of the receipts and payments account are debited to the income and expenditure account.

The next step is to adjust the receipts and payments for any accruals and prepayments which are revealed by enquiries made about them. Once expenditure has been adjusted to show expense the account can be tidied up, and in this respect it is important to show separately the effect on income of the separate ventures undertaken by the organization. Transactions of a capital nature shown in the receipts and payments account should be posted to accounts in the general ledger and thus appear in the balance sheet. Any surplus of assets over liabilities at the beginning of the accounting period will be balanced in the general ledger by the amount in the accumulated fund account, to which any surplus or profit made during the period is added.

The production of accounts for a non-trading organization is not always straightforward, since certain problems can arise. In some cases the accumulated fund is not the only capital account of the organization; there may also be an account for life members' subscriptions or for a building fund. Some clubs and societies may hold part of their accumulated capital in such separate funds since they have been raised separately from the main capital of the society for a distinct purpose.

The treatment in the accounts of the subscriptions of life members is sometimes a source of confusion. A life member makes a large single payment instead of paying a subscription each year and for this he is allowed to be a member of the club or society until his death. Thus a life fund can be built up from these subscriptions which is represented, as is the accumulated fund, by the general assets of the club. As new life subscriptions are made they should not be taken to the credit of the income and expenditure account, but should be added to the balance on the life members fund, and when a life member dies that part of the life fund represented by his payment should be transferred to the credit of the accumulated fund.

A similar difficulty concerns entrance fees to a club where these are separate from the annual subscription. There is some confusion about whether these are of an income or of a capital nature. Opinion is divided on this point, the only principle to guide the accountant being that their treatment should be consistent from year to year. A major argument in this debate is that if entrance fees are written off to the income and expenditure account the profit of the club or society could be distorted in a year when many new members join.

Another problem encountered in this type of accounting concerns the position of subscriptions in arrears. Such subscriptions are technically debtors of the club, but in many cases they are likely never to be received. Thus a decision has to be made as to whether this asset should be ignored or revealed, the criterion for the decision being an objective and realistic review of the probability that subscriptions in arrears will eventually be paid. Such subscriptions can also have an impact on the income and expenditure account, since, although it is wrong to credit that account with subscriptions which are not likely to be received, if such subscriptions are not taken into account in one period they could distort the profit of a subsequent period if many arrears are paid in that year and counted as income of that period.

Example

This example combines the incomplete records technique with the production of the accounts of a non-trading organization.

The following balances were taken from the books of Paddington Green Golf Club, as at 1 January.

	£	£
Course at cost		80 000
Clubhouse at cost		20 000
Building fund, represented by investments		
£20 000 4 per cent consolidated stock	7 400	
Deposit with East Acton Building Society	12 000	19 400

	£	£
Subscriptions in advance (this year to 31 Dec.)		400
Creditors for bar supplies		350
Life membership fund		5 000
Subscriptions in arrears		600
Bar stock		4 850
Clubhouse equipment at cost		3 400
Cash in hand	100	
Cash at bank	950	1 050

An analysis of the bank account operated by the club showed the following summary of receipts and payments during the year ended 31 December.

		£
Receipts	Subscriptions	26 000
	Life members	2 000
	Sale of instruction manuals	800
	Green fees	200
	Sale of old carpet from clubhouse	22
	Bar takings	28 600
	Consolidated stock interest	800
Payments	Upkeep of course	17 150
	General clubhouse expenses (including bar wages of £4200)	12 150
	Petty cash, expenses paid to treasurer	1 550
	Bar supplies	23 150
	Purchase of instruction manuals	350
	Piano	700
	Deposited with East Acton Building Society	800
	Replacement carpet for clubhouse	1 260

The following information is relevant to the preparation of club accounts.

1. The club maintains a building fund separate from the capital fund and life membership fund. The building fund is invested in consolidated stock and a building society, while the capital fund and life membership fund are represented by the general assets of the club.
2. The East Acton Building Society has been instructed to credit the interest on the club's account direct to the account at each half year. The Society computes interest half yearly on 30 June and 31 December. This year the interest amounted to £840. Interest paid on the consolidated stock is also added to the building fund by paying it into the building society account.
3. There were five life members at the beginning of the year, one of whom has since died. Two other life members have joined the club.
4. Renewals of clubhouse furnishings are to be treated as revenue expenditure.
5. Outstanding at 31 December were:

	£
Creditors for bar supplies	1 600
Subscriptions in advance (next year)	900
Subscriptions in arrears (this year)	300
Bar chits not yet settled	65

6. Bar stocks at 31 December were valued at £4350.
7. It is a rule of the club that a cash float of £100 should be maintained in the treasurer's hands. To this end an imprest petty cash account is operated.
8. An insurance premium of £480 has been paid by cheque during this year for the year to 31 March next year.

Produce an income and expenditure account for the year ended 31 December, and a balance sheet as that date, ignoring taxation.

The best method of approaching this problem is to compute as 'workings' some significant figures, using the process of deduction already described, and then build them into the accounting statement.

1. *The Opening Accumulated Fund.* This is the recorded amount of the net assets of the club at the start of the accounting period.

	£	£
Course and clubhouse at cost		100 000
Subscriptions in arrears		600
Bar stock		4 850
Equipment		3 400
Cash (at bank and in hand)		1 050
		109 900
Less Creditors	350	
Subscriptions in advance	400	
Life fund	5000	5 750
		£104 150

2. *Subscriptions.* During the year.

	£	£
Amounts paid in cash		26 000
Plus Opening subscriptions in advance	400	
Closing subscriptions in arrears	300	700
		26 700
Less Opening subscriptions in arrears	600	
Closing subscriptions in advance	900	1 500
		£25 200

3. *Renewals.*

	£
Cost of a new carpet	1260
Less scrap value of old	22
	£1238

4. *Bar Trading Account.*

	£		£
Paid to creditors	23 150	Opening stock	4 850
Less owed at start	350	Plus purchases	24 400
	22 800		29 250
Plus owed at end	1 600	Less closing stock	4 350
Purchases	£24 400	Cost of sales	24 900
		Wages	4 200
Takings Banked	28 600		29 100
Chits	65		
Total takings	£28 665	Bar takings	28 665
		Loss	£ 435

5. *General Expenses.*

	£
Payments less bar wages	7950
Petty cash	1550
Less prepayment (3/12 × 480)	(120)
	£9380

6. *Instruction Manuals.* Sales £800 − Costs £350 = Profit £450. Note: No closing stocks.

7. *Life Fund.* Opening balance, £5000, minus one deceased plus two new members, £6000. (Life membership £1000.)

8. *Building Fund.*

	£
Opening balance	19 400
Add Interest on stock (£20 000 ×4 per cent)	800
Building society interest	840
Closing balance	£21 040

Note: £1640 of interest is added to building society deposit.

9. *Bank Account.*

	£
Opening balance	950
Add total of receipts	58 422
Less total of payments	(57 110)
Closing balance	£ 2 262

Note: A petty cash float of £100 appears on the balance sheet.
Once these 'workings' are completed, the accounts can be produced as follows.

Paddington Green Golf Club

Dr.   *Income and Expenditure Account Year ended 31 December*   Cr.

	£	£		£	£
Course upkeep		17 150	Subscriptions		25 200
General expenses		9 380	Green fees		200
Renewals (net)		1 238	Profit on manuals		450
Bar loss:			Deficit for year		2 353
Cost of sales	24 900				
Wages	4 200				
	29 100				
Takings	28 665				
		435			
		£28 203			£28 203

Paddington Green Golf Club Balance Sheet as at 31 December

	£	£	£
Capital fund as at 1 January			104 150
Transfer from life membership fund			1 000
			105 150
Less deficit for the year			2 353
			102 797
Building fund as at 1 January		19 400	
Add interest consolidated stock		800	
East Acton building society		840	
			21 040
Life members fund as at 1 January		5 000	
Less transfer to capital fund		(1 000)	
Add new life members		2 000	
			6 000
Funds employed			£129 837
Represented by:			
Fixed assets			
Course at cost			80 000
Clubhouse at cost			20 000
Clubhouse equipment at cost		3 400	
Additions: piano		700	
			4 100
Investments, building fund			
20 000 4 per cent consolidated stock at cost		7 400	
Deposit with East Acton building society		13 640	
			21 040
Current assets			
Bar stocks		4 350	
Subscriptions in arrears		300	
Prepayments		120	
Debtors		65	
Bank		2 262	
Cash in hand		100	
		7 197	
Less current liabilities			
Subscriptions in advance	900		
Creditors for bar supplies	1 600		
		2 500	
			4 697
Net assets			£129 837

ADJUSTMENTS TO ACCOUNTS

Mistakes often occur in the accounting system, and when they are discovered the books and accounts have to be adjusted. Some adjustments will have an effect on the profit figure, some on items in the balance sheet, and some on both the position and income statements. In some cases a compensating error will be found, the adjustment of which shows no change in a figure on an accounting statement; for example, if money received from debtor A is posted to debtor B's account, when this is adjusted the overall debtor figure on the balance sheet will not have changed. Such adjustments can be used as a test to prove the ability of an accountant to understand the impact and extent of mistakes and to see what is needed to correct them. For this reason this has been a fertile source of examination questions.

The major types of adjustment are as follows.

The Capital/Revenue Allocation. It often happens that items which should be capitalized are written off to the income statement as revenue expenses, so they have to be adjusted by increasing the asset in the balance sheet and reducing the charge in the income statement, thus increasing the profit for the period. If the fixed assets are increased the depreciation charge for the period which has been set against profit must be updated to include the newly capitalized amount, so an extra depreciation charge will have to be made, with a consequent reduction of the profit figure. A common example of this type of adjustment occurs where a company uses its own labour to install a new machine. In this case the wages account must be credited and the asset account debited with the cost of labour so used.

Drawings of the Proprietor Charged in the Salaries Account. It must be recognized that an amount drawn out by a proprietor is an appropriation of profit and not a charge to be borne before that profit is computed. In this case salaries must be reduced and thus profits increased, but at the same time drawings increased so that the amount of ploughed-back profit remains the same.

Prepayments or Accruals Omitted when the Accounting Statements were Made up. An expense large enough to be considered material may be discovered after the income statement has been completed. Such an expense must be debited to the profit and loss account, thus reducing the profit figure, and shown in the balance sheet as an accrual or creditor among the current liabilities. If the accountant has forgotten to apportion a payment such as rent, rates or insurance premium, which concerns a time period other than the accounting period, the appropriate part of the expense to be carried forward must be calculated, credited to the profit and loss account, thus increasing the profit, and shown in the balance sheet as a prepayment or debtor among the current assets.

Credit Sales Understated. If sales made to some customers on credit terms have been omitted the amount of such sales must be credited to the trading account, thus directly increasing the profit while debtors are similarly increased in the balance sheet. Note that the profit is increased by the full amount of this transaction, since the cost of goods sold has already been debited to the trading account as the closing stock was taken after the goods had been sold.

Depreciation at the Wrong Rate, or on the Wrong Basis. If depreciation was charged on the written-down value instead of on the cost of the asset, the adjustment required would need a computation of the correct amount so that the difference could be added to or subtracted from the costs, with a consequent effect on profit, and also shown as an adjustment to accumulated depreciation in the balance sheet.

Goods on Sale or Return Counted as Sold. Such goods are placed with an agent in the hope that they will be sold, but until the agent sells them they are still the property of the business and should be counted in the closing stock shown in the balance sheet. The adjustment required in this case is to reverse the entries made, so that sales are reduced, stock is increased, and the profit figure is reduced by the profit margin on this transaction.

A Stock Write-down. If stock is old or has lost its value for some other reason a realistic value must be placed upon it, which may be less than the figure shown in the balance sheet. In this case stock in the balance sheet is reduced and the amount of the reduction is written off against profit in the income statement.

Errors in the Cash Book. There are many errors which can be made when a cash book is written up, for example, an amount of £86 posted as £68, in which case the appropriate increase must be made, or a payment posted on the receipts side, in which case the adjustment is to post double the amount to the payments side.

Loan Interest Outstanding. If this expense has been omitted it must be debited to the profit and loss account, thus reducing profit, and shown among the creditors on the balance sheet. Sometimes interest is paid half-yearly so that the first instalment may appear in the trial balance, but an accrual is needed for the remainder. The loan and interest rate must be checked to find out how much has been paid.

A Vehicle Sold Without any Record of the Transaction Entered in the Books. The asset account for vehicles must be reduced and the accumulated depreciation on the vehicle sold must be written out of the depreciation account. Both these items are transferred to a vehicle disposal account so that the written-down value can be set against the price received for the vehicle which has been posted from the cash book to the credit of the vehicle disposal account. This adjustment will affect the profit figure and the balance sheet.

A Debtor Balance which Goes Bad after the Accounting Date. An extra provision must be raised to reduce the profit and to appear as a deduction from debtors among the current assets of the balance sheet.

Cost or Appropriation Omitted when the Profit Figure is Struck. Sometimes an amount for taxation due to be paid, or salary, or manager's commission computed after the profit figure has been struck, is forgotten. The provision is debited to the profit and loss account (appropriation section for taxation), thus reducing profit, and the amount thus provided appears on the balance sheet among the creditors, since payment has not yet been made.

Debit Balances Listed as Credits, or Debits Posted as Credits. The adjustment in this case is to reverse the wrong posting, remembering to double the amount involved.

Casting Errors. Pages in the ledger may be under- or over-cast, in which case the difference between the wrong figure and the right figure must be calculated, and this amount added to or subtracted from cost (and profit), or the appropriate asset account as the case may be.

The list of likely adjustments shown above is not exhaustive, since the practical application of double entry book-keeping produces many types of error. Suffice it to say that a cool head is needed to work out the impact of mistakes and see what is required to correct them.

JOURNAL ENTRIES

The means by which adjustments are made in the books is the journal entry. The journal is written up in a two-column ledger so that the dual aspect of each adjustment can be seen. It is customary to explain the reason for each adjustment by means of a 'narration' or 'narrative'. In a well organized system only authorized persons are allowed to make journal entries, and a file of journal vouchers is maintained as a form of internal control.

A typical journal ruling is:

Date	Narration	£	£
1.4.19 ..	Plant and machinery Direct labour Being cost of own labour used to install plant, capitalized	1423	1423

SUSPENSE ACCOUNT

Where a trial balance will not balance it is sometimes the practice to open a suspense account, entering therein the difference. As errors are found they can be posted to the suspense account and the difference will gradually be eliminated.

CONTROL ACCOUNTS

In most businesses a number of suppliers provide materials on credit terms and a number of customers purchase goods on credit. Thus the asset debtors and the liability trade creditors which appear in the balance sheet are the total figures for a number of debtor balances and a number of creditor balances. To record this situation properly a subsidiary ledger is maintained for debtors and creditors. The individual account of each debtor is kept in the debtors ledger while the total figure for amounts owed by all the debtors is shown in the general ledger.

When there is a large number of accounts for debtors or creditors book-keeping mistakes are bound to be made, so the device of the control or total account is used in an attempt to reveal them. Suppose there are 5000 customers of a business all buying goods on credit terms, so that 5000 individual debtor accounts must be maintained. Goods purchased will be debited to each individual's personal account and the sales account will be credited. Cash paid by customers, discount allowed to them and goods returned by them will be credited to the personal account of each customer and debited to cash discounts and returns.

If the amounts for the goods bought, goods returned, cash paid and discount allowed for all debtors are totalled and the total figures entered into a control account, the balance of this account must equal the total of the balances of the individual accounts. If it does not, then a book-keeping mistake has been made which must be sought and rectified. Total figures from the daybooks and cash book can be used for this purpose, since they summarize the transactions entered from those books to the individual debtor or creditor accounts.

A total account can be used to control the situation wherever a large number of postings are made to individual accounts in a subsidiary ledger, for example the cost ledger control, or the handwritten control used to check the accuracy of amounts entered into a mechanized or computerized book-keeping system. The balance on the control account will appear in the trial balance taken out from the general ledger, while the total of balances in the subsidiary ledger must be reconciled to this figure. Thus the trial balance can be extended and accounts produced without delay while petty mistakes on the personal ledgers are located.

Another advantage of the control account is that errors are localized within one section of the books so that the area of search for a mistake can be reduced to only those accounts covered by the control.

Typical Entries in a Creditors Ledger Control Account

Dr.	Creditors Ledger Control Account	Cr.
	£	£
Cash paid	Opening balance b/d	
Discounts received	Purchases	
Returns outwards		
Closing balance c/f		

The totals for the month are entered into the account from the following sources: purchases from the daybook, returns from the returns daybook (written up from credit notes received), cash and discounts from the cash book.

Typical Entries in a Debtors Ledger Control Account

Dr.	Debtors Ledger Control Account	Cr.
	£	£
Opening balance b/d	Cash received	
Credit sales	Discounts allowed	
Dishonoured cheques	Returns inwards	
(written back)	Bad debts written off	
	Closing balance c/f	

The amounts entered in the account are totals for the month (hence the name total account) and are posted from the following books: cash received and discounts allowed from the cash book, returns inwards from the sales daybook or a separate book for credit notes if one is maintained, bad debts written off from the journal, sales from the daybook, cheques written back from the cash book. The procedure when a customer's cheque 'bounces' is to reverse the entry made when it was first received, credit the cash book and debit the customer's account in the debtors ledger. If the control account is to reflect the total of accounts in the personal ledger, then it too must be debited. At first glance this seems to be two debits for one credit, but the debtors ledger is now treated as a subsidiary ledger for memorandum purposes only, to give a detailed analysis of the total debtors figure shown in the control account. It is this total figure which appears in the trial balance and which is used in the computation of accounting statements.

Example

Shaw and Steadfast Ltd keep a debtors control account in their general ledger, and maintain individual accounts for each customer in a subsidiary debtors ledger. There are 150 accounts in the debtors ledger. The first eight are as follows:

	Balance at 1 January
	£
T. R. Andrews & Co.	126
Arnold & Palmer	264
Ankler Ltd	20
Bageholt & Drew	–
Bell Garages Ltd	300
T. C. Belling	60
Bright and Co.	136
Broadbent & Neames	240

The total of the balances outstanding at 1 January (including the above) is £19 284.
Transactions during January affecting these accounts were:

	Sales	Returns	Bad Debts	Cash Received	Cash Discounts
	£	£	£	£	£
T. R. Andrews & Co.	280	–	–	126	–
Arnold & Palmer	–	–	–	200	–
Ankler Ltd	164	28	–	154	2
Bageholt & Drew	70	–	–	48	2
Bell Garages Ltd	–	–	–	294	6
T. C. Belling	–	–	60	–	–
Bright and Co.	128	–	–	136	–
Broadbent & Neames	70	6	–	236	4
All other accounts	13 560	174	84	14 862	206
	14 272	208	144	16 056	220

Head up accounts for the debtors control and for the first eight accounts in the debtors ledger. Add a further account to represent all the other customers' accounts. Enter the above transactions. Balance all the accounts and check that the total of the balances in the debtors ledger agrees with the control account balance at 31 January.

Dr.	T. R. Andrews & Co.		Cr.
Balance b/d	126	Cash	126
Sales	280	Balance c/f	280
	£406		£406
Balance b/d	280		

Dr.	Arnold & Palmer		Cr.
Balance b/d	264	Cash	200
		Balance c/f	64
	£264		£264
Balance b/d	64		

Dr.	Ankler Ltd		Cr.
Balance b/d	20	Returns	28
Sales	164	Cash	154
		Discount	2
	£184		£184

Dr.	Bageholt and Drew		Cr.
Sales	70	Cash	48
		Discount	2
		Balance c/f	20
	£70		£70
Balance b/d	20		

Dr.	Bell Garages Ltd		Cr.
Balance b/d	300	Cash	294
		Discount	6
	£300		£300

Dr.	T. C. Belling		Cr.
Balance b/d	£60	Bad debts	£60

Dr.	Bright & Co.		Cr.
Balance b/d	136	Cash	136
Sales	128	Balance c/f	128
	£264		£264
Balance b/d	128		

Dr.	Broadbent & Neames		Cr.
Balance b/d	240	Returns	6
Sales	70	Cash	236
		Discount	4
		Balance c/f	64
	£310		£310
Balance b/d	64		

Dr.	All Other Accounts		Cr.
Balance b/d	18 138	Returns	174
Sales	13 560	Bad debts	84
		Cash	14 862
		Discount	206
		Balance c/f	16 372
	£31 698		£31 698
Balance b/d	16 372		

Dr.		Debtors Ledger Control		Cr.
Balance b/d	19 284	Returns	208	
Sales	14 272	Bad debts	144	
		Cash	16 056	
		Discount	220	
		Balance c/f	16 928	
	£33 556		£33 556	
Balance b/d	16 928			

List of Balances	£
T. R. Andrews & Co.	280
Arnold & Palmer	64
Bageholt & Drew	20
Bright and Co.	128
Broadbent & Neames	64
Others	16 372
Total debtors per personal accounts	£16 928

BANK RECONCILIATIONS

At the end of an accounting period a statement will be received from the bank showing all amounts paid into or drawn out of the business bank account. The balance on this statement represents the funds of the business held at the bank or the amount overdrawn. It is rare for the balance on the statement to agree with the balance in the cash book maintained at the office of the business. It may seem strange that two records made up from the same basic documents should disagree as to the bank balance at a particular time, but this is because certain items which appear on the bank statement are not in the cash book, and vice versa.

One such item concerns cheques drawn by a company in favour of its creditors and entered in its cash book, but not yet presented at its bank for payment by those creditors. A cheque is drawn, it is entered on the payments side of the cash book, and then put into an envelope and sent off to the creditor. There is a time lag while the cheque is in the post, while it is at the creditor's office, and while it is filtering through the banking system from the creditor's bank, where it has been paid in, to the debtor company's bank, where it is presented for payment. Thus cheques not yet presented are payments made by a business but which have not yet been paid out of its bank account.

Another difference concerns cheques received from debtors and entered into the cash book on the receipts side, but not yet entered on the bank statement because of the time lag while they are entered on a paying-in slip, taken to the bank and deposited, and then entered by the bank on to the appropriate bank statement page.

The third difference between cash book and bank statement is caused by receipts or payments made by banker's order, standing order or direct debit. These are payments made not by cheque but by an instruction to a bank to make the payment.

Thus the transaction is completed within the banking system by the transfer of funds from one bank account to another. If no prime document is produced to inform the recipient that the payment has arrived, he discovers this only when he receives his bank statement. In this case the bank statement itself acts as the document of prime entry which evidences the transaction and initiates its entry into the cash book.

Occasionally miscellaneous income of a business is collected by its bank and will therefore appear on the bank statement rather than in the cash book. Dividends from an associate company, or the interest on a loan, can be paid by a warrant sent directly to the bank of the recipient, so that if no separate notice is sent to the office of the recipient no entry will be made in the cash book until the item is picked up from the bank statement. Many companies make routine payments by standing order, and these are posted on the credit side of the cash book from the bank statement, and from there debited to the appropriate expense account. Other items which are first notified to the company through its bank statement concern the costs of running the bank account itself, i.e. bank charges and interest charged on overdrawn balances. Once again these amounts must be identified on the bank statement and entered from there into the cash book.

When a cheque received from a debtor and banked is dishonoured, this too will appear on the bank statement but not in the first instance in the cash book. The company receives the cheque, enters it in its cash book, and posts it from there to the credit of the debtor's account. The cheque is then banked and presented by the creditor company's bank to the debtor's bank for payment. If the debtor does not have sufficient funds in his account to meet that cheque his bank will return the cheque to the creditor company's bank marked 'refer to drawer'. This means that the cheque has 'bounced', i.e. that it has been returned from the debtor's bank. The creditor company's bank will therefore write it back out of their client's account, so that it appears on the payments side of the bank statement to contra its earlier appearance on the receipts side. The bank will notify its client of its action, but often such dishonoured cheques are found to be a source of difference between the bank statement and the cash book.

Thus the differences between the cash book and the bank statement have two main causes. These are items not yet processed completely through the banking system, and items not yet notified by the bank to the business so that they are not in the cash book. At the end of each month, when the cash book is closed, cross cast, and posted to the accounts in the general ledger, a bank reconciliation must take place. This means that all the items causing a difference between the cash book and the bank statement must be identified, those not yet entered in the cash book must be entered, and the remaining difference must be set out in the form of a reconciliation statement so that no items are 'lost' between the bank and the business, and the cash book total as entered in the accounts shows the correct amount for cash belonging to the business. Such a reconciliation will also eliminate errors in the cash book.

The procedure is a simple one. First the items in the cash book and in the bank statement are checked off against one another to find the transactions which are not shown on both statements. A list of cheques sent out to creditors but not yet presented by their recipients can be computed and deducted from the bank balance or added to the overdraft. The amounts paid in before the end of the period but not yet shown on the bank statement must be added to the bank statement total, which should then agree with the cash book. It is important to list these outstanding amounts so that at the end of the next month it can be easily ascertained that they have gone through the system correctly and are not still outstanding for some other reason. At this time extraordinary items, such as cheques on the bank statement which do not correspond with the cheque number sequence used by the company, or standing orders not authorized by the company, can come to light.

Example

A book-keeper has written up the cash book of Nolling Ltd for the month of June but the balance shown by his work does not agree with the corresponding amount on the bank statement. Check the cash book for errors, reconcile it to the bank statement, and comment briefly on any matters you discover which might merit further investigation.

Dr.   Cash Book of Nolling Ltd   Cr.

	Receipts				Payments		
June	Account	£	June	Cheque	Accounts	Ref.	£
6	Dawson & Co.	47.50	2		Opening balance b/d		2761.75
7	James	29.29	6	473	T. Maint	M13	32.00
15	Shaw	10.00	6	474	L. Brock	B7	25.00
24	Dingle Ltd	70.00	8	475	IKI Ltd	I2	18.20
24	Weather Ltd	36.32	9	476	Clumber Ltd	C4	59.14
28	Mitchells	41.29	13	477	Crackle Ltd	C7	40.00
28	Ronalds	88.00	16	478	Lamp & Co	L17	39.98
	Total lodgements	322.40	19	479	Print & Co	P42	100.25
30	Balance c/f	2496.59	20	480	Bandelle Ltd	M3	22.67
			25	481	Petty Cash	PC14	50.00
			27	482	Crumble	C4	35.00
			27	483	Anderton	A7	30.00
			29	484	Nimble Ltd	N21	105.00
		£3318.99					£3318.99
			July 1		Opening balance b/d		2469.59

Eastmid Bank Ltd, Statement of Account with Nolling Ltd

Particulars	Debit £	Credit £	Date June	Balance £
Balance forward			2	2761.75 (o/d)
Lodged		47.50	9	2714.25
476	59.14		10	2773.39
473	32.00			
S.O.	16.32		12	2821.71
477	40.00			
475	18.20		13	2879.91
Lodged		29.29	20	2850.62
478	39.98		22	2890.60
S.O.	36.00		23	2926.60
Lodged		70.00	24	2856.60
C.T.		23.34	25	2833.26
481	50.00			
9437	21.50		26	2904.76
482	35.00		29	2939.76
C.T.		46.32	30	2893.44

S.O. = Standing Order
C.T. = Credit Transfer

Note that the cash book shows payments in excess of receipts, which means an overdrawn account at the bank. The cash book balance has been computed in error. There has been a transposition of figures when the balance was carried down and a casting error in the balance calculation. The correct balance carried forward should be £2996.59.

	£	£
Correct balance per cash book (overdrawn)		2996.59
Deduct lodgements not entered in cash book (credit transfers)	23.34	
	46.32	69.66
		2926.93
Add payments not entered in cash book	16.32	
	36.00	
	21.50	73.82
Correct balance per cash book (overdrawn)		3000.75
Less cheques not yet presented	105.00	
	30.00	
	25.00	
	22.67	
	100.25	282.92
		2717.83
Add lodgements not yet credited	36.32	
	10.00	
	41.29	
	88.00	175.61
Balance per bank statement		£2893.44

The following points should be noted.

1. Cheque 9437 is out of sequence on bank statement. Enquire of bank whether this is the correct account.
2. Reference C4 is used twice on the payments side of the cash book. Is there a misposting? The accounts of Clumber Ltd and Crumble are not likely to be on the same page in the creditors ledger.
3. £29.29 was received from James on 7 June according to the cash book but was not banked until 20 June according to the bank statement. Why was there a delay in banking funds when the account is overdrawn?
4. Check authority for standing orders.
5. Bandelle Ltd is given posting folio M3 in the cash book. Is this correct? Should it not be a 'B' posting?

SEMINAR EXERCISES 7

1. Mr Feckless holds the view that a system of stock record cards is an expensive luxury for a business such as his. He says, 'When quarterly accounts are compiled, all that is needed for accuracy is a physical stock-take and the extension of the physical totals at cost to provide the figure for closing stock.' Stock was taken on 30 November, but Mr Feckless has lost his briefcase containing the stock sheets.

The quarterly accounts are needed urgently. It is now 15 December, so stocktaking carried out now would not necessarily reflect the position at 30 November, and in any case would take time and effort to undertake.

Your enquiries uncover the following facts:

(a) Sales invoiced to customers during the months September, October and November amounted to £85 627, but this figure includes £7346 which relates to goods despatched in August.

(b) Goods despatched in November but not yet invoiced total £7912 at selling price.

(c) Stocks at 31 August were £53 278.

(d) An examination of the stock sheets for 31 August reveals the following errors. The total of page three was £24 690, but it had been carried forward on to page four as £26 490. 400 items which had cost £17 each had been extended at £1.70 each. Page five had been overcast by £81.

(e) The mark-up on stock sold is $33\frac{1}{2}$ per cent.

(f) Items in stock at £725 on 31 August had been scrapped in October.

(g) Purchase invoices entered in the bought daybook during September, October and November totalled £64 539, but included goods received in August totalling £2643. Goods received in November but not yet entered in the daybook totalled £3129.

(h) Sales returns during the quarter recorded in the sales daybook were £796 and purchase returns in the bought daybook were £958.

Compute the stock figure as at 30 November for inclusion in the accounts and make a brief comment on stock levels in the firm.

2. A summary of the cash book of Reconcile Ltd for the year to 30 September is as follows:

Dr.		Cash Book		Cr.
	£			£
Opening balance c/d	912	Payments		175 638
Receipts	176 614	Closing balance c/f		1 888
	177 526			177 526

After investigation of the cash book and vouchers you discover that:

(a) Standing orders appearing on the bank statement have not yet been entered in the cash book.
   (i) Interest for the half year to 31 March on a loan of £30 000 at 8 per cent per annum.
   (ii) Hire purchase repayments on the managing director's car, 12 months at £61 per month.
   (iii) Dividend received on a trade investment, £1248.

(b) The company owes £789 to the Electricity Board.

(c) A cheque for £112 has been debited to the company's account in error by the bank.

(d) Cheques paid to suppliers totalling £830 have not yet been presented at the bank, and payments into the bank of £780 on 31 May have not yet been credited to the company's account.

(e) An error of transposition has occurred in that the opening balance of the cash book should have been brought down at £921.

(f) A cheque received from a customer for £167 has been returned by the bank marked 'refer to drawer', but it has not yet been written back in the cash book.

(g) A cheque drawn for £69 has been entered in the cash book as £96, and another drawn at £341 has been entered as a receipt.

(h) Bank charges of £213 shown on the bank statement have not yet been entered in the cash book.

(i) A page of the receipts side of the cash book has been undercast by £400.

(j) The bank statement shows a balance of £757.

Produce well presented statements to adjust the cash book in the light of the above discoveries, and reconcile the adjusted cash book to the bank statement.

3. The books of account of Naunton Knitwear are handwritten with great care by a small team of book-keepers under the eagle eye of the office manager. However, the manager has recently taken extended leave to visit relations abroad, with unfortunate results, since the month end trial balance will not balance, credits exceeding debits by £1227.

   You are asked to help and after inspection of the ledgers discover the following errors:

(a) A balance of £57 on a debtors account had been omitted from the schedule of debtors, the total of which was entered as debtors in the trial balance.

(b) A small piece of machinery purchased for £1138 had been written off to repairs.

(c) The receipts side of the cash book had been undercast by £400.

(d) The total of one page of the sales daybook had been carried forward as £3209, but the correct amount was £3292.

(e) A credit note for £271 received from a supplier had been posted to the wrong side of his account.

(f) An electricity bill for the sum of £78, not yet accrued for, was discovered in a filing basket.

(g) Mr Exe, whose past debts to the company had been the subject of a provision, at last paid £311 to clear his account. His personal account has been credited but the cheque has not yet passed through the cash book.

Write up the suspense account and make the entries to clear the balance thereon. State the effect of each error on the accounts.

4. The balance sheet of Harold Darby as at 30 June is as follows:

	£	£		£ Cost	£ Accumulated Depreciation	£ Net
Capital		48 500	Fixed assets			
Profit	12 500		Buildings	40 000	–	40 000
Less drawings	9 500	3 000	Plant	22 000	11 000	11 000
		51 500	Vehicles	9 000	6 000	3 000
Loan at 12 per cent p.a.		20 000		£71 000	£17 000	54 000
Current liabilities			Current assets			
Creditors	27 500		Stock	23 000		
Tax payable	6 000	33 500	Debtors	19 000		
			Cash	9 000		51 000
		£105 000				£105 000

Scrutiny of the accounts revealed the following information:

(a) The company's own workmen were employed to construct the foundation for a new machine. No adjustment has been made in the books for the labour cost of £2930.

(b) Interest on the loan for the half year to 30 June is outstanding, and has not yet been recorded in the books.

(c) Goods costing £2400 have been sent to an agent on a 'sale or return' basis. These goods have been invoiced at a mark-up of 25 per cent on cost and are included in sales for the year. The goods also appear in stock.

(d) Repairs in the sum of £179 made to a flat occupied by Mr Darby have been charged to maintenance expenses.

(e) A vehicle, four years old, has been sold at its written-down value, but no entry has been made in the books to record this transaction. The original cost of the vehicle was £1600. Depreciation on vehicles is at 25 per cent on reducing balance.

(f) A debtor of the firm who owes £800 has gone bankrupt. Reliable evidence confirms that his estate is likely to pay 50p in the pound.

Draft the journal entries required to adjust the books in the light of the above information, and produce a statement to reconcile the present profit figure to the true profit for the year.

5. Dear Mrs Jones,   31 December 19..

I am very pleased that you have agreed to help me to sort out the accounts of my second-hand business, which as you know commenced on 1 January last. Such records as I have kept are, unfortunately, to be found on tattered scraps of paper kept in an old cardboard box. I expect you will want to examine these records for yourself, but I thought it might help you if I were to summarize my business dealings up to 31 December 19.. as I recall them.

I was lucky enough to win £10 000 on the football pools, and with this and £2000 lent to me by an aunt (I agreed, incidentally, to pay her 10 per cent per year interest) I started my business. I put £11 000 into the bank immediately, in a separate business account. I needed a lorry to enable me to collect and deliver the second-hand goods, and I'm pleased to say I made a profit of £920 here; a dealer was asking £2600 for a second-hand lorry, but I beat him down to £1680. I've paid by cheque only £400 of this so far, but as I will finish paying the full £1680 in three years, it will be mine before it falls to pieces in another five years from now.

I rent an old shed with a yard, and I pay only £700 a year. I've paid by cheque this year's rent and also £100 in respect of next year.

My first deal was to buy a job lot of 4000 dresses for £12 000. I've paid a cheque for £8000 so far and my supplier is pressing me for the rest. To date I've sold 3000 dresses and received £11 600, which I promptly banked as it was all in cheques. I reckon I'm still owed £1000, most of which I should be able to collect.

I bought 2000 ties for £2400 out of my bank account. I've sold 1500 of these for cash (£3000 in all) but as the remainder have been damaged I'd be lucky if I got £100 for them.

I managed to get some cigarette lighters cheaply – 100 of them cost me only £800. I'm rather pleased I haven't paid for them yet, as I think there is something wrong with them. My supplier has indicated that he will in fact accept £400 for them, and I intend to take up his offer, as I reckon I can repair them for £2 each and then sell them at £16 a time – a good profit.

I haven't paid my cash into the bank at all, as the cash I got for the T-shirts and my initial float enabled me to pay for my diesel, £800, and odd expenses, £500. Also it enabled me to draw £40 per week for myself. As I've done so well I also took my wife on holiday. It made a bit of a hole in the bank account but it was worth all £1200 of it.

Perhaps from what I've told you you can work out what profit I've made – only keep it as small as possible as I don't want to pay too much tax.

Yours sincerely,
Don Lerr

(a) From the data provided by Mr Lerr prepare a business trading, and profit and loss account for the period ended 31 December and a balance sheet as at that date. Show clearly all your workings and assumptions as notes to the accounts.
(b) Write a short report to Mr Lerr highlighting what you consider to be the most important features revealed by the accounts you have prepared.

6. Your friend John Grey is in business as a sole trader, and you act as his accountant. His book-keeper draws up the accounts each year and you check them for mistakes. The balance sheet as at 31 May is as follows:

John Grey, Balance Sheet as at 31 May 19__

	£	£ Accumulated Depreciation	£
Fixed assets	Cost		
Buildings	100 000	–	100 000
Plant	111 346	44 554	66 792
Vehicles	24 838	11 212	13 626
	£236 184	£55 766	£180 418
Current assets			
Stock		49 080	
Debtors	73 102		
Less provision	8 000	65 102	
Cash in safe		1 446	115 628
			£296 046
Financed by			
Capital account			174 000
Add profit for the year			52 944
			226 944
Less drawings			(18 614)
			208 330
Long-term loan			
Mr Green			
(interest			
11 per cent)			60 000
Current liabilities			
Trade creditors		21 254	
Overdraft		6 462	27 716
			£296 046

When the accounts are checked the following facts emerge:

(a) Part of the stock is considered to have a net realizable value of less than its cost, necessitating a stock write down of £8000.

(b) A debt of £12 000 owed by Mr Black is considered to be bad. The provision for doubtful debts is to be maintained at 10 per cent of debtors after this bad debt is written off.

(c) Machinery costing £10 000 was bought on credit from Mr Black during January but no entry has yet been made in the books.

(d) John Grey has taken goods costing £1032 for his own use during the year.

(e) Loan interest for the half year to 31 May is outstanding.

(f) Bank charges and interest of £1260 are shown on the bank statement but have not yet been entered in the cash book.

(g) A vehicle was sold on 31 May at book value £400. Its original cost was £2400. No entry has yet been made in the books for this transaction.

Raise journal entries in good form for the above adjustments and prepare a balance sheet in vertical form, after the adjustments have been made.

10 | Partnership

Partnership has been defined as 'the relation which exists between persons carrying on a business in common with a view to profit'. Case law abounds with instances where an attempt has been made to prove a partnership, and it is clear that three essentials must exist before partnership can be established. These three essentials are (a) carrying on a business, (b) in common, and (c) with a view to profit. It is sometimes important to know whether a partnership exists, since if such a business ceases trading because of lack of funds, there is no limited liability to protect the private assets of the partners. If creditors can establish that somebody is a member of a partnership they can use his private assets to make good the debts of the partnership, or if a person can establish a claim to partnership, that person can also claim a share of the profits and a share of the assets of the business when it ceases trading.

Partnership, of course, means that there is a mutual agency in existence between the partners. Each partner can act as an agent for the other, and also as a principal for the business. Thus a partner, by his own acts on behalf of the business, can bind his partners in law. A partnership in the United Kingdom is governed by the Partnership Act of 1890 and by the Limited Partnership Act of 1907. The Act of 1890 lays down that partnerships shall be limited to a maximum of twenty partners, unless the partnership is a banking partnership, in which case the limit is ten partners. Partnerships in banking can apply to the Department of Trade to extend the partnership to twenty. Under the Companies Act of 1967 firms of solicitors or accountants qualified to audit public companies, or members of stock exchanges, may have any number of partners.

Because the action of a partner, whether careless, inefficient or dishonest, can affect the future of others in the partnership, the relationship between partners is one 'uberrimae fidei'. This means that the utmost good faith must exist between partners, and that one partner can rely on information given by other partners when he enters the partnership and during the term of the partnership. If such information is found to be false a claim for damages can be sustained in the courts. Partnerships can be established for a limited period by agreement, or 'at will', which means they can be wound up by the partners at any point in time, subject to reasonable notice being given.

A partnership can trade under any name it wishes to use, unless that name is similar to a name already used by an established business. Trading under such conditions would be an attempt to hoodwink customers, and the business already using the name could gain an injunction from the courts to restrain the partnership from imitating it. The Registry of Business Names Act of 1916 was passed to inhibit such conduct. Any partnership using a name other than the names of the partners must register under the Act, giving the name, the nature of the business, the place of business, the present and past names, nationality and residence of the partners, and any other occupations that the partners may have. Armed with this information and the date on which they commenced business, the Registrar can then see whether their name infringes a name used by another established business and require them to change.

A partnership is a relationship which exists between the partners, and it may be expected, therefore, that some agreement between the partners will be used as an instrument to govern this relationship. The Partnership Act lays down the rules to be applied in a partnership in the absence of an agreement, but wherever there is a partnership agreement, the rules in the Act are subordinated to the terms of the agreement.

THE PARTNERSHIP AGREEMENT

Partnership agreements vary according to the partnership concerned, but in general they cover the following matters.

Capital. Is capital per partner to be a fixed amount settled at the beginning of the partnership or is it to vary from year to year?

The Division of Profits. The profit-sharing ratio which exists between the partners states what proportion of the business profit each partner is to receive.

Current Accounts. These are maintained to record the remuneration of partners by means of salary, interest and share of profits, and to set against this remuneration the amount of drawings made by each partner. It is usual in a partnership agreement to decide that capitals will be of a fixed amount, and that the shares of profit etc. and drawings shall be passed through a current account.

Interest on Capital or Drawings. The agreement should specify whether partners are to be entitled to interest on their capital, and the rate at which such interest is to be computed. Where partners have contributed widely different amounts of capital, interest is seen as a method of compensating the partner who has contributed most. Alternatively, it may be agreed among the partners that they should pay interest on their drawings, so that any partner who draws out part of his profit share before it is earned and is thus overdrawn will still contribute to the partnership.

Interest on Current Accounts. If partners leave their share of profits in the business and do not draw them out entirely, this is equivalent to the profits ploughed back into the reserves of a limited company. If one partner contributes more to the partnership than his fellows, it would seem right that he should be paid interest on his current account balance, which is an extension of his fixed capital amount.

A Limit to Drawings. The partners may wish to stop any one of their number from drawing out of his current account more than there is in it, or alternatively they may put a limit on the amount by which partners can overdraw.

The Remuneration of Partners. Some partners may work harder for the business than others, and thus the profits are more attributable to their efforts than to those of their fellows. The senior partner has probably contributed more in capital to the partnership, but the junior partner with a much smaller capital probably works harder. Accordingly if interest is paid on capital it is only right that salaries should be paid to those partners who contribute most in terms of effort. It must be stated, however, that such partnership salaries are an appropriation of profit, and not a charge thereto, but that both interest on capital and partners' salaries must be deducted from profit before the figure to be divided in the profit-sharing ratio is computed.

The Preparation of Accounts. The agreement will often contain a clause about the preparation of accounts, usually stipulating that they should be produced once per annum. This part of the partnership agreement also stipulates that the accounts shall be binding on the partners once they are agreed inter se.

Goodwill. Goodwill arises from time to time in partnerships when a new partner joins the original team or when one of the original partners leaves. In order to ensure that a new partner pays a fair price for his share of the partnership assets, or that a retiring partner takes with him the appropriate amount, goodwill is valued on these occasions. There are many different ways of making such a valuation, and the method to be used for each particular partnership should be contained in the agreement.

Retirement. The agreement should state how the amount to be paid to a partner on his retirement shall be determined, and what steps shall be taken to pay him out at this time.

THE PARTNERSHIP ACT

At all times in partnership the terms of the Act of 1890 are subordinated to those in the partnership agreement, but where there is no agreement or where the agreement is silent on any point, then the terms of the Act apply. Section 24 of the Act lays out the terms which are to apply in partnership accounts.

1. Partners are deemed to have an equal share of capital on cessation of business and to share equally any profits or losses made during periods of trading.
2. The partnership firm undertakes to indemnify a partner for payments made by him on behalf of the partnership business. This means that if a partner pays a partnership expense out of his own bank account he has a right to draw that money from the partnership bank account, although usually such an adjustment is made through the current account. This indemnity extends to payments or contracts made by partners on behalf of the firm in the ordinary course of business or in order to preserve the business. Thus if a partner buys raw material for the business his partners cannot refuse in the name of the partnership to accept what he has purchased in the normal course of business. Payments made to preserve the business are more difficult to define, but if a partner sees vacant shop premises near those already occupied by the partnership business and decides to lease them on behalf of the partnership, this action could be construed as an act to preserve the business, since the partner could claim that he acted to deny the premises to a rival and allow the partnership business to expand, and though he did not consult his partners before taking action they would have to ratify what he has done.

3. Interest to be paid on loans made to the business by partners at a rate of 5 per cent. A loan in this context is defined as an advance beyond the amount of a partner's agreed capital.
4. Interest on capital is not payable.
5. All partners are allowed to play an equal part in managing the business.
6. Partners are not to be paid salaries.
7. Before a new partner can be admitted to the business all existing partners must consent to the change. One dissenting voice will be sufficient to keep out the joining partner.
8. In all decisions of the partnership the majority is seen to rule. However, in any decision which changes the nature of the business all partners must agree before that change can take place.
9. The books of account of the partnership must be maintained at the partnership office, and all partners must be able to view them on request.

THE APPROPRIATION ACCOUNT

The appropriation account is used in partnerships to make adjustments for the rights of partners inter se, so that the accounting profit is reduced by any interest payable on the capital of the partners, by any salaries payable to the partners, and by other similar adjustments before the profit to be divided among the partners in their profit-sharing ratio is revealed. Once the accounting profit has been appropriated, the amounts debited to the appropriation account are credited to the current account, drawings are set against them, and the balance of undrawn profits is carried forward and shown on the balance sheet. If there are several partners a current account in columnar form will be easy to assimilate, and can also be used to show up adjustments between the partners, such as where partner A guarantees partner B a certain minimum income. In such a case, if partner B's income does not reach the guaranteed minimum, he will be credited with the appropriate amount and partner A will be debited.

Example

There are three partners, Frank, Fearless and Bold, who agree to share profits in the ratio 3:2:1. Their partnership agreement stipulates that partners will receive interest on their capital at 10 per cent per annum, that Bold is entitled to a salary of £1000, and that 10 per cent interest is to be charged on drawings. Frank has guaranteed Fearless a minimum income of £4000 per annum. The last agreed capitals of the partners were: Frank, £50000; Fearless, £10 000; and Bold, £15 000. The opening balances on their current accounts stood at £1300 for Frank, £200 for Bold and £600 overdrawn for Fearless. The net profit as disclosed by the accounts was £14 500 for the year. Partners' drawings during the year to date were Frank £5000, Fearless £3000 and Bold £3000. The accounts to record these circumstances would appear as follows.

Calculation of income of Fearless:

		£
Profit share		2367
Interest on capital		1000
		3367
Less interest on		
drawings		300
		3067
From Frank		933
		4000

Frank, Fearless and Bold, Appropriation Account

		Year Ending
	£	£
		14 500
Net profit per accounts		
Add interest on drawings		
Frank	500	
Fearless	300	
Bold	300	1 100
		15 600
Deduct salary, Bold		1 000
		14 600
Deduct interest on capital		
Frank	5000	
Fearless	1000	
Bold	1500	7 500
		7 100
Deduct share of profits		
Frank (3/6)	3550	
Fearless (2/6)	2367	
Bold (1/6)	1183	
		7 100

Frank, Fearless and Bold, Current Accounts

	Frank	Fearless	Bold		Frank	Fearless	Bold
	£	£	£		£	£	£
Opening balance b/d	–	600	–	Opening balance b/d	1300	–	200
Transfer to Fearless per agreement	933			Salary			1000
				Interest on capital	5000	1000	1500
Drawings	5000	3000	3000	Share of profit	3550	2367	1183
Interest on drawings	500	300	300	Transfer from Frank per agreement		933	
Balance c/f	3417	400	583				
	£9850	£4300	£3883		£9850	£4300	£3883
				Balance b/d	3417	400	583

CHANGE OF PARTNERS

Accounting for a partnership becomes slightly more complicated when there is a change in the personnel involved in the partnership, either by the addition of one or more extra partners or by the retirement or death of an existing partner. Often the retirement of one partner is accompanied by the addition of a new partner. Before such an addition can take place, however, all the existing partners must agree about the person involved and the terms on which he joins the group. The legal position is that the partnership ends when an existing partner retires or dies and a new partnership is started by those remaining, with or without a new partner to replace the one who has retired.

The incoming partner usually introduces capital of his own into the firm, often in the form of cash or assets such as cars or plant, but occasionally in the form of goodwill. The accounting entry here is to debit the appropriate asset account and credit the capital account of the new partner with the agreed value of the items he has introduced. It is important to revalue assets whenever there is a change of partner, since if the real value of the assets is more or less than their book value, the true value must be used in transactions between the partners at this point. An incoming partner will be entitled to a share of the assets and, if there is a surplus of real value over book value, he will receive a share of this surplus without paying for it, unless the surplus is recognized when he joins the firm.

A retiring partner will wish to ensure that the assets are properly valued when he retires, so that his share is accurately computed and he receives adequate compensation, from those who are going to continue the business after he has left it, for the items which he is leaving behind. Goodwill is a significant item in such a valuation. Sometimes a business is worth more than the value of all its individual assets. This surplus is called goodwill, and arises from a number of factors, which will be discussed in a later chapter. Goodwill is generated because a business is a going concern with established customers, or because its owners have knowhow and experience, or because it makes more profit than is expected from the assets involved.

There are several methods by which the revaluation of assets and the creation of goodwill can be treated in the accounts of a partnership. The most common method is to recognize the true value of the assets and the existence of goodwill, and to apportion the surplus or capital profit to the existing partners in their profit-sharing ratio before a new partner joins the firm. This involves the creation of a revaluation account to which the debit balances of the asset accounts are written off, while the newly agreed values of the assets are credited to the revaluation account and debited in turn to the asset accounts. A credit balance on the revaluation account means that there is a surplus on revaluation which is divided among the partners in their profit-sharing ratio and credited to their capital accounts.

An alternative method is to compute the share of goodwill or revalued assets attributable to an incoming partner and make him pay for this share when he enters the business by debiting his capital account and crediting the capital accounts of the other partners from whom he is buying this part of the surplus. If the partners do not wish a revaluation or goodwill account to be raised in their books, the matter can be settled by a payment from the incoming partner in cash direct to the existing partners.

The third way of dealing with this situation allows the new partner to earn his share of the goodwill over a period of years without paying for it. In this case a goodwill account is raised and written off against the old partners' capital accounts over a period of years, in the profit-sharing ratio which existed before the arrival of the new partner. Thus, when goodwill is valued at a later date, it can be apportioned between all the partners in their new profit-sharing ratio.

Example

Albert and Brian are in partnership sharing profits in the ratio 2:1. Albert has capital of £17 000 invested in the business, while Brian's capital is £7000. This means that the net assets of the business have a book value of £24 000. The partners agree that Charles shall join them as a partner, and that in return for introducing capital of £3000 in cash and £2000 in the form of machinery, he is to receive a fifth share of future profits. The net assets are revalued at £27 000 at this point, and a goodwill account of £6000 is also to be created.

A balance sheet before revaluation of the assets would show:

	£	£
Capital		
Albert	17 000	
Brian	7 000	£24 000
Represented by		
net assets		£ 24 000

Goodwill is computed as three years' purchase of the superprofits, which are defined as the excess of past weighted average profits over the profits that should be earned by a business when the risk involved is considered. Albert and Brian reckon a 15 per cent return is needed to compensate for the risk they are taking, so on capital employed of £24 000 they should earn £3600. The profits of the last three years are as follows:

	£		£
This year	6000 ×weighting 3	=	18 000
Last year	5500 ×weighting 2	=	11 000
Year before last	4600 ×weighting 1	=	4 600
Total	6		33 600 ÷ weights (6) = £5600

Past weighted average profit of £5600 less required profit of £3600 = superprofit of £2000. Three years' purchase of superprofit gives goodwill a value of 3 × £2000 = £6000.

The greatest weighting or significance in the calculation was given to the most recent year because that is most likely to reflect the current situation and the amount of profit which will probably be made in the immediate future.

The journal entries to record the transactions are as follows.

Journal Entries

	Dr. £	Cr. £
Asset accounts	3000	
Revaluation account		3000
Being surplus on revaluation of assets		
Revaluation account	3000	
Capital account		
Albert		2000
Brian		1000
Being apportionment of surplus on revaluation to partners' capital accounts in the ratio 2:1		

	£	£
Goodwill	6000	
Capital account		
Albert		4000
Brian		2000
Being creation of a goodwill account and its apportionment between the partners in their profit-sharing ratio 2:1		
Cash	3000	
Assets	2000	
Capital account: Charles		5000
Being capital introduced by Charles		

A balance sheet at this point would show:

	£	£
Capital		
Albert	23 000	
Brian	10 000	
Charles	5 000	£38 000
Represented by		
Goodwill		6 000
Net assets		29 000
Cash		3 000
		£38 000

The new profit-sharing ratio is computed as follows. At present A and B share 2 : 1 and C is in future to get one fifth. Thus four fifths will be left for A and B to share in ratio 2 : 1 (3 × 5 = 15). In future A gets $\frac{8}{15}$, B gets $\frac{4}{15}$ and C gets $\frac{3}{15}$

With the alternative method of accounting for goodwill on the admission of a new partner, no goodwill account is raised but part of the cash introduced by the new partner is deemed to be to pay for his share of goodwill. The entries are to debit cash and credit the old partners' capital accounts in their original profit-sharing ratio.

If the partners do not want any entry in the books concerning goodwill the amount can be paid direct to Albert and Brian by Charles.

If the goodwill is valued at £6000, Charles will be entitled to a fifth share as a partner, and must therefore pay £1200 to Albert and Brian, in the ratio 2 : 1, from the £3000 of cash which he introduced into the business.

Appropriate journal entries are:

	Dr. £	Cr. £
Cash	1200	
Capital account		
Albert		800
Brian		400
Being payment from Charles for a fifth share of goodwill apportioned between Albert and Brian in their profit-sharing ratio.		
Cash	1800	
Assets	2000	
Capital account: Charles		3800
Being capital introduced by Charles		

A balance sheet would now show:

	£	£
Capital		
Albert	19 800	
Brian	8 400	
Charles	3 800	£ 32 000
Represented by		
Net assets		29 000
Cash		3 000
		£32 000

If the goodwill is now valued at £6000, it will be shared by the partners in the ratio 8 : 4 : 3, and Charles will get what he has paid for. The balance sheet will then show:

		£	£
Capital			
Albert	(19 800 + 3200)	23 000	
Brian	(8400 + 1600)	10 000	
Charles	(3800 + 1200)	5 000	£38 000
Represented by			
Goodwill			6 000
Net assets			29 000
Cash			3 000
			£38 000

When a partner dies or retires the assets, including goodwill, are revalued to compute accurately his share of the business. If he is not paid out in cash, for which the entries are credit cash and debit the capital accounts of the remaining partners in their capital ratio, then the balance on his capital account will be transferred to a loan account.

Example

Suppose, in the partnership above, Brian decides to retire and goodwill is valued at £7500 at this point. His share will amount to $\frac{4}{15}$ of the extra value placed on the goodwill, or £400. If the partners do not wish to change the goodwill account the entries would be:

	Dr. £	Cr. £
Either (a)		
Goodwill	400	
Capital account: Brian		400
Being Brian's share of increase in value of goodwill		
Or (b)		
Capital accounts:		
Albert	291	
Charles	109	
Brian		400
Being Brian's share of increase in value of goodwill paid for by his partners in the ratio 8:3		

With either alternative Brian would receive £10 400 on his retirement. Until he is paid, the balance sheet would show, for alternative (a):

	£	£
Capital:		
Albert	23 000	
Charles	5 000	£28 000
Represented by		
Goodwill		6 400
Net assets		29 000
Cash		3 000
		38 400
Less loan account: Brian		10 400
		£28 000

Perhaps under these circumstances it is better to revalue goodwill at £7500 and distribute the extra £1500 to the partners in the ratio 8:4:3.

In law a retired partner is liable for the debts of the partnership as at the date of his retirement. He may offset this liability by persuading the remaining partners to indemnify him against such claims, or by the use of a contract of novation whereby the creditors of the firm agree to look to a new partner, as a substitute for the retiring partner, to meet their claims. In certain circumstances a retired partner could be liable for debts of the business incurred after his retirement, for example if a creditor did not know of his retirement and lent money to the partnership because he still believed him to be a partner. In the example quoted above, Brian should give specific notice of his retirement to all present creditors of the firm and past creditors who may advance credit again in the future, so that he is not 'held out' as a partner and 'estopped' from denying liability if existing partners cannot repay.

DISSOLUTION OF A PARTNERSHIP

A partnership is dissolved whenever there is a change of partners, but often the business carries on and a new partnership comes into existence. If there is bankruptcy or all partners retire the business will cease when the partnership is dissolved. The assets are sold for cash (and/or shares if they are sold to a company), the debts are collected, the liabilities are paid and any funds remaining are repaid to the partners. Profit or loss on the sale of the assets is apportioned in the profit-sharing ratio and posted to the credit of the capital accounts.

Section 44 of the Partnership Act 1890 lays down rules for the disbursement of partnership funds on a dissolution. The assets of the firm are to be applied first to repay the debts and liabilities of the firm to persons who are not partners, second to repay partners' loans to the firm, third to repay partners' capital balances, and last to pay out any surplus on dissolution to the partners in their profit-sharing ratio. If the assets are insufficient to meet the liabilities of the firm the deficiency shall be met out of profits and, if they are insufficient, out of capital, and if that is still not enough then the partners must contribute to the remaining deficiency in their profit-sharing ratio. If at this stage one partner is bankrupt and is unable to contribute his share of the deficiency, under the rule in Garner v. Murray, a case decided in 1904, the solvent partners must make up the share of the deficiency of an insolvent partner, in the ratio of their capital accounts before the dissolution commenced.

Example

Alan, Ben and Chris share profits equally. Their balance sheet is as follows:

Balance Sheet of Alan, Ben and Chris as at 31 December

	£	£
Capital:		
Alan	5000	
Ben	2000	
Chris	500	
		7500
Current accounts:		
Alan	1000	
Ben	1000	
Chris	(1600)	
		400
Loan account: Alan		2000
		£9900
Represented by:		
Assets:		
Cash		7800
Losses on realization		2100
		£9900

Chris is found to be bankrupt and cannot contribute his share of the loss. The cash would be apportioned among the partners as follows:

	Loan	Capital and Current Accounts		
	Alan	Alan	Ben	Chris
	£	£	£	£
Opening balances	2000	6000	3000	(1100)
Share of loss	–	(700)	(700)	(700)
	2000	5300	2300	(1800)
Chris deficit, apportioned in opening capital ratio 5:2		(1286)	(514)	1800
Cash paid out	£2000	£4014	£1786	Nil

These amounts equal the cash of £7800.

SALE OF PARTNERSHIP TO A LIMITED COMPANY

When a partnership is sold to a company and the partners either retire or carry on in business as directors of the company, a realization account is used to sort out the transactions. First the fixed asset accounts are closed off to the realization account, i.e. credit fixed assets and debit the realization account. Care must be taken to ignore any assets which are not being sold. Sometimes retiring partners may take certain assets in lieu of cash, and if they agree to take such assets at a price in excess of their book value, this constitutes a sale at a profit. The appropriate entries are: credit the asset with the agreed price, debit the partner's capital account, and transfer the balance on the asset account to the realization account (as a credit if it is a profit and a debit if it is a loss).

The next step is to compute the price or consideration to be paid. This may be in cash or in the form of shares, or a mixture of cash and shares. The amount should be debited to the purchaser's account and credited to the realization account. When the price is paid, the purchaser should be credited and either shares or cash should be debited.

The debtors and any investments should next be realized for cash. A profit on the sale of investments should be posted from the debit side of the investment account to the credit side of the realization account, but if debtors do not realize the book amount (some bad debts are encountered or discounts allowed for early payment) then the difference is debited to the realization account. When creditors are paid (credit cash and debit creditors) any discount received will go to the credit side of the realization account. The costs of realization will be credited to cash and debited to the realization account. A credit balance on the realization account means that the consideration is greater than the book value of assets sold, and a profit on realization has been made. The profit is apportioned in the profit-sharing ratio and posted to the credit of the partners' capital accounts. The balance on the capital account is then settled in cash or shares, or both, and at this point all accounts will be closed.

Example

William and Samuel were in business as partners sharing profits in the ratio 3 : 1. A summarized balance sheet for their business as at 31 December is as follows:

	£	£
Capital accounts:		
William	30 000	
Samuel	10 000	
		£40 000
Represented by:		
Fixed assets (net)		18 400
Investments		4 800
Current assets:		
Stock	9 000	
Debtors	16 800	
Cash	2 520	
	28 320	
Less trade creditors	11 520	
		16 800
		£40 000

Included in the fixed assets were two motor cars at book values of £1800 and £1340 respectively.

The partners have decided to cease trading as a partnership and have sold their stock and fixed assets to Stockholders Ltd for a price of £44 000, to be satisfied by a payment in cash of £16 000 and the issue to the partners of 28 000 ordinary shares of £1 each in Stockholders Ltd. The two vehicles mentioned above were excluded from the sale, since William had agreed to take over the first car at a valuation of £2200, and Samuel had agreed to take over the other car at £1280.

On final realization £16 600 was received from the debtors, the investments were sold for £5200, and creditors settled for £11 400. The costs of dissolving the firm were paid in cash for £240.

The partners agreed that the ordinary shares were to be allocated in proportion to the capitals shown in the balance sheet above, with any final balance to be settled by cash.

Record the above transactions to close the books of the partnership.

Dr.   Realization Account   Cr.

	£	£		£	£
Fixed assets			Stockholders Ltd		
£(18 400 − 3140)		15 260	Purchase consideration:		
Stock		9 000	Shares	28 000	
Dissolution costs		240	Cash	16 000	44 000
Debtors and bad debts		200	Profit on sale of		
Loss on Samuel's vehicle		60	investments		400
Profit on realization:			Profit on William's vehicle		400
William (3/4)	15 120		Creditors'		
Samuel (1/4)	5 040		discounts received		120
		20 160			
		£44 920			£44 920

Note: The profit on William's vehicle arises since he has agreed to take it over at a valuation in excess of its book value. Samuel takes over his car at a value which is less than its book value, so a loss is made. The investments were sold for more than their book value. The accounting entries are:

Dr.   Investment Account   Cr.

	£		£
Balance	4800	Cash	5200
Profit to realization			
account	400		
	£5200		£5200

Dr.   Cash Book   Cr.

	£		£
Balance b/d	2 520	Creditors	11 400
Stockholders Ltd	16 000	Dissolution costs	240
Sale of investments	5 200	William's capital account	21 920
Debtors	16 600	Samuel's capital account	6 760
	£40 320		£40 320

Dr.		Stockholders Ltd		Cr.
	£			£
Purchase consideration	44 000	Cash		16 000
		Shares in Stockholders		28 000
	£44 000			£44 000

Dr.		Shares in Stockholders Ltd		Cr.
	£			£
Stockholders Ltd	28 000	William's capital account		21 000
		Samuel's capital account		7 000
	£28 000			£28 000

The shares are apportioned between the partners according to their capital ratio, i.e. 30:10.

Partners' Capital Accounts

	William	Samuel		William	Samuel
	£	£		£	£
Motor cars	2 200	1 280	Balances b/d	30 000	10 000
Shares	21 000	7 000	Profit on		
			realization	15 120	5 040
Cash	21 920	6 760			
	£45 120	£15 040		£45 120	£15 040

The capital account tells a simple story: how much each partner had before realization, what his share of profit was on realization, and how he withdrew his capital – shares, cash and goods.

The partnership assets will now be recorded in the books of Stockholders Ltd. If the consideration paid for them exceeds their book value, the amount of the excess will appear as an extra asset, goodwill.

CONVERSION OF A PARTNERSHIP TO A LIMITED COMPANY

Sometimes partners may decide to change the form of their business to a limited company. The accounting entries for this manoeuvre are similar to those for the sale of a partnership to a company. The fixed and current assets and current liabilities are transferred to the company, and shares are issued to the partners in place of their capital accounts. Often the partnership books are used for the company's accounts and in some cases the conversion entries are not made until after the event. If the conversion takes place during an accounting year it is necessary to apportion the profit for the year to a partnership period, when it will be divided in profit-sharing ratio, and a company period, when it will be divided pro rata to share holdings. If a partner retires on the conversion date he will not be a shareholder and cannot receive a share of post-conversion profits, but if his capital was not repaid to him on the conversion date it will appear as a loan in the company's accounts and interest thereon would normally be provided.

Partnership assets are usually revalued at the conversion date. The consideration for net assets in the partnership is the amount of shares issued to the partners. It seems logical to allocate the shares on the basis of partners' capital accounts, but if this is done profits in the company will be shared on a different basis from that ruling in the partnership. Agreement can be reached if partners become directors and draw salaries or fees which will compensate for any loss of income.

Example

Frank, Victor and Jon are in partnership sharing profits and losses equally. Their balance sheet as at 30 October is as follows:

Frank, Victor and Jon, Balance Sheet as at 30 October

	£		£	£
Capitals:		Fixed assets (net of		
Frank	40 000	depreciation):		
Victor	20 000	Buildings		20 000
Jon	4 000	Fixtures and fittings		4 000
	64 000			24 000
Current liabilities:		Current assets:		
Creditors	6 000	Stock	25 000	
		Debtors	15 000	
		Cash	6 000	46 000
	£70 000			£70 000

The partners decide to convert their business to a limited company, Factors Ltd, as from 1 November, but Jon decides to retire on that date, leaving his capital in the business as a loan at 10 per cent interest per annum. The buildings were revalued at £29 000, and £1 ordinary shares in Factors Ltd were issued to Frank and Victor in settlement of their capital accounts.

A profit of £9000 is disclosed on revaluation and divided equally among the partners. Frank and Victor now have capitals of £43 000 and £23 000 respectively, so shares issued by Factors Ltd equal £66 000.

Factors Ltd Balance Sheet as at 1 November

	£		£	£
Share capital:		Fixed assets net of depreciation:		
66 000 ordinary shares		Buildings		29 000
of £1 each	66 000	Fixtures and fittings		4 000
				33 000
Long-term loan:		Current assets:		
Owed to Jon at 10 per cent		Stock	25 000	
interest	7 000	Debtors	15 000	
Current liabilities:		Cash	6 000	46 000
Creditors	6 000			
	£79 000			£79 000

The business uses the same set of books until the year end of 31 August in the following year, when a trading and profit and loss account is prepared:

	£	£
Sales		42 000
Less cost of sales		22 200
Gross profit		19 800
Expenses:		
Selling expenses	2202	
Carriage outwards	460	
Management salaries	8400	
Rates	560	
Office expenses	688	
Directors' fees	500	
Preliminary expenses'	200	13 010
Net profit		£6 790

Depreciation on buildings is at 5 per cent on book value and on fixtures 10 per cent on book value.

The next problem is to compute a true profit and apportion it between the partnership which existed until 31 October and the company. Your enquiries reveal that the goods sold in the year are of one kind and have been priced at the same level throughout the year. The average monthly sales for the first two months (September and October) were half those of the average monthly sales for the remaining months in the accounting year. This means that the gross profit can be apportioned as follows:

$$\text{September and October: two months at half each} = 1 = \frac{1}{11}$$

$$\text{November to August: ten months at 1 each} = 10 = \frac{10}{11}$$

Ratio 1:10

Further information available is that £600 paid to partners as salaries is included in management salaries.

Remember to provide loan interest ($£7000 \times 10$ per cent $\times \frac{10}{12} = £583$) and depreciation: buildings ($£29\,000 \times 5$ per cent $\times \frac{10}{12} = £1208$); and fixtures ($£4000 \times 10$ per cent $\times \frac{10}{12} = £333$). The buildings and fixtures were taken over at a valuation, so no depreciation can be charged against the partnership profit. Any depreciation so charged would merely increase the profit on revaluation.

Factors Ltd, Statement showing apportionment of Profit for Year Ended 31 August

	£	£	Basis of Apportionment		Partnership		Company	
Gross profit		19 800	Turnover	1:10		1800		18 000
Selling expenses	2202		Turnover	1:10	200		2002	
Carriage outwards	460		Turnover	1:10	42		418	
Salaries:								
Partners	600		Actual		600		–	
Others	7800		Time	2:10	1300		6500	
Rates	560		Time	2:10	94		466	
Office expenses	688		Time	2:10	114		574	
Directors' fees	500		Company		–		500	
Preliminary expenses	200		Company		–		200	
Depreciation:								
Building	1208		Company		–		1208	
Fixtures	333		Company		–		333	
Loan interest	583	15 134	Company		–	2350	583	12 784
Net profit		£4 666				£(550)		£5 216

The partnership period shows a loss which would be divided equally among Frank, Victor and Jon as £183.30 each.

JOINT VENTURES

A trading agreement where two or more parties already in business in their own right agree to act together for a specific transaction is known as a joint venture. The transactions concerned are usually of a trading nature, where one venturer, perhaps a sole trader, consigns goods to the other, who sells them. Joint ventures are not, however, confined to small operations, since this form of trading can be adopted when companies co-operate to undertake a large project, perhaps with one partner providing expertise and the other providing local production facilities.

The difficulty of accounting for such transactions concerns the recognition of expenses of the venture borne by the venturers, and the computation of the profit made. Sometimes a separate set of books is kept for the joint venture, but the more usual method employed is for each venturer to record his own transactions in a joint venture account in his books and then these accounts are brought together in a memorandum joint venture account which will disclose the profit made. Each venturer's share of the profit is posted back to the joint venture account in his own books, and the balance on that account will disclose the cash to be received from, or paid to, the other venturer.

Example

Charles and Rodger agreed upon a joint venture to buy up a bankrupt's stock, with a view to selling it later at a profit. The stock was valued by the receiver at £8000, and Charles agreed to contribute £3000 towards its cost, leaving Rodger to find the balance. Other expenses were paid by Charles and Rodger as they occurred. The venturers agreed to share profits equally, but decided to credit a 10 per cent commission to each party on the sales he made. A separate set of books was not opened for the venture.

The following transactions took place:

May 1 Stock purchased.
2 Charles bought a van to transport the stock, £1500.
3 Advertisements were placed: by Charles, £70; by Rodger, £90.
5 Sales were made: Charles, £2500; Rodger, £2600.
9 The van broke down and Rodger paid a repair bill, £100.
12 Sales were made: Charles, £1300; Rodger, £800.
16 Sales were made: Charles, £2800; Rodger, £3000.
18 Petrol bills were settled by Charles, £80.
20 The venture being over, Rodger agreed to take the van at a price of £1100.
25 Settlement was effected between the partners, after the agreement that petty cash expenses paid out for travelling should be £30 each, and for general expenses, Charles £70 and Rodger £120.

These transactions would be recorded as follows:
Charles' Books:

Dr.		Joint Venture Account with Rodger		Cr.
	£			£
Stock	3000	Sales		2500
Van	1500	Sales		1300
Advertising	70	Sales		2800
Petrol	80			6600
Travelling	30			
General expenses	70	Balance – cash from Rodger		165
Commission	660			
Share of profit	1355			
	£6765			£6765

Rodger's Books:

Dr.		Joint Venture Account with Charles		Cr.
	£			£
Stock	5000	Sales		2600
Advertising	90	Sales		800
Van repairs	100	Sales		3000
Travelling	30			6400
General expenses	120			
Commission	640	Van taken over		1100
Share of profit	1355			
Cash to Charles	165			
	£7500			£7500

Dr.	Memorandum Joint Venture Account				Cr.
May		£	May		£
1	Stock purchased	8 000	5	Sales	5 100
2	Van purchased	1 500	12	Sales	2 100
3	Advertising	160	16	Sales	5 800
9	Van repairs	100	20	Sale of van	1 100
18	Petrol	80			
25	Travelling	60			
25	General expenses	190			
25	Commission				
	Charles 10 per cent of £6600	660			
	Rodger 10 per cent of £6400	640			
		11 390			
Net profit:		£			
Charles ($\frac{1}{2}$)		1355			
Rodger ($\frac{1}{2}$)		1355			
		2 710			
		£14 100			£14 100

SEMINAR EXERCISES 8

1. (a) The books of Check and Mate, who are equal partners, are balanced annually on 31 December. Before profits are ascertained and divided, 5 per cent interest is allowed upon partners' capital. Depreciation (based on cost) is written off plant at the rate of 5 per cent per annum and off motor vehicles at the rate of 25 per cent per annum. A provision of 5 per cent on debtors is to be made for bad and doubtful debts. One year's interest at the rate of 6 per cent is due on the loan, and has not yet passed through the books. The stock in hand as on 31 December was valued at £3225. The following are the final balances as on 31 December:

	£		£
Purchases	16 450	Carriage inwards	400
Manufacturing wages	2 150	Motor vehicles (at cost £3200)	2 400
Sales	24 800	Sundry creditors	15 345
Check's capital	5 000	Loan on mortgage	5 000
Check's current account			
(overdrawn)	550	Freehold land and buildings	8 000
Mate's capital	2 000	Plant (at cost £6000)	4 000
Mate's current account		Provision for bad and doubtful	
(overdrawn)	350	debts (1 January)	600
Stock (1 January)	3 000	Sundry debtors	13 100
Salaries	820	Cash at bank	1 200
Rates	325		

Check is to receive a salary of £575 but guarantee Mate a profit share of £1300. Prepare a trading, profit and loss and appropriation account for the year ended 31 December, and a balance sheet as at that date. Show current accounts as a working.

(b) Distinguish between appropriations of profit and charges made against profit. Use examples from (a) above to illustrate your answer.

2. Hope and Crosby are in partnership and have been trading as The Utopia Road Nurseries for several years. Neither partner is skilled at accounting. They have presented you with such books and vouchers as they have kept and have asked you to prepare the annual accounts. You discover the following:

(a) *Bank Account*

	£		£
Balance 1 April		Purchases	81 035
last year	1 200		
Bankings	101 349	Drawings	
		Hope	6 000
		Crosby	5 500
		Rates	2 400
		Cash	3 000
		Electricity	1 660
		Balance this year	2 954
	£102 549		£102 549

(b) *Bankings.* Cash takings have been paid into the bank twice a week. Payments made from takings were:

	£
Wages	16 080
Repairs	670
Insurance	835
Sundries	2 982
Electricity	1 300
Purchases	2 900
Tractor expenses	877

Cash in hand at 1 April last year was £92 and at 31 March this year £110.

(c) *Partners.* Crosby is to be credited with a salary of £2500 and the partners will be credited with 10 per cent interest on their capital as at 1 April last year. Hope owns the freehold land and a notional rent of £1500 is to be charged in the accounts. The partners took, at retail prices, some goods for their own consumption. They amounted to £350 for Hope and £520 for Crosby. Profits are shared in the ratio Hope 60 per cent and Crosby 40 per cent. At 1 April last year the capital amounts were Hope £10 000 and Crosby £5000.

(d) *Assets and Liabilities.* Debtors and creditors are:

	This Year	Last Year
	£	£
Purchases: creditor	3250	2820
Electricity: creditor	300	180
Sales account: debtor	352	773
Stocks of goods and plants		
for resale	9080	7935

Fixed assets at 1 April last year were:

	Cost	Accumulated Depreciation	Depreciation Rate
Tractor	1 800	600	25 per cent on cost
Greenhouses	12 000	5200	10 per cent on cost

Present the trading and profit and loss account for the year ended 31 March and a balance sheet as at that date.

3. Leek and Bean were in partnership as lawnmower manufacturers, Leek being responsible for the factory and Bean for the warehouse. Completed lawnmowers were transferred from the factory to the warehouse at agreed prices. Profits are to be shared as follows:

	Factory	Warehouse
Leek	75%	25%
Bean	25%	75%

The following trial balance was extracted from the books on 30 June this year.

	£	£
Capital accounts:		
Leek		48 000
Bean		49 000
Drawings:		
Leek	6 000	
Bean	5 000	
Freehold factory at cost	42 150	
Factory plant at cost	25 750	
Provision for depreciation to 30 June last year		6 050
Delivery vans at cost	8 050	
Provision for depreciation to 30 June last year		3 450
Stocks at 30 June last year:		
Raw materials	4 028	
Work in progress	3 400	
Lawnmowers completed (1200 @ £40 each)	48 000	
Sales (1820 lawnmowers)		111 020
Purchase of raw materials	28 650	
Factory wages	15 020	
Warehouse wages	6 030	
Expenses:		
Factory	12 070	
Warehouse	10 020	
Provision for doubtful debts		1 600
Trade debtors and creditors	18 000	6 000
Bank overdraft		7 048
	£232 168	£232 168

1520 lawnmowers at £45 each were transferred to the warehouse in the year; lawnmowers in stock at the end of the year were to be valued at £45 each. Closing stock of raw materials was £3180 and work in progress was valued at £5050.

Accrued expenses outstanding on 30 June this year were:

	Factory	Warehouse
Expenses	£2090	£1080
Factory wages	£ 280	–

The general provision for bad debts was to be maintained at 10 per cent of the trade debtors.

During the year Leek bought a new car for £4000 out of his own money and brought it into the partnership business, but this has not yet been entered in the books. It is to be charged against the warehouse.

Provision for depreciation is to be made as follows: factory plant 10 per cent per annum on cost; motor vehicles 20 per cent per annum on cost.

Interest is to be charged on drawings at 10 per cent and paid on capital at 5 per cent, and satisfied by a contra entry between the partners' profit shares.

Prepare manufacturing, trading, profit and loss and appropriation accounts for the year ended 30 June this year and a balance sheet as at that date.

4. The following is a trial balance of a partnership at 31 December last year.

	£	£
Capital accounts as at 1 January last year		
Henrietta		10 000
Maud		8 000
Nellie		2 000
Freehold property	20 000	
Fixtures and fittings	4 000	
Stock	5 000	
Debtors	1 000	
Cash at bank	2 500	
Creditors		2 500
Net profit for the year		
to 31 December		10 000
	£32 500	£32 500

The net profit for the year is to be divided as follows: Henrietta $\frac{1}{2}$, Maud $\frac{1}{4}$, Nellie $\frac{1}{4}$, after allowing for interest at the rate of 10 per cent per annum on the capital account balances at 1 January and after allowing a salary of £1000 per annum to Maud.

On 31 December Henrietta retired from the partnership. On this date the assets were revalued as follows:

	£
Freehold property	25 000
Fixtures and fittings	2 000
Stock	3 000

Goodwill was valued at £6000. On this date and after adjusting for the foregoing, Henrietta received payment of the amount due to her.

On 1 January this year Emma was admitted to the partnership, sharing profits equally with the two remaining partners. It was agreed that she should introduce capital of £5000 in cash and that goodwill should not appear in the balance sheet of the new partnership. Emma also brought a car worth £2000 into the business.

Draw up the balance sheet of the new partnership on 1 January this year after the admission of Emma.

5. (a) Red, Green and Blue are in partnership sharing profits and losses equally. At close of business on 31 May Green decided to retire, and Red and Blue agreed to continue in partnership sharing profits and losses in the ratio of 2:1. The balance sheet at 31 May before the retirement of Green was:

	£	£		£	£
Capital accounts			Freehold property		1 500
Red	13 000		Plant and machinery		4 000
Green	5 000				5 500
Blue	7 000				
		25 000			
			Stock	9100	
			Debtors	6900	
Sundry creditors		5 000	Bank	8 500	24 500
		£30 000			£30 000

The partners also agree the following:
  (i) In computing the amount due to Green, goodwill is to be valued at £9000 but no goodwill account is to be opened in the books.
 (ii) Revaluation of assets is to take place, which results in revised amounts as follows: freehold property £2500, plant and machinery £3000, stock £7300.
(iii) Green is to be paid £4000 in cash and it is agreed that the balance due to him is to be retained in the form of a loan.
Prepare the partners' capital accounts recording the above and also the balance sheet of Red and Blue after Green has retired.

(b) In drawing up a partnership agreement provision is often made for the partners to be entitled to salaries and interest on the capital invested in the firm, as well as the balance of profits to be shared in an agreed ratio. Why is this so?

11 | The Financial Accountant as an Auditor, and Accounting Systems

A well proven definition of an audit is 'the examination by an auditor of the evidence from which the income statement and balance sheet have been prepared, to ascertain that they represent a true and fair view of the transactions under review, and of the financial state of the organization at the closing date of the period'. An auditor is one who asks questions, listens to answers, checks facts, eventually forms an opinion about the correctness of the financial statements, and then reports his views to the shareholders of the company. The evidence he uses is in the accounting records, and especially the vouchers which provide the basic data from which the accounting records have been written up. He is interested in invoices, goods received notes, orders, sales invoices, wage sheets and bank statements, all of which provide him with evidence to confirm that the books properly represent the transactions which have taken place and that the accounts are based firmly on those book entries. Apart from this paper evidence the auditor must examine the actual assets themselves, where possible, to ascertain that they really exist and are correctly shown in the books and the accounts.

Part of the object of an audit is to reveal errors in the accounts, and to discover any fraud which has taken place, but another objective of equal importance is to prevent error and fraud from taking place. It is the professional duty of an auditor to report to those who employ him on the accounting systems in operation in the business. He tests the system to see whether it is good enough to account adequately for the transactions which take place and to ensure that it is being operated properly. If he thinks that the system is weak, or that the operation of a good system is less than thorough, he makes his views known to his client in what is called a 'letter of weakness'. When working for a company the auditor is employed by the shareholders to comment to them on the accounts prepared for them by the management, but the letter of weakness is sent to the management of the company so that they can act to put matters right.

TYPES OF AUDIT

It is customary to classify audits according to their type, i.e. private, statutory and internal. The private audit takes place when an accountant acts as auditor to a sole trader or partnership. In this case he will operate to an agreed limit of work, the task to be undertaken being the subject of an agreement between himself and his client, who is the sole trader or the partners. It is wise to formalize the nature and scope of the work to be undertaken in a written agreement in order to protect the auditor from difficulties which can arise at a later date. In a private audit the auditor works directly for the manager, who may also be the owner of the business, and therefore the extent of his work can be limited to what the client requires. Often this requirement is to certify the accounts, so that they can be used as reliable evidence for tax purposes or for the valuation of a business if it is to be sold. The client may ask the auditor to verify the accounts, but stipulate that a full stock audit is not required. If the stock figures are later proved to be wrong, then the client cannot seek redress from the auditor for damage he has suffered from this mistake.

The second type of audit is the statutory audit, so called because it is carried out under the provision of the Companies Acts. Such an audit is undertaken for a public limited company, i.e. one whose shares are traded on the stock exchange. In this type of audit the auditor is working for the shareholders and commenting to them on the accounts produced by their management for their company. The general investing public may also rely on the audited accounts to guide their investment policy. For this reason the auditor must do whatever he considers necessary to a satisfactory audit, and there can be no restriction on what he checks and the amount of work he does. There can be no agreement between the auditor and the management to limit his powers of investigation or the area of his search. Because the auditor accepts no restrictions he alone is responsible for determining how much work needs to be done for a proper audit.

The third classification is the internal audit. In this case the auditor is an employee of the company and reports to its managers. His task is to review the systems set up in the business, to ensure that they are efficient, to comment on the safety and security of the assets, and to discover and prevent fraud where possible. The work of the internal auditor is very detailed, involving much checking and vouching of prime documents, and he is often closely connected to the organization and methods department. The relationship of the internal auditor and the external auditor is one of friendly co-operation. The external auditor can, if he wishes, completely ignore the work undertaken by the internal audit department, but usually he satisfies himself as to the abilities and standards of the internal auditor, and then is able to avoid the duplication of much detailed checking by relying on some of the work undertaken by the internal auditors, whose programmes of work he may have helped to design. Vouching is a term used to describe the substantiation of a transaction by the inspection of a voucher which provides evidence to support the entry made in the books.

AUDITING METHODS

There are several different methods of undertaking an audit. The traditional method is that of the final audit, where the auditor attends the business premises after the accounts have been produced and checks and vouches them thoroughly at one sitting. This may take several weeks or, in a large company, even several months. With a small business the practising accountant may find that he has to produce accounts from incomplete records and then audit them as a separate task.

The final audit has been shown to be impractical for large businesses, since it concentrates the work into one period, and the fact that it may take many weeks to complete the checking required can delay the publication of the company's accounts. Also, concentration into one period, for example in February after a year-end date of 31

December, creates a peak demand for auditors' services and may cause difficulties in an accounting practice. For these reasons the interim audit has been developed. This method entails the attendance of the auditors on two or three occasions in the year. They work through the books, checking and vouching according to their audit programme, until they have checked the transactions of, for example, the first six months of the accounting year, and then they stop, carefully noting the point at which their checking ceases, and return later in the year. Thus the device of the interim audit accelerates the production of audited accounts at the year end and enables companies to produce audited accounts at the half-way stage, on the basis of which the board can decide to pay an interim dividend to the shareholders.

In some very large organizations, however, even the interim audit has proved inadequate from a timing point of view, and has been replaced by the continuous audit. This method necessitates the attendance of auditors throughout the year at various parts of the organization. The small permanent team of auditors will constantly check the transactions which have taken place so that when the year end approaches most of the checking has been completed. The auditor of a large group of companies, perhaps with subsidiaries in many different countries, may find that a continuous audit is the only way in which he can check the many thousands of transactions which have taken place in time to meet the deadline of the annual general meeting for which the published accounts are produced.

The audit of a large volume of transactions requires the application of special techniques. The auditor cannot check everything, since this would be too time consuming. To save time auditors have adopted two techniques, sampling and depth checking. Sampling, to the auditor, is the selection of a statistical sample of the transactions which have taken place and their careful checking and vouching by the auditor. The auditor knows that he can rely on this sample, if it is large enough, as being representative of the whole, so that if the transactions in the sample are found to be correct it is probable that the remainder, which have not been checked, are also correct. The success of sampling is largely dependent on the selection of the sample, and it should be ensured that the sample is large enough to be a significant guide to the whole 'population'.

Depth checking is a term used to describe the audit method whereby a single transaction is selected and checked in depth, which means that the auditor follows the transaction from beginning to end in great detail. For example, the auditor may select the purchase of a certain delivery of raw materials, and he will check every prime document and every entry in the books needed to record that transaction from the moment that the purchase is requisitioned right through until the point at which the supplier is paid by cheque. This will show him whether the system is operating correctly, and if he selects a large enough sample of transactions for this depth checking he can rely on the accuracy of his findings and therefore he need not check in depth every transaction.

It must be emphasized that the extent to which the auditor can rely on his work depends upon the selection and size of the sample.

APPOINTMENT OF AN AUDITOR

It is considered a matter of professional ethics that when a new auditor takes up his appointment to audit the accounts of a company he should ascertain from the retiring auditor whether there is any reason why he should not act. The new auditor should not accept nomination for the post without having had written communication with the retiring auditor to ensure that all is well. This simple stratagem ensures that a new auditor is given full information by the previous auditor of any disagreements he has had with the management over the production of the accounts, or of any pressure which the board may have tried to put on the auditor to accept certain accounting policies which he considered to be undesirable. This will inhibit the ability of a board to change its auditors in order to gain acceptance of questionable accounting policies. The shareholders have a right to change their auditors, and it is their votes at the annual general meeting which will be needed to make the change, but they will often accept the advice of the board of directors when a change of auditors is proposed by the board.

The auditor has a right to act independently, since he is employed by the shareholders to comment on what the management have done so far as the accounting statements are concerned. He must therefore be able to form and express his opinion openly. This principle is supported in the appointment, rights and duties of auditors which are laid down in the various sections of the Companies Acts.

Section 14 of the Companies Act 1967 deals with the appointment of auditors. It lays down that the auditor of a public company shall be appointed by the shareholders at the annual general meeting, and shall be entitled to hold his appointment from the end of that meeting until the end of the next annual general meeting. This ensures that an auditor will have the right to attend the AGM and speak in his own defence if necessary.

If no auditor is appointed at the annual general meeting, the Secretary of State for Trade has the right to appoint an auditor to serve until the next annual general meeting and the company must notify him that this power has become exercisable within one week of the event. In the case of the first auditor of a company, the directors are empowered to appoint him to serve until the first annual general meeting of the shareholders.

The directors are also empowered to fill a casual vacancy caused by the death or retirement of an auditor during the accounting year. The auditor's fee for his services is fixed by the shareholders at the annual general meeting, unless the Secretary of State or the directors have appointed him. It is also stated in the 1948 Act that only professional accountants who are members of accounting bodies recognized by the Department of Trade can act as auditors of a public company. The Institute of Chartered Accountants and the Association of Certified Accountants are the only bodies recognized for this task in the United Kingdom, although a few individuals who are not members of these bodies are licensed by the Department of Industry to act as auditors.

Some persons are forbidden by law to act as auditors to public companies. Section 161 of the Companies Act 1948 states that an officer or servant of the company cannot act as its auditor. The term 'officer of the company' applies to directors and the company secretary, while a 'servant of the company' is somebody in its employ. It is also stated that the partner or employee of an officer or servant of the company cannot act as auditor to that company. These measures are written into the law to ensure the independence of the auditor and to prohibit the appointment as auditor of any person who owes a debt of loyalty to those running the company and who are the subject of the auditor's investigation. Neither can a body corporate (another company) act as an auditor.

RIGHTS AND DUTIES

The auditor has certain rights which are embodied in Section 15 of the 1967 Act. In the case of the audit of a private company the rights of an auditor depend on his agreement or contract with the person who is employing him as auditor, i.e. the principal shareholder. An auditor has a lien on the books of the company for any unpaid audit fees. This means that in the event of non-payment of the fee for his services, the auditor can withhold the books and papers of the company in his possession until his fee is paid. Under Section 147 of the Companies Act 1948 the auditor who claims such a lien on the books of his client would have to give reasonable facilities for the directors to inspect those books.

The auditor has a right at all times to have access to the books, accounts and vouchers of the business which he is auditing, and he is expected to use all information at his command to carry out his duties. He also has a right to such explanations as he shall require from the officers and employees of the company, and he must be invited to all meetings of the company, i.e. the annual general meeting and any special meetings held for the shareholders. Any officer of a company who knowingly or recklessly makes a misleading statement to an auditor is guilty of an offence.

The rights of the auditor are especially significant when it is suggested that he should be removed from office or replaced by another auditor. In order to protect him from pressure from management the auditor has the right to receive special notice of a resolution to appoint as auditor a person other than the retiring auditor, or to remove the auditor before the expiry of his term of office, and on receipt of such a notice he can make representations of a reasonable length to the company, and these must be sent out to all shareholders. Even after he has been removed an auditor has the right to attend the annual general meeting at which his term of office would have expired or a meeting held to fill a casual vacancy, and to be heard at such meetings.

An auditor may resign his office by written notice deposited at the company's registered office. Such notice must contain a statement to the effect that there are no circumstances connected with his resignation which should be brought to the attention of shareholders or creditors or an appropriate statement. This statement must be circulated to all shareholders and the resigning auditor can convene an extraordinary general meeting to consider it.

Whenever rights are granted to a person it is proper that he also should have certain duties which he must undertake and standards which he must maintain. The main duties of an auditor are to make a proper investigation of the books and vouchers of the company, and to form an opinion as to whether proper books have been maintained and whether the accounts are in agreement with those books. To quote Lindley L. J. in the London and General Bank Case of 1895, 'He must be honest, that is, he must not certify what he does not believe to be true, and he must take reasonable care and skill before he believes that what he certifies is true'. Having formed an opinion, the auditor has a duty to report to the shareholders at the annual general meeting that the accounts have been properly prepared in accordance with the law, and that they show a true and fair view. A typical auditor's report might read as follows:

'I have obtained all the information and explanations which, to the best of my knowledge and belief, were necessary for the purpose of my audit. In my opinion proper books of account have been kept by the company so far as appears from my examination of those books. I have examined the above balance sheet and profit and loss account, which are in agreement with the books of account. In my opinion and to the best of my information and according to the explanations given to me, the said accounts give the information required by the Companies Acts of 1948 and 1967 in the manner so required, and the balance sheet gives a true and fair view of the state of the company's affairs as at . . . and the profit and loss account gives a true and fair view of the profit for the year ended on that date.'

An auditor's report phrased in such a manner will be found appended to the published balance sheets of all public companies.

QUALIFICATION OF AN AUDITOR'S REPORT

The most powerful weapon in the armoury of the auditor is the threatened qualification of his report. This consists of a threat to comment in his auditor's report on matters which he considers to be improper, unless the directors and management of the firm take his advice and act to set matters right. When an auditor is not satisfied with an accounting policy, or a system, or certain transactions, it is his duty to say so in his report, so that the shareholders and potential shareholders are made aware of factors which may adversely affect their interest.

An auditor will qualify his report if the accounts are not drawn up in conformity with recognized accounting principles. He must also mention it in his report if in any respect the standard accounting practices agreed by the major accounting bodies in the United Kingdom within the Accounting Standards Committee have been ignored. Not all companies agree with the recommended treatment of some accounting transactions laid down in the standards, and their boards of directors sometimes set the standards aside when drawing up their accounts. The auditor must draw the attention of the shareholders to this fact, but some large and influential companies who cannot be rightfully accused of accounting malpractice have chosen to account in ways not approved by the accounting standards. When their accounts are qualified by an auditor for this reason this tends to increase the number of qualifications made to accounts during a calendar year, and reduces the impact of a more serious qualification made by the auditors of another company. In the past a qualification by the auditor was considered a very serious matter, but nowadays, as qualifications increase and are often the subject of disagreement with the terms of a technical accounting standard, the significance of a qualification has been lessened.

If the accounts have been drawn up to follow a policy or method which is inconsistent with past accounting statements of the company, the auditor must mention this in his report, unless an adequate explanation by way of a note to the accounts has been made. Such an explanation should, of course, reveal the extent of the impact on profits or balance sheet items of a change to a different accounting policy. If the auditor does not agree with the amount stated in the balance sheet for an asset, or with an item shown in the profit and loss account, he must say so. Qualifications of this nature often concern the directors' valuation of investments in subsidiary companies or fixed assets such as buildings. Another reason for qualification is where the accounts fail to disclose some information which the auditor feels is significant if a true and fair view of the position is to be read from the accounts.

Thus the auditor has a duty to ensure that all pertinent information is revealed and that the accounts are free from bias. Indeed, the auditor has a duty to qualify the accounts by revealing any inconsistencies where, for example, a note to the accounts changes the view given by the accounting statements themselves. Such qualifications should be concise, clear and specific, and should express the auditor's opinion in such a way that his comments cannot be misinterpreted.

LIABILITY OF THE AUDITOR

Because the auditor holds himself out as a professional expert he must take great care to ensure that the work he does is absolutely correct. Shareholders and potential investors will rely to some extent on the auditor's certificate to confirm to them that the accounting statements show a true and fair view. If it can be proved that an auditor did not bring to his work the normal skill expected of a professional man, and as a result of this negligence some other person suffered, then the auditor may be held liable under both civil and criminal law to make good any loss so suffered.

Under common law the auditor is considered as an agent of the company, and as a professional person he must bring to his work a high standard of care, skill and diligence. If it can be proved that he has been negligent in discharging this duty, he will be liable to his clients for any losses they may suffer as a result. Under Section 333 of the Companies Act 1948 the auditor is considered to be an officer of the company, and any wrongful performance of his fiduciary duty to the shareholders will be regarded as misfeasance. This section, however, applies only in the case of the winding-up of a company, and under a later section there is provision for the auditor to apply to the court to be relieved of this liability if he has acted honestly and reasonably and should be excused under the circumstances.

In one leading case, re London and General Bank 1895 (CH 673), the auditor informed the directors that loans had been made on poor security, but they did not act on this advice. The auditor qualified his report by saying that the value of the assets was dependent on the realization of these loans. It was held, however, that such a qualification was not in sufficiently strong terms and acted only as a hint. In the Kingston Cotton Mill case of 1896 (CH 279), the stocks were overvalued and profits thus inflated. In the course of his judgement, Lord Justice Lopes remarked that an auditor must use reasonable care and skill in the execution of his duties, but was not a detective, next making his now famous remark that the auditor is a watch-dog but not a bloodhound. The relevance of his remark in this case was that the auditor was justified in believing the trusted servants of the company in whom confidence is placed by the company, and is entitled to assume that they are honest. In later cases, however, it has been held that the auditor must, to the best of his ability, use all available information when he forms his opinion, and should make an attempt to check the accuracy of information given to him by employees of the company.

If an auditor is negligent he may be liable to third parties if they have relied on his statements and suffered damage by so doing. The leading case here is that of Hedley Byrne v. Heller and Partners 1963, which does not directly concern an auditor. In this case a banker gave a negligent reference about a client, and the plaintiff suffered loss by relying on this reference and sued the bankers. From the result of this case it appears that an auditor is not now immune from a liability to make good the losses of third parties caused by his negligence.

DIVISIBLE PROFITS

One important consideration of the auditor when he seeks to determine a true and fair profit is that profit shall not be overstated, because if it is the directors of the company will get a false impression of the efficiency of their organization, and of the amount which they can distribute in the form of dividend. In an extreme case the directors may distribute in dividend more than the true profit, thus paying part of the dividend out of capital rather than profit. Such action is imprudent financially since it reduces the capital employed, and does not have regard to the long-term survival of the business. It is also illegal, since it prejudices the rights of the creditors of the business if capital is repaid to shareholders by way of dividend before the claims of creditors have been met. As we have seen, the amount of a true profit is often the subject of estimate and argument, and the amount of profit available for dividend is subject to the requirements of statute, case law, and prudent accounting policy. Prudence dictates that the profit available for dividend shall be a surplus left after adequate provision has been made for items such as depreciation and doubtful debts, and after sufficient funds have been set aside in the reserves to finance expansion or ensure the long-term survival of the business. The Companies Act 1948, section 66, states that no dividend shall be paid other than out of profit. From the requirements of the statute and of good business practice, a body of case law has developed some general rules to be followed.

Some of the leading cases date from the late nineteenth century, but the principles which they established still hold true today. In the 1890s, even though it was accepted that profit was the surplus of current income over current expenditure, after allowing for losses made on fixed or current assets during the period, it was nevertheless held that a dividend could be paid before past losses of a capital nature had been made good. So long as the existence of a current profit was established the articles permitted such a payment, and the rights of creditors were protected by establishing that sufficient assets remained after the payment of the dividend to meet all liabilities and claims.

Another important rule established early in this century is that the directors can, if the articles permit, allocate profit to reserves before the payment of a dividend. In the case of Bond v. the Barrow Haematite Steel Company Ltd 1902 (1 CH 353), the preference shareholders tried to compel the company to pay their dividend out of the balance on the profit and loss account, before making such reserves as the directors considered necessary and prudent. They failed, but the case is complicated by the fact that losses of a capital nature had been made which the judge considered should be made good before a divisible profit could be established.

The next case of interest is the Ammonia Soda Company v. Chamberlain 1918 (1 CH 266), which established that a board could pay a dividend out of current profits without first writing off losses which had been made in the past. The company had written off the loss made on boring an unsuccessful well against a revaluation of some of its other property. It was claimed in this case that the loss should have been written off against profits before dividends were paid, rather than against the revaluation. This claim was denied, a significant factor in the case being that the facts concerned had been adequately reported to the shareholders in the accounts and had also been mentioned in the auditor's report. This judgement was supported by the case of Stapley v. Read Brothers Ltd 1924 (40 TLR 442), in which it was held that goodwill previously written off against profits could be recreated and used to offset past losses, so that a dividend could be paid from current profits. The judge in this case made the point that the original goodwill was written off against profits which would otherwise have been divisible.

A problem which has been the subject of some activity within the courts is to establish the position of capital profits and to determine whether they are available for dividend. Some early cases at the turn of the century established that capital profits could be distributed in the form of dividend if they were realized, that is turned into cash rather than a paper profit, if they remained after all other assets had been realistically valued, and if the articles permitted such a distribution. It is interesting, however, to note that two more recent cases have had a significant effect on this position. In 1960 the Westburn Sugar Refineries case supported the traditional view that a capital profit could not be distributed until it was realized. This position has, however, been eroded by the decision in the case of the Dimbula Tea Company v. Laurie, which sought to determine the correct treatment for unrealized reserves. When assets are revalued the corresponding credit is placed in a reserve not available for distribution, but such a reserve can be used to pay up unissued shares so that they can be distributed to the shareholders as a 'bonus' or 'scrip' issue. Thus, although it still has not been established that a capital profit can be distributed *in specie* unless it has been realized, it is now possible to distribute it in the form of extra shares on which dividend can later be paid.

Over the past seventy years a series of cases have set out to show what can be distributed. At the time of writing the Government is being pressed to produce a statutory definition of realizable profits. Such a task is fraught with difficulties, not the least being the definition of value so far as assets are concerned. An intriguing suggestion is that distribution of a dividend can be made only from profits shown in accounts which bear an auditor's certificate that they show a true and fair view.

THE CLASSIFICATION AND LOCATION OF ERRORS

Once a trial balance is extracted from the books a check on the accuracy of the book-keeping is available, since if every debit has a credit, then the two columns of the trial balance should add up to the same figure. If they do not, then an error has occurred and a search must be organized to locate the error and correct it. Errors which occur in book-keeping can be classified according to their type.

First, there are errors of omission, which concern the complete omission of a transaction from the books. Such an error will not affect the balance of the books, since both the debit and credit elements have been omitted. If, for example, an invoice for goods sold has been overlooked and is discovered after completion of the accounting statements, the books will not record the sale or the existence of the debt as an asset. An efficient system to record transactions, especially sales, will reduce the incidence of such errors. If, in the example above, the sales invoices had each been given a serial number, the fact that one of the series was missing would have been recognized and a search initiated.

Next there are errors of commission, which occur when transactions are wrongly recorded in the books. Such errors may or may not affect the trial balance, according to the circumstances. A sale amounting to £5000 may be recorded as £500 in both the sales account and the debtors account without disrupting the balance of the books, but if it is correctly recorded as a sale, but is shown as £500 in the debtors account, then the trial balance debits will not agree with the credits. Other errors of commission concern mistakes in casting when columns are added up, posting errors when items are posted to the wrong account or to the wrong side of the right account, and errors of transposition when figures are changed before they are entered or carried from one page to another as the wrong amount, e.g. £8950 carried forward or entered as £8590.

A third class is errors of principle, which, although they do not affect the balance of the books, will certainly influence the validity of accounting statements computed from the books. Such errors concern the incorrect treatment of a transaction in the books of account; for example, where a revenue expense is capitalized by being posted to a fixed asset account, the profit will be understated and the balance sheet will also be wrong.

Compensating errors are mistakes which take place when, by coincidence, two mistakes of similar amounts are made on opposite sides of the books. Such errors are not discovered immediately, since they cancel each other out, and the trial balance appears to be correct; e.g. a total of £910 carried forward as £900 on the credit side will compensate for £10 undercast on the debit side. Mistakes which nearly compensate can also cause problems, since if an error of £5000 on the debit side is accompanied by an error of £4800 on the credit side, the book-keepers will be searching for an amount of £200 which they will not find. It is important to understand that some mistakes can occur which will not be shown up by the trial balance.

The location of errors is a science in its own right. A common practice is to open a suspense account and post the amount of the difference to it. Then, as successive errors are discovered, they too can be posted to the suspense account so that the outstanding amount is readily available to the team who are searching for the error. A useful step is to try to trace the difference to a control account, to isolate it and reduce the area of the search. If a control account total is proved to be correct, the accounts can be produced using that figure, while a search is continuing to find the mistake in a subsidiary ledger and adjust it to the control account total. An early step to locate an error is to check all balances from the ledger to the trial balance, and to check the accuracy of the opening balances in the books. If the amount of the difference is divided by two, a figure is provided which, if posted to the wrong side in the books, could account for the error. A check should be made for transposition of figures; e.g. £15 posted as £1.50 gives a difference of £13.50. All totals carried forward from one page to another should be checked, and if the error is still not located then columns and crossfooters should be recast in case an error of addition or subtraction has taken place. If the error still cannot be found, it is necessary to check the postings from the daybooks to the ledger, checking for badly formed figures which may give rise to a mistake.

In a well organized business the system will be designed to minimize the occurrence of error.

INTERNAL CONTROL AND INTERNAL CHECK

The term 'internal control' is given to the whole system of controls existing in an organization, which have been set up to ensure that the accounting records are accurate and reliable, and that the assets of the organization are adequately protected. Such controls may not be entirely financial, but will arrange the systems of working within the business to achieve the aforementioned goals. A system of stock control or credit control and the existence of internal checks built into the system will, together with an internal audit department, lead to the appropriate level of control, whereby management are sure that all revenue to which they are entitled is received and recorded, and that no expenditure is made without proper authorization. If the assets of the business are adequately accounted for they cannot be lost, stolen or misused, and if liabilities are systematically recorded it will be difficult to ignore such claims or to fail to provide for known losses when the accounting statements are produced.

Internal check comprises the routine checks on the day-to-day transactions which operate as part of the system. A major feature of internal check is to ensure that the work of one person is proved independently or is complementary to the work of another, so that errors are found and prevented, or at least detected, at an early stage. It is virtually impossible to prevent all fraud, but a well planned system can reduce temptation, increase the difficulties encountered by the fraudulent employee and improve the chances of his being detected. Internal check seeks to define the responsibility of individuals with a view to arranging matters so that no one person can undertake all the activities involved in any one transaction. If a single clerk can order goods, check their receipt, pass the invoice for payment, and then draw a cheque, he is in a position of great temptation, since it would be comparatively easy for him to pass fictitious entries through the books and make payments to his friends and accomplices. If more than one clerk is involved in the system, however, collusion must take place before fraud can be effected, and if employees are frequently rotated within the system then any collusion will not last long.

There is more to internal check than the prevention of collusion between employees. Test checks can be built into the system so that one record provides an independent confirmation of another, e.g. comparison of order with invoice. A well organized accounting system will ensure that costs are classified and coded so that they are entered in the correct accounts, and that control accounts are maintained for sections of the books (especially the personal ledgers) so that mistakes or differences can be isolated. If the debtors ledger control account is written up by a senior clerk he can check the accuracy of the clerk who maintains the debtors ledger, and collusion must take place between the two before fraud can be accomplished. The simple tactic of putting serial numbers on invoice pads will highlight any missing documents, and colour coding will serve to show where a copy of an accounting record, say an order, has strayed to the wrong department.

Authorization is an important feature of internal check, since it limits the ability of employees to act irresponsibly with the company's assets. If all orders, discounts, cheques, bad debts written off, etc. must be authorized by the signature of a trusted employee, judgement will be exercised before the company is committed in any way. The safe custody of order pads, cheque books, and receipt books is part of the system. A close check is particularly important at the points where transactions enter the accounting system. There must be a prime document to support each entry, and it must be authorized before an accounting record is made. The existence of the internal audit department will ensure that the system is reviewed from time to time to test its efficiency, and, most important, to test that an efficient system, once established, is operated properly by all concerned.

SOME SYSTEMS EXPLAINED

The Payment of Wages

This is a function which is to be found in most enterprises. The basic records are as follows:

a. the employee's record card, which shows personal details of the employee, including rate of pay;
b. the clock card, which the employee punches through a time clock when starting and stopping work to provide a record of working hours;
c. the wage sheet, which is written up from the clock cards, to show for each employee the wage earned and deductions such as tax, national insurance, holiday savings scheme, pension deductions etc; totals from the wage sheet give the amount to be drawn from the bank for wages, and the amounts for Schedule E tax deduction etc;
d. if the wage sheet is produced using a carbon copy system, the tear-off slip for each worker's pay packet is produced, and the individual's tax deduction card is written up at the same time.

The system could operate as follows:

a. Alterations to rates of pay should be initialled on the personal record card by a senior manager.
b. Time clocks should be installed to record hours worked on clock cards. Precautions should be taken to ensure that one employee does not clock in for another as well as himself. The foreman or gateman can carry out this check.
c. Overtime should be separately recorded and authorized by a senior manager.
d. Wage sheets should be ruled in columns to record any pay details and deductions, e.g. national insurance and tax. Each employee should have a line on the wage sheet. The wage sheet should be written up from the time cards and then extended. This work should be undertaken by two clerks, one to check the work of the other. Thus collusion will have to take place if fraud is to remain undetected.
e. A separate cheque for the total wages should be drawn, and the amounts put into the wage packets with the individual pay slips. All cash should be accounted for in this operation.
f. Payment of wages should be made by a person who has no part in making them up, and to whom all employees are known, e.g. the departmental foreman. All unclaimed packets should be recorded and returned to the wages office. In this way 'dead men' or non-existent employees injected into the system will be discovered.
g. The system should be strictly adhered to, and supervised by those responsible for the business. The management should review the wage sheet frequently and attend the payment of wages from time to time.

The Purchase of and Payment for Raw Materials

As a matter of internal control all purchases must be made through the buying office, which should be the only department allowed to place orders. When goods are required by the stores or by another department, a requisition signed by a responsible official must be submitted to the buying office. The requisition will contain details of quantity, quality, delivery date and address, as well as a full description of the goods. The buyers negotiate a price with the supplier and place an official order, which contains the information on the requisition and any variations. All orders must be countersigned by the chief buyer. A copy of the order is sent to the requisitioning department, the gatehouse or goods receiving bay, and the invoice department, for information. A copy is filed for reference in the buying office.

When the goods arrive they are checked against the order for type, quantity and quality before being stored, and a goods received note is raised by the checker, to accompany the goods to the store. Copy GRNs are sent to the buying office and to the invoice department, and a copy is filed for reference in the receiving bay. Next the invoice arrives and is checked by the invoice department against the order and the GRN, and only when this check proves satisfactory is the invoice passed and entered in the creditors ledger. This check is to ensure that the quantity, quality and price on the invoice are as agreed, and that only those so authorized can pledge the firm's credit. It is important that in the system so far the buyer, checker, stores clerk and invoice clerk are separate, so that collusion must take place before fraud can occur.

The next step in the system occurs when a statement of account is received from the supplier. This is compared with the ledger and if they agree, and if the period of credit has expired or the appropriate discount has been taken, the account can be passed for payment and a cheque drawn. If possible the clerk in charge of the creditors ledger should be separated from the cashier who draws the cheque. The cheque sent to the supplier will be accompanied by a remittance advice which explains the various items covered by the cheque. The cheque should be signed by a trusted official of the firm who is appointed as a signatory. This system can be expressed as a flow chart (Figure 5).

Cash Sales

The system to account for the handling of cash must be designed with care, since it is at this point that the company's assets are often most vulnerable to misappropriation. The selling points at which cash is received may be remote from the central administration or

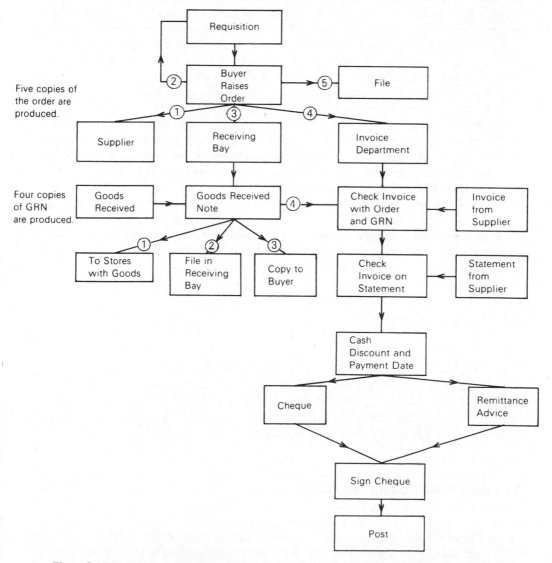

Figure 5. Flow Chart to Illustrate a System for the Purchase of and Payment for Materials.

accounts department, so control is difficult to achieve. The operation should be divided into spheres of responsibility, with a particular employee responsible for each area and reporting to a trusted manager.

For a branch shop with, for example, five counters, each counter selling a different product, the system might be designed as follows. All goods should be invoiced to the shop at selling prices, with a record of goods despatched maintained at head office. Therefore stock at the shop plus cash banked must equal the amount sent to the shop. An internal auditor should visit to make spot checks on the stock at random intervals, when each counter should have cash collected and banked, or goods, equal to the amount issued to it by the manager. The shop as a whole should also pass this test.

Sales should be evidenced by a bill given to the customer and a copy retained by the assistant. Cash received should be put into the till immediately, and tills emptied every day, when the amount removed, net of float, must equal the total shown on the till roll and the total of the copy bills. The assistant should initial the till roll amount and date, and this should be countersigned by another assistant, in order to prevent collusion between the manager and the assistant. The amount from each till should be entered daily by the manager in a cash book, amounting to a total to be banked per the paying-in slip. A copy paying-in slip should be sent to the main office, for entry in the main cash book. Pads of bills should be printed with serial numbers and issued to assistants by the manager only. The internal auditor should check that all the numbered pads are accounted for. No refunds should be made unless authorized by the manager.

The total of the copy bills should be entered each day in a sales journal analysed for each counter, and a summary sent to the main office each week for entry in the sales account. A trusted clerk at the head office should check cash banked against the bank statement and against sales. All cash takings should be banked, and local expenses and wages dealt with by a separate imprest system. Head office should check the date on which bankings appear on the bank statement against the date on the copy paying-in book, so that cash received on one day cannot remain in the possession of the branch manager for several days before being banked. Thus the manager cannot use this cash for his own purposes and make it up from takings at a later date (teeming and lading) without detection.

Sales on Credit Terms

A system to account for this type of transaction must contain steps to check the credit-worthiness of the prospective customer and to check whether the goods required are in stock. Multipart stationery can be used to distribute copies of documents such as the sales invoice, to ensure that important information is received by all persons working in the system. Follow the system through on the flow chart in figure 6.

TUTORIAL DISCUSSION TOPICS

11.1. 'The prime reason for employing an auditor is to discover and prevent fraud.' 'The purpose of an audit is to test the lines of communication.' Discuss these two views.

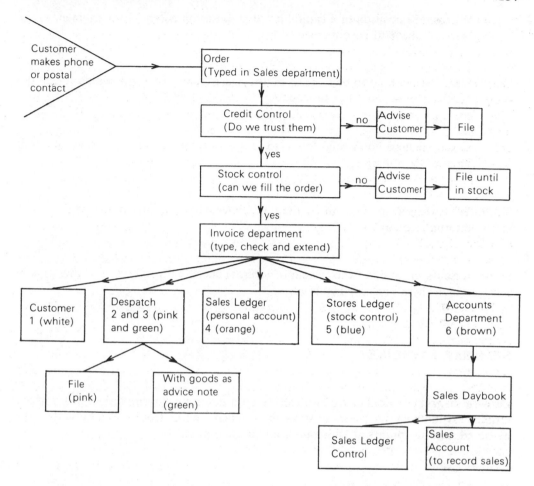

Figure 6. Flow Chart of a Sales Accounting System. The sales ledger records what is owed by each customer and should check with the total of the sales daybook as entered in the sales ledger control account. Note that the invoice department could type the invoices on a six-part stationery set, colour coded to ensure proper distribution.

11.2. What action should an accountant take before accepting the audit of a limited company? What information would he require on commencing the audit if he were subsequently appointed?

11.3. What are the main statutory duties of an auditor of a limited company, and what powers does he have to enable him to carry out these duties?

11.4. Discuss the ability of an auditor to withstand pressure put upon him by management with special reference to the weapons he can use in his defence.

11.5. How far can an external auditor rely upon the work of an internal auditor and what relationship should exist between these two parties?

11.6. What is the position of a capital profit so far as its potential for payment in the form of dividend is concerned?

11.7. Describe, with examples, each of the major types of error which affect the accuracy of accounting statements.

11.8. Trace the steps you would follow to locate an error when the two sides of a trial balance do not agree.

11.9. What do you understand by the term 'internal check' and how is it related to internal control?

11.10. Discuss the aims of the system of internal check with reference to the ways in which those aims are achieved.

SEMINAR EXERCISE 9

Draw a diagram or flow chart to illustrate an accounting system with which you are familiar. Annotate your charts to show the original records from which basic data are gathered, and the points at which internal check applies.

12 | An Introduction to Taxation

Taxation is levied by the Government to meet the expenses of governing, administering and protecting the country. The Government uses its revenue to provide education, the health service, social security, defence and roads, and to pay for the administration of Government schemes. A secondary use of taxation is as an instrument of economic policy, to encourage saving instead of consumption, to inhibit inflation, to increase economic activity to avert a recession, and to give aid to newly established and growing industries or declining industries so that employment opportunities are safeguarded. Tariffs can be used to reduce the competitiveness of imports and thus influence the balance of payments. Taxation can also be used to redistribute wealth for political and social reasons.

A taxation policy must be based on the need to structure taxes in such a way that their effects are beneficial to the economy. An understanding of the incidence of taxation, by recognizing the class on which the weight of a tax falls, is important to this end; for example, if a local government body, a county council, increases the local rates on shop premises, the shop-keepers will pay the tax, but may pass it on to the consumer in the form of increased prices. Their ability to pass on the tax is influenced by supply and demand, and the availability of substitutes to which customers can transfer their trade when prices are increased. It is also important to realize the limits to which taxation can be successfully levied. If business profits are taxed too heavily the net of tax return for risk taking will not compensate for the risk, and this will affect enterprise and the provision of venture capital to finance business undertakings. The Government itself participates in the provision of goods and services within the economy, through its control of the nationalized industries and other agencies. The public sector of the economy contains many basic industries, but the Government may use fiscal policy to influence events in the private sector also. Capital grants or tax concessions may persuade companies to site new factories in areas of high unemployment.

A direct tax, e.g. income tax, is levied directly on the individual, but an indirect tax, e.g. value added tax (VAT), is levied on goods or services and is paid when the item is consumed. For example, an individual pays VAT when he buys a television set or pays for a hair-cut. The indirect tax is collected by the seller of the goods on behalf of the Government and paid over at a later date. An indirect tax can usually be passed on to the ultimate consumer in the form of a price increase by the collecting agency. Indirect tax can be avoided by forgoing the consumption of the items on which it is levied. Direct taxes may be passed on to the consumer by manufacturers who raise their prices to maintain their net profits after tax, when corporation tax rises. The ability to transfer the incidence of tax depends on the elasticity of demand for the product.

PROGRESSIVE AND REGRESSIVE TAXES

The effect of taxation is not felt to the same extent by all taxpayers. Those with higher incomes can probably afford to pay more than those who earn less. The annual road fund licence of £50 paid by the owner of a Rolls Royce means little to him, whereas the same sum paid by the owner of a Mini may be equal to a half or more of his weekly income. For reasons of fairness it is suggested that taxation should be progressive, and that each should pay according to his means and ability to pay. Income tax is progressive, because incomes up to a certain level are exempt and then the rates of taxation get higher as income increases. As a matter of administration it is not worth the cost of collecting small amounts of tax from the lower income brackets, but as a matter of political policy progressive taxes can be used to transfer income from one class, the richer members of society, to another, the poor.

In the case of the road fund licence, however, a poll tax (so much per head) is levied on all road users. The man who drives 50 000 kilometres a year pays the same as another who drives only 10 000 kilometres, and the owner of a large car pays the same as the owner of a small car. This tax is regressive, since the higher the income the lower the proportion of it which is paid for putting a car on the road.

It has been suggested that there should be a negative income tax whereby those who receive low incomes should receive a subsidy to bring their standard of living up to a set minimum level, but if progressive taxation is carried too far it can have unfortunate effects on the economy. The impact of high marginal tax rates will inhibit the willingness of wage earners to forgo leisure in order to work overtime, will reduce the desire for promotion among managers if they do not consider the extra salary net of tax to be worth the burden of increased responsibility, and may decrease the supply of venture capital if the net of tax return is considered inadequate to compensate for the risks taken.

Indirect taxes, such as VAT, may be considered to be slightly regressive, since the tax per article is the same irrespective of the purchaser's ability to pay and if it is true that the rich spend a smaller proportion of their income than the poor. For this reason it is suggested that higher rates of VAT should be levied on luxury items to add a progressive element to VAT.

FORMS OF TAX

Income is an obvious base on which to compute an individual's liability for taxation. Some members of society, however, may not receive their income in monetary form, e.g. a farmer providing his own food, so it may be difficult to measure. This dilemma can be solved by placing an arbitrary value on business drawings in kind.

Other problems associated with income tax are that it ignores the existing wealth of the individual and the effort he has made to earn his income. In the UK unearned income (mainly from invested wealth) is taxed more rigorously than earned income, and assets held for capital gain are also subject to taxation when gains are realized (capital gains tax). The income tax system has also tried to take into account the various needs of individuals by developing a system of allowances which consider the circumstances of each case. A taxpayer with children or a dependent relative is allowed to earn more before he starts to pay tax than a taxpayer without such liabilities. Other allowances concern expenses 'wholly and exclusively' paid out in order to earn the income. The income of a company is subject to corporation tax, but a number of allowances embodied in tax law will be applied to convert net profit to taxable profit.

A wealth tax has been considered, as a supplement to income tax rather than as an alternative, but the suggestion has encountered the difficulty of measuring wealth at frequent intervals. At present, wealth is taxed, by means of capital transfer tax, when it is transferred, either on the death of its owner or when he gives it away during his lifetime.

The following diagram shows the various taxes levied by the British Government.

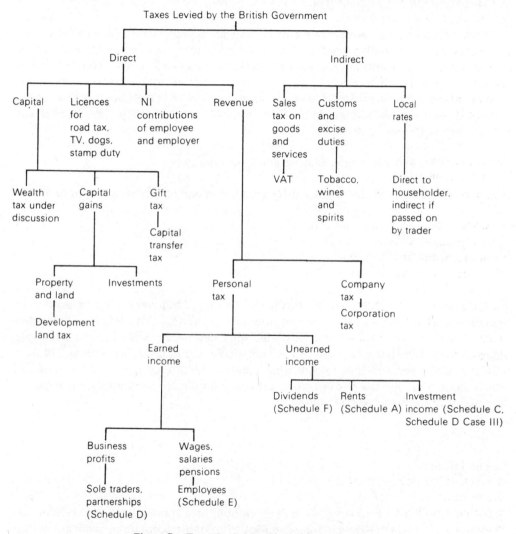

Figure 7. Taxes Levied by the British Government.

THE SCHEDULES

An individual may have income under more than one schedule.

Schedule A. This covers income from rent received (less statutory repairs) from land and buildings. This schedule used to cover a notional rent for owner/occupiers.

Schedule B. This covers income from the occupation of land other than through its trading uses. This schedule mainly concerns woodlands, since farms are now treated as businesses under Schedule D.

Schedule C. This covers income from investment in Government securities. This is taxed at source and the net amount paid to the recipients.

Schedule D. Cases I and II concern income from trades, professions and vocations. Case III concerns income from interest, annuities and other annual payments. Cases IV and V concern income from abroad. Sometimes UK taxation can be levied only on that part of the income that comes to the UK, and sometimes under a double taxation agreement with a foreign government such income is treated as franked investment income, and is not taxed again since it has already been taxed in its country of origin. Case VI concerns miscellaneous income.

Schedule E. This covers wages, salaries and pensions.

Schedule F. This covers dividends received from companies, advance corporation tax.

TAXABLE PROFIT

Business income is subject to corporation tax, if it is earned by a company, and income tax Schedule D Case I if it is earned by a sole trader or partnership. The definition of taxable profit is not the same as accounting profit, since certain expenses are not allowable against the taxation liability. Therefore the taxation computation of a company will start with net profit, and will then list the adjustments needed to convert it to the profit to which the corporation tax rate or income tax rate is applied to compute the tax payable. The major adjustments are as follows.

Depreciation

This cost is added back to net profit and an amount for capital allowances is deducted. Thus the rate at which depreciation is applied to compute accounting profit cannot be influenced by taxation. All businesses are treated the same so far as long-lived assets are concerned. Taxation policy allows 100 per cent of the cost of plant to be set off against profit in the first year after the plant is purchased, to encourage industrial concerns to install modern plant and equipment. When a capital asset is sold a balancing charge may be set off against capital allowances on new purchases that year. If the original cost less allowances received is less than the scrap value, the difference is the balancing charge.

Domestic Expenditure

Any disbursements or expenses of maintenance of the partners, their families or establishments, or any sums expended for domestic or private purposes distinct from the purposes of the trade, are not allowed to be set against taxable profit. Thus, for a partnership or sole trader, domestic expenditure must be identified in the accounts and added back to profit. However, some expenditure may lie in a grey area between business and domestic purposes, and this must be negotiated between the tax inspector and the accountant representing the tax payer. If a car is used partly for business purposes, part of its running costs will be an allowable expense. The same logic can be applied to private telephones used for business purposes and premises used for domestic as well as business purposes, e.g. a flat over a shop or office.

Entertaining

This can be expensive, but for some years now it has not been a tax allowable expense. It can be argued that entertaining a customer is a legitimate tactic of the salesman who is seeking an order, but the system can easily be abused and the Inland Revenue made to contribute to items of consumption rather than allowing the expense of a justifiable business activity. Only entertainment for overseas customers with the aim of gaining export orders can be set against profit for tax purposes.

Miscellaneous Items of Expenditure

These may be disallowed if it cannot be proved that they are 'wholly and exclusively' for the purpose of the business. Fines for parking etc. incurred by salesmen but paid by their employers are a case in point. Some companies will pay their employees' subscriptions to golf clubs etc. to encourage them to meet potential customers, but these expenses are disallowed, although subscriptions to trade associations are allowable. An accountant's subscription to his professional body is a tax deductible expense. Gifts to charities and donations to political parties are not tax deductible. Charitable donations made over a period of seven years under a deed of covenant are deemed to be net in the hands of a registered charity which can then claim a refund of the tax.

Debtors

A general provision for doubtful debts based on a percentage of debtors is not allowed as a deductible expense for tax purposes, relief in this direction being limited to provisions against specific debts which are considered doubtful. If a bad debt which has been written off is later paid, then it would be treated as business income in that year.

Stocks

The amount at which stocks are included in the accounts can have a significant effect on the profit figures. Although there is no strict legal definition of how stocks are to be valued for tax purposes, a business must be consistent in its use of one method or another. Case law has developed over the years, and the general rule is that stocks are to be valued at the lower of cost or market value, and that FIFO is favoured as a method of deriving cost whereas LIFO is not acceptable.

Example

The firm of Terry's Taxis has been in existence for a number of years. The proprietor lives on the premises. The income statement for the twelve months to 31 March this year was:

	£	£
Gross profit (after charging petrol, oil, drivers' wages)		19 630
Add		
Profit on sale of old taxis	300	
Football pool winnings	2350	
Advertising fees received	60	
Rent for sub-letting part of premises	400	
		3 110
		22 740
Less		
Office:		
Salaries (part-time staff)	1800	
Rent and rates (25 per cent private)	800	
Lighting and heating (30 per cent private)	250	
Postage and stationery	130	
Advertising	340	
Telephones (20 per cent private)	600	
Repairs:		
Premises (5 per cent private)	120	
Vehicles	910	
Loss on sale of office equipment	10	
Audit fee	150	
Depreciation	2100	
General expenses	970	
		8 180
Net profit		£14 560

Notes:
1. Capital allowances of £1600 have been agreed with the Inland Revenue.
2. General expenses include:

	£
Taxi Proprietors Association subscription	20
Golf club subscription	25
Fines for speeding and illegal parking	130
Entertaining	60
Employees' Christmas gifts	45
Donation to RSPCA	10

Prepare a statement showing the profits adjusted for Schedule D Case I purposes.

Terry's Taxis, Schedule D Case I Taxation Computation

	£	£
Net profit		14 560
Add back disallowed items		
Office:		
Rent and rates (25 per cent of £800)	200	
Lighting and heating (30 per cent of £250)	75	
Telephones (20 per cent of £600)	120	
Repairs to premises (5 per cent of £120)	6	
Loss on sale of office equipment	10	
Depreciation	2100	
General expenses:		
Golf club subscription	25	
Fines	130	
Entertaining	60	
Christmas gifts	45	
Donation to RSPCA	10	
		2 781
		17 341
Deduct receipts not taxable, already taxed, or taxable under another case or schedule		
Profit on sale of old taxis	300	
Football pool winnings	2350	
Rent for sub-letting	400	
		3 050
Taxable profit		14 291
Less capital allowances		1 600
Schedule D Case I assessment		£12 691

THE IMPUTATION SYSTEM

The treatment of taxation in company accounts is closely connected to the imputation system whereby advance corporation tax (ACT) is levied on dividends paid by companies. SSAP 8 has been issued to lay down the agreed procedure.

Company income, whether distributed or not, is subject to corporation tax. If no dividend is paid, the whole amount of this tax is payable, depending on the circumstances, as a single sum from 9 to about 21 months after the end of the accounting period to which it relates.

If a company pays a dividend, the 'qualifying distribution', as it is called, necessitates an amount of advance corporation tax (ACT), equal to tax at standard rate on the notional gross dividend, to be paid to the Inland Revenue within thirteen weeks of the dividend payment date.

The standard rate applied is that in force at the date of the dividend payment (which of course may be different from that obtaining at the date of the dividend declaration when the provision for ACT would be raised).

Example

Share capital 100 000 £1 ordinary shares. A dividend of 20 pence per share is proposed, which calls for an entry in the appropriation account and a pay out of £20000. This is deemed to be net of tax, so to find the amount of tax due on the dividend it must be 'grossed up' to tax. If the income tax rate is 33 pence in the £1, then the ACT payable on the dividend would be $\frac{33}{67} \times £20\,000 = £9851$. The amount is proved by the fact that 33 per cent of £29 851 = £9851, so this is the amount of tax at the standard income tax rate that shareholders would have paid on this dividend if they had received the gross amount.

The amount is deemed to have been collected from them by the company when the dividend was paid, and must therefore be paid over to the Inland Revenue by the company within thirteen weeks of the date of payment of the dividend. Thus at the year end the company will show, as current liabilities, £9851 ACT payable and £20 000 dividend payable. However, the company has the right to set off ACT paid against corporation tax payable in a future period, so the £9851 should also appear in the balance sheet as an asset. In practice ACT is usually included in the balance sheet as a deduction from a liability, the deferred tax account.

When the ACT is set off against corporation tax, the net amount payable is termed mainstream corporation tax (MCT). ACT can be recouped in the first instance from corporation tax payable on the taxable income of the year in which the dividend is paid. Thus if a company makes a profit in year 1, and pays a dividend and ACT on that profit during year 2, the ACT can be recovered from corporation tax on the profit of year 2 when that tax is paid, which may be in year 3 or year 4. Until the ACT is recovered it appears in the balance sheet as a deduction from other deferred tax liabilities. If ACT cannot be recouped because corporation tax on future years' profits is insufficient, it can be carried back for two years or carried forward indefinitely, unless recoverability is uncertain, when it should be written off to the profit and loss account as a separate item.

In the balance sheet ACT recoverable that year is netted off against the corporation tax charge on the profit for the period, and the net (MCT) liability is shown. Where dividends have been proposed but not paid at the date of the balance sheet, the related ACT is provided and shown as a current liability.

PAYMENT OF MAINSTREAM CORPORATION TAX

In 1965 the taxation system was changed, and companies which previously had paid income tax were subject to corporation tax from then onwards. Corporation tax, like income tax, is payable after the end of the accounting year in which the profit arose. An accounting year can be timed to end on any date; many companies use 31 December. The tax year runs from 6 April to 5 April, and companies pay corporation tax on 1 January in the next tax year after the tax year in which its accounting year ended.

Example

The accounting year ending 31 December 1979 is in the tax year ending 5 April 1980, and corporation tax on those profits would be payable by the company on 1 January 1981. A

Schedule D income tax payer who has been in business for some years would pay his tax in a similar year but in two equal instalments on 1 January 1981 and 1 July 1981.

However, for companies incorporated after 1 April 1965, or established companies which have changed their accounting period after that date, corporation tax is payable nine months after the end of the accounting period or one month after the issue of an assessment, whichever is the later. In the example above the tax would be payable in these circumstances on 1 October 1980.

Tax payable within twelve months of the balance sheet date should be treated as a current liability, but tax payable more than twelve months into the future should be shown separately as 'future taxation payable on . . .', with the appropriate date.

DEFERRED TAXATION

The account under this name contains the total of tax liabilities arising from various transactions which may or may not have to be paid at some future date. These tax liabilities arise in a number of ways.

First, capital allowances at accelerated rates such as 100 per cent in the first year will exceed the depreciation charge in that period. This difference is called a timing difference because after a number of years the depreciation charged each year will have caught up with the capital allowance. If the asset is sold before this time, a balancing charge will be made in the tax computation, so that the liability to tax in that year will increase. The tax attributable to the timing difference is held in the deferred tax account until the difference no longer exists, in case the asset concerned is sold for more than its tax written-down value. This can be a significant amount for a company with a large capital investment programme spread over several years.

Second, 'stock relief' is held in the deferred tax account. The Inland Revenue will not accept LIFO as a means of valuing stock, and profits may be overstated in a period of inflation if the FIFO method is used. Thus relief against a tax on inflation has been devised, on the basis of the physical increase in the size of stocks. This stock relief is subject to 'clawback', which means that if stocks fall the tax relief received in an earlier period must be refunded to the Inland Revenue. This conditional liability is covered by an amount set aside in the deferred tax account.

Third, certain items may be dealt with in different time periods for the accounts and for the tax computation, and are held in the deferred tax account. For example, a provision for bad debts may not be tax deductible until the debts go bad in a subsequent period, or a provision for interest receivable may not count as taxable income until the period in which the interest is actually received.

A fourth reason for the creation of a deferred taxation account arises from the revaluation of buildings and other fixed assets. If the assets were sold at their enhanced value, a capital gains tax liability might arise, and a provision must be made against this eventuality. Some businessmen do not agree with this provision, since the accounts are drawn up on a going concern basis, and this implies that basic fixed assets such as buildings are not likely to be sold in the future. Capital gains are taxed in the hands of a company at corporation tax rates.

A fifth reason for creating a deferred tax account concerns fixed assets which are sold for a capital gain. Usually this gain would attract capital gains tax, but if the funds produced by the sale are used immediately to replace the assets sold, there is a dispensation termed 'roll over relief', which delays the payment of capital gains tax until the funds so employed are no longer invested in replacement assets. Clearly there is a case here for a provision against this deferred taxation liability.

The impact of timing differences and the creation of a deferred taxation account have met with so much opposition in industry that SSAP 11, which deals with these matters, has been suspended. It is argued that some of the reasons for creating the account are not likely to occur, but it is suspected that at the root of the opposition lies the depressing effect of a provision to the deferred tax account on profits and the price/earnings ratio, which is used as a stock exchange indicator.

TUTORIAL DISCUSSION TOPICS

12.1. Explain how taxation can be used as an instrument of economic policy.

12.2. What is the difference between progressive and regressive taxes? Give examples of each type.

12.3. What is the imputation system and how does it affect the balance sheet of a company?

12.4. State the rules which govern the payment of corporation tax and Schedule D income tax in the UK.

12.5. 'Deferred taxation is an account in which are accumulated tax savings of varying degrees of permanence. The balance of the account thus represents the aggregate of tax liabilities arising from sundry individual transactions which may have to be discharged at diverse times over future periods.' Explain the reason for having a deferred taxation account and the transactions referred to in the above quotation.

13 | The Accounting Requirements of the Companies Acts 1948 and 1967

The Companies Acts of 1948 and 1967 lay down certain rules about what information companies must disclose in their annual accounts. The requirements of the Acts represent the legal minimum for disclosure, and many companies show more than is required by law in their annual accounts. The Acts do not lay down any special form in which the information is to be presented, and different companies adopt different forms of presentation.

The information specified in the Acts can be shown either on the face of the profit and loss account or balance sheet, or in the form of notes appended thereto. It is fairly common for companies to show their profit and loss account and balance sheet in published form as an austere statement with as few figures and as little information as possible. The bulk of the information is provided in the form of notes appended to the accounting statements. One item of information which is always shown in published accounts is data concerning the previous year's statement, so that a comparison can be made.

THE PUBLISHED PROFIT AND LOSS ACCOUNT

On the published profit and loss account there are certain items which must be shown. These are as follows.

1. Depreciation. The account must show as one figure the amount charged for depreciation, renewals, or the diminution in value of the fixed assets. Thus only one figure to represent all depreciation for the year has to be shown, but in the notes appended to the profit and loss account the position is further explained.

2. The figure for interest payable on loans and overdrafts must be analysed among those repayable otherwise than by instalment and due within five years, loans repayable by instalments, the last instalment being within five years, and other loans. Thus shareholders can see the impact on the profit and loss account of interest on the various types of loan.

3. The remuneration (including expenses) of the auditors. Since the auditors are employed by the shareholders it is right that the published accounts should show the shareholders what they are paying for the service they receive.

4. Amounts, if material, for the hire of plant and machinery and revenue in rents from land, after deduction of expenses. We have already seen that what is considered material

is determined by the circumstances of each case. When the cost of plant hire is disclosed, this will help the investor to see whether a company is making a significant profit from a small amount of fixed assets, and is thus very efficient, or whether hired assets are being used to supplement plant etc. owned by the business.

5. Directors' emoluments. One figure only is shown for these emoluments. This figure covers directors' and past directors' pensions and compensation for loss of office paid to directors, as well as all fees, salaries and commissions paid to directors during the year. An analysis of this figure appears as a note to the statement.

6. Any charges or credits arising in consequence of events in a preceding financial year. Thus the profit from this year's trading can be isolated by the investor and the impact of past mistakes or windfalls can be seen.

7. Income from investments must be analysed between income from quoted and unquoted investments. A quoted investment consists of shares in a public company or some other type of security traded on a stock exchange. On the balance sheet the cost and current value of such investments will be shown, analysed again between quoted and unquoted investments, so that the shareholder can see the return such investments make and can decide whether the company's funds are best laid out in this direction or elsewhere.

8. Under the heading taxation the charge for United Kingdom corporation tax, double taxation relief and taxation imposed outside the United Kingdom should be shown.

9. Any amount set aside for the redemption of share capital and loans must be shown separately.

10. Any amounts appropriated to or withdrawn from reserves or provisions must be shown and, if it is material, any amount withdrawn from a provision and not used for the purpose for which the provision was originally made must be individually stated.

11. The amount of dividend paid or proposed must be shown, analysed for the various classes of capital in the balance sheet.

The items detailed above usually appear on the face of the published profit and loss account, and are supplemented by the following data, usually shown as a note appended to that account.

1. A figure for turnover (or the total of sales or other income) must be shown, together with a note about the method by which the figure has been computed. There is provision in the Act for a company with a turnover of less than £250 000 for the year to omit the figure. It is also allowable to omit turnover if it has been earned from banking operations. Thus a bank need not disclose its turnover, and a group which has a banking subsidiary can omit banking turnover from the figure it discloses. This concession to the banks has been made to protect the confidentiality of their figures. It is felt that if the general public see a decrease in the turnover of a bank their confidence in its ability to meet repayments of deposits they have made with it may be reduced, so that a 'run' on the bank could be initiated. The figure for turnover is often shown on the face of the profit and loss account right at the top, and then underlined to denote that it is not part of the computation.

2. The basis on which taxation has been computed and any special circumstances affecting the liability to tax now and in the future must be shown as a note.

3. An important note to the profit and loss account concerns the directors' emoluments. If the total emoluments exceed £7500 they should be analysed to show the emoluments of the chairman, the emoluments of the highest-paid director and the number of directors with emoluments in succeeding 'bands' of £2500. There is no liability on a company to name the highest-paid director or the other directors in the bands referred to above, but some companies do show how much each director receives, and also show his shareholding in the business. This demonstrates the fact that the accounting

requirements of the Companies Acts are minimum requirements, and that companies can, if they wish, give further information. The requirements of confidentiality over and above the basis needed to comply with the Acts are thus left to the discretion of the company concerned. A further note concerning directors' emoluments is needed to show those emoluments waived by directors, and the number of directors who have waived their rights. Pension contributions made by the company for present or past directors are excluded from this analysis, but are included in the figure shown on the face of the profit and loss account.

4. Employees' emoluments are shown to the extent that the number of employees earning above £10 000 per annum in succeeding 'bands' of £2500 must be noted. Both directors and employees working mainly outside the United Kingdom are excluded from these last two notes.

5. A note concerning depreciation is required where additional charges for renewal have been made, or where amounts have been provided for the replacement of fixed assets other than by a depreciation charge. The facts that no provision for depreciation has been made, or that the depreciation is based on amounts other than those shown in the balance sheet or computed other than by a normally accepted method, must also be revealed.

6. Special circumstances must be noted. Material amounts caused by transactions not usually undertaken, or exceptional or non-recurring circumstances, and changes in the basis of accounting must be noted. Auditors are particularly vigilant here, with special reference to the disclosure of accounting policies under SSAP 2. A separate note dealing with this item is usually appended to the accounts.

Example

A typical published profit and loss account might appear as follows:

Anyfirm Limited Profit and Loss Account for the Year ended 31 December 19 _ _

Last year's figures £		£	£
15 485 760	Turnover for the year net of returns		17 412 583
521 603	Net profit		572 619
	After accounting for the following expenses and revenues:		
76 231	Depreciation	89 412	
2 000	Interest on loans repayable by instalments within five years	2 000	
4 000	Interest on other loans	4 000	
61 750	Directors' emoluments	62 750	
4 900	Remuneration of auditors	5 800	
6 547	Income from unquoted investments	8 934	
	Less charge for UK corporation tax		
201 684	based on profit for the year		219 472
319 919	Net profit after tax		353 147
35 781	Add unappropriated profit brought		65 800
355 700	down from last year		418 947
100 000	Less amount set aside for redemption of debentures	100 000	
89 900	amount set aside to general reserve	120 000	
100 000	amount set aside proposed to be paid as dividend	140 000	360 000
£65 800	Balances of unappropriated profit carried forward		£58 947

THE BALANCE SHEET

The following items must be shown either on the face of the balance sheet or by way of note.

Share Capital

The amount for authorized and issued capital must be summarized. The authorized capital is the amount which the company is authorized to raise, under its Memorandum and Articles of Association, and the issued capital is the proportion of authorized capital which has been issued to subscribers. Where redeemable preference shares have been issued, the details of redemption dates, whether the redemption is optional, and any redemption premium which may be payable must be shown. Obviously such details cannot be shown on the face of the balance sheet, and are usually revealed in the form of a note. A further note is required to give details of any arrears of fixed cumulative dividend. Further information concerning share capital, which does not often appear in the accounts, covers particulars of share capital on which interest has been paid out of capital, together with the rate, and details of any loans made by the company for the purchase of its shares, with particulars of options outstanding to any person to subscribe for the company's shares.

Reserves and Provisions

The sources from which increases in reserves and provisions have been made must be shown, as must the ways in which any reduction of a reserve or provision has been applied, unless this information has already been revealed in the profit and loss account or the notes appended thereto. If there is a share premium account this should be shown separately. Such an account arises in circumstances where a company issues shares at more than their face value. If there is a strong demand for its shares, a company will be able to offer a new issue of fresh shares to the general public at a premium, i.e. the public would be willing to subscribe, say, £1.50 for every £1 ordinary share they take up. If 100 000 shares are the subject of such an issue, then the capital will increase by £100 000, the share premium account will increase by £50 000 and, on the other side of the balance sheet, cash will go up by £150 000. It must be remembered that a share premium account is equivalent to a reserve not available for distribution, and the uses to which such an account can be put are severely limited. Any amount taken from the taxation equalization reserve account and used for some other purpose should be noted.

Loans

Loans repayable within five years of the balance sheet date must be separated from other loans, and their repayment terms and rate of interest shown. A note should reveal any debentures of the company which have been redeemed and which the company has power to re-issue, together with details of any debentures of the company held by a nominee for the company. Any loans or other liabilities which are secured on the assets of the company must be the subject of a note, but there is no need to specify the assets concerned in such a security. In cases where there is a charge on the assets of the company to secure the liabilities of another person, this too must be stated.

Current Liabilities

The Acts say little about how current liabilities should be shown, but since the introduction of advance corporation tax under the imputation system there has been a significant change in the way in which proposed dividends are shown. Dividends proposed, but not yet paid, are creditors of the company. The amount to be paid to the shareholders is thus shown as a current liability. Under the imputation system advance corporation tax on dividends is liable to be paid to the Inland Revenue within thirteen weeks of the payment of that dividend, but it can be reclaimed later by being set off against mainstream corporation tax. Thus advance corporation tax liable as a result of a dividend must be shown as a current liability on the balance sheet, although in fact it is an asset, since it can be reclaimed later. It does not, however, appear on the balance sheet as an asset, but as a deduction from the deferred taxation account.

Contingent Liabilities

These must be noted. They are not part of the balance sheet computation, since they are not owed at the balance sheet date, but they relate to transactions which took place before the balance sheet date and which may or may not become liabilities after the balance sheet date, contingent upon some further circumstance which cannot be accurately forecast. Separate figures must be shown for capital expenditure authorized by the board and not yet contracted for, separate from authorized capital expenditure for which contracts have been placed.

Intangible Assets

Any amount not yet written off for preliminary expenses, goodwill, patents and trade marks, and share and debenture issue expenses and commissions, must be stated.

Fixed Assets

The method by which the fixed assets have been valued must be stated. It is usually sufficient to show on the face of the balance sheet the cost less depreciation to date. However, a note is required to reveal the date of any revaluation of the fixed assets, and in the year when the revaluation is made the identity of the valuer or his qualifications to value must be stated. Thus the shareholders and potential investors can assess the validity of any new value set upon the fixed assets of the business, and can also see how outdated the balance sheet values for such assets are. Any significant differences between the book value and the real value of such assets should also be the subject of a comment in the director's report appended to the published accounts.

The aggregate figure for fixed assets acquired during the year and disposals during the year must be shown. There must be a distinction on the balance sheet between freehold and leasehold property, and a further distinction between long- and short-term leases. A short lease is one which has less than fifty years to run from the balance sheet date. Most companies show one figure for their fixed assets in the published balance sheet, and comply with the requirements shown above by giving a detailed statement of movements of fixed assets and depreciation during the year appended as a note.

Investments

The total costs of quoted and unquoted investments must be shown separately. A note of the current market value of quoted investments is required (this is taken to be the mid-market price between the jobber's buying and selling quotations) and the directors' valuation of unquoted investments must also be shown. Here again the auditors will be concerned with testing the validity of such a valuation.

A further note concerns the amount of capital gains tax payable if investments are realized at these values.

Current Assets

Stocks and work in progress are shown at cost, but a note about the basis of their valuation is required. If, in the director's opinion, any current assets have a lower realizable value than that shown, this fact must be stated. The basis of conversion to sterling of any foreign currency included in the accounts must be stated if this is a material factor.

Loans Made by the Company

A company may not lend money to a person who intends to use that money for the purchase of its own shares, unless it is a money-lending company and the loan is made in the ordinary course of business, or unless the loan is made under a scheme whereby trustees are buying the shares on behalf of employees. Loans made under such schemes must be shown in the accounts. A note must also reveal the amount of loans made during the year to any officer of the company, or to a person who became an officer of the company after the loan was made, whether the loans were made by the company or a subsidiary. The amount of any such loans made before the beginning of the financial year and still outstanding at the year end must also be shown.

THE DIRECTORS' REPORT

Once again a minimum of information is required by the Acts, but many companies exceed these limits in the cause of good public relations. The manner in which the required information is presented often reflects the character of the board. The report should be attached to the balance sheet, and should cover the following matters:

1. the names of the directors, whether they have been on the board for the whole or part of the year;
2. the principal activities of the company, with notes on any significant changes during the year;
3. any important changes in fixed assets which have occurred during the year;
4. whether the market value of the company's interest in land and fixed assets differs materially from the book value shown in the accounts at the year end;
5. details of any issue of shares or debentures made during the year, including the reason therefor and the consideration received;
6. the interest of any director in any contracts the company has entered into;
7. the directors' rights to acquire shares or debentures in the company;
8. directors' interests in shares or debentures of the company at the year end;
9. any other matters which may be material to enable the members to appreciate the state of the company's affairs (unless in the directors' opinion such information could harm the company's business);
10. an analysis of the company's turnover and profit or loss before taxation analysed for each class of business carried on;
11. the average number of employees per week if this exceeds 100;
12. the aggregate remuneration paid or payable to employees for the year, if the number of employees exceeds 100;
13. the aggregate of both political and charitable contributions made during the year, with details of any political payment which exceeds £50;
14. the value of the company's exports during the year, or the fact that no goods have been exported;
15. recommended dividends and amounts recommended to be carried to reserves.

STATEMENTS OF STANDARD ACCOUNTING PRACTICE

Statements of Standard Accounting Practice (SSAPs) describe methods of accounting practice approved by the councils of the major professional accounting bodies in the United Kingdom, for application to all financial accounts intended to give a true and fair view of the financial position, or profit or loss. Professional accountants, whether acting in the capacity of director, executive, or auditor, must observe the requirements of these standards and explain departures from them. Failure to do so renders that person liable to disciplinary proceedings for unprofessional conduct, and is often the subject of an auditor's qualification in his report on published accounts.

SSAP 2 deals with the disclosure of accounting policies. In the absence of an explanatory statement of facts to the contrary, the four fundamental concepts, i.e. going concern, accruals, consistency and conservatism, are presumed to have been observed in the preparation of the accounts. The accounting policies, i.e. the specific accounting basis used, followed for dealing with items judged to be material in determining profit or loss for the year and in stating the financial position, should be disclosed by way of a note to the accounts. Disclosure of policy adopted would be required for such matters as depreciation of fixed assets, treatment and amortization of intangible assets, research and development expenditure, stocks and work in progress, long-term contracts, deferred taxation, hire purchase and instalment transactions, and repairs and renewals.

SSAP 6 deals with extraordinary items and prior-year adjustments. In this standard extraordinary items are those material items which derive from events or transactions outside the ordinary activities of the business. They do not include prior-year adjustments or those items which, although exceptional as to their size and incidence, arise from the ordinary activities of the business and which should be reflected in the net profit (before tax) for the year and disclosed separately if necessary. The profit and loss account should show the net profit (after tax) before extraordinary items, then the extraordinary items themselves, with their nature and amounts specified, less any tax liability attributable to such items. The statement can conclude with the net profit after tax and after extraordinary items. Prior-year adjustments in this context are limited to the effects of changes in accounting policies and the correction of fundamental errors. They do not include corrections and adjustments to previous periods' estimates. In the cases of correction of fundamental errors and change in accounting policy, such as a change in the basis of depreciation of fixed assets, or in the basis of stock valuation, the cumulative adjustments relating to prior years should not be included when calculating a current year's profit. Such cumulative amounts should be adjusted in the opening balance of retained profits with an adequate note to disclose the nature of the adjustment and separate amounts where necessary.

Example

Grande Ltd has an authorized share capital of £280 000 consisting of ordinary shares of £1 each. The company prepares its accounts as on 31 March in each year, and the trial balance, before final adjustments, extracted on 31 March this year showed:

	£	£
Ordinary share capital, issued and fully paid		220 000
Retained profit as on 1 April last year		41 000
6 per cent debenture stock (secured on leasehold		
factory)		45 000
6 per cent unsecured loan stock		5 000
Leasehold factory:		
Cost at beginning of year	190 000	
Accumulated depreciation		75 000
Plant and machinery:		
Cost at beginning of year	90 000	
Accumulated depreciation		31 000
Additions in year	12 000	
Interest on debenture stock	2 700	
Interest on loan stock	300	
Directors' remuneration	23 000	
Auditors' remuneration	1 500	
Creditors and accrued expenses		145 000
Stock as on 31 March this year	150 000	
Debtors and prepayments	174 000	
Balance at bank	76 000	
Sales: invoiced value less allowances		995 000
Material consumption, direct and indirect expenses	837 500	
	£1 557 000	£1 557 000

You ascertain the following.

1. The debenture stock is repayable at par by five equal annual drawings starting on 31 December next year.
2. The unsecured loan stock is repayable at par on 31 December this year.
3. The lease of the factory has forty years to run.
4. Directors' remuneration comprises: (a) salaries of chairman, £5000, managing director, £8000, sales director, £8000; (b) fee of non-executive director, £500; and (c) pension contributions, £1500.
5. The managing director is entitled to a commission of 5 per cent per annum on the net profit, after deducting all charges except taxation and the commission.
6. Annual deprecation is calculated as to: leasehold factory, 2 per cent on cost; plant and machinery, 20 per cent on net book value on 1 April last year plus additions in year.
7. Stock has been valued consistently at the lower of cost and net realizable value.
8. A dividend of 20 per cent (20 pence per share) is proposed.
9. Corporation tax on the profit of the year has been computed at £40 000 and is payable on 1 January next year. The current standard rate of income tax is 34 per cent.
10. The directors have placed contracts for new plant costing £5000 and have authorized further expenditure on new plant costing £10 000.

You are required to prepare, in a form suitable for publication and in conformity with the provisions of the Companies Acts 1948 and 1967:

(a) a balance sheet as on 31 March this year;
(b) a profit and loss account for the year ended 31 March;
(c) notes to the accounts.

The auditor's report and comparative figures are not required. The accounts should be presented concisely and informatively in columnar form.

 The first step is to compute the trading profit, since it is not shown in the trial balance.

	£	£
Sales		995 000
Less:		
Materials and expenses	837 500	
Interest on debenture	2 700	
Interest on loan	300	
Audit fee	1 500	
Depreciation (2 per cent of 190 000) + (20 per cent of (90 000 + 12 000 − 31 000))	18 000	
Directors' remuneration	23 000	883 000
		112 000
Managing director's commission (5 per cent)		5 600
Net trading profit		£106 400

The next step is to identify those items which need to be revealed in the published accounts. It should be remembered that the commission has not yet been paid, so it appears as a creditor in the balance sheet. The figure for sales will be shown, together with the basis on which it was computed, either on the face of the profit and loss account or as a note appended to it. The notes above, except 5, 6, 8 and 9, provide information relevant to the notes to the accounts.

Only one figure is required in the profit and loss account for depreciation, or for the directors' remuneration, but a note to the accounts explains these figures. Total directors' remuneration is shown in the profit and loss account, but the analysis in the note excludes pension contributions.

The accrued commission to the managing director must be added to the trial balance figure, to compute the total emoluments in the published profit and loss account.

The 6 per cent unsecured loan stock has now become a current liability, since it is repayable within a year.

The ACT is computed as 34/66 of £44 000.

A change of income tax rate merely changes the fraction used. A 30 per cent rate would be applied as 3/7 of £44 000.

There has been no change of accounting policies during the year, such as a different stock valuation or depreciation method. If there is no depreciation of leasehold land and buildings this fact is worthy of a note, or should be shown in the analysis of fixed assets. The absence of such depreciation may attract an auditor's qualification of the accounts as being in contravention of SSAP 12.

Grande Ltd, Profit and Loss Account for the year ended 31 March

	£	£
Turnover (sales at invoiced value less allowances)		995 000
Trading profit		106 400
After charging:		
Directors' emoluments	28 600	
Depreciation	18 000	
Interest on loans repayable within five years	300	
Interest on loans repayable five years hence	2 700	
Audit fee	1 500	
UK corporation tax based on profits for the year		40 000
Net profit after taxation		66 400
Less dividend proposed, 20 per cent		44 000
		22 400
Add unappropriated profit b/d		41 000
Unappropriated profit c/f		£63 400

Grande Ltd, Balance Sheet as at 31 March

	£	£
Share capital:		
Authorized, ordinary shares of £1		280 000
Issued, ordinary shares of £1 each, fully paid		220 000
Reserves: unappropriated profit c/f		63 400
		283 400
Long-term liabilities:		
6 per cent debentures (secured)		45 000
Net capital employed		£328 400

	£	£	£
Represented by:			
Fixed assets			168 000
Deferred asset: ACT, recoverable			22 667
Current assets: Stock		150 000	
Debtors		174 000	
Cash		76 000	
		400 000	
Less current liabilities:			
6 per cent unsecured loan stock	5 000		
Creditors	150 600		
Corporation tax	40 000		
Advance corporation tax	22 667		
Proposed dividend	44 000		
		262 267	
			137 733
Net assets			£328 400

Notes to accounts:

1. Directors emoluments: chairman, £5000; highest paid director, £13 600; others, scale 0 – £2500, one, £7501 – £10 000, one.
2. Fixed assets

	Land and Buildings	Plant	Total
	£	£	£
Cost	190 000	90 000	280 000
Additions during year	–	12 000	12 000
	190 000	102 000	292 000
Depreciation to date	78 800	45 200	124 000
	£111 200	£56 800	£168 000

3. 6 per cent unsecured loan stock is repayable on 31 December this year. 6 per cent debentures are repayable at par by five equal annual drawings starting on 31 December next year.
4. The land and buildings are now a short-lease property.
5. Stock is shown at the lower of cost or market value.
6. Capital commitments: contracts placed, £5000; contracts authorized, £10 000.

STATISTICAL SUPPLEMENTS TO PUBLISHED ACCOUNTS

Many companies present a statistical supplement to their published accounts. The purpose of such extra data is to highlight the salient features of the accounts, to put current events in the company into perspective, and to provide background information to help shareholders and potential shareholders to interpret the accounting statements. Advantage is often taken of such statements to undertake a public relations exercise and, in the process of simplification and explanation, to ensure that the company's activities and performance are shown in the best possible light. This type of appendix to the published accounts can help to maintain the price of the shares by showing the company to be a good investment.

Statistics of this type should be easy to assimilate. Companies often work to the nearest

£1000 and use percentages and ratios so that comparisons can be made easily, trends revealed, and key figures accentuated. A good statistical supplement avoids presenting a mass of figures by using forms of visual presentation other than tables of figures. Such devices as graphs, bar charts and pie charts are very useful in this respect. For example, an international company may show a map of the world with a dot or company emblem in every area in which the group has an interest.

A pie chart is a useful device for showing the proportion of parts to a whole. An example of the use of such a chart is in demonstrating how the profit figure is appropriated. A large slice of the pie would go in taxation, another large slice would be ploughed back into the company, and a comparatively small slice would be dividend to the shareholders. Such a pie diagram might be useful in undermining the arguments of trade union officials for higher wages based on the large return achieved by the shareholders.

SEMINAR EXERCISES 10

1. Sandal Ltd, a company which sells footwear, makes up its accounts to 31 December in each year. The company has an authorized share capital of £300 000 divided into 150 000 $7\frac{1}{2}$ per cent preference shares of £1 each and 300 000 ordinary shares of 50p each.

    The following draft accounts for the year ended 31 December were presented to the auditors for consideration.

Dr.		Profit and Loss Account		Cr.
	£			£
Cost of sales	353 871	Sales		606 740
Motor expenses	78 482	Discounts received		685
Depreciation on		Income from investments		–
motor vehicles	6 509	Trade		800
Overhead expenses	40 240	Quoted		1 170
Wages and salaries	61 179			
General expenses	6 564			
Audit fee	1 050			
Depreciation on fixtures and				
fittings	540			
Pension to former director's				
widow	950			
Superannuation scheme	6 250			
Corporation tax	13 104			
Debenture interest	800			
Preference dividend	7 500			
Net profit for year	32 356			
	£609 395			£609 395

Dr.	Balance Sheet		Cr.
	£		£
8 per cent debentures 1990/2001	10 000	Cash in hand	1 763
Ordinary share capital	100 000	Balance at bank	59 149
Preference share capital	100 000	Stock in hand, at cost	105 246
Creditors	73 105	Motor vehicles	12 800
Provision for doubtful debts	7 500	Fixtures and fittings	5 560
Profit and loss account	84 691	Debtors	170 022
		Freehold land and buildings	85 000
Corporation tax	29 244	Investments at cost	15 000
General reserve	30 000		
Share premium	20 000		
	£454 540		£454 540

You are given the following additional information:

(a) The issued share capital is all fully paid.

(b) The charge for wages and salaries includes the salaries of the managing director, £6500, and sales director, £6000. The superannuation scheme also includes £858 on their behalf. Provision is to be made for directors' fees of £7500, being £2500 for each director, including the chairman, who does not receive a salary.

(c) The charge for corporation tax in the profit and loss account is the amount estimated to be payable on the profits for the year, at 45 per cent, and due on 1 January next year.

(d) There have been no additions to, or sales of, motor vehicles or fixtures and fittings, but freehold land and buildings includes an amount of £20 000 spent on a new extension built during the year. The cost of fixed assets was: freehold land and buildings, £85 000; motor vehicles, £25 600; and fixtures and fittings, £10 400.

(e) The quoted investments, which cost £10 000, had a market value on 31 December of £17 582. The trade investment represents $12\frac{1}{2}$ per cent of the issued ordinary share capital of Slipper Ltd, a private company incorporated in England with an issued share capital of 40 000 ordinary shares of £1 each. The shares were purchased at par and are valued by the directors at £2.50 each. If the investments were realized at the market and directors' values respectively it is estimated that taxation amounting to £9000 would become payable.

(f) Provision for doubtful debts is to be adjusted to £7918.

(g) The directors recommend payment of an ordinary dividend of 10 per cent.

Prepare the company's profit and loss account for the year ended 31 December, and a balance sheet as on that date, in a form suitable for publication.

Corresponding figures are not required, and the information given may be taken as if it included all that is necessary to satisfy the requirements of the Companies Acts 1948 and 1967.

2. Milton Ltd is a manufacturer of knitted garments. The following is the trial balance at 31 March this year:

	£	£
Sales		843 800
Cost of sales	505 810	
Administrative expenses	200 250	
Debtors/creditors	190 340	116 040
Provision for bad debts		5 150
Directors' remuneration	30 650	
Debenture interest	1 500	
Half-year preference dividend	990	
ACT paid on 14 October last year (re above)	510	
Freehold land and buildings at cost	113 000	
Provision for depreciation on freehold land and buildings		11 320
Plant and machinery at cost	325 500	
Provision for depreciation on plant and machinery		197 060
Motor vehicles at cost	48 200	
Provision for depreciation on motor vehicles		20 760
Stock in trade and work in progress at 31 March this year	174 000	
Cash	192	
Bank overdraft		28 154
Profit and loss account balance at 1 April last year		176 658
Ordinary share capital		132 000
Preference share capital		20 000
$7\frac{1}{2}$ per cent debentures 1996/1991		40 000
	£1 590 942	£1 590 942

The following information relates to the accounts for the year ended 31 March this year.

(a) The directors' remuneration is divided among the five directors of the company as follows:

Mr Newall, Chairman	£6 800
Mr Edmund, Managing Director	£6 500
Mr York, Sales Director	£6 100
Mr Price, Finance Director	£6 000
Mr Park, Production Director	£5 250
	£30 650

In addition provision is to be made for bonuses of £1000 to the managing director and £500 to the sales director, and fees of £500 to each of the five directors.

(b) Depreciation is to be provided for the year as follows: freehold land and buildings, 2 per cent on cost; plant and machinery, 10 per cent on cost; and motor vehicles, 20 per cent on cost. The only changes in fixed assets during the year were an extension to the factory which cost £8000 and the purchase of a car for the chairman which cost £9000. Depreciation is to be provided in full in the year of purchase of the asset.

(c) The provision for bad debts is to be increased to 5 per cent of gross debtors at the year end.

(d) A provision of 4 per cent of the value of stocks and work in progress at the year end is to be made to provide for slow-moving and damaged stocks.

(e) Provision is to be made for the audit fee of £1300 and expenses of £80.

(f) Administrative expenses include bank overdraft interest of £2079 and the cost of hire of delivery vans of £1500.

(g) A provision of £21 173 is to be made for corporation tax at 52 per cent based upon the profits for the year. This will be payable on 1 January next year.

(h) The half-year preference dividend to 31 March and a dividend of 11.5 pence per ordinary share are to be provided in the accounts.

(i) The authorized preference share capital is £20 000 in shares of £1 each.

(j) The authorized ordinary share capital is £150 000 in shares of £1 each. All shares in issue are fully paid.

(k) Assume that the standard rate of income tax is 34 per cent.

You are required, within the limits of the information given above, to prepare a profit and loss account and balance sheet in a form suitable for presentation to members and which comply with the Companies Acts 1948 and 1967.

3. Sampler Ltd, which manufactures electronic circuits, makes up its accounts to 30 June in each year. The following trial balance was extracted from the company's books as on 30 June this year.

	£	£
Share capital, authorized and issued:		
100 000 7 per cent preference shares of £1 each, fully paid		100 000
400 000 ordinary shares of £1 each, 50 pence paid		200 000
Share premium account		25 000
Freehold land and buildings, at cost	223 000	
Plant and machinery at cost, including additions during the year, £16 000	146 000	
Provision for depreciation on plant and machinery		103 200
Investments, at cost	43 500	
Corporation tax, due 1 January next year		20 000
8 per cent unsecured loan stock, 1995/99		150 000
Stock in hand as on 30 June (at cost £80 000; at net realizable value £24 000)	104 000	
Profit and loss account balance as on 30 June last year		24 755
Trading profit for year ended 30 June this year		85 480
Unsecured loan stock interest (gross) to 30 June this year	12 000	
Work in progress (at works cost) as on 30 June	150 000	
Bank overdraft (secured on freehold property)		44 160
Income received from investments		
Quoted		2 500
Unquoted		3 500
Dividend on preference shares for half year, paid 31 December last year	3 500	
Debtors and prepayments	97 655	
Trade creditors and expenses accrued		21 060
	£779 655	£779 655

You are also given the following relevant information:

(a) The investments consist of:

(i) 17 000 £1 ordinary shares in Simon Ltd, an unquoted company incorporated in England, which has an issued share capital of 70 000 £1 fully paid ordinary shares. The shares cost £27 000 and are valued by the directors at £48 000;

(ii) 12 000 50p. fully paid ordinary shares in a quoted company, which has an issued share capital of £6 million. On 30 June the stock exchange closing price for the shares was 220p. – 230p.

It is estimated that if the investments were realized at the directors' and market values respectively, taxation amounting to £9000 would become payable.

(b) Trading profit for the year ended 30 June is stated after cha.. ing:

	£	£
Depreciation		33 200
Audit fee		950
Provision for doubtful debts		700
Bank interest		1 460
Directors' salaries		
Chairman	5000	
Managing Director	8000	
Sales Director	5300	
Pension to former director	1500	19 800

Sales for the year totalled £1 560 000.

(c) A contract has been entered into for capital expenditure amounting to £38 740.

(d) Corporation tax, £20 000 represents the provision made on 30 June last year. The liability has now been agreed at £28 104. Corporation tax based on profits for the year ended 30 June is estimated at £27 000.

(e) Provision is to be made for directors' fees, £2500 to each of the directors.

(f) The directors recommend the payment of the half-year's preference dividend and an ordinary dividend of 10 per cent.

Prepare the company's accounts for the year ended 30 June, complying with the requirements of the Companies Acts 1948 and 1967.

Corresponding figures are not required, and the information given may be taken as all that is necessary to satisfy the requirements of the Companies Acts.

4. Golf Ltd manufactures sports equipment. The following is the trial balance at 31 December:

	£	£
Sales		945 300
Cost of sales	595 299	
Administrative expenses	256 432	
Debtors/creditors	156 444	123 674
Provision for bad debts		7 500
Directors' remuneration	30 500	
Audit fee	1 000	
Debenture interest	2 500	
Half-year preference dividend paid on 30 June	650	
ACT paid on 30 June (re above)	350	
Freehold land and buildings at cost	200 000	
Plant and machinery at cost	45 000	
Provision for depreciation on plant and machinery at 1 January		20 000
Motor vehicles at cost	18 000	
Provision for depreciation on motor vehicles at 1 January		8 000
Stock in trade and work in progress at 31 December	94 176	
Trade investment at cost in Swing Ltd	24 000	
Bank overdraft		118 176
Profit and loss account balance at 1 January		21 701
General reserve		10 000
Ordinary share capital		100 000
Preference share capital		20 000
10 per cent debentures (1990/93)		50 000
	£1 424 351	£1 424 351

The following information is also related to the accounts for the year to 31 December.
(a) The bad debt provision is to be increased to an amount which is equal to 1 per cent of the turnover for the year.
(b) The directors' remuneration is divided among the four directors of the company as follows:

	£
Mr Andrews, Chairman	8 000
Mr Turnberry, Managing Director	10 000
Mr Wentworth, Finance Director	6 500
Mr Stoylake, Sales Director	6 000
	£30 500

In addition provision must be made for directors' fees of £1000 to each of the above directors.
(c) Depreciation is to be provided for the year as follows: plant and machinery, 10 per cent on cost; and motor vehicles, 25 per cent on written-down value. The only change in fixed assets during the year was an addition to plant and machinery in early January, costing £10 000.
(d) A provision of £20 000 is to be made for corporation tax at 52 per cent, based upon the profits for the year. This will be payable on 30 September next year.
(e) The half-year preference dividend to 31 December and a dividend of 13 per cent on the ordinary share capital are to be provided in the accounts.
(f) The sum of £5000 is to be transferred to general reserve.
(g) The authorized preference share capital is £20 000 in £1 shares.
(h) The authorized ordinary share capital is £200 000 in 50p. shares. All shares in issue are fully paid.
(i) Assume the standard rate of income tax to be 35 per cent.
(j) Administrative expenses include £1748 interest on the overdraft.
(k) The directors consider the value of the trade investment to be £5000.

Within the limits of the given information, prepare the accounts of Golf Ltd in a form suitable for presentation to the members and which complies with the Companies Acts 1948 and 1967.

PART THREE | Some Aspects of Accounting Theory

14 | The Recognition of Revenue

Our discussion of the measurement of income covered the accruals principle, by which the costs of a product are matched against the revenue from its sale. A development of the accruals principle is that revenue for one accounting year brought into the income statement is not necessarily the total of the cash received in that year, since some payments may have been made for goods sold in a previous year, while other payments may concern goods not yet delivered. Care must be taken, therefore, to differentiate between cash received during a period and that part of the cash which can be counted as revenue. A further step in the measurement of income is to define the point in a transaction at which profit can be taken. A good accountant is conservative and will not wish to show a profit in his income statement for a period unless he is certain that that profit has been made, and that circumstances which may transpire in a later period will not reduce that profit. For this reason there is a well defined rule about when revenue can be recognized as available for crediting to the income statement and, like most general rules, it has a number of exceptions.

The earning of revenue is a gradual process, sometimes termed a cycle. A manufacturer will change raw materials into finished goods during the production process, then transport, store and sell them. At this point an asset, stock, is exchanged for another asset, debt, the difference between the values of the two being the profit. The debt is eventually collected and thus the asset, stock, is translated into cash. The recognition of revenue concerns the definition of the point in the cycle at which profit will be recognized and considered, for accounting purposes, to have been made. Only when a profit is safely made can it be distributed in the form of a dividend. Profit is the reward for enterprise or risk-taking. Some accountants hold that the point in the cycle when the most critical decision has been made or the most difficult task completed is the point at which profit can be recognized, and this is usually taken to be the time of sale. At this point profit has been earned, since the revenue-earning activity is complete, and the profit can be measured objectively since it has undergone the test of the market. Even though the price may not yet have been collected from the customer the basic transaction is complete, and any doubt about the eventual payment of the price can be dealt with in the accounts by a provision for doubtful debts.

The certainty theory holds that revenue can be recognized at the point beyond which there is no further uncertainty about the completion of the transaction, while the completed contract theory holds that revenue can be recognized only when the transaction is complete. A new idea, that of the critical event concept, holds that for every transaction there is a critical event in the cycle which acts as a decision point for the recognition of revenue from the transaction.

The basic conditions for the recognition of revenue can be summarized as follows.

1. Has the revenue been earned, i.e. has the value generated by the transaction been added to the assets of the business?
2. Can that revenue be measured objectively, i.e. has it undergone the test of the market or of an 'arm's length transaction'?
3. Has the critical event taken place?

For most transactions these three conditions can be said to exist at the point when the sale is made, and this is the general rule which accountants follow when recognizing revenue. In England the law is quite precise about the moment at which the property in the goods passes from seller to buyer and a sale can be said to be made. It is a matter between the buyer and the seller when they intend the property to pass. For specific goods, i.e. the goods identified by the buyer and the seller as those concerned in the transaction, the buyer is bound to take delivery when the seller sends the goods to his place of business. Thus delivery is not the critical event, but rather the agreement between the buyer and the seller for the transaction to take place. However, with 'unascertained' goods (goods not identified when the contract was made) property passes when the goods of that description are unconditionally appropriated to the contract by the seller with the assent of the buyer. Delivery instructions from the buyer are construed as assent to such an appropriation. Thus, when a warehouseman separates a specified lot from the bulk in his warehouse and instructs the carrier to load, on receipt of delivery instructions, the critical event has taken place, since the goods will not be returned unless they are not of merchantable quality. It is, however, normal commercial practice to confirm receipt of an order in writing.

EXCEPTIONS TO THE RULE

The first exception to the general rule concerns long-term contracts. In the building and civil engineering industries it could take five years or more to complete a job for a client. It is wrong to take all the profit on a five-year job at the end of the five-year period, since if in any one accounting year no jobs are completed then no profit will be shown that year, but in another year, when more than one job is completed, profits will be high. Thus fluctuations in profit will occur unless the profit is spread over the years of the contract. The price for the work is usually determined in advance, so once part of the contract is completed it is possible to take profit on that part. The quantity surveyors in the building industry will decide with the architects how much of the contract is completed, and the management will be given technical advice about what could go wrong on the contract before it is finalized, so that an estimate of profit to date can be made. Sometimes it is possible to take a percentage of the final expected profit based on the percentage of the job completed to date. Such methods are uncertain, so conservatism is important when profit is measured in this way. However, the value is added, the revenue is objectively measured, and if acceptance by the architect is considered to be the critical event, then the profit on work to date covered by an architect's certificate can be recognized.

SSAP 9, referring to work-in-progress stocks on long-term contracts, lays down that the profit recognized, if any, should reflect the proportion of the work carried out at the accounting date and any known inequalities of profitability of various stages of the contract. If the outcome cannot be reasonably assessed before the work is completed then no profit should be taken. Conservatism should be exercised at all times and future estimated costs compared with future estimated revenues in case losses may accrue. Progress payments received to date are to be deducted from the figure for cost plus profit allocation to date. The profit computation would include costs to date plus future estimated costs to completion, including estimates of future rectification costs and work under any guarantee scheme, and amounts to provide for any penalties which might arise out of the contract. Once the total cost has been estimated, having taken into consideration likely increases in wages, materials and overheads, the amount can be set against the sales value of the contract to show what profit is likely to be made, and an appropriate proportion of this figure, less any profit already taken in previous years, can be taken to the credit of the profit and loss account.

A second exception to the general rule concerns accretion, where the value of work in progress increases gradually through natural growth or an ageing process. Examples of this are timber, which gradually increases in value as it grows year by year, animals, for the same reason, and commodities such as brandy or whisky which mature over a long period. It is possible to value the stocks of such items at the beginning and end of an accounting period and to gauge the increase in value achieved during the year. This increase is an income even though it has not arisen from transactions, and has yet to be realized. Such an income cannot be made available for distribution, but this does not mean that it cannot be recognized, if realization and the realization price can be estimated with certainty and provision can be made for costs yet to be incurred. A prudent accountant might show such a profit as a note to his accounts rather than credit it to the income statement. If the stocks are shown at their current value in the balance sheet the increase in the value of this asset during the accounting period could be balanced by the creation of a reserve not available for distribution as part of the equity interest.

A third exception to the general rule concerns sales made on instalment or hire purchase terms. The sale is made at one point in time and the customer is obligated to pay for the goods over a period. Revenue could be recognized at the time of sale, but since customers are sometimes poor credit risks it is more conservative to spread the profit over the period of the instalments. In practice this is usually accomplished by the use of percentages, i.e. when 70 per cent of the total price has been paid, then 70 per cent of the profit to be made from the transaction can be credited to the profit and loss account. Goods on hire purchase should not be confused with goods on a 'sale or return' basis. In this case the goods might be consigned by a wholesaler to a retailer but revenue cannot be recognized at this point since, if the retailer is unable to sell the goods, he will return them to the wholesaler and owe nothing. Transactions of this nature are merely the movement of the wholesaler's stock from his warehouse to another place. The stock still belongs to him and property in it passes only when the retailer makes a sale to a customer.

A fourth exception to the general rule is that in some cases revenue is recognized only when cash is received from a sale. This is an extension of the third exception, but occurs in slightly different conditions. If the customer has a poor credit rating, or if circumstances outside the control of the parties to the transaction can interfere with the payment of the price, the critical event for the transaction must be considered to be collection of the price. In this case it is conservative not to recognize the revenue until the price is paid.

A fifth exception to this rule concerns interest on a loan. If a loan contract is arranged between borrower and lender, it could be argued that the interest payable on the loan is earned once the contract is signed, and the full amount could be taken to the credit of the profit and loss account at once. It is, however, a much more prudent practice to spread the interest over the period of the loan. A similar argument is expressed for the treatment of profit on a leasing transaction, but once again income is spread, by one means or another, over the period of the lease.

In some transactions payment is made before delivery of the goods, but this is no case for the recognition of revenue, since a successful delivery, and in some cases production of the goods, must take place before the transaction is completed. In this case it is not payment, but delivery, which is critical. An example of this case is subscriptions to a monthly magazine. Such subscriptions are usually purchased a year in advance and then the magazine is printed and delivered monthly throughout the period of the subscription. If production costs are certain then there is a temptation to recognize revenue at the time of sale rather than at the time of delivery, but this is not conservative practice. Some accountants try to make out a special case for the recognition of revenue at the completion of the production process. They argue that at this point the costs are no longer uncertain, since they have been incurred, and if the product is covered by a contract for its sale, or is to be sold in a market where the price is fixed, then uncertainty is removed and revenue can be recognized before the point of sale. This exception to the general rule concerns only products which conform to the above conditions, and examples of these are difficult to find. American textbooks give as an example the production and refining of gold, where the market is certain and the price is fixed by the Government.

TUTORIAL DISCUSSION TOPICS

14.1. Discuss the basic conditions for the recognition of revenue.

14.2. Explain the differences between the certainty theory, the completion of transaction theory and the critical event concept.

14.3. What is an 'arm's length' transaction? Give examples of transactions which are, and are not, in this category.

14.4. What are the exceptions to the general rule for the recognition of revenue?

14.5. How would you determine the amount of profit to be taken in any one year on a five-year civil engineering contract?

15 | A Critical Appraisal of Accounting Principles and Statements

CONCEPTS IN THE REAL WORLD

There is still much mystery attached to accounting, almost to the extent that its practitioners behave somewhat as though it were a medieval guild from which intruders must be excluded.

In accounting, despite recognition of the fact that accounting statements should be easily assimilated and understood by those for whom they are prepared, there remains a great deal which is not properly explained, and a tendency for the accountant to use his own jargon to confuse those who are attempting to argue with him.

The misuse of the accounting or tax terms in this way has done much to create a reputation for accountants in some parts of industry as being obstructive, over-cautious and entirely involved in their own subject. Gradually, however, this view of the accountant is being dispelled as accountants do their best to translate their subject for those who use it, and merge themselves more with the management team in industrial concerns.

Accounting concepts are criticized as being merely matters of convention, relying on their acceptance by practitioners, and as such cannot support a coherent theory of accounting. The historic cost principle is the one which is most criticized today. The balance sheet shows the original cost paid for an asset and its allocation to the various accounting periods, but the layman, seeing the figures in the balance sheet, attributes value to them and concludes that the unexpired portion of the capital cost is in fact the current worth of the asset shown. It is hard to convince him that the balance sheet is not a statement of value and that if it were a certain degree of bias and uncertainty would be inevitable because of the methods by which such figures would be produced. The impact of inflation on accounting statements has all but sunk the cost principle. The unreality of using historic figures which mean different amounts in real terms at current prices is now apparent to accountants and the users of accounting statements, but inflation-adjusted accounts are still only a supplement to the historic cost statements.

The realization postulate, under which an increase in value is not recognized until realized, can cause distortion in accounting statements. Thus only when stock is sold can the difference between the price and the cost be taken as profit. If a fixed asset shows a permanent increase in value over and above its cost, it would seem short-sighted to continue to show the owners of the business what it cost rather than what it is now worth. For this reason a company will have its property revalued from time to time by an expert.

If the increase is deemed to be permanent and the estimate is a conservative one, then the asset can be written up to current value. The surplus has not been realized and so it cannot be distributed, but the increase in value can be recognized and shown on both sides of the balance sheet, on the liability side as a reserve not available for distribution, but part of the equity interest in the business.

The going concern postulate has been criticized as being more a matter of common sense than a postulate, in that if fixed assets are held for future production and not for resale it seems obvious that they should be accounted for as though the company is going to continue using them, rather than at their second-hand market price. This means, however, that the charge for using the asset during the year is a proportion of the historic cost and not the fall in value or loss to the company experienced as a result of holding that asset during the year. One question which still has to be answered is how to decide whether a company is a going concern. Opinion may differ on this point. If it can be established that the market for the firm's product is steady, that there is sufficient working capital to prevent liquidity problems, that the company is able to compete with its rivals, to attract sufficient labour, and to replace equipment when necessary, then it is true and fair to assume that it is a going concern which will survive through the next accounting period.

The matching or accruals principle is often misunderstood by non-accountants who seek to equate net cash income with profit. Expense is not always matched with revenue when, for example, development costs or advertising expenditure are written off before the benefits derived from them are received in full, or when the fall in value over a period of time of a fixed asset differs from the amount written off the asset in the form of depreciation. Prudence and caution are often mistaken for pessimism or a lack of dynamism in these circumstances.

Accountants themselves cannot agree about the principles to be followed. There is no complete set of accounting principles to cover every eventuality, and there is no international agreement about the areas which should be covered by accounting principles and what those principles should be. In the United Kingdom, the Accounting Standards Steering Committee has produced exposure documents which have become standards, but the committee is often defied by companies which do not wish to follow these standards in the accounts that they prepare for their shareholders.

The multiplicity of practice among accountants in the EEC and the contrasts between American and European practice are evidence of the wide differences that still confront accountants. Even within the United Kingdom there are often different applications of accounting principles. The assumptions behind the valuation of stock, the treatment of research and development expenses, the inclusion or exclusion of goodwill in the balance sheet, and the various methods of depreciation are all matters about which accountants may not agree. Many of these differences are matters of opinion or judgement of each situation, but they can still lead to considerable differences in the figures entered in the accounting statements. The opinion of one accountant about the amount to be provided for bad and doubtful debts will not necessarily be the same as that of another accountant reviewing the same debtor balances.

Probably the concept which causes more differences of opinion than any other is the concept of materiality. For example, one accountant may consider that an alteration required by another (perhaps the auditor) is not material to the overall view shown by the accounting statements and should therefore be ignored. Recently an accountant commenting on a loss of £5 million made by a subsidiary of a group excused the fact that the loss had not been shown separately in the accounts by saying that it was not material to the overall view of the position of the business. Obviously size is important for materiality, but often this is used as an excuse for not presenting the facts explicitly in an accounting statement.

The scope of business is wide, and its operations are complex, so no single set of rules could cover all the situations to be found in business, and the accountant often has to treat each circumstance as best he can. The rule of consistency prevents such diversity from becoming chaos, but it is also often used as an excuse to continue to use out-dated methods and to avoid change that is perhaps overdue. The cost principle has proved inadequate in the current period of inflation. While the reports, exposure drafts and standards of accounting practice reflect a careful search for an alternative, the amount of argument and discussion suggests a rearguard action in defence of the cost principle by those who are opposed to change.

As has already been stated, the limitation of accounting principles is that they cannot show a complete and accurate picture of the complexities of business within the accounting statements. Reporting in monetary terms is necessary, but the statement cannot show the impact of matters which cannot be quantified in monetary terms. Estimates of the future have to be built into the statements, but since they are subject to human error it is sometimes deemed more accurate to exclude them. Accountants are aware of these limitations, but non-accountants may not realize their impact. To overcome this problem accountants produce, along with accounting statements, a number of notes explaining the accounting policies followed when the accounts were computed. Also published with the accounting statements is a chairman's report which deals with items not quantified in the accounts. Naturally a chairman reporting to his shareholders will try to use his report to show the business in the best possible light, and while the Companies Acts give strict legal control over what the chairman's report should cover, this report is often used to promote good public relations.

Even when accounting statements have been certified by an auditor as showing a true and fair view, they still have their limitations. They do not always show the reader what is required, but rather provide information which can be used to draw conclusions if the reader is skilled enough to interpret them. Investors require information about the future, but accountants steadfastly refuse to forecast, and report only what has happened. In any case an accounting statement must be read with caution, and it is important for the reader to realize its shortcomings.

THE BALANCE SHEET

The balance sheet has been criticized for many reasons, not least the fact that it shows up the position of the company at one point in time, and this can be very different from the position of the same company only a few days earlier or later than the balance sheet date. Some accountants see the balance sheet as a type of photograph catching the image of the business for a fleeting moment only, and are aware that some photographs are not at all representative of their subject matter. The term 'window dressing' is used to describe the action taken by a company to temporarily improve its balance sheet position at or near to the year end, with a view to showing a healthy balance sheet in the published accounts, although of course there are limits to what can be done to make a poor position appear a much better one.

The balance sheet gives no information about the past or the future, it does not tell the reader how the business reached its present position, and it provides little information from which a trend can be deduced unless comparison is made with figures from previous years. The fixed assets of the business are recorded at historic cost less depreciation, leaving the unexpired portion of the capital cost. This historical record is not a statement of current worth of the assets, but many investors confuse the book value of the assets with their real or market value. The balance sheet may be consistent and drawn up along conservative lines, but it is not a realistic guide to the value of the business. Some companies revalue their assets from time to time so that their balance sheets are updated to meet the changes in the value of assets owned by the business, but such valuations are expensive and liable to personal bias on the part of the valuer, so they are not carried out annually and the asset values shown in the balance sheet soon become outdated again. Even though the terms 'owner's equity' and sometimes 'net worth' are used when a balance sheet is drawn up, it is misleading to think of the balance sheet as a means of valuation, since the value of shares in a business depends upon the financial climate in the market where they are likely to change hands, and the potential which a likely buyer sees in the business. The figure for owner's equity or shareholders' funds is an amalgam of accretions over the years when profits have been ploughed back at varying price levels.

Not all the assets of a business are shown in the balance sheet; those which cannot be quantified, such as good labour relations, know-how, or a team of hard-working executives, are ignored. Some liabilities are also excluded; for example, the rentals due in future years on a contract made by the business will be excluded since they are not outstanding at the balance sheet date, but if the business were to cease the other party to the rental contract would no doubt seek assurance that arrangements would be made for the amounts due under the contract to be paid at the proper times. In a recent case of a large group of companies in financial trouble, the liquidator who was turning the enterprise into cash to pay the creditors was presented with a demand for £30 million from a leasing company for future rentals under contract. These items were omitted from the balance sheet because they were not immediately payable, and yet that balance sheet was claimed to show a true and fair view of the current position.

Accountants often disagree about matters of accounting policy or the treatment of items in the balance sheet. They may have opposing views about the treatment of intangible assets, the valuation of freehold property, the rate for plant depreciation, the method by which stocks of raw materials or finished goods are to be valued, the valuation of unquoted investments owned by a business, or the provision for doubtful debts. When such differences occur (usually between the auditor and the firm's accountant) they undermine the general public's confidence in the veracity of the position statement.

Some of the terms used in a balance sheet can limit the value of the statement; the term 'net worth' has been dealt with above. A simple term such as capital employed has four basic definitions. It is sometimes used to describe the aggregate of share capital and reserves, being the capital employed in the business by its legal owners and separate from capital used which has been borrowed from others. A second definition is that of net capital employed, where the capital contributed by the owners is combined with the long-term loans. This definition excludes the current liabilities as part of the capital employed and therefore leaves out bank overdrafts, taxation owed and trade credit, all of which are important sources of funds. A third definition of capital employed considers the book value of all the assets under the control of management as being the capital employed by them in the business. This is known as the 'gross assets' definition of capital employed. It is, however, unreal because some of the assets are included in the balance sheet at historic cost, so their true current value is not revealed. A fourth definition of capital employed attempts to arrive at the full value of the funds used by the management in the business by taking the gross assets and valuing them at current replacement cost.

THE INCOME STATEMENT

The income statement is also often the subject of critical comment. Some authorities take the view that, while this statement shows the profit or loss that has been made, it makes no mention of the risks taken to make that profit or the potential of the business in terms of what profit could or should have been made during the period under review. The income statement summarizes the past year's trading but makes no comment about the maximization or optimization of profit. Nor does it give any forecast for the future to assist those who have to decide on future policies. The idea of the accounting year could also be considered as a limitation of the income statement, since a year is hardly a long enough period over which to make a worthwhile comment about a capital project with a life of perhaps ten or fifteen years.

The task of the income statement is one of profit measurement, not profit determination. The profit calculation is, however, affected by the accounting policies adopted and by the estimates made in its computation, so accountants using different bases could produce different profit figures for the same period for the same business. Once again the rate and method of depreciation, the basis of stock valuation, the method of absorption of overheads (whether they should be carried forward or written off during the period) and the treatment of advertising or research and development expenditure are all matters where the judgement, outlook, or view developed by the accountant can have an impact on the profit figure. In the face of such criticism of accounting methods the alternative method of computing profit advanced by the economists, that of viewing the business at two points in time and considering any increase in value over a period as the profit made, seems attractive, until the practicalities of its operation are considered.

The major weaknesses of the profit figure shown by the income statement derive from the multiplicity of measurement practices in use, an over-reliance on the stability of the monetary unit, and a failure to incorporate contemporary values into the statement. Conservatism acted in the past to prevent optimistic claims of solvency in position statements laid before creditors, but in recent times this concept, together with those of realization and objectivity, has acted to obscure the true profit. What the accountant shows as a profit in the income statement is not the full gain attributable to the period, but only that part of the gain which has been realized, and to this he adds gains from previous periods realized this year, and deducts unrealized losses which he estimates may be experienced in the future. It is difficult to support such a heterogeneous collection of items as the product of a coherent theory of income measurement, yet it is accepted by practitioners as the most useful measure of income.

In recent years a dynamic view of accounting has moved the published profit and loss account into a more central position of attention than that of the published balance sheet. There are many reasons for this change of emphasis, not least of which are the short-comings of the balance sheet, where fixed assets, long-term liabilities and share capital are shown at historic monetary values, stocks and work in progress may be valued on a number of bases, and the reserves are a combination of accretions over a number of years at varying price levels. The concept of conservatism only accentuates these shortcomings, while in the current economic climate of inflation investors will pay more attention to the profit and loss account, since this shows performance from which a price/earnings ratio can be computed. Also, profit is of course the motivating force of business, and therefore the profit and loss account can be expected to assume major importance for those who have risked their funds and are seeking a return. While the balance sheet is a 'snapshot' of the financial position at one point in time, the profit and loss account summarizes the figures for a whole period and is a better vehicle for the extrapolation of trends. If losses are made by a business they will be shown in the profit and loss account, but will not be visible on the balance sheet, since they are covered by reserves; it may even be possible to pay a dividend out of reserves rather than profits without a marked impact on the balance sheet. The profit and loss account owes its greater significance partly to the fact that the appropriation section reveals the policy of management so far as the payment of dividend and the retention of profits in the business is concerned.

These two accounting statements should really be considered as a pair rather than separately, but even when they are combined their limitations are such that many companies now find that they need to show a movement of funds statement in their published accounts to further interpret what has happened in the business during the accounting year. The market value and book value of a company are very different, so what is shown in the balance sheet is of secondary importance to investors, but if the value of a business is computed as the present value of future profits, then a statement which reveals current profits will be of some interest.

THE POSITION STATEMENT VERSUS THE INCOME STATEMENT: AN ACADEMIC VIEW

There has recently been some academic argument about whether the position statement or the income statement is the embodiment of the most fundamental elements of accounting theory. To those who use accounting statements, the income statement is probably the more important, but the argument here is not one of practicality but rather to determine which of these two statements is nearer to the theoretic base of accounting.

Some accountants see the balance sheet as merely a sheet of balances which are left in the books after the measurement of income has taken place, and for them accounting theory stems from the income statement, with the accruals or matching principle as the most important part of the entire system. They reject the economist's view of income as the increase in wealth or the owner's interest during a period, preferring to match cost against revenue in the profit and loss account to show a profit on a transactions basis. These accountants seek to divide the flow of costs by channelling some of them into a pool to be deferred and used up in a future period, while the balance of the flow is channelled into the income statement. According to this theory the balance sheet is created as a by-product of the matching process, and the assets shown therein are merely items which are not yet required as costs in the income statement. The opponents of the sheet-of-balances view hold that income is best measured as a change in value during a period, and that the accruals principle leads to nothing more than a set of estimates made in an attempt to match costs with revenue. Such estimates, they say, are value judgements, depending on individual preference and bias, and cannot be part of a consistent theory. The supporters of the accruals principle, however, reply that estimates are made only where uncertainty exists, and that the accountant's response to uncertainty is conservatism, consistency, disclosure and objectivity, and this, they argue, is a sound theoretic base for the principle. Matching seems to emerge from this argument not as a principle but as a system which is adopted because it works. Its success depends upon the ability of the accountants who operate it, so rules such as conservatism have had to be made as parameters within which the accountant is able to exercise his judgement.

A second view of the balance sheet is as a statement of static funds, showing the sources from which capital has been obtained and the ways in which that capital is used in the business to finance assets. Here the balance sheet is seen as a statement of what is owed and what is owned by the business. This view corresponds closely to the 'commander' theory, whereby the balance sheet is seen as being prepared for the chief executive of the business, showing the sources from which capital has been recruited and the ways in which that capital is employed. The accountant preparing a balance sheet as a statement of static funds is acting as a steward, explaining the current position of the business to the owners or managers. The opponents of the static funds view of the balance sheet point out that some of the items included cannot be conveniently classified as either sources or uses of funds. Some liabilities arise as a result of transactions which have nothing to do with the raising of funds; for example, when a dividend is declared but not yet paid, a liability is created, but this can hardly be viewed as a source of funds to the business. The treatment of taxation due in the balance sheet as a current liability is also used as an argument against the static funds view, since it is argued that because tax due has not yet been paid this is not a source from which there has been an inflow of funds. However, this is a difficult argument to maintain, since credit taken from taxation authorities is an important liability in most companies, and it can be argued that funds set aside to meet future taxation which are ploughed into the business up to the point when payment is made are a source of finance just as much as trade credit is. The opponents of the static funds view also turn their attention to the assets of the business and argue that when fixed assets are revalued and a reserve is created on the liabilities side of the business this cannot be said to be a source of capital. They further state that a movement of funds statement will show up the flow of funds in and out of the business during a period in a far more vivid manner than can a balance sheet as at one point in time.

A third view of the balance sheet is as a statement of financial position, showing the assets and liabilities of the business. An asset can be defined as something owned by the business from which future economic benefits or rights will be derived, while liabilities are described as obligations to convey assets or perform services at a future time. Liabilities, it is said, arise from past transactions which have to be settled at some future date. This idea of assets and liabilities goes much further than the concept of them as merely balances remaining in the books. The net assets of the business can be equated to the owner's equity, and when during a period the net assets increase, the consequent change in owner's equity is seen as the income of the business. Thus the measurement of income, it is argued, is dependent upon the measurement of the value of assets and liabilities. Transactions therefore should be analysed in terms of their effect on the assets, the liabilities and the owner's equity of the business, so the revenue account is needed only as an analysis of the sources from which income is received.

Another argument in favour of the financial position view of the balance sheet is that the items therein can be so arranged as to give information and ratios which help to interpret the financial position, for example the working capital and acid test ratios. The balance sheet as a vehicle for the interpretation of the financial position is far more important than a mere dumping ground for surplus balances remaining in the books at the year end. The critics of this view, however, argue that the financial position and static funds views of the balance sheet are very similar, and that the financial position is of more interest to creditors than managers or past investors. The counterpoint to this argument is of course that anything which has a bearing on the view taken by the creditors of a business is important for the owners and the managers, since both these groups rely heavily upon trade credit to finance the operations of the firm.

To summarize these arguments, one view is that the revenue account is a summary of one class of transactions only, that the measurement of income depends upon the measurement of assets, and that it thus follows that the concept of income is dependent upon the concept of assets and liabilities as shown in the position statement. The counter-argument is that the balance sheet is sometimes seen as a summary of stocks or residual items left after the measurement of income has taken place. This argument is supported by the belief that the value of an asset depends on the future income it can provide and that current earnings are the best guide to this future income. Thus it is argued that the concept of assets is dependent upon income, and the position statement is therefore of secondary importance to the income statement.

There are of course some very original views held by academics. One such view is that the balance sheet should be seen as a statement of resources and future commitments of the business, resources being seen as items likely to produce a future cash inflow and commitments as items likely to produce a future cash outflow. Those who hold this view of the balance sheet say that it need not balance, since at any one time the resources available to a business may be more than the future commitments made on its behalf, or indeed less than those commitments, since the term commitment implies a future use of resources and there is thus time to increase resources to meet commitments at a future date or to commit surplus resources.

THE CORPORATE REPORT

In 1975 the Accounting Standards Committee issued this consultative document in an attempt to initiate a debate on the objectives and form of published financial statements. New ideas for appendices to company accounts were suggested, including, among others, the value added statement.

The report first attempts to analyse the users of accounting statements and investigate the special needs of each group of users. The fundamental objective of accounting statements is to communicate economic measurements of, and information about, the resources and performance of an enterprise, in a form that is useful and understandable to those who need this information. To fulfil this aim statements should contain certain basic characteristics:

1. Relevance. The information provided should be what the users need, not what the accountant thinks they should have. Users of statements may develop different requirements for information as time goes by, and accountants must be ready to provide for changing requirements.
2. Understandability. Complex business affairs cannot be simplified, but accountants must balance the need to disclose against the danger of confusion arising from a detailed presentation. Perhaps what is required is a simple presentation for the less sophisticated and a more detailed statement for those who need more detailed information. To some extent statements fulfil this need by including notes to explain in depth some of the figures in the statement.
3. Reliability. The fact that an accounting statement has been verified by an independent auditor will increase the user's confidence in that statement. Audited information should be clearly segregated from unaudited information. High standards on the part of auditors will help accountants to achieve reliability. The reputation of the accounting profession is important if users are to rely on the statements accountants produce.

4. Completeness. Accounting statements should show all aspects of the enterprise.
5. Lack of bias. This means that accountants should not bias their statements towards the need of one category of user. Accounting standards are helpful in this respect.
6. Timeliness. Accounting statements should be published as soon as possible after the end of the accounting period to which they relate, to provide users with up-to-date information. This is especially important for accountants providing information for managers.
7. Comparability. Information is more meaningful if comparisons are made, so that the significance of a particular piece of information can be measured. Accountants should therefore prepare statements in a form which facilitates comparison with other enterprises and, if possible, also provide figures for comparison, e.g. those of a previous period.

The profit and loss account and the balance sheet are criticized because, although the information they provide is of great use to shareholders and creditors, it is of much less use to other users of accounting information. The profit figure is given great prominence, but it is a short-term measure of the result of one slice of the life of the business, and as such may mask the significance of the long-term view. If too much emphasis is placed on making a profit in the short run, this may obscure the long-term aim of management, which is to ensure the survival of the enterprise and maximize the value of the business in the future.

The auditors who certify that the accounting statements show the true and fair view give the impression that this is the only view, whereas, as we have already seen, the use of different bases of accounting and estimates can show a very different profit figure. The chairman of one public company was irritated when the accounts of his company were qualified by the auditors since they did not comply with SSAP 9 but adopted a more conservative view of stock valuation. He sought Counsel's opinion and received the advice that it was possible to have more than one true and fair view, and that the one he had adopted was as good as the view proposed by the auditor. Therefore, although accounting standards can help to reduce the multiplicity of practices used in the production of accounting statements, if they are applied too rigidly this can lead to public argument, which reduces the users' confidence in the figures produced by accountants.

The Corporate Report suggests that the disadvantages of accounting statements might be reduced if additional statements were produced to give a more comprehensive picture of the economic activities of the enterprise. The fact that under SSAP 10 a funds flow statement is to be appended to the published accounts of a company is an improvement, but other additional statements recommended are as follows.

Value Added Statement

The profit of an enterprise is seen as the product of the combination of capital, labour and management. Value added is the wealth created by the efforts of managers, employees and shareholders, and it provides a fund from which shareholders, employees, the state and the company, through re-investment, receive a share. This form of presentation underlines the interdependence of the elements in the enterprise which have combined to make it successful.

Example

All that is required to produce a statement of value added is to rearrange the data already available in the books.

Note the use of percentages to bring out the significance of the figures as parts of a whole and for comparison between years.

Tinpot Manufacturing Co. Ltd, Statement of Value Added

	Year to 31 December		Last Year	
	£ (000s)	%	£ (000s)	%
Turnover	217.5	100	186.8	100
Less materials and services bought outside the organization	146.9	68	131.4	70
Value added	£70.6	32	£55.4	30

Applied as follows:				
To pay employees: (wages, pensions, fringe benefits)		49.8	70.5	38.7	69.8
To pay providers of capital:				
Interest on loans	1.9		1.2	
Dividends to shareholders	2.1		1.7	
		4.0	5.7	2.9	5.2
To pay the Government:				
Corporation tax		8.3	11.8	6.5	11.7
To provide for maintenance and expansion of assets:				
Depreciation	3.9		3.2	
Retained profits	4.6		4.1	
		8.5	12.0	7.3	13.3
		£70.6	100%	£55.4	100%

Employment Report

The workforce in an enterprise is its human asset, but accountants do not show that asset on the balance sheet because it is difficult to value the asset and prove ownership rights to it. This does not prevent the provision of information about the workforce in the published accounts. An employment report would include statistics about the number of employees, labour turnover, age and sex distribution, and geographical location of the workforce. Details of hours worked, rates of pay, pension contributions by the company, and training and safety costs should all be included in such a report.

Statement of Money Exchanges with the Government

Such a statement can reveal the contribution made by a company to the activities of the state, and the help given to the Government by the company in its role as a collector of taxes. Income tax deductions collected from employees and VAT collected from customers should be shown, as well as corporation tax and local rates paid by the company. Figures for capital grants and employment subsidies received should also be shown on this statement.

Other Statements

Other statements which the Corporate Report suggests are:

1. a statement of transactions made in foreign currencies to show the impact of the enterprise on the balance of payments;
2. a statement of future prospects;
3. a statement of corporate objectives.

The last two of these three might be of interest to investors, but from the accounting point of view they would be difficult to compute objectively and to audit. If a statement of future prospects were to be made a compulsory appendix to published accounts, managers would lower their sights and try to achieve less, so that they could be certain of meeting their profit forecasts. As for corporate objectives, many firms would object to being asked to reveal their goals to rival organizations.

STANDARD ACCOUNTING PRACTICES*

The Need to Standardize

The Accounting Standards Steering Committee was established in 1969 to 'narrow the areas of difference and variety in accounting practices by publishing authoritative statements', and this they have tried to do. Accounting principles, unlike the laws of natural science, are man-made, and they rely on the fact that accountants accept each principle because they consider it to be correct and a matter of good practice. The publication of accounting standards seeks to codify some existing methods and prohibit other methods which are considered to be of doubtful validity. A cynical view is that the publication of standards was motivated by a need to improve the image and reputation of the profession after several well publicized cases in which the accounts of companies had been questioned and shown to present neither a true nor a fair view; and was also an attempt to head off moves by government authorities to impose some sort of control over the profession. A more charitable view, however, might be that the standards are an attempt to produce basic rules for accountants to follow in sensitive areas of practice where doubt and confusion are present. There is a need to standardize if those who use published accounts are to understand them properly, and to be able to compare the accounting statements of one company with those of another, and if those who produce accounting statements are to be encouraged to improve their performance. The standards

* This section quotes extensively from an article written by the author which appeared in the *Certified Accountant* of April 78 entitled 'Accounting Standards – Are We Trying Too Hard?'.

also give accountants and auditors some means of protection from those who may try to pressurize them into accepting methods of which they do not approve.

A number of criticisms are now being made, suggesting that accounting standards are not achieving their objectives. Critics point to the range of topics covered by the standards, some of which are in very contentious areas of accounting. Acceptability has always been the keynote of accounting principles, and to impose standards which are not accepted by some, and to ban methods which are seen as perfectly proper by others, would seem to have departed from this basic idea.

More Flexibility

In order for the accounts to be prepared and checked in accordance with the standards, the workload of accountants and auditors has increased, but it is questionable whether the informativeness and accuracy of the final product have improved enough to warrant the extra cost involved. If one accepts standardization as an answer to the need to convey essential financial information to a wide range of consumers, the point remains that perhaps the attempt to impose uniformity of practice on disparate operations has gone too far. Accountants offer their expertise to many different industries, and it seems foolish to suppose that what is good practice in one situation will be acceptable in another. Accounting methods should fit the circumstances of the industry or company, and when ideas which work well elsewhere are imposed by standard in places where they do not quite fit a difficult situation is bound to develop. The difficulties produced by SSAP 9 are a good example. Perhaps consistency and a statement of accounting policies, as proposed by SSAP 2, would be a preferable course of action when there is a strong objection by a company to a practice laid down by a standard.

A further criticism of the standards is that they are applied with too little flexibility by those in the auditing profession. In the past, when a set of accounts was qualified it meant that something was seriously wrong, but the impact of qualification has been eroded by its use as a sanction against companies whose accounts do not conform to standards. It has not improved the reputation of the accounting profession for auditors to be seen to be in public contention with their clients, invariably companies of high repute, over what must seem to the onlooker to be a too rigid application of an inappropriate rule. An explanatory foreword written when the Accounting Standards Committee was being set up said 'Accounting practitioners involved in the preparation of financial statements must ensure that, if the standards are not observed, significant departures are disclosed and explained in the accounts and their effect, if material, is disclosed', and a later statement contained the words 'all significant departures from accounting standards should be referred to in the audit report'. There is, however, no firm definition of the word 'significant', and in some cases rather trivial infringements have been the subject of an auditor's qualification, and hence its devaluation in the eyes of investors and others. Perhaps we should try to return to the position laid out in the Statement of Intent of 1969, which proposed that 'only departures from definitive standards which are not disclosed in the accounts should be mentioned in the auditor's report'. In spite of the standards, there are still too many unfortunate occurrences where published accounts fall short of excellence, and it is suggested by some critics that these lapses are more the result of poor auditing than poor accounting.

Statements of Standard Accounting Practice Issued

1. Accounting for the results of associated companies, January 1971, revised August 1974.
2. Disclosure of accounting policies, November 1971.
3. Earnings per share, February 1972, revised August 1974.
4. The accounting treatment of government grants, April 1974.
5. Accounting for value added tax, April 1974.
6. Extraordinary items and prior-year adjustments, May 1974, revised April 1975.
7. Accounting for changes in the purchasing powers of money, May 1974 (provisional, withdrawn January 1978).
8. The treatment of taxation under the imputation system in the accounts of companies, August 1974, revised December 1977.
9. Stocks and work in progress, May 1975.
10. Statements of source and application of funds, July 1975.
11. Accounting for deferred taxation, August 1975, withdrawn October 1978.
12. Accounting for depreciation, December 1977, amended December 1978.
13. Accounting for research and development, December 1977.
14. Group accounts, September 1978.
15. Accounting for deferred taxation, October 1978.

Exposure Drafts still Outstanding

ED 3   Accounting for mergers.

ED 16   A suggested supplement to Standard 6.

ED 21   Accounting treatment of overseas currencies.

ED 22   Post balance sheet events.

ED 23   Accounting for contingencies.

ED 24   Accounting for inflation.

TUTORIAL DISCUSSION TOPICS

15.1. What criticisms have been made of the balance sheet as a useful accounting statement? Does such criticism make out a valid case?

15.2. Some accountants see the balance sheet as simply a sheet of balances, and therefore of secondary importance to the profit and loss account. The opponents of this view seek to demolish the accruals principle to gain victory in the debate. How and why do they do this?

15.3. 'A balance sheet is mainly a historical document which does not purport to show the realizable value of the assets' (ICA N18). Comment on this statement.

15.4. What criteria are used to establish the fact that a business is a going concern?

15.5. Discuss the basic characteristics which you consider to be desirable in an accounting statement.

16 | Economic Ideas and Accounting Practices

THE ACCOUNTANT AND THE ECONOMIST

The accountant and the economist both study the workings of a business and use such terms as income, expenditure, profit, capital and value. However, from a common starting point they face in opposite directions, and from the same basic data they produce very different end products. The economist uses information produced by the accountant to attempt to answer some of the questions which his subject poses, but he usually sees the information in a different perspective. For example, an accountant will attempt to measure a profit, but to the economist profit is the motive force in the market system which guides the allocation of resources between competing purposes. Profit to an economist is not necessarily the same as profit computed by an accountant.

The accountant and the economist are closest together when the firm is discussed, but here again there are different perspectives. The accountant sees each firm as an entity and to be accounted for as such, while the economist views the firm as a small part of the whole which comprises the market. A major difference is in their views of the position statement, where the economist would prefer to see all assets of the business included and those assets shown at their current value, while the accountant records only those which are quantifiable, and records them at cost. In his financial statements the accountant shows what has happened in the past and what the current position is, while the economist is more interested in what might have occurred and how the optimum position for the business can be defined and achieved. The businessman is sometimes caught between these two opposing views, when the economist talks about the future potential and an optimum, but is unable to measure them with any accuracy, while the accountant is accurate in his measurement of past events but hesitant when asked to predict the future.

The accountant shows in the income statement and balance sheet what has actually happened. The economist, however, deals in variables, always seeking to define an outcome under differing conditions so that potential and an optimum position will emerge. Perhaps it can be said of profit that the accountant seeks to measure what the economist seeks to improve, but this is a little unjust since, as management accountants have moved more into the area of business decision-making, they have become concerned with the evaluation of future cash flows and the selection of the best alternative. The economist often assumes perfection either in the market or in knowledge of future events, so that it is conceivable to him that at one point in time the best alternative can be chosen. The accountant, however, is far more concerned with the real world and has to produce his accounting statements for firms which are working under conditions of oligopoly, imperfect competition, etc. The motives of the entrepreneur interest the economist in that he investigates whether a firm is seeking to maximize its profits or whether it is a 'satisficer' (content with less than a maximum profit). The accountant, however, is content to measure what the firm has actually achieved, and his conception of this measurement is limited by the assumption of accounting within the terms of real-life situations. He is unable, like the economist, to assume perfection and carry his analysis to its logical conclusion. Although the accountant is reluctant to comment on subjective measurements in terms of potential and optimum, he will compare the actual result with a budget or a pre-set plan and show variances which have occurred.

Incremental analysis for decision-making, where only costs which change as a result of a decision are considered significant for that decision, is another point at which accountant and economist converge. The accountant, however, will want to measure the marginal or incremental cost so that he can see the impact on total cost of a particular decision, whereas the economist sees the margin as a small increment which brings into balance a delicate economic mechanism, for example the price mechanism.

Accountants and economists also differ in their attitudes towards inflation. The economist will investigate the reasons which have caused inflation to develop and the ways in which inflationary pressure can be controlled within the economy as a whole. The accountant, on the other hand, is interested in inflation only in so far as it affects the individual business for which he is accounting, and he seeks to determine the impact which inflation will have upon his accounting statements and on the capital structure and future of the business whose accounts he is preparing.

CAPITAL, INCOME AND VALUE

The accountant and the economist certainly have different ideas about capital and income and, so far as value is concerned, the economist has many ideas and suggestions, but the accountant is unwilling to be involved with the subjective theories put forward.

Capital

To an investor capital is important as the amount of his wealth which he has committed to a certain economic project and from which he hopes an income will flow. The investor has given up control over the use of his funds and sees profit as the return for risk and use forgone. The capital has probably been created in the first place by saving, which represents consumption of income forgone in order to accumulate wealth. This is the stock and flow concept, with capital as the stock and income flowing from it. The accountant sees capital as the amount invested in an enterprise by its legal owners (share capital plus reserves saved out of profits), or lent to the firm over a long period (debentures). The shareholders' interest in the firm is of a residual nature, since they are entitled to whatever is left after all liabilities have been met. The accountant's concept of capital is derived from the assets owned by shareholders, from which it is hoped that an income will be earned, and which are recorded on the basis of the transaction undertaken to own them, i.e. historic cost or book value. Capital, then, is the book value net of liabilities of those debit balances left on the books after the income measurement exercise has taken place. It represents payments not yet matched as expenses against revenue, but left over after the profit figure is struck. All assets will eventually become expenses when they are used up by the business.

In economics, capital is considered to be the present value of future earnings derived from an asset or enterprise as a whole, so capital and income are again linked together. An economist might prefer a broader definition of capital employed, and might suggest that some assets, such as human resources, are ommitted by accountants because they cannot be quantified and recorded in the books. The accountant measures capital with reference to tangible assets whose existence, ownership and cost can be verified. To the economist capital is an expression of the potential future earning power of the enterprise, and is measured in order to derive income from the change in capital between two points in time. If the capital value of the business has increased during the year this is an income, and should be included when profit is determined.

Income

Thus the concept of income is a significant point of difference between the accountant and the economist. Accountants measure income and try to ensure that their measurements are as accurate and near to the truth as possible, but economists sometimes take the view that income is used for several purposes, and that perhaps a different method of measuring income should be applied according to the purpose for which the income measurement is required. Income is seen as a determinant of company dividend policy, since the rights of creditors would be prejudiced if a dividend was paid when losses had been made. Accounting income is a surplus derived from business activity and is measured by the use of the matching principle, when cost is set against revenue for a given time period. This is an 'ex post' measurement, since it is made from objectively recorded amounts after the event has taken place.

Economists and accountants see profits as a guide to future investment in a business, using the past to assess future prospects. The best investment, of course, is the one which leads to the greatest future benefits, and these can be discounted and measured at their present value. Thus capital investment is oriented towards the improvement of the present value of future receipts from the investments made by the company. From this premise it is only a short step for the economist to regard income as growth in the present value of future receipts, or the capital value of the business. An economist called Hicks defined income as the maximum amount an individual could consume during a period while remaining as well off at the end of the period as at the beginning. The success of this idea depends upon the definition of the term 'well off', which can mean possession of capital, or wealth. It follows, therefore, that income is the amount by which capital or net worth has increased during a period plus what has been withdrawn for consumption, less new capital that has been introduced into the business. For the economist, then, the net worth of the business is the capital value of expected future receipts, and any increase in the value of those future receipts will be a profit. This valuation-based idea is very different from the accountant's view of net assets, which is the unexpired portion of the capital cost, stemming from recorded transactions.

An economist would hold that the accountant's definition of income is of little use as a measure of business success because it ignores value changes, other than to write off depreciation and adjust stock values downward if required. Unrealized profits are ignored by accountants unless there is a certainty of their permanence, since it would not be conservative to distribute them. The accountant, however, might ask the economist how he would attempt to compute a profit figure from the concept he has developed, how far into the future receipts are to be forecast, and how accurate such a forecast should be, and would also wish to know the criterion for the selection of the discount factor on which the present value calculation is based. The Hicksian concept of income can be linked to the idea of maintaining the capital invested in the enterprise, if income is defined as the maximum amount that can be consumed in a period without a reduction in the expected level of consumption in the next period.

Value

When a value is attributed to an asset or a whole enterprise, the asset or enterprise is appraised and ranked in order of preference against other items which have greater or lesser values. These preferences are expressed in money terms, so value allows us to measure an asset against others in terms of the amount of purchasing power we must sacrifice to possess the valued item. Money shows what must be paid to exercise economic choice and to show a preference for one item over another, since money spent cannot be used to purchase alternatives which are competing for scarce resources in the market.

The accountant records as objective the value laid out to purchase an asset, i.e. historic cost, but will use current market value if it is lower than historic cost for reasons of conservatism (the lower of cost or market rule for stocks) or if a permanent increase in value above historic cost is established (a building revalued and written up in the books). Many accountants do not trust value, since it implies a subjective judgement or estimate which may be influenced by bias on the part of the valuer and may not be permanent, although it should be remembered that accountants themselves make subjective judgements when providing for doubtful debts or accrued expenses, and when fixing a rate of depreciation. Many users of balance sheets mistakenly believe that they are reading a statement which discloses the value of the business, and the use of the term 'net worth' to describe net capital employed only serves to strengthen this belief.

As we have seen, the economic or capital value of an asset is the present value of the future income stream expected to be derived from the asset. The price of the asset is the value set on it in the market place by the interaction of supply and demand. This is an exchange value for the asset whereby its worth is expressed in money, so that when that price is compared with the price of other assets its worth can be measured. The economic value computed for an asset simply reflects the expectations of the company or individual and sets the maximum price they would be willing to pay for it on the market. Therefore individuals with different expectations of the potential of an asset to produce income would value it at different amounts.

An asset may have different values according to the purpose for which the valuation is made. For example, the following are different ways of valuing an ocean-going liner.

1. Scrap value, i.e., what it is worth at break-up value. This reflects the intrinsic value of its parts less the cost of dismantling them.
2. Going concern value i.e., what it is worth to the shipping company that owns it. They

intend to operate it together with other ships in their fleet and other assets which they possess (docks, know-how etc.). This value approaches economic value, as it is the present value of the expected income stream.

3. Historic cost. This is an input value – what was spent when the asset was acquired. This value is soon outdated and does not represent earning potential.
4. Book value, i.e. the asset as recorded in the books. Usually this is historic cost less depreciation to date, the unexpired portion of the capital cost. The depreciation profile adopted by the enterprise may not reflect the real fall in value from use and/or the passing of time.
5. Net realizable value or market value. This is an exit value, since it represents what another ship-owner would be willing to pay for the liner if he intended to use it as part of his fleet. It is impractical, however, to put assets up for sale simply to value them. The market price of specialized assets with a narrow market will not be easy to establish. The difference between this value and (2) above is the difference in the expectation of future income between its present owner and the potential buyer, and the cost of the transaction. Supply and demand will affect this value.
6. Replacement value, i.e., the cost of another liner to do the same job. It will be difficult to establish a price for an exactly similar asset, and also to appraise the amount to be deducted for years of expired service since the liner is not new.
7. Opportunity cost. This is a value based on the returns expected from the asset in its next best alternative use, for example as a cruise ship rather than in passenger service. This could be the same as net realizable value.

Faced with so many different bases on which a valuation can be made, accountants hesitate to incorporate valuation in their statements, preferring to use the objective basis of recorded historic cost adjusted for conservatism.

TUTORIAL DISCUSSION TOPICS

16.1. What are the different meanings of the term 'capital'?

16.2. Discuss the relationship of income to capital from the point of view of both an economist and an accountant.

16.3. How does the Hicksian concept of income differ from the profit computed by an accountant? How far do the rules concerning depreciation and the payment of dividends only out of profit help to bridge this gap?

16.4. Accountants are loathe to use the 'value' of assets in a balance sheet. Why is this so?

16.5. How many different values can you define for the same asset, for example a large item of industrial machinery?

17 | Accounting in a Period of Rising Prices

THE IMPACT OF INFLATION ON ACCOUNTING STATEMENTS

During a period of inflation prices rise, so a fixed amount of money buys less in terms of goods and services after inflation than it could before. Thus the 'real' value of money is said to fall in an inflationary period. However, accountants still record transactions in the money terms applying at the date of the transaction, even long after the date of that transaction. This is called historic cost accounting. The historic cost convention claims to use values which have been derived from actual events, so this system has the advantage of objectivity. It is suggested that if assets and costs are accorded estimated current values rather than values recorded when accounting statements are compiled, they could become matters of opinion, where uncertainty and bias influence the figures. It is argued that conservatism in accounting supports the historic cost convention, since it is prudent to ignore increases in value of an inflationary nature, but if such actions cause an accountant to set historic costs against sales at current prices, profit will be overstated, and will certainly not have been computed on a conservative basis. Accountants in the UK would not add together assets or costs expressed in dollars, yen, marks and francs, but would take care to convert them to pounds, yet they are willing to mix pounds of 1970 with pounds of 1980, although the difference in the amounts of goods and services commanded by them is as great as the difference in the amounts of goods and services commanded by the pound and the dollar. There are four major points at which inflation can influence the accounting statements.

[handwritten: Shouldn't mix £s of 1970 with £s of 1980 — there is a difference in the amt of goods & services commanded by them.]

① Fixed Assets and Depreciation

First, as the value of money falls, fixed assets recorded at historic cost will not reflect the purchasing power of capital invested in them at current prices, and depreciation based on historic cost will fail to set aside a large enough amount out of profit to replace the investment that has been used up at current prices. Thus depreciation based on historic cost will overstate profit and can lead to the depletion of capital in the business if such profit is distributed. For example, if an asset purchased ten years ago for £1000 is depreciated at £100 per year, although at the end of its ten-year life the original £1000 invested in it will have been set aside out of profits, after ten years of inflation £1000 can command less in terms of goods and services than could the original amount. So although the capital of the business has been protected in money terms, this amount means less in real terms. Assets stated in the balance sheet at historic cost fail to show the shareholders the current value of what the company owns, and cause the capital-employed figure to be understated.

✓ *Example*

A. Mann is in the haulage industry on his own account and owns his own lorry. He started business with £5000 in cash, which he invested in the vehicle. His opening balance sheet would be:

Dr.		A. Mann	Cr.
	£		£
Capital	5000	Vehicle	5000

During his first year of trading revenue is £20 000 but he charges £10 000 for his services and pays £8000 as expenses. The vehicle has a life of five years, and no scrap value, so depreciation of £1000 per annum is provided, and a net profit of £1000 is computed. A balance sheet at the end of the first year would show:

Dr.		A. Mann	Cr.
	£		£
Capital	5000	Vehicle	5000
Undistributed		Less accumulated	
profit	1000	depreciation	1000
			4000
		Cash	2000
	£6000		£6000

At the end of five years, if no profit is distributed, the balance sheet might show:

Dr.		A. Mann	Cr.
	£		£
Capital	5 000	Vehicle	5 000
Undistributed		Less accumulated	
profit	5 000	depreciation	5 000
			Nil
		Cash	10 000
	£10 000		£10 000

The statement shows the vehicle as being fully depreciated and the funds set aside by depreciation held in the form of other assets, cash. But what if A. Mann tries to replace his fixed asset and finds that a similar vehicle now costs £8000. His balance sheet, after replacement, will be:

Dr.		A. Mann		Cr.
	£			£
Capital	5 000	Vehicle		8 000
Undistributed profit	5 000	Cash		2 000
	£10 000			£10 000

He is now in exactly the same position as when he started in business five years ago, except that he has £2000 of cash. He might question the validity of the measurement technique which shows him to have made a profit of £5000 in that period. Depreciation based on historic cost has replaced the original investment in money terms but not in real terms. If A. Mann had withdrawn his profits year by year he would not now be able to continue in business without recruiting fresh capital to help pay for the replacement vehicle. Capital depletion would have taken place.

The Cost of Sales

The second point at which the impact of inflation is felt on accounting statements concerns the measurement of profit when costs incurred in one period are set against revenue received in a later period. The revenue will be counted at higher (post inflation) prices, while the costs, for example raw materials, will be charged at low (pre-inflation) prices, and an enlarged profit will thus be disclosed. If, however, the raw material used up in the transaction is charged in the profit computation at replacement cost rather than historic cost, then both the revenue and cost side of the sum will be expressed in current price terms and the true profit will emerge. Some accountants argue that the next in first out (NIFO) assumption should be used to compute profit in an inflationary period.

Example

John Green is a trader. He buys 500 shirts at £1 each and sells them one month later for £2 each. His expenses are £200, so a profit is calculated at £300. He returns to his supplier for another batch of 500 shirts, but this time they cost £1.50 each. John Green asks himself how much better off he is now than he was a month ago. Then he had 500 shirts and no cash, and now he has 500 shirts and £50 in cash. The profit of £300 has been overstated, since it sets historic cost of sales against current selling price. A calculation using replacement cost of sales shows a truer profit during an inflation.

(Hasn't really made £300 profit if he is going to continue in b/s)

Stocks
valued at replacement cost

Historic Cost	£	£	Current Cost	£	£
Sales		1000	Sales		1000
Cost of sales	500		Cost of sales	750	
Expenses	200		Expenses	200	
		700			950
Net profit		£300	Net profit		£50

Perhaps the current cost profit is also distorted if sales during the year are set against a cost of sales calculated at an end-of-year price. The cost of sales might be more suitable if computed at the average cost ruling during the year, weighted for quantities involved.

③ Monetary Items

Third, certain items in the balance sheet, termed monetary items, such as creditors, debtors and cash, are shown in the accounting statements in current terms so that they appear to be correctly stated at a time of inflation. However, if a firm holds its assets in a monetary form, i.e. cash and debtors, during a period of inflation, when it eventually turns its monetary assets into tangible assets such as machinery or stock, prices will have risen, so it will get less for its money than if it had spent the money earlier. Thus to hold a monetary asset is to make a loss during a period of inflation. By the same token a company which obtains its funds from borrowing will gain during an inflationary period, since when it repays its creditors, overdraft, or long-term loans, the amount paid out will equal the amount borrowed, but since inflation has taken place during the period of the loan the amount paid out will mean less in terms of goods and services than it meant when the loan was made.

Example

The sole asset possessed by an investment company is an investment of £100 000 lent to a client at 10 per cent interest and repayable after one year. At the end of the year the client repays £100 000 of principal plus £10 000 interest. The investment company's balance sheet now appears as follows:

Dr.		Investment Company		Cr.
	£			£
Capital	100 000	Cash		110 000
Undistributed profit	10 000			
	£110 000			£110 000

If, for the sake of argument, inflation at 10 per cent has been experienced during the year, the cash of £110 000 can now buy exactly the same quantity of goods and services as the original capital of £100 000 could have bought a year ago. It is difficult to see how a profit has been made in these circumstances, since the company is no better off in real terms than it was at the beginning of the year. The client, however, is in a favourable position, since he has repaid (including interest) the same amount in real terms as he borrowed, and the use of the money for a year has cost him nothing.

④ Capital and Growth

The fourth point at which inflation affects accounting statements concerns the way in which conventional accounting protects the money capital of the business but fails to show how that money capital is being eroded in terms of purchasing power during a period of inflation. The original investment by the shareholders in a business is shown by the amount of the share capital, and the amount of their investment since the inception of the business is represented by ploughed-back profits or reserves in the balance sheet. If 100000 £1 shares were raised by a company in 1930 it seems wrong to show that amount as £100000 in a current balance sheet, since the quantity of goods and services which can be commanded by that amount has fallen since the capital was first raised. At the same time profits have been ploughed back into the reserves year after year since the company began. The accountant records this by adding to the reserves each year, but when he does so he adds an amount of profit computed at the price level of each year, so the figure for reserves is an amalgam of many different price levels shown as one figure, below the share capital, which is stated in a single but outdated price level. In this way the true growth of the owners' equity in the business is not shown, and the amount required to equal at current prices the shareholders' original investment is obscured.

SHOULD HISTORIC COST ACCOUNTS BE ADJUSTED?

The points made above show that there is a case for adjusting accounting statements to show the impact of inflation, and the case is strengthened as follows. Historic cost is a true view of the cost of an asset only at the time when the asset is purchased. If the historic costs of a number of assets purchased at different dates are added together, the total cannot be said to express the cost in terms of one monetary unit. Historic cost accounting will cause profits to be overstated, while the capital employed, as shown by the balance sheet, will be understated, so the use of the ratio of net profit to capital employed as a measure of managerial efficiency is impaired.

Example

A company purchases a plot of land for £5000. Three years later an adjacent plot of the same size comes up for sale and the company buys it for £10000. Two years after this a third similar plot is purchased for £15000. The balance sheet would show the historic cost of these assets as £30000, yet at the time of purchasing the third plot the market value of the three plots would be £45000 (3 × £15000). If a net profit of £4500 is made in year six, and the land is the only asset possessed by the company, the return on the capital employed recorded at historic cost would be $\dfrac{£4500}{£30000} \times \dfrac{100}{1} = 15$ per cent, but the return on the current value of the assets used would be only $\frac{\pounds 4500}{\pounds 45\,000} \times \frac{100}{1} = 10$ per cent.

If a company pays out a high proportion of its profit in dividends, and if the profit is overstated because historic costs have been set against revenue computed at current prices, then there is a danger that a dividend could be paid out of capital if the dividend exceeds the amount of the real profit made. If insufficient profit is retained in the business to maintain the purchasing power of the original capital investment, capital depletion in real terms will have taken place. It is necessary, therefore, in a time of inflation, to identify that proportion of the reserves of the business which is needed to maintain the purchasing power of the original investment, and that proportion of the reserves which represents real growth. When profits are overstated this gives a false picture to investors and employees alike, and thus the former are encouraged to expect high dividends and the latter to submit high wage demands. If the accounting statements are computed in terms of current rather than historic costs they become more realistic, and when inter-firm comparison takes place it will be possible to judge the capital structure best suited to inflationary conditions.

[handwritten margin note: Need to separate]

Thus the true position of long-term loans repaid in post-inflation pounds becomes apparent. The case against adjusting accounting statements for the effect of inflation is a weak one, and is no longer considered to hold good. Its arguments centred around the fear that such adjustments could have a depressing effect on profits, and that if investors could see the real return their funds were earning, the supply of risk capital might be inhibited. The refusal of the Inland Revenue authorities to accept for taxation purposes accounts which have been computed in other than historic terms has also long delayed implementation of this much needed reform. The main argument remaining between accountants and others on this subject concerns the methods by which the accounting statements are to be adjusted for the impact of inflation. Some suggest that assets and costs should be updated at the accounting date so that they are expressed in current purchasing-power terms, but they cannot agree how it should be done.

[handwritten margin note: But How should you adjust for the impact of inflation?]

THE REMEDIES PROPOSED

The Current Purchasing Power (CPP) system suggests that a supplementary statement should be added to the historic cost accounts to reveal the impact of inflation on the figures. This statement should be produced by converting the historical figures to current purchasing-power terms by applying an appropriate price index. A general index, the retail price index (RPI), is suggested as appropriate, since it reflects the general movement in prices of goods and services. The critics of this system argue that the impact of inflation is not general in its nature, and that it depends on what assets and costs are involved. For example if a business consumes a material whose price has not changed then it has not suffered inflation, but if the raw material it uses has increased in price at twice the rate of the RPI, then this index is of little use as a measure of the effect of inflation on that particular company. The supporters of CPP, however, claim that when the shareholders come to spend the profits, they would be able to buy less after inflation, and thus profit should be stated in CPP terms. Their opponents also criticize the RPI, saying that it is based on the family budget and has little to do with the assets or consumption of large industrial enterprises. What is required, they say, is the updating of historic cost to current terms by the application of price indices which are specific to the assets or expenses which are under review.

[handwritten margin note: Suggested – should adjust by using gen index (RPI) but not all Ps rise by same amt ∴ not all assets & costs are involved.]

[handwritten margin note: ← Also]

The production of two sets of accounting statements is complicated, and those who support current cost accounting (CCA) suggest that a CCA system should replace historic cost accounting, with one set of accounts expressed in terms of current costs. The CCA system proposes the use of specific indices and other devices for measuring current value, so that the inflation adjustment would be more closely related to the assets or costs concerned. For example, some assets may fall in value during an inflationary period, or may inflate faster than the movement of general purchasing power. The values used in accounting for the assets held by a company under CCA could be based on entry prices (replacement cost), or exit values (realizable market value), or economic value (capital value of future earnings). There are, of course, difficulties in computing these values and $\leftarrow$ combining them. For example, some machines do not have a current replacement model with which to compare them, and how would one account for expired service in the replacement cost of an old machine? The capital value of future earnings depends on a number of estimates and assumptions, and can hardly be said to be an objective measure. A workable system of detailed specific indices has yet to be provided.

Drawbacks

MONETARY ITEMS

One of the major differences between CPP and CCA is in the treatment of monetary items. The CCA system at first denied the gains and losses attributable to monetary liabilities and assets. This was unfortunate, since it obscured the fact that differences of capital structure could influence profit during an inflationary period. As a compromise a monetary adjustment was included in the Hyde guidelines, but this was only a short-term solution to the problem and in any case did not meet with universal acceptance.

It is difficult to find an index which is specific to monetary items, unless the RPI is used. A useful suggestion is that the gains or losses on monetary items should be separated from the operating profit, if only to make sure that they do not attract the attention of the Inland Revenue.

The fact remains, however, that debts and cash in a balance sheet will cause an element of loss during inflation, since when they are eventually spent on goods or services they will command less than if they had been spent at an earlier date. Companies with long- or short-term liabilities gain during an inflation, since they repay a fixed amount of money which means less in terms of purchasing power after inflation. This is an important matter for banks with deposits and loans, and for highly geared companies with a large proportion of loan capital in their capital structure.

EXPOSURE DRAFT 24

This draft is the most recent attempt by the Accounting Standards Committee to produce a workable system of accounting in an inflationary period. It favours current cost accounting, but limits the mandatory application of the system to enterprises with an annual turnover of £5 million or more, with the exception of property companies, insurance companies and investment and unit trusts. It is intended that the historic cost accounts would still be produced, accompanied by a current cost profit and loss account, a current cost balance sheet and explanatory notes.

with many provisos

Three major adjustments to the historic cost profit are proposed, to arrive at a current cost operating profit, and a fourth adjustment is then made.

1. **Depreciation adjustment**, to allow for the impact of price changes when determining the charge against revenue for that part of the fixed assets consumed in the period. The amount will be the difference between the value to the business of fixed assets used up and historic cost depreciation for the year, and will be deducted from the historic cost profit.

2. **Cost of sales adjustment**, to allow for the impact of price changes when computing the cost of stock used up in the period. The difference between the value to the business of stock consumed and the historic cost charge therefore will be deducted from the historic cost profit.

3. **Monetary working capital adjustment**, to recognize the need to maintain the real value of the monetary assets in the business. Sales made on credit terms cause the business to finance any inflationary price changes which take place in the credit period before the goods are paid for. Conversely, any purchases on credit terms reduce the working capital belonging to the firm which is tied up in stocks and debtors, so that the real value of this proportion of funds invested in current assets does not need to be maintained by the business. It is suggested that cash or overdrafts should be excluded from the monetary working capital adjustment unless the exclusion will give a misleading result.

4. **Gearing adjustment.** If liabilities, long-term and current, other than trade creditors, exceed current assets other than those in adjustments (2) and (3) above a net borrowing situation exists. The proportion of net operating assets financed by net borrowing must be determined, and this proportion applied to the total of adjustments already made. This final adjustment, it is hoped, will account for long-term and other credit used by the business, which the business need not repay at current real values, but at a fixed amount borrowed in the past. When the gearing adjustment reduces the impact on profit of the other adjustments it is recognizing the profit made on borrowed funds repaid after inflation.

Current Cost Profit and Loss Account

	£	£
Historic cost profit before interest and tax		xxxx
Less:		
Depreciation adjustment	xx	
Cost of sales adjustment	xx	
Monetary working capital adjustment	xx	
		xx
Current cost operating profit		xxx
Add gearing adjustment	xx	
Less interest	x	
		xx
Current cost profit before tax		xxx
Less taxation		xx
Current cost profit attributable to shareholders		xx
Dividend		xx
Retained for the year		£xx

The current cost balance sheet will contain:

1. fixed assets and stock at their value to the business;
2. investments in associated companies – the company's proportion of the current cost net assets of the subsidiary company;
3. other investments at directors' valuation;
4. intangible assets and goodwill at current replacement cost but if this is impracticable historic cost basis;
5. current assets other than stocks at historic cost;
6. all liabilities at historic cost;
7. capital maintenance reserves which will reflect revaluation surpluses on fixed assets, investments and stocks, and the working capital and gearing adjustments.

Examples of the four adjustments suggested to mitigate the impact of inflation on financial statements are as follows.

Cost of Sales Adjustment

The purpose of the adjustment is to revise the opening and closing stock figures to the average current cost for the year. An index, specific to the raw material in stock, is used in the adjustment. Suppose the index stood at 100 on 1 January, and at 120 on 31 December, that the average index over the year is 110, and that raw material purchases are spread evenly over the year.

	Historic Cost Data	Index	Current Cost Data
	£		£
Opening stock	700	$\times \dfrac{110}{100}$	770
Add purchases	4600		4600
	5300		5370
Less closing stock	1080	$\times \dfrac{110}{120}$	990
Cost of materials used	£4220		£4380

This adjustment would reduce profit by £160. It is an attempt to isolate the inflationary effect of setting costs at historic prices against sales at current prices.

The adjustment can be computed in a more complicated manner using the formula:

$$\left(\frac{\text{Historic cost closing stock}}{\text{Closing index number}} \times \text{Average index number} \right) - $$

$$\left(\frac{\text{Historic cost opening stock}}{\text{Opening index number}} \times \text{Average index number} \right)$$

$$\left(\frac{1080}{120} \times \frac{110}{1} \right) - \left(\frac{700}{100} \times \frac{110}{1} \right) = 990 - 770 = 220.$$

This amount is deducted from the historic cost stock increase for the period. $380 - 220 = 160$ as the adjustment.

Depreciation Adjustment

The value to the business of a fixed asset is its net current replacement cost. This amount is computed by applying relevant indices to the original historic cost of the asset and deducting therefrom a proportion for the expired life of the asset. First it is necessary to find an appropriate index, which is specific either to the industry concerned or to the assets involved, then to apply it to gross book value and then subtract the expired service proportion from the figure calculated. The adjustment is the difference between the depreciation on the revised cost and the historic depreciation for the year.

A machine was bought a year ago for £10 000 and it has a ten-year life. The appropriate index has moved from 100 to 120 during the year.

	Historic Cost Data	*Index*	*Current Cost Data*
	£		£
Cost	10 000	$\frac{120}{100}$	12 000
Depreciation	1 000	$\frac{120}{100}$	1 200
Net book value	£9 000	$\frac{120}{100}$	£10 800

This adjustment would reduce profit by £200. The increase of £2000 in the cost of the asset as stated in the current cost balance sheet would be balanced by £2000 transferred to the capital maintenance reserve, part of the equity interest on that balance sheet.

Monetary Working Capital Adjustment

This adjustment represents that part of the change in working capital which has resulted from a change in prices and eliminated changes in volume. Stocks are excluded since they are adjusted under cost of sales, and amounts owed to the Inland Revenue are excluded since they form part of the gearing adjustment.

Debtors (£1000) less creditors (£500) at start = £500 MWC.
Debtors (£1400) less creditors (£600) at end = £800 MWC.
This represents an increase of £300 on the year. The formula is:

$$\left[\frac{\text{Closing MWC}}{\text{Closing index}} \times \text{Average Index} \right] - \left[\frac{\text{Opening MWC}}{\text{Opening index}} \times \text{Average Index} \right]$$

$$= \left[\frac{800}{120} \times \frac{110}{1} \right] - \left[\frac{500}{100} \times \frac{110}{1} \right]$$

$$= 733 - 550 = 183$$

This amount is deducted from the increase for the year. 300 – 183 = £117 as the adjustment.

The total increase (£300) less the volume increase (£183) equals the increase in **MWC** caused by price changes.

The Gearing Adjustment

Net borrowings are the total of long-term liabilities, deferred taxation, hire-purchase creditors and bank overdraft less any cash balances. The gearing proportion is derived from the formula:

$$\frac{\text{Opening Net Borrowings} + \text{Closing Net Borrowings}}{(\text{Opening} + \text{Closing Net Borrowings}) + (\text{Opening} + \text{Closing Equity Interest from Current Cost Balance Sheet})} \times \frac{100}{1}$$

This proportion is applied to the amount of the first three adjustments, and the current cost profit is increased by the figure produced. The effect of this adjustment is to add back to profit the proportion of the other adjustments which has been financed by interests other than those of the shareholders.

$$\frac{8550 + 9650}{(8550 + 9650) + (24\,230 + 25\,310)} \times \frac{100}{1}$$

$$= \frac{18\,200}{18\,200 + 49\,540} \times \frac{100}{1} = 27 \text{ per cent}$$

	£
Cost of sales adjustment	220
Depreciation adjustment	200
Monetary working capital adjustment	183
Total adjustments	603
Gearing adjustment adds back 27 per cent of 603	163

HOLDING GAINS

The controversy over holding gains and losses is an extension of the argument between the specific and general index concepts. If a company holds an asset which rises in price faster than the general rise in prices, the company is said to have made a holding gain. The CCA system tries to separate the holding gain from the operating profit and calculates the holding gain as the amount by which costs have been saved because stocks were purchased at pre-inflation prices instead of at prices current when the sales took place. This element of profit has not come from operations but from stock holdings. The CPP system relates the cost of materials used to the current value of money, and shows as a profit any surplus of sales over the current purchasing power equivalent of the original cost. Thus under CPP real holding gains are included with operating profit and fictional holding gains are ignored. A fictional holding gain is the amount by which an asset must increase in price to be worth the same amount of purchasing power (not money) that it represented when it was first purchased.

Example

Fictional Ltd sells goods for £150 000 during the year. The historic cost of goods sold was

£100 000, but to replace the goods it has sold Fictional must pay £130 000. The RPI has risen by 10 per cent during the year. An income statement for Fictional Ltd could be produced on the following bases.

	Historical	*CPP*	*CCA*
	£	£	£
Sales	150 000	150 000	150 000
Cost of sales	100 000		
Adjustments for RPI		110 000	
At current cost			130 000
Profit	£50 000	£40 000	20 000
Holding gain (replacement cost minus historic cost)			30 000
			£50 000

In terms of the Hicksian concept of income, which seeks to maintain the 'well-offness' of the company before showing a profit, the CPP system is trying to maintain capital in terms of what money can buy in general, but the CCA system is trying to maintain the real value of those assets owned by the company. This distinction is sometimes expressed as the difference between real capital (what money can buy) and physical capital (the assets of a firm irrespective of their original cost). This example can be shown on a graph (figure 8).

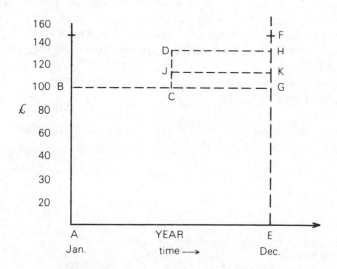

Figure 8.
Historic cost = AB
Inflationary increase in value of materials = CD
Sale price = EF
Holding gain = GH
Operating profit = HF
Historic accounting = GF

Fall in purchasing power of money as shown by:
RPI = CJ
CPP profit = KF

TUTORIAL DISCUSSION TOPICS

17.1. Why should accountants adjust historic cost accounts for the effects of inflation?

17.2. How does a cost of sales adjustment reduce the effect of inflation on profit?

17.3. Why should accounts be adjusted for the effect of inflation on monetary items?

17.4. What is a holding gain? Should accountants include it with the profit they measure?

17.5. What is the difference between a general index and a specific index? How does the use of either affect the profit adjusted for inflation?

SEMINAR EXERCISE 11

For several years Mr Grant has been employed as branch manager of a butcher's shop owned by a retail chain store. Last year he received an inheritance, and this provided him with sufficient funds to buy a shop in the main street of the town for £30 000.

At the end of his first full year of business he thought he had done moderately well, and he was therefore somewhat annoyed when his accountant sent him figures which indicated he had operated at a loss.

His accountant requested him to submit the accounts for inspection. Schedule I shows the figures which Mr Grant prepared.

Schedule I, James Grant, Statement of Profit for First Year's Trading

	£	£
Sales		53 000
Cost of goods sold		41 000
		12 000
Gross profit		
Salaries and wages	4800	
Advertising	800	
Stationery and postage	500	
Insurance on and improvements to shop (£700)	900	
Heat, light and power	300	
Depreciation of equipment	250	
Sundry expenses (including rates, £250)	800	
Income tax	1550	
Repairs to flat above shop	112	10 012
		£1 988

The accountant asked for more information concerning salaries and the rent value of the building. Mr Grant answered as follows:

'I own my own business so there is no point in my charging a salary. I drew £3000 from the business last year and paid my wife £20 per week from the till. My salary as a manager was £3200 per annum, although I don't see what relevance this figure has.

I thought I made it clear to you that I own my own shop. It would cost me £2400 a year to rent a similar building, and you can see I save a lot of money by not being forced to rent, as well as living on the premises rent free, since flats in this area cost £400 a year.'

On the basis of this information the accountant revised Mr Grant's figures and sent him the revised statement shown in Schedule II.

Schedule II. James Grant, Statement of Loss for Year

	£	£
Sales		53 000
Cost of goods sold		41 000
		12 000
Gross profit		
Salaries and wages	8000	
Advertising	800	
Stationery and postage	500	
Rent	2000	
Insurance	200	
Heat, light and power	300	
Depreciation	320	
Sundry expenses	800	12 920
Net loss		920
Add drawings in excess of salary charged		840
Capital depletion		£1 760

(a) How much profit did Mr Grant's shop earn in the year? How do you explain the difference between the profit of Schedule I and the loss of Schedule II?
(b) What, if any, accounting principles are violated in either statement?
(c) Does either statement show an 'economic' profit?
(d) Should Mr Grant continue to operate his own shop? Has he been successful?

PART FOUR

Business Units: Their Finance and Valuation

18 | Types of Business Organization

There are many ways in which a business enterprise can be organized, the main difference between the forms being the number and types of owners who join together in a business.

THE SOLE TRADER

In the case of a sole trader there is one proprietor who both owns and operates the business. He acts as manager and is responsible to himself as owner. However, although he is free of the control of others his business success is limited to what he can achieve by his own ability, and the finance of the business is limited to what he himself can raise. This form of business organization is very flexible in that business decisions can be made quickly and with a minimum of delay. Because the sole trader is responsible to himself he tends to work very hard, since the success of the business depends on his efforts and all the profits belong to him. Certain types of business where there is a high degree of skill or professional content e.g. an accountant or a dentist, are perhaps best organized in the form of a proprietor or sole trader.

THE PARTNERSHIP

The success of the business of a sole trader may be limited by his ability and by the amount of capital he can invest, but these limitations are to some extent overcome by the amalgamation of two or more sole traders into a partnership. The business can expand if more principals join it and bring capital with them, while each partner will bring a measure of expertise to the running of the business. Decisions in a partnership are no longer the responsibility of an individual, but are usually the outcome of discussion among the partners. It is necessary for partners to have absolute trust in one another, and therefore it is important to select one's partners with care. This is very important, because one partner can bind the whole of the partnership by his actions and, as in the case of a sole trader, the debts of the business can be recovered by the creditors from the private resources of the partners. The Limited Partnership Act 1907 allowed a certain class of partners, who provided capital but took no part in the management of the business, to have their liability for its debts limited to their investment.

THE COMPANY

The company is a 'body corporate' comprising persons who have united together to form a separate legal entity. A company is considered to be a legal person, separate in law from the people who own and manage it. As such it can sue or be sued in its own right. A creditor or any other person seeking to establish a legal right against a sole trader or a partnership must sue the trader or the partners as individuals. (The legal liability of a partnership is 'joint and several', which means that it is possible to sue individual partners or the group as a whole.) A person with a debt or legal right to establish against a company must sue the company, and cannot sue its members, the shareholders. It follows from this idea of legal personality that the law gives a company perpetual succession. The company itself will continue even though the composition of the group of people who own it is changed. This is a distinct advantage over partnership as a form of business organization, since a partnership is deemed to be discontinued when one or more partners join or leave the group. A shareholder in a company can sell his interest in the business, die or go bankrupt, but the company itself still continues. Since the company is a separate legal person it has a seal to signify its will. There is a divorce of management from ownership, with a board of directors elected by the members or owners to control on their behalf the day-to-day operations of the business. For certain types of contract the board will agree to bind the company, and the company secretary will affix the seal of the company to the contract, thus expressing this decision.

As a form of business organization, the company allows a large number of people to be organized to own and finance the business, while a small committee, the board, manages it on their behalf. The shareholders, or owners, have the privilege of limited liability, which means that if the company's ventures are unsuccessful the liability of the shareholder for the debts of the company is limited to the amount of his original investment plus any amount unpaid on his shares.

It has long been a cardinal principle of English law that no corporation or company can be formed without the permission of the Crown. In historical times companies which were formed required a royal charter to establish their existence. Such companies as the Hudsons Bay Company and the East India Company are examples of this type of company formation. In the nineteenth century, with the establishment of the principle of limited liability, the company form of business organization became more common, and companies began to be incorporated by Act of Parliament. Many of the early railway companies and water and electricity authorities were established by private Act of Parliament in this way. The most common form for the incorporation of companies, however, is by registration under the terms of the Companies Act 1948. A memorandum and articles of incorporation are prepared and submitted to the Registrar. Once he has approved these documents he will issue a certificate of incorporation which proves the existence of the company. The memorandum includes an objects clause which sets out what the company proposes to do. Any transaction undertaken by the company which is not within the scope of its objects will be considered as 'ultra vires', which means that it is beyond the powers of the company to undertake it. The articles of the company contain the rules under which the company is to operate, and will cover such matters as the regulations for the issue of shares, the rules concerning directors and managing directors, the proceedings and powers of the board, the rights of the members inter se (between themselves) and the extent of the company's borrowing powers.

There are three main types of company. First, there is the most common type, which is the company limited by shares. In this type, as explained above, the liability of the members for the debts of the company is limited to their investment in the company. The creditors can levy no further contribution from the shareholders to meet their claims against the business. The second type of company is that limited by guarantee. This form of organization calls for the members of the company to undertake to contribute a specified sum to the liabilities of the company if it ceases to trade and has insufficient funds to meet its creditors. They are not so much shareholders as members who have promised to pay a stated amount towards the debts of the company if required. This arrangement provides the business with a measure of security which it can offer to normal trade creditors. Guarantee companies are not a normal form of business undertaking; this type is usually restricted to non-profit-making organizations such as charities. The third type of company is the unlimited company. In this form the members or shareholders have the same liabilities as partners and cannot claim the protection of limited liability if the creditors wish to pursue their debts to the full extent of the shareholders' private fortunes. However, this form of business undertaking does give the advantages of a body corporate, of transferability of shares, and of perpetual succession.

In companies limited by shares there is yet another division. Such companies can be either private or public. A private company, as defined by Section 28 of the Companies Act 1948, is one which, by its articles, restricts the right of members to transfer their shares (usually by stipulating acceptance by the board as a condition of such a transfer), limits the number of its members to fifty, and prohibits any invitation to the public to subscribe for its shares or debentures. If these clauses appear in the articles of the company it is deemed to be a private company and has certain privileges. These privileges can be summarized as follows:

1. A private company can be formed with only two members, whereas a public company requires at least seven.
2. A private company can have only one director, whereas a public company must have two.
3. A private company need not issue a prospectus, and can commence business immediately on incorporation, whereas a public company has to obtain a trading certificate from the Registrar of Companies after fulfilling conditions laid down in Section 109 of the 1948 Act.
4. A director of a private company is not forced to retire when he reaches seventy years of age, whereas in a public company such directors must retire and be re-elected each year.
5. The directors of a private company can be appointed as a board by a single resolution, whereas in a public company directors must be appointed individually by separate resolutions.
6. A public company must have a statutory meeting and a statutory report, but these are not required by law for a private company.
7. In a private company proxy holders may speak at meetings. A proxy holder is somebody who attends the meetings of a company to represent one of its shareholders and to vote on his behalf. In a public company the proxy holder cannot speak, although he can vote.

The major differences between the company form of business organization and the partnership may be summarized as follows:

1. A company is a legal person in its own right, whereas a partnership is not a separate legal entity from its members. This gives to the member of a company the right to transfer his share in the company without the termination of the business, as would happen with a partnership. This is known as perpetual succession.
2. Shareholders in a company are protected by limited liability, whereas in a partnership each partner may be made liable for the debts of the firm to the full extent of his private fortune.
3. A limit of twenty is usually put upon the number of partners who can engage in a partnership business, but in a public company the only limit to the number of shareholders is the number of shares authorized. This means that a public company can recruit capital from a much wider market than can a partnership or a private limited company.
4. Only two people are needed to form a partnership or a private limited company, while a minimum of seven shareholders is needed to start a public company.
5. In a partnership all partners have a right to join in the management of the business and have access to the books and vouchers, but in the company form of business organization management is delegated by the shareholders to the board, and once that delegation has taken place the shareholders have only a statutory right to the information specified in the Companies Acts 1948 and 1967.
6. Since a company is incorporated by registering under the Companies Act, it must file certain information about its accounts etc. with the Registrar. A partnership, however, does not have to disclose information about itself to the public.
7. The Partnership Act of 1890 lays down the rules within which a partnership is administered, unless there is an agreement among the partners which can override the Act. The Companies Acts 1948 and 1967 lay down rules by which companies must abide, even though in some cases they might wish to vary those rules.
8. The capital of a company is authorized by the terms and conditions laid down in its memorandum. It is an administrative matter to increase the capital, but to reduce capital is a matter for the court. In a partnership, however, capital is fixed only by agreement and can be changed if the partners so wish.
9. Under the Companies Acts, a company must appoint an auditor and must maintain certain books. There is no such requirement for the audit of a partnership and nowhere in the Partnership Act is a list of statutory books laid down.
10. The profit of a partnership business is divided among the partners according to their agreed profit-sharing ratio, and can be withdrawn by them if they so wish. The profit of a company is distributed as a dividend pro rata to shareholding at a rate determined by the company in a general meeting. The board decides how much of the profit is to be paid out in dividend and recommends its decision to be adopted by the shareholders.

CO-OPERATIVE SOCIETIES

This form of enterprise occurs when groups of consumers or producers band together to form an organization to represent them in the market. A co-operative of farmers may develop in order to purchase seeds and fertilizers for the group as a whole. In the retail field a co-operative society is set up to sell goods to customers, who may or may not be members, and to pay back some part of the profit made by the co-operative to its members in the form of a dividend based on the amount of goods purchased by the member in the period. A consumers' co-operative attempts to cut out the middleman and provide supplies at a cheap rate.

A co-operative is a business enterprise, and as such will need the services of competent managers. Whereas in a company the board is elected by the shareholders, in a co-op the members elect a governing body to which managers will report, and which is responsible for overall policy decisions. Under the Industrial and Provident Societies Act 1965 each society is constituted as a corporate body with limited liability, with a maximum shareholding for each member of £1000.

BUILDING SOCIETIES

This form of enterprise brings together the saver and the borrower in the domestic property market. The object of the society is to take deposits or subscriptions to share accounts from those members who wish to use the society as a means of saving, and then to lend out the funds accumulated to other members, on the security of freehold or leasehold property.

The Building Societies Act 1962 governs the operation of this form of enterprise. Depositors and shareholders are paid a rate of interest on their funds invested in the society and can withdraw their investment at short notice, e.g. on demand, or else they can receive a slightly higher rate of interest if they agree to give three months' notice of withdrawal. Building societies are seen as a safe form of investment for the small saver who has little fear of loss, since he will be repaid at par and knows in advance what rate of interest he will receive, subject to fluctuations in the rate from time to time on the initiative of the society. The interest received by the investor is deemed to be net of tax at the standard rate. There is a limit of £20 000 on the amount invested by an individual in any one society, but a husband and wife are seen as two individuals for this purpose.

At first sight it appears a doubtful commercial practice to borrow on short-term repayment terms and lend to a householder for a twenty-year period. The societies do, however, note carefully the amount of funds flowing in to them each month from deposits and repayments from borrowers and, if withdrawals increase, they can increase the rate of interest they offer to tempt more deposits and discourage withdrawals. When this occurs the increase in the rate is passed on to the house buyers who have outstanding mortgage loans with the societies.

UNIT TRUSTS

This is another form of savings institution, established under a trust deed. Investors buy units in the trust, and the board of management invest the funds in a portfolio of securities, which are usually specified in the trust deed. A trust may invest only in certain shares, e.g. of banks and insurance companies, or the deed may specify companies in a specific area, e.g. Yorkshire, or with a particular emphasis, e.g. growth or income. The idea is that the small investor can obtain a stake in a large and prosperous business, can spread his risk across the portfolio of the trust, and can receive the benefit of the expertise of the trust managers. The 'managers' are usually a company associated with a number of trusts, to which they make a management charge for their services. This charge is passed on to the unit holders by a loading charge, applied when they buy their units, and an annual service charge. The actions of the trust managers are overseen by the trustee, usually a large corporation whose task it is to hold the investments of the trust. Some unit trusts are quoted on the stock exchange, but in others the buying and selling prices of the units are specified from time to time by the managers.

NATIONALIZED INDUSTRIES

A number of enterprises are under the control of the Government. Such undertakings usually provide important public services such as transport, electricity or water, or operate in a strategically important area of the economy, e.g. the production of steel, oil and coal. The Government controls the operation of these undertakings, through the responsibility of management to a minister of state and through him to Parliament. Each nationalized industry produces an annual report which can be debated by MPs, but it is unusual for a minister of state to face questions on the day-to-day running of a nationalized industry. A nationalized industry is expected to operate as efficiently as possible, but often there is a claim for it to be run in the national interest, which usually implies the provision of a service at less than its cost, the subsequent loss being recouped by a grant out of revenue raised from taxation. Industries under Governmental control should be free of political pressure in order to make sensible commercial decisions, e.g. British Airways may prefer to buy an American airliner rather than one built in the UK. However, in practice the effect of political manoeuvre is often obscured when their accounts are drawn up and their efficiency discussed. The Government can control a nationalized venture by setting up an authority or corporation under statute, by holding shares in a company, e.g. Cable and Wireless Ltd, or by taking a share stake in a company and vesting it in the National Enterprise Board.

TUTORIAL DISCUSSION TOPICS

18.1. What advantages accrue to the sole trader form of business organization and what further advantages can be achieved if a sole trader joins with a partner?

18.2. Discuss the different types of company that can be found in the UK.

18.3. What privileges are accorded to a private company which a public company cannot obtain?

18.4. What are the major differences between a company and a partnership?

18.5. Discuss the function of a building society.

19 | Capital Structure and Gearing

CAPITAL STRUCTURE

The funds used to finance the assets of a company can be recruited from several sources. In most companies a combination of share capital, long-term loan capital, and short-term facilities is used. It is important that a significant proportion of the finance is provided by ordinary shareholders, who are the legal owners of the business. The existence of a sizeable fund of permanent capital invested in the business will increase the confidence of other lenders, whereas overdependence on finance provided by sources other than the legal owners is seen as a sign of weakness. The authorized capital of the business is the number of shares stated in its memorandum of association which it has authority to issue to investors. The proportion of that capital which has been taken up by the public and subscribed for is termed the issued capital, and is usually in the form of ordinary or preference shares.

Ordinary Shares

An ordinary share is a fixed unit of the common fund of the company, and it gives its holder a right to a proportionate interest in the company as to a share of the profit or loss, and as to the return of his capital in the event of a winding up. When business ceases the assets are realized and the funds used to repay claims on the business. Thus the term 'equity shares' means that ordinary shareholders have a right to share pro rata to their holdings, the profits made by the business, and any surplus available on a winding up. Most ordinary shares carry with them the right to attend and vote at all meetings of the company. Thus the shareholders elect the board and the auditors, and approve or disapprove the level of dividend which is proposed by the board. They can also vote to accept or reject a take-over offer made by another company. There are, however, some ordinary shares, sometimes known as 'A' shares, which do not possess voting rights. Some companies have ordinary shares and 'A' ordinary shares in issue at the same time and it is interesting to note the low value set on the vote by the investors, which is shown by the small difference in price between the shares. Yet another class of shares is sometimes called 'founders' shares. These are issued to members of the family which built up the business before it changed from a private to a public company, or others who founded the company. Such shares usually carry enhanced voting rights such as ten votes per share, and are used as a means whereby a small group of people can maintain control over an old family business after it has expanded. Needless to say, the stock exchange disapproves of these various classes of shares with different voting rights, and encourages the issue of shares on a one vote per share basis.

In the final analysis the ordinary shareholders with their votes can approve or disapprove the board's policy. Anyone who possesses over 50 per cent of the voting shares is said to have a controlling interest in a company, while the other shareholders in this instance comprise the minority interest. It is, of course, possible to maintain control of a company by owning a share stake with less than 50 per cent of the votes if the other shares are disposed over a large number of small holdings whose owners find it difficult to join together to formulate a policy of concerted action.

The ordinary shareholder has a right to sell his shares on the market, and the company has a duty to record this transfer in its share register and issue the appropriate share certificate. The marketability of shares in a private limited company is restricted, since such shares cannot be traded on the stock exchange. Financial managers see the issue of ordinary shares as advantageous, since there is no liability to repay the investment on the part of the company, and the rate of dividend can fluctuate with profits. If losses are made the dividend on ordinary shares can be 'passed'. Investors see other advantages in holding ordinary shares, such as the possession of the right to participate in all surpluses remaining after prior right capital (preference shares) has been satisfied, and the potential capital growth from profits retained in the business to buy assets, which provides a hedge against inflation. Of course any increase in the value of ordinary shares is subject to capital gains tax when the shares are realized, but an investor with a large income would prefer to pay this rather than high marginal rates of income tax on distributed profits. The main disadvantages of issuing ordinary shares are that the creation of extra votes may change control in a company and give more investors the chance to join in the distribution of large profits.

When an issue of ordinary shares is floated on the market it is first advertised in what is called a prospectus. The terms of this document must be absolutely correct and within the rules laid down by the Council of the Stock Exchange and the Companies Acts so that the potential investor is not misled in any way. The investor will apply for shares which are to be issued, sending in his application money as he does so. The terms of the issue of a £1 share may be 25p. on application and 25p. on allotment, with one call thereafter. This means that when a potential shareholder applies for shares in the issue, he must send application money of 25p. per share for all the shares he wants. The board of the company will review the applications for their issue, and if it is oversubscribed (more applications for the shares than there are shares available) they will scale down applications by lottery or selection, selecting only those potential shareholders whom they wish to be members of the company. An investor who is not allotted shares has his application money returned with a letter of regret, while the successful subscriber is sent a letter of allotment whereupon he must pay a further 25p. on allotment of the shares. Often application and allotment money is paid when the application is made. Once share certificates have been issued to the new shareholders the company may, at its discretion, 'call up' the remainder of the capital. They send a letter to the new shareholders asking them for a further 50p. per share, so that they have all contributed £1 for every share issued to them. Sometimes if a share is popular with the investing public it is possible to issue it at a premium, i.e. a £1 share can be issued for £1.50. If 10 000 such shares are issued the ordinary share capital of the company is increased by £10 000 and a share premium of £5000 is also created. This is a reserve not available for distribution, since it is the same as the ordinarily subscribed capital. There is little which can be done with this type of reserve, except to use it to pay up new shares to be issued as a bonus or scrip issue, or to write off against it the expense of an issue or the premium on repayment of a debenture.

Bonus Shares

Bonus shares are extra shares issued to ordinary shareholders pro rata to their holdings. They do not need to be paid for since they represent reserves which are already part of the equity interest of the business. A bonus issue is a means by which the share capital of a company can be brought more into line with the value of assets owned by the company, since reserves not available for distribution can be used to 'pay up' the issue.

Example

Dr.		Balance Sheet of Bonus Ltd (before bonus issue)	Cr.
	£		£
Capital		Fixed assets	120 000
100 000 £1 ordinary shares	100 000	Current assets	80 000
Capital redemption reserve fund	20 000		
Share premium account	5 000		
Reserve arising on revaluation			
of fixed assets	5 000		
General reserve	50 000		
	180 000		
Current liabilities	20 000		
	£200 000		£200 000

A bonus issue of three new shares for every ten now held is made. The new shares are to be paid up out of reserves not available for distribution.

Dr.		Balance Sheet of Bonus Ltd (after bonus issue)	Cr.
	£		£
Capital		Fixed assets	120 000
130 000 £1 ordinary shares	130 000	Current assets	80 000
General reserve	50 000		
	180 000		
Current liabilities	20 000		
	£200 000		£200 000

The shareholders have been given nothing except what was already theirs. They will, however, benefit if the existing rate of dividend is maintained on the newly increased capital.

Preference Shares

Another class of shares, separate from ordinary shares, is preference shares. These shares are so termed since they have a preferential right to receive their dividend if profits exist, and repayment of capital before other shareholders. The exact rights of preference shareholders will be found in the articles of association of the company. The dividend on such shares is, however, limited to a fixed percentage of the face value (nominal or par value) which is stated on the share certificate. We can thus speak of 8 per cent preference shares, being shares whose owner has a right to a dividend of 8 per cent each year, but no more. If a company has issued 10 000 8 per cent preference shares, and has made a profit of only £800, then the preference shareholders will have a right to receive their dividend before any payment is made to the ordinary shareholders, who in this case will receive nothing. The same rule applies in the event of a winding up, so that the preference shareholders are repaid the face value of their shares before any money is paid to ordinary shareholders. However, the ordinary shareholders have a right to all the profits that are made after the preference dividend has been paid, and a right to divide equally among themselves the entire value of the business on a winding up after the preference shareholders have received the face value of their shares. Thus the ordinary shareholders take the greater risk, since they are the last group to receive their share of profit or their money back on a winding up, although they do have a right to all the surplus that is earned. This is why ordinary shares are often referred to as risk or venture capital. Preference shares also suffer by restriction of their voting rights. Normally they carry no right to vote at a general meeting of the company, but if an extraordinary meeting is called to discuss matters which prejudice their preferential rights, e.g. a capital reorganization scheme, then it is usual for preference shareholders to be allowed to vote.

Some companies will issue cumulative preference shares to avoid the difficulty which occurs in a year when profits are too small to pay either the preference or ordinary share dividends. In this case a normal preference shareholder will receive nothing, and will have to wait until next year for his normal fixed percentage dividend. The holder of a cumulative preference share will, in a subsequent year, receive his arrears of dividend which have accumulated in the past, before any dividend is paid on the ordinary shares. Yet another variation of the preference share is the participating preference share. A holder of such a share has a right to his fixed preference dividend, and then has a further right to participate in exceptionally high profits when they are made and divided. The terms of issue of such a share usually state that when the ordinary shares have received a dividend of, for example, 30 per cent, the participating preference shareholders will receive an extra x per cent for every further y per cent paid to the ordinary shareholders. Thus the preference shareholder is in a safer position than the ordinary shareholder because of his preferential rights but, since he takes less risk, he also receives a lower return, since the entire surplus of the business, after the preference shareholders and creditors have had their due, belongs to the ordinary shareholders. For this reason the equity interest in the business comprises the ordinary share capital and the reserves which belong to the ordinary shareholders.

Some classes of preference share are redeemable. This means that the capital sum can be repaid by the company to the shareholders. The normal rules for such a redemption state that it can be made out of profits or reserves available for distribution, or it can be financed by a fresh issue of shares. If the redemption is made out of reserves, then a capital redemption reserve fund must be established. In effect this means that part of the reserves available for dividend are transferred to a capital redemption reserve fund, which is a reserve not available for dividend. Thus if a company repays part of its share capital without raising fresh capital it must establish a reserve not available for distribution to replace the share capital repaid, so that the rights of the creditors etc. are not prejudiced in any way. In a similar way to a share premium account, the capital redemption reserve fund can be used only to pay up new shares which can be issued as a bonus or scrip issue, or to offset the effect of writing off preliminary expenses or the premium paid on the redemption of a debenture, or to write off discounts on issue of shares or debentures.

Debentures

A debenture is the written acknowledgement of a debt. When this acknowledgement is made by a company it is a contract made under seal of the company, providing for a fixed rate of interest to be paid on the sum loaned to the company and specifying terms for the repayment of the principal at the end of the period. The debenture, therefore, is a long-term loan. There is, however, some confusion about terminology. In the legal sense the term debenture is used to describe any long-term loan, whether it is secured or not, but in the financial press the term debenture is usually restricted to cover only long-term loans which are secured, while unsecured long-term loans are called loan stock. A debenture deed has a trustee whose task it is to protect the interests of the debenture holders or lenders. In normal circumstances the trustee has little to do, since the interest will be paid on the due date regularly each quarter or half-year as specified in the agreement. However, if the interest is not paid, then the trustee can act to demand its payment or, in the event of the collapse of the borrowing business, he can demand the repayment of the debenture holders' principal. If the debenture is secured, then the trustee can take charge of the security and sell it to provide funds from which the debenture holders will be paid. Often the security will be fixed on a specific asset of the company, e.g. the buildings, and it is these which will be taken over by the trustee and sold to meet the repayment. Sometimes, however, the security is of a floating nature, which means that the trustee can take control of any of the assets of the business when the need arises. The term used in this case is that the floating security 'crystallizes' on a certain asset. A naked debenture is one which has no security at all. The holder of a naked debenture will rank pari passu with the ordinary creditors of the business at the time of a winding up.

A debenture holder is not a member of a company, but a creditor thereof. As such the fixed interest is paid on this debt whether or not a profit has been made and this interest is considered a charge against, not an appropriation of, profit. This means that such interest is held by the Inland Revenue to be an expense of the business allowable as a deduction against profits for corporation tax purposes. In effect the burden of debenture interest will be borne partly by the state, since for every pound of interest paid taxable profit will be reduced and corporation tax at, say, 50 per cent in the pound will be saved. Thus it is cheaper to finance the business by means of debentures, whose holders are not members of the company, than by the issue of fixed return preference shares which do not have this tax advantage.

From the viewpoint of the investor a debenture with its priority right and certainty of interest and repayment is much less risky than preference or ordinary shares. A debenture holder can sell his holding on the market, but the price offered for a fixed return security will fluctuate with the general rate of interest. Debentures with a coupon rate of 10 per cent will be worth 10/8 of their face value when the market rate of interest stands at 8 per cent. Debenture holders do not possess voting rights, so there will be no dilution of control with the issue of debentures. The need to repay the debt eventually, and the cost of interest up to that time, may prove a burden if profits fall, and will act to reduce cash flow.

Sometimes a debenture carries with it the right to convert to an ordinary share at the option of the holder. Conversion rights state a date or dates by which the option must be exercised, and the number of ordinary shares to be acquired for each £100 worth of debentures. Usually fewer shares are offered as succeeding dates are passed. The debenture holder gains the advantage that, if he thinks the company has good growth prospects, he can switch his investment to equity, or, if he is doubtful about future results, he can stay safe with loan capital. In return for this advantage he usually receives a slightly lower rate of interest.

CAPITAL GEARING

Gearing or leverage, as the American textbooks call it, is the relationship between the fixed return capital and equity capital used to finance the operations of a business. It is sometimes expressed as a ratio whereby one sets fixed return capital against equity, or alternatively against the aggregate of fixed return and equity capital. As one would expect, there is some debate among accountants as to the precise definition of the parts of this ratio. The capital structure of the business is built up by recruiting capital from ordinary shares, preference shares and long-term loans, and gearing is the relationship between the fixed return and equity proportions of this structure. Fixed return capital is generally taken to mean preference shares, debentures and loan stock, all of which are serviced by a fixed rate of dividend or interest. Some authorities, however, argue that bank loans and overdrafts receive a fixed rate of return and should be included in the definition. There is some degree of acceptance for this idea, but much less for the suggestion that loans from trade creditors should be included, since they are of a fluctuating nature and bear no interest charge at all. Equity capital is sometimes included as the par value of ordinary shares only, while in other cases the reserves are added to this amount to change it to the equity interest in the business.

Gearing is said to be high when there is a large proportion of fixed return capital in the capital structure of a company, and low when the equity interest comprises a large proportion of the capital. The following example shows the effect on the return to equity of profit fluctuation in a highly geared situation.

Example

Capital structure	Distribution of Profit		
	Year 1	Year 2	Year 3
	£	£	£
10 000 ordinary shares	3000	5 000	Nil
10 000 5 per cent debentures	5000	5 000	5000
Profit before interest	£8000	£10 000	£5000

A profit of £8000 in year 1 is distributed between debentures and ordinary shares in the manner shown. An upward fluctuation in profit (a 25 per cent increase from £8000 to £10 000) will result in a disproportionately greater increase in the return to the ordinary shareholders. In year 1 they were paid a 30 per cent dividend, $\left(£\dfrac{3000}{10\,000} \right)$, but in year 2 a 50 per cent dividend is possible. Thus dividend has increased by 66 per cent (from 30 per cent to 50 per cent equals an increase of 20 on 30) as a result of a profit increase of only 25 per cent. This disproportionate increase in the profit available to one class of capital providers is the consequence of the highly geared capital structure whereby profit is made from the fixed return funds invested in the business, and any surplus of that profit over the interest required to service the fixed return capital can be used to increase the return on the ordinary shares. Another benefit is that debenture interest is a tax deductible expense, and the cost net of tax is much less than the coupon rate.

Thus we are led to the conclusion that if the management of a company are able to raise the gearing of the company by recruiting fresh fixed return capital, and make more in profit from the use of that capital than is needed to service it, then the surplus will increase the return available to ordinary shareholders. The equity interest is thus claimed to benefit from a highly geared situation. However, this is not always true. What if profits were to fluctuate in a downward direction? The fixed return would still need to be serviced, and if, as in year 3 of the above example, there were no surplus after interest had been paid, then the dividend would be passed. Real problems would follow if profit in one year was not sufficient to cover the fixed return, as interest must be paid whether or not a profit exists. It seems, therefore, that although the ordinary shareholder who bears the risk in the company receives all the superprofits when they are made, he will also be the first to suffer if profits fall away.

A final point with regard to raising the gearing in a company concerns the repayment of capital and the risk borne by the ordinary shareholders. When the gearing is raised by increasing fixed return capital, perhaps using the fixed assets as security, this new group from whom finance has been raised now has a prior right to interest or dividend out of profit and repayment of principal before the claims of ordinary shareholders are met. Because this group has been interposed in front of the ordinary shareholders, the risk borne by the ordinary shareholders may be said to have increased and thus the return they would expect for taking a greater risk would also need to increase.

TUTORIAL DISCUSSION TOPICS

19.1.

Balance Sheet of X Ltd

	£		£
£1 ordinary shares	40 000	Fixed assets	70 000
7 per cent £1 preference			
shares	16 000	Current assets	20 000
Reserves	24 000		
Liabilities	10 000		
	£90 000		£90 000

(a) Distinguish between the ordinary and the preference shares as regards dividend, return of capital on winding up, and voting rights.

(b) What does the expression 'cumulative' mean in connection with preference shares? Are the above preference shares cumulative?

19.2.

Balance Sheet of Y Ltd			
	£		£
Ordinary shares, par value	60 000	Fixed assets	100 000
7 per cent preference			
shares	20 000	Current assets	60 000
6 per cent debentures	24 000		
Reserves	36 000		
Liabilities	20 000		
	£160 000		£160 000

(a) Distinguish between the preference shares and the debentures as regards security of holders' investments, return on investments (certainty and treatment in accounts), and status of holders.
(b) Why is the rate of interest on the debentures lower than the dividend on the preference shares?

19.3. Ordinary share capital is sometimes referred to as the equity of a company. Why?

19.4.

Balance Sheet of Z Ltd			
	£		£
Ordinary shares, par value	60 000	Fixed assets	140 000
Share premium			
account	20 000	Current assets	60 000
Revenue reserves	100 000		
Creditors	20 000		
	£200 000		£200 000

(a) How will the share premium account have arisen, and for what purposes can it be used?
(b) If the company was to declare a dividend of $33\frac{1}{3}$ pence per share on £1 ordinary shares, how could you reply to the criticism that shareholders were getting their money back in three years?
(c) What are the arguments for capitalizing part of the reserves?

19.5. The promoters of a new company estimate that it will initially need £100 000 in long-term funds to finance its activities. The following capital structures have been suggested:

	(1)	(2)
	£	£
Ordinary shares	80 000	30 000
8 per cent cumulative		
preference shares	10 000	20 000
7 per cent debentures	5 000	50 000
6 per cent convertible loan		
stock (repayable 1980)	5 000	–
	£100 000	£100 000

(a) Discuss the advantages and disadvantages of the above alternatives.
(b) What additional information would you require in order to advise the promotors on the two alternatives suggested?

20 | Major Sources of Finance for Business

Business finance is concerned with the provision of funds for investment in business enterprise. Whatever is invested in this way must be provided by an investor, and this means that the investor must forgo consumption and save to provide the funds. Savers and the users of their funds come together in the market for finance, where the normal rules of supply and demand apply unless there is Governmental interference with interest rates. The price of money is the rate of return paid for its use. If the demand for investment funds is greater than the funds offered for investment by savers, then the rate of interest will rise until people in the economy are induced to forgo consumption and make their savings available for investment. The money market is worldwide, and is limited only by communication difficulties and problems of transferring funds from one economy to another. Within each country the money market tends to be concentrated in one place, where the important institutions of the market have their offices, e.g. in the City of London there is the Stock Exchange, the banks, and pension and life assurance companies. However, finance is also local, e.g. the banks have established a network of branches nationwide.

The mechanics of the market for finance are not as simple as, for example, a local country market for eggs or butter, where buyers and sellers meet. The market for finance involves the use of many intermediary institutions such as banks, stockbrokers, unit trusts, pension funds and life assurance companies, which are geared to accepting the savings of many individuals and channelling them to the businesses which need the funds for investment. Savers can invest their funds in a wide range of different industries and companies, and at different levels of risk. They can also choose from many types of investment, e.g. an ordinary share in or a loan to a company, or a deposit in a bank, which is lent in turn by the bank to a company in the form of an overdraft or loan. In this way the saver may not be directly connected to the business which uses his money. An important influence in the financial market is the Government, which borrows in advance of tax revenue, and sometimes in excess of tax revenue, in order to pay for its current expenditure.

A small business may be limited to the amount of money that the proprietor can invest in it. If it is to expand extra funds must be recruited from elsewhere, and the return for the use of these funds must be met out of profits. The proprietor may offer a share of the business and its profits to tempt a saver to entrust his funds to the firm, but on the other hand the saver may prefer to lend his money to a firm on the understanding that the interest is to be paid whether a profit is made or not, and that the funds can be disinvested and returned to him on a certain date. This depends perhaps on the investor's need to use the funds at a future time, or perhaps on his psychological make-up, i.e. whether he is a risk seeker or a risk averter.

The risks encountered in business can be caused by natural hazards such as drought, flood, or the death of a key employee, or calamities such as war or revolution. Other risks encountered are of an economic nature, for example a fall in demand for a product because of a change in taste or fashion, or losses as the consequence of inefficient management, bad product design, or strikes caused by poor industrial relations. The causes of some types of risk are thus outside the control of the business, while others are a direct consequence of circumstances within the business. If an investor is to take a risk there must be the chance of high reward as well as the chance of failure.

The funds needed to finance a business can be divided between fixed capital and working capital. The fixed element of the capital employed is sunk into fixed assets such as machinery and buildings, while the working capital is turned over in the short term, in a cycle from cash to stock, work in progress, finished goods, debtors and back to cash again. Some funds will be provided to finance current assets from bank overdrafts and trade creditors for goods supplied, thus reducing the amount of funds from the firm's own resources needed to finance stocks, debtors etc. The level of stocks and debtors in the business may fluctuate over time, but usually an amount below which they will not fall can be established. It is necessary, therefore, when reviewing the capital structure of a business, to compute the amount of funds which will be needed permanently in the business and thus discover the amount of funds needed during peak periods of activity only.

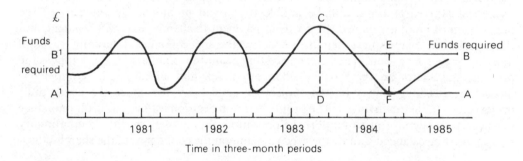

Figure 9. The fluctuations of funds required are caused by varying levels of stocks, debtors and work in progress, in what appears to be a seasonal trade. If the company grows over the period the lines A^1A and B^1B will slope upwards from left to right.

The business must determine whether to raise long-term funds up to level A^1A or B^1B. If finance is raised up to level A^1A then the amount DC will be needed as short-term funds at peak periods of activity. In the situation where short-term borrowing is more costly than long-term finance, this could be expensive. However, if long-term funds are borrowed up to level B^1B, while the expensive short-term requirement is reduced, some of the long-term finance may lie idle during periods when business activity slumps (FE). Even though they are not utilized to earn a profit, such funds will still need to be serviced by way of interest. The decision as to the form of the company's financial structure is one in which the flexibility of expensive short-term finance must be set off against the cost of servicing long-term funds during periods when they are not fully employed. Another factor which influences this decision is the ability to raise short-term funds at the precise time when they are needed.

The cost of long-term finance will vary according to when it is raised. If it is raised at a time when interest rates are high the company, once it is committed, will have to pay these rates for many years. It may therefore be preferable to borrow short term and delay a long-term commitment until rates improve.

PROFIT RETENTION AS A SOURCE OF FUNDS

A large and well established business will have access to the market of the Stock Exchange as a means of raising funds, since, as a public company, it can offer its shares to investors in general. Despite the presence of this wide market for funds, the fact remains that the most significant source of capital for British industry is ploughed-back profits, or profits retained in the business. The appropriation of profit is in three main directions: a proportion is paid to the Inland Revenue as corporation tax; a proportion is paid out to the shareholders as dividends; and the remainder is reinvested in the business. Profits retained in the business are shown in the balance sheet as reserves, and the funds they represent are invested in the general assets of the business. The board of directors decides how much of the profit available for dividend is to be paid out. This decision is important, since it involves a fine calculation of the amount needed to satisfy the shareholders and thus maintain the price of the shares, while ensuring that sufficient funds are reinvested in the business to maintain its financial health. If too little profit is retained the business may find itself starved of funds and be unable to expand or modernize while if a large proportion of profit is retained the dividend payment to shareholders will be small, and the shareholders may express their dissatisfaction through comment at the annual general meeting or by selling their shares and reinvesting in another company. If this happens the price of the shares on the Stock Exchange will fall and, although the company is financially healthy, it may be the subject of a takeover bid, since the share price undervalues the assets involved. The profit-retention decision is thus a difficult one, since the need to modernize or to support the present level of activity during an inflationary period must be balanced against the need to maintain the confidence of the shareholders.

THE LONG-TERM CAPITAL MARKET

A public company can raise fresh capital from the market by an issue of shares, debentures or loan stock. Sometimes loan stock is issued with a conversion right which allows the owner to convert his stock to ordinary shares at a future date. The decision about whether to issue shares or fixed-return securities such as debentures will be determined by the ability to provide security for the debentures, the need to retain control so that the issue of voting shares is avoided, and the impact of a new issue on the gearing of the business.

There are several methods by which a public company can issue shares, but the best known one is a *public issue by prospectus*. In this activity the company is helped by an issuing house, usually a subsidiary or department of a merchant bank, which organizes the issue. A prospectus is compiled which gives full details of the shares to be offered, the company and its prospects, and what it intends to do with the funds once they are raised.

The prospectus is accompanied by an advertisement, strictly governed by the rules of the Stock Exchange, and special bank accounts are opened for the application and allotment monies. The advertisement ends with an invitation to the public to apply for the shares, loan stock or debentures. The issuing house has given advice about the timing of the issue and the price at which the shares or fixed-return stock are to be issued. If the shares of a company are popular it will be possible to issue them at a premium, but if the market is dull or there is some doubt about the success of the issue, then debentures or loan stock (but not shares unless sanctioned by the High Court) may be issued at a discount, e.g. £97 for a £100 stock certificate. Such an issue is usually underwritten by a firm of professional underwriters who contract to take up any shares or debentures not subscribed for by the public. In this way the company is guaranteed a successful issue so far as raising its funds is concerned, but since the underwriters will try to unload the blocks of shares or stock they have taken up from an unsuccessful issue, the price of these securities could be depressed for some months. A public issue by prospectus is an expensive method to use, since underwriting, bank commission, advertising, legal and accounting fees, capital duty and issuing house expenses must be paid, and it has been estimated that as much as 6 or 7 per cent of the money raised by the issue goes to meet these costs.

Another method of raising funds which has now to some extent superseded the prospectus method is an *offer for sale*. In this case the company issues shares directly to an issuing house, which then offers them for sale to the public at a fixed price. This is also an expensive method, and is best used when the size of the issue is too small to merit a public issue by prospectus, or when a significant shareholder in the business decides to retire or sell his interest. In cases where the company requiring the finance is not well known to potential investors it will rely on the reputation of the issuing house to attract funds. The issuing houses are very particular about the shares they offer to the public, since an unsuccessful issue could harm their reputation from which their ability to act is derived. Sometimes the technique of a *rights issue* is used. In this case the shareholders of the business are circularized and told of the offer, which is made to them at what appears to be an advantageous price. They are then able to take up the offer and subscribe for the shares or sell their rights to the offer to another investor.

The technique of a '*placing*' is one which can be used in both private and public companies. The shares to be issued are placed with a number of investors by an intermediary. In the case of a large placing a merchant bank or issuing house will be used, and it will communicate with other institutions such as pension funds and insurance companies in order to place the shares with them without the expense of a public issue. A placing on a smaller scale can be undertaken by a solicitor or broker who has contacts with companies or individuals who will take up a share stake in the business if it is offered at the right price. A placing avoids the expense of going to the market and allows a smaller amount of funds to be raised than is economic for a public issue. The Stock Exchange authorities keep a close watch on placings by public companies, since these avoid the mechanism of the market. The current ceiling on such issues is £1 million.

An *offer by tender* is sometimes used as an alternative to a public issue by prospectus. In this event shares or loan stock are offered to the public with a prospectus attached, but the offer is not made at a fixed price. The investors are left to tender or offer the price at which they are willing to invest in the shares or debentures. The company states a minimum price below which shares will not be offered, but the shares are issued at what is termed the striking price, which is the lowest price offered by those tendering for the shares at which the shares on issue are all taken up. This means that if an investor offers to take up shares at a price above the striking price he will receive those shares at the striking price, but if an investor offers below the striking price he will be unsuccessful.

The mechanism of the finance market so far as the flotation of share issues is concerned is really open only to larger companies, because the costs of an issue are too great to make it economic for small issues. When the small company expands it can do so by recruiting finance from short-term sources, but a point is reached when it can expand no further from these sources, and requires an injection of long-term funds. If such a company has not grown to a size which makes it economic to come to the market, it will find it difficult to obtain finance for further expansion. Many large private companies seek to change to public status by a Stock Exchange introduction, which is effected by an offer for sale or a public placing, after the strict regulations of the Exchange have been met. A company may expand by using short-term finance, which it later replaces by a funding operation. Long-term funds are raised and used to repay the short-term finance, which is then available for use in the next stage of expansion.

THE INSTITUTIONAL INVESTORS

There seems to be a size beyond which companies cannot grow without an injection of long-term funds, but sometimes there is a gap between the size to which they can grow by the use of their own resources and the size which they need to be before they are big enough to make a public issue. To help small companies to expand across this gap or step (the MacMillan gap), other financial institutions have been developed. First there is Finance for Industry, which has taken over the Industrial and Commercial Finance Corporation. This was a body set up under the auspices of the Bank of England which made available to small companies money provided by the major banks. A subsidiary of ICFC was Technical Development Capital Ltd, which still uses funds provided by the major banks to encourage technical innovations and improvements. A similar institution is the Estate Duties Investment Trust which uses its funds, provided by insurance companies and investment trusts, to help private companies over the awkward period when the payment of capital transfer tax consequent upon the death of a major shareholder causes problems of cash shortage within the family who run the business. 'Edith', as this institution is known, acts as an investment trust to buy a share stake in such businesses to encourage them to grow, and then to sell its share stake when eventually the business is large enough to go public.

A number of other institutions have also developed to assist the small company to grow until it becomes large enough to go public. Foremost among these are the merchant banks, which are large banks in private ownership (their shares can be bought and sold on the Stock Exchange) which, as their name implies, used to be involved in the finance of foreign trade by means of bills of exchange. Over the last twenty years, however, they have changed the market in which they operate and, although the bill market is still important, they are now more involved in the provision of finance to growing businesses. Most merchant banks have an issuing house department, and some provide an underwriting service. They also provide advice and financial assistance in takeover battles on the sides of both the attacker and the defender. A merchant bank likes to make contact with a small growing company early in its existence and help it to expand by providing loan capital or by taking a stake in its shares. Sometimes a merchant bank will appoint a director to the board of the company to watch over its interests and to provide helpful financial advice. When the company has grown large enough to cross the gap and apply to the Stock Exchange for a public quotation of its shares with a view to making a public issue, the issuing house department of its merchant bank will organize the issue. Later in the life of the company, when amalgamations or takeover negotiations take place, the merchant bank gives help and advice.

A similar institution in the finance market is the investment trust, which is not a trust in the normal sense of the word, but is really a public company whose shares can be traded on the Stock Exchange. An investment trust is a company which holds the shares of other companies. Its task is to invest its funds in a portfolio of other companies, both large and small, so that it spreads its risk and makes a profit from the investment expertise of its directors.

There is often no clear line of demarcation between merchant banks and investment trusts, since both will operate what are called 'city nurseries', where a number of small but profitable private businesses are encouraged to expand and then are helped to go public.

Unit trusts are institutions within the finance market whose task it is to channel savings from their many unit holders to be invested in companies. The unit trusts, the life assurance companies, and the pension funds collect the savings of many people and convert them to investment by buying shares and debentures both privately and on the market. These institutions spread their risk and do not want to dominate any company in which they invest, but during a takeover bid the institutions, with their large block holdings of shares, are the ones whose votes are most significant in deciding whether or not the bid is successful. When a merchant bank has a block of shares to place it contacts unit trusts, assurance companies and pension funds, and is usually able to place the shares with them without much difficulty.

OTHER METHODS OF FINANCE

There are ways in which a company can finance the purchase of an asset which it needs without borrowing the money. A company may undertake a sale and lease back operation, which is a financial technique to set free some funds that are tied up in fixed assets so that they can be used elsewhere in the business. For example, suppose a company owns a large office block as its headquarters, and wishes to invest £500 000 in new plant for its factory. The company may contact a city institution or property company with a view to selling its headquarters office block to the institution, a term of the contract of sale being that the company can lease back the premises for the payment of a rent. In this way the manufacturing company can continue to use the building, while at the same time it now has the funds it needs to purchase the machinery. The property company or city institution has a good investment, since it now possesses a prime piece of property let to a reputable company at a fair rental, and it also gains any increase in value achieved by the property because of inflation or other reasons. This technique thus has advantages for both parties. If the company had mortgaged its office block it could have borrowed the required funds and retained ownership of the building, but the payment of interest and repayment of the loan may have created cash flow problems. Sale and lease back releases the full market value of the asset, whereas a mortgage only raises funds equal to a proportion of this value. The mortgage alternative does, however, mean that the company retains the ownership of the property, so any increase in value falls to the company rather than the financier.

The practice of leasing is another way in which a company can gain the use of an asset without having to pay for it. Instead of borrowing money to buy an asset it can lease or rent the asset from a leasing company. In the United Kingdom it is possible to lease a wide range of assets, from typewriters for a period of months, through vehicles for several years, to large pieces of plant for longer periods. There is usually a distinction between an operating lease for a short period and a capital or finance lease for a large item over a long period. The leasing company, which is usually a subsidiary of one of the larger banks or insurance companies, buys the asset and owns it, but the lessee company uses the asset in its business in return for paying a rental or hire charge. The accounting procedure involved in leasing means that, since the asset does not belong to the user company, it does not appear in the balance sheet. Nor does the liability to pay the rental under the lease agreement, although this is certainly a liability which exists at law. Thus the balance sheet fails to show the asset and the liability, and it is suggested that changes should be made so that the accounts of the lessee company reflect the true situation.

It is also possible for a company to enter into a hire-purchase agreement with a finance company, whereby it can pay for assets which it uses, not before it possesses them, but out of the profits created while it is using them. With hire purchase the asset eventually becomes the property of the user company, whereas with leasing the asset remains the property of the lessor, unless there is a clause in the lease whereby the lessee can purchase the asset at some time. The significance of the difference is that under the Inland Revenue rules capital allowance can be claimed by the owner of the plant, which in leasing is the lessor company and under a hire-purchase agreement is the user company.

SHORT-TERM FINANCIAL REQUIREMENTS

There are several sources of short-term capital available to companies. First, the commercial banks provide short-term funds to finance working capital items, either by loans repayable at short notice or by overdraft facilities. An overdraft is usually considered to be preferable to a loan, since interest is payable only on the overdrawn amount, whereas with a loan interest is payable on the whole amount, whether or not it is used in its entirety in the business. The rate of interest payable on such short-term facilities offered by the banks depends on the credit-worthiness of the borrower, and is also linked to the minimum lending rate of the Bank of England. In some cases commercial banks require security for such a short-term loan, and with a small business it may be that the security needed is a guarantee on the part of the proprietor to repay the loan if the business fails to do so. In this way the banks can avoid the difficulties they would encounter if, once they had lent money to a company, the owner of the company claimed protection as a shareholder under the limited liability rule.

Another important source of finance for all businesses is trade credit advanced by suppliers. This is usually governed by the terms of trade in a particular industry and by the contract between the purchaser and supplier of its goods. The amount of credit advanced to a company by its suppliers depends on their view of the company's credit-worthiness, and whether the company is an important customer. Trade credit is often viewed as being a source of interest-free funds, since apparently there is no rate of interest attached to it. This is not always true, since if a cash discount is offered by the supplier, the fact that the customer does not pay early net of the discount shows the amount he is prepared to forgo in order to extend the payment period. Although a business should try to maximize the amount of trade credit it takes from its suppliers, there is a limit at which its reputation as a good payer begins to suffer, and at which the creditors begin to emerge as a significant pressure group in the running of the business. Both bank finance and trade credit are important sources of finance for the small firm, but they can also be the reason for its sudden demise if they withdraw their financial support at a crucial moment.

Another source of short-term finance is invoice discounting or factoring. If a company makes sales to a number of customers on credit terms it will have to wait for two or even three months before its debtors pay what they owe. This means that the debtors must be financed by the company, and the idea of factoring is to pass over the finance of debtors from the selling company to a special factoring or finance company. The factoring company, after reviewing the amount of the debts and the credit-worthiness of the debtors, will pay the selling company, at the end of the month in which the sales were made, the amount it can expect to receive from the debtors (less a percentage). In this way the selling company receives its money one or two months earlier than would normally be the case. The factoring company will then collect the debts from the selling company's customers when they fall due. A company with sales of, for example, £20 000 a month can release up to £40 000 of working capital for use elsewhere in the business if it sells its debts to a factoring company. However, debt factoring has some disadvantages, such as the expense of the discount charged by the factoring company, and the procedures whereby the factor collects the debts from debtors who are not his customers. The factor may not be too courteous in the way he collects his money and therefore an element of goodwill on the part of the selling company may be lost. Factoring companies are very particular about what debts they are willing to buy, and will often accept only balances owed by the larger and more reputable customers, so the selling company may be unable to factor all its debtor balances, and will also have to bear the cost of all bad debts involved. Some companies like to hide the fact that they factor their debts in case this harms their financial standing, while others factor their debts with a company which not only undertakes collection later, but also takes on the task of recording sales and book-keeping.

Thus there is a range of facilities open to a company to raise funds in both the long and short term, and it is up to the business itself to select the source of funds which is cheapest and most convenient for it. Often, however, a decision cannot be made on this basis, since once the cheapest and most suitable source has been utilized the business still needs finance, and less suitable and more expensive methods must be used.

TUTORIAL DISCUSSION TOPICS

20.1. Why is the decision about how much profit to retain in the business an important one?

20.2. Outline the institutions which operate in the long-term capital market.

20.3. What methods are open to a company which intends to raise long-term funds on the capital market?

20.4. What facilities are available in the market to meet the short-term financial requirements of a business?

20.5. What role is played by merchant banks in the progress of a company from its early days to financial maturity?

21 | Working Capital

The working capital of a business is computed by deducting the current liabilities from the current assets at any point in time. It is sometimes expressed as a ratio of current assets to current liabilities. The current assets of a business, as shown on the balance sheet, consist of stock, valued at the lower of cost or net realizable value, debtors, less a provision for doubtful debts, short-term investments, prepayments and amounts of cash and bank deposits. The current liabilities show the sources from which short-term funds have been recruited by the business, and are trade creditors, accrued charges, short-term loans, amounts owed to the Inland Revenue, bank overdraft and any dividends which are payable in the near future. The amount owed to the Inland Revenue may consist of corporation tax to be paid within twelve months, or amounts of value added tax, or income tax deductions made from wages paid to employees, which are collected by the company and later paid over to the revenue authorities. Thus the working capital of a business shows the amount of the firm's own funds which have been used to finance the current assets, and also shows the extent to which short-term borrowings have been used for this purpose. From the viewpoint of a creditor, the existence of working capital denotes a safety margin of current assets over current liabilities, which he sees as a pool from which his short-term loan to the business can be repaid. In the past the current or working capital ratio shown above has been thought to be satisfactory if a relationship of two to one existed. This idea has now fallen into disrepute and now it is considered that the extent of a satisfactory margin of current assets over current liabilities depends upon the company concerned, the trade, and the season of the year, as well as other factors.

Working capital is often viewed by accountants as that portion of the finances of the firm which is used to 'oil the wheels of business'. The funds employed as fixed assets are directly concerned with the production of the goods which the business sells, but it is the function of working capital to facilitate that production and selling activity. For example, working capital invested in stock eases production problems, since production without stock would be difficult, and working capital invested in debtors allows the sales force of the company to support their activities by offering trade credit. Where negative working capital exists, this means that current liabilities exceed current assets, and that short-term funds are used not only to finance short-term assets, but also to finance some long-term assets. Such a situation is financially imprudent, since it will be difficult to disinvest from fixed assets if repayment is required.

The importance of adequate working capital for a business is demonstrated by the disadvantages suffered by firms which operate with insufficient working capital. Such firms are in a financial straitjacket, as their operations are hindered and their growth stunted by a lack of funds to finance extra stock and debtors. The weakness of such firms is also demonstrated by their dependence on short-term sources of funds to finance their operations, since at times of great dependence the providers of funds may begin to dictate the policy of the business and, in extreme cases, may bring profitable operations to a halt by calling a creditors meeting and appointing a liquidator. A business must always have adequate funds to finance the continuity of its operations. If it can be proved that the directors or managers authorized the company to borrow money at a time when they knew it was already insolvent, they can be charged with fraud.

DISADVANTAGES OF INSUFFICIENT WORKING CAPITAL

The disadvantages suffered by a company with insufficient working capital are as follows.

The company is unable to take advantage of new opportunities or adapt to changes. Since it does not have sufficient financial elbow-room, it is unable to finance the development of new products or the alteration to production techniques needed when new opportunities occur. A company which has used up all its overdraft facility is unable to take advantage of a cheap line of raw material when a supplier offers it.

Trade discounts are lost. A company with ample working capital is able to finance large stocks and can therefore place large orders. The bigger the order the more generous the trade discount offered by the supplier, who uses it as a method of reducing his price so that the company is induced to order from him. If a company is unable to place large orders it will find that the prices it has to pay for raw materials and components are higher than those paid by its rivals, so it is at a competitive disadvantage in the market. Large stocks also act as a cushion against the disruption of production consequent upon a 'stock out', if there are supply problems.

Cash discounts are lost. Some companies will try to persuade their debtors to pay early by offering them a cash discount off the price owed. Discounts of $2\frac{1}{2}$ per cent for cash in one month (instead of taking two or three months' credit) or even $3\frac{3}{4}$ per cent for cash within seven days are not uncommon. A discount of $2\frac{1}{2}$ per cent for payment one month early is equivalent to an annual rate of interest on the money of about 30 per cent,

i.e. $\dfrac{2\frac{1}{2}}{97\frac{1}{2}} \times 12 = 30.67$ per cent.

The advantages of being able to offer a credit line to customers are forgone. If the sales force can back up their efforts by making credit available to the customer this will give them an advantage over rival organizations whose credit facilities are less extensive. In the case of contracts for large items of heavy engineering plant where the goods offered for sale are of equal efficiency, the credit line may be the deciding factor.

Financial reputation is lost. A company with ample working capital is able to pay its bills to suppliers and other creditors in good time. Thus it achieves a reputation as being a good payer, and this will enhance the goodwill of the business. A company with a good reputation can expect co-operation from trade creditors at times of financial difficulty; for example it would be possible for a firm that is well known in the trade to negotiate with suppliers as much as two or three months' extra credit at a time when funds are short because a large item of capital equipment has been purchased. Suppliers will value their connection with a company with a good reputation and may be willing to offer advantageous prices to maintain the connection. Conversely, a company with a bad reputation can expect credit controllers in the trade to be on their guard if it attempts to exceed the credit limits they have set. At such times a credit controller may cut off supplies of raw materials to a factory, thus seriously disrupting production.

There may be concerted action by creditors. If the working capital of a business is grossly inadequate it will be forced to finance its operations more and more by short-term borrowings such as overdraft and trade credit. Eventually the point will be reached beyond which the short-term lenders are not willing to extend credit, and it is at this point that the policy, and indeed the continuation of the business, is dependent not on the wishes of the owners, shareholders or directors, but on the actions of the creditors. Even though the business is a profitable one, at this weak stage in its development a creditors meeting can decide that, in the absence of repayment, the creditors will apply to the court to appoint a liquidator or force the company to commence a voluntary winding-up.

Over-trading is often the reason for the development of such adverse credit conditions in a business. In simple terms, to over-trade means to attempt to finance a large volume of production and sales with inadequate working capital. If the company does not have enough funds of its own to finance stock and debtors it is forced, if it wishes to expand, to borrow from creditors and from the bank on overdraft. Sooner or later such expansion, financed completely by the funds of others, will lead to a chronic imbalance in the working capital ratio. At this point the creditors and the bank may withdraw their support and a creditors meeting will take place.

CONSERVING THE RESOURCES OF WORKING CAPITAL IN A BUSINESS

A much used measure of the profitability of a business is to set net profit against the capital employed and show it as a percentage thereof. This is known as the return on capital employed. A good accountant or financial manager will attempt to manage the resources of the business in such a way that the capital employed is used efficiently and not wasted. If the capital employed can be reduced and profit maintained, then an improved return on capital employed will be achieved. Conversely, if the capital employed in current operations is reduced, funds are released for use in other activities, and the profit on capital employed is increased. The financial manager should review the asset structure of his business to seek out idle, under-utilized and non-profitable assets, so that he can recommend that they be turned back into cash which can then be re-employed in the business, or elsewhere, at a much greater return. Fixed assets are as important in this operation as are current assets, since when they are squeezed, liquidity, or funds for use elsewhere in the business, is the result. Some fixed assets, especially plant of a specific nature, may not be easy to sell unless at a price well below book value, and there will also be redundancy payments if staff are involved.

The land and buildings belonging to and used by the company should be investigated. The accountant must attempt to find out whether they are fully utilized, and to discover idle or underused space or space being used for wasteful or unprofitable purposes. He must then initiate discussions with the technical experts in the business to rearrange the factory area, to re-route goods and stocks of work in progress which travel round the factory so that some space is released. Such space can then be sold, rented out, or used to house a new operation; any of these courses of action should improve the cash flow of the business.

A review of machinery used in the business should be made to discover the level of idle time experienced each week or day by individual machines. This survey will reveal whether the plant and machinery is working at full capacity, whether the same volume of work could be produced from a smaller number of machines, and how much extra work could be undertaken using the existing plant and machinery. Once again, the level of spare capacity, if it exists, will be shown, so that it can be put to work or sold. Care must be taken in such economy reviews that back-up capacity is not seen as an idle resource, but as a form of insurance against breakdown.

Vehicles should also be brought under scrutiny. Investigation, with the transport manager, into routes and mileages driven per week or per month would pinpoint those vehicles which do not earn their keep, and perhaps produce ideas so that fewer vehicles can be used to undertake the work of the company.

Investments made by the business also tie up capital, and therefore they too should be analysed. The return received from an investment should be set against its current value to determine whether it is worthwhile. In cases of low return perhaps the investment is held for strategic reasons, e.g. a share stake in a supplier or customer company. It is difficult to quantify such strategic benefits, but an attempt should be made to find out whether the benefit is considered to be worth tying up the amount of capital in the investment. Perhaps the same strategic benefit could be gained by holding a smaller share stake, thus releasing some funds for use elsewhere in the business.

CONSERVING FUNDS INVESTED IN CURRENT ASSETS: STOCKS

So far the accountant's activities to husband the capital at his disposal have been directed towards achieving the same volume of turnover and activity from a reduced quantity of fixed assets. A review of the current assets of the business should also be made to ascertain whether levels of stocks and debtors could be the subject of economy measures.

The stocks of a manufacturing business are usually of three types. They consist of stocks of raw material waiting in the store to be used in the productive process, stocks of work in progress or semi-finished goods being worked on in the factory, and stocks of finished goods waiting to be sold. The computation of ratios is a useful device to determine the stock-holding period. In the case of raw material, the stock should be set against the usage of each material. If the amount of stock is divided by the average weekly issue a figure for the number of weeks' usage held in stock will emerge, and this can be compared with the lead time between placing an order and receiving delivery in order to find out whether the stock held is excessive. For example, if one can buy raw material at a fortnight's notice, it seems wrong to finance two months' usage of that raw material in stock. The executive responsible for this is the buyer and, if the raw material stock-holding period is increasing, he must be called to account for the change. It may be that the rate of production has slowed down while he has continued to buy material at the same rate, or that he is buying more than is required for production quantities. On the other hand, the buyer may be attempting to build up stocks in anticipation of a forthcoming seasonal demand or as a hedge against inflation.

The ratio of stocks of work in progress to the cost of production when computed as a number of days or weeks will show how long it takes for semi-finished articles to progress through the factory. This time period must be compared with the normally expected production cycle and discrepancies analysed. If, for example, there are fifty working weeks in the year and it takes a week to complete the production process, but work-in-progress stocks are $\frac{4}{50}$ of the production cost for a year, then there is too much work-in-progress stock in the factory, and the bottlenecks which are disrupting production must be discovered and eliminated.

The ratio of finished goods to the cost of goods sold will, when expressed as a time period, show how long the finished goods wait in the stores before they are sold. In this way one can discover whether production is co-ordinated properly to sales, or whether the factory goes on producing at its normal rate while sales are falling away. For example,

$$\frac{\text{Stock}}{\text{Cost of sales}} \times \frac{52}{1} = \text{The number of weeks.}$$

These ratios are discussed, with examples, in Chapter 22.

The establishment of a correct stock level is a decision affected by many different factors. The management team must trade off the advantages of holding large stocks against the disadvantages. The advantages of holding large stocks can be summarized as follows: that large orders can be placed with suppliers so that trade discounts are secured, that there is a reduction of buying costs if orders are placed less often, and the advantage of a smooth flow of production, since a large buffer stock of raw materials will reduce the possibility of a 'stock out'. The disadvantages of holding a large stock of raw materials stem from the costs of financing and maintaining the stock. Interest paid on overdraft used to finance the stock, the cost of running the stores, i.e. rent, rates, light, heat, insurance, the costs of spoilage, spillage and pilferage, the losses inherent in the operation of breaking bulk, and the fear of obsolescence followed by a stock writedown must be set against the advantages shown above.

The accountant must ensure that stocks are examined to discover slow-moving and obsolescent items so that the quantities involved can be reduced to realistic levels and funds released. Any action taken to improve the flow of products through the factory will reduce the time lag involved in the conversion of raw material to a sold product.

The working capital cycle can be expressed in terms of the number of days it takes to convert raw materials to finished goods, and then after they are sold to collect the price from the company's debtors. Such a computation will reveal the time period in which the company must finance the working capital cycle, and from this period it is possible to deduct the amount of credit received from suppliers. For example, if the raw material waits thirty days in the stores before being used, is then transferred to the factory for a ten-day production cycle, then waits for fifteen days in the finished goods store before being sold, and the person to whom the goods are sold delays a further sixty days before he pays his bill, it will take 115 days to change the funds invested in raw materials into cash or liquid resources. This means that the company will have to finance this period, but if it in its turn takes ninety days of credit from the supplier of raw materials, the period to be financed is reduced to 25 days. Thus the amount of working capital tied up in raw materials for this transaction will be the cost of 25 times an average day's usage of raw materials.

Example

	Days
Storage	30
Production	10
Finished goods store	15
Payment delay	60
	115
Less credit from suppliers	90
Days to finance	25

This simple sum emphasizes the importance in the working capital cycle of the management of debtors and creditors, since if debtors can be induced to pay sooner and creditors can be persuaded to wait for their money, the amount of the company's own funds tied up in the transaction will be reduced. Any other factor which can shorten the time period, such as a shorter production cycle or a reduced lead time between the delivery and use of raw material stocks, will also reduce the amount of working capital required. Thus planning and the reduction of production bottlenecks can help to turn over stocks faster and allow the same amount of money to finance more transactions, and earn more profit margins from each transaction, in an accounting period.

DEBTORS AND CREDITORS

The accountant must approach debtors with some caution if he wishes to conserve the working capital of the company. He has less control over debtors than, for example, over stock, since the period of credit which the company must give depends to some extent on the activity of the other party to the transaction, i.e. the customer. The volume of funds required to finance debtors may grow without an increase in the volume of transactions, merely because in a period of inflation prices rise and more capital is needed to finance the same number of transactions.

Many companies employ a credit controller in an attempt to economize on their working capital tied up in the form of debtors. The credit controller has four main tasks. It is his job to vet new customers and set a credit limit (an amount beyond which goods will not be sold to the customer without the payment of previous bills), to review the credit position of old customers and set new credit limits for them, to ensure that credit limits are not exceeded, and to hasten the slow payers by means of carefully worded letters encouraging them to pay. The credit controller is in a delicate position, since he wishes to collect the firm's money from its customers, but does not wish to be rude to them while collecting the money, since this may discourage them from buying from the company in the future. Thus he is the rope in a tug of war between the accounting department, who wish to collect debts and reduce working capital wastefully tied up in debtors, and the sales department, who wish to extend the credit line and maintain customer goodwill. A useful device in the control of trade credit is the ageing debtors list. This is merely an analysis of all debtor balances to show how long they have been outstanding. Thus the poor payers are revealed and the credit controller can do his best to make them pay. The danger with debtor balances which are four or five months or more overdue is that they may, unless the credit controller is careful, become bad debts.

Another aspect of the management of working capital which a financial accountant must monitor with care is the amount of trade credit which he can take on behalf of his company from the suppliers of raw materials. The general rule is to take as much as possible, since it is free, but not too much, since slow payment of bills harms the reputation of the company and its goodwill, and may affect future prices charged to the company for raw materials. Long delayed payment may result in a stop on the delivery of vital raw materials to the factory. Some companies adopt the policy of always paying promptly where they are offered a cash discount, while others, through careful programming with their suppliers, organize the deliveries to co-ordinate with the needs of the factory and thus reduce the stock-holding period.

Cash balances, or funds lying in the bank, are viewed by many companies as idle assets, since they are earning nothing. They are, however, a useful safety margin to ensure that urgent bills can always be paid. Forward planning in the form of a cash budget can show up the impact of future transactions on the cash balance, so that when an overdraft is required it can be requested well in advance.

CASH BUDGETS

A matter of such importance as the amount of liquid funds available to the company cannot be left to chance. Cash planning or budgeting implies that as part of the general budgeting procedure an accountant will forecast the flows of cash into and out of the company's bank account, so that any excess of payments over receipts will show up well in advance, and action can be taken to provide for a shortfall of liquid funds. This can be done on a quarterly, monthly, or even weekly basis, according to the needs of management and the situation of the company. It is especially important if the firm has an overdraft and wishes to ensure that the limit placed by its bank is not exceeded. Also, it is a useful tactic to be able to approach a bank for overdraft facilities well in advance of the date on which the funds will be needed, since such evidence of financial planning and control will improve the credit-worthiness of the company in the eyes of the bank. Finance cannot be raised at short notice without extra expense. It is preferable to make arrangements in good time so that funds are available when required.

The technique of cash budgeting is a simple one. The accountant needs to discover the receipts and payments of cash which are likely to take place in the future, and the dates on which they will happen, so that a forecast of the balance at the end of the month or week can be computed. The accountant must find out the length of lead time between incurring an expense and paying for it, and the time lag between making a sale and collecting the price from debtors. The art of cash budgeting is to work out accurately the timing of receipts and expenditure. If, for example, a firm takes two months' credit on its purchases, materials delivered in January will need to be paid for in March, and so on. The same applies to cash collected from credit sales. If a firm gives three months' credit to its customers, then cash from January credit sales will be received by the end of April. Care must be taken in this forecast to take into account the likely percentage of bad debts which will reduce the cash received, and to separate cash sales from credit sales, since these will be banked at once.

With labour costs the timing is a little more predictable, but difficult to compute, since some companies pay a week in arrears. This means that in a monthly cash budget each quarter, divided into thirteen weeks, must be analysed for the number of weeks in each month. If January and February each contain four pay days then March will cover five weeks of wage payments. If the firm pays one week in arrears the cash paid out in February will equal one week of January's wages $(\frac{1}{4})$ and three weeks of February's wages $(\frac{3}{4})$, whereas in March the wages paid out will be a quarter of February's labour cost and four fifths of March's labour cost. It must be remembered that in cash budgeting the actual wage sheets are not available and figures must be assessed from estimates of monthly costs.

Expenses are usually easier to forecast, since they are often paid one month in arrears, e.g. salaries. Certain expenses are paid quarterly, e.g. rent, or half-yearly, e.g. loan interest and rates, or annually, e.g. insurance premiums or annual bonus. Some expenses, such as depreciation, do not cause an outflow of cash and therefore should be ignored for cash budgeting purposes. Care must be taken when budgeting for miscellaneous items, both receipts and payments. Dividends received from an investment should be allotted to the correct month, together with projected receipts from the sale of fixed assets, while the amount and date of capital expenditure and payments of tax and dividend should be entered on the statement. It then remains only to set off the receipts against the payments each month to compute the surplus or deficit, and to show the impact of this cash flow on the bank balance or overdraft. A columnar approach facilitates the compilation of a cash budget.

Example

The CB Co. Ltd has a balance of £150 000 in its bank account on 1 January. The company has negotiated overdraft facilities of £100 000 with its bankers. Materials, all purchased on credit, usually cost £500 000 per month, but a reduction of £100 000 is planned during December. Suppliers allow two months' credit terms to the company. Labour costs for December, January, February and March are £250 000, £280 000, £320 000, and £400 000 respectively. Wages are paid one week in arrears, and December and March are considered to be five-week months. Expenses paid monthly in arrears amount to £80 000 each month, the rent of £60 000 is paid on each quarter day, and rates of £12 000 per annum are paid half yearly on 31 December and 30 June. An annual insurance premium of £45 000 falls due on 30 January and corporation tax of £205 000 must be paid in January. Capital expenditure to purchase new machinery for £400 000 is planned, and a progress payment of 25 per cent is to be made in March.

A dividend from an associated company is expected to be received in February, and should amount to £200 000. The company expects to raise a long-term loan of £250 000 by a mortgage on its property during March.

Expected sales are as follows: October, £800 000; November, £750 000; December, £1 090 000; January, £650 000; February, £800 000; and March, £900 000. 10 per cent of sales are for cash, and the remainder are on terms of three months' credit. Bad debts are expected at the rate of 5 per cent on credit sales.

Compute a cash budget for January, February and March.

Note: A simple way of remembering the quarter days is as follows:

> 25 March (five letters in March)
> 24 June (four letters in June)
> 29 September (nine letters in September)
> 25 December (Christmas)

CB Co. Ltd Cash Budget (£000s)

	January	February	March
Receipts:			
Cash sales	65	80	90
Debtors	684 (95% ×720)	641.25 (95% ×675)	931.95 (95% ×981)
Loan			250
Investment income	–	200	–
Total receipts	749	921.25	1271.95
Payments:			
Materials	500 (Nov.)	400 (Dec.)	500 (Jan.)
Labour	50 (1/5)	70 (1/4)	80 (1/4)
	210 (3/4)	240 (3/4)	320 (4/5)
Expenses	80	80	80
Rent and insurance	45	–	60
Taxation	205	–	–
Capital expenditure	–	–	100
Total payments	1090	790	1140
Surplus/deficit	(341)	131.25	131.95
Opening balance	150	(191.00)	(59.75)
Closing balance	(191)	(59.75)	72.20

Therefore the overdraft limit will be exceeded during January, but the situation will be under control by the end of February, and the facility will not be required by the end of March.

Note that the quarter day for rent is 25 March and that rates are ignored since they are not paid during this period. This computation shows month-end balances, based on the assumption that receipts and payments flow in and out evenly during each month. A substantial payment early in a month could upset this computation.

In conclusion, the differences between a cash budget and a profit and loss account must be discussed, since the two are often confused. A cash budget does not contain the non-cash expenses found in the profit and loss account, such as the provision for depreciation. The provision for doubtful debts cannot be included in the cash budget, but actual bad debts will reduce the cash received from sales. Conversely, income and expenditure of a capital nature will appear in the cash budget but not in the profit and loss account. Appropriations of profit for tax and dividend will cause an outflow of cash, but cannot influence the profit figure before it is struck.

TUTORIAL DISCUSSION TOPICS

21.1. What is working capital and why does a creditor see it as a significant figure on the balance sheet?

21.2. Why is it so important for a business to have an adequate fund of working capital?

21.3. What is the working capital cycle and how can an accountant use his understanding of this cycle to benefit his firm?

21.4. Discuss the task of a credit controller, with specific reference to the pressure to which he is subjected.

21.5. Outline the advantages of a cash budget.

SEMINAR EXERCISES 12

1. From the two balance sheets of Ginger Ltd shown below calculate the change in working capital over the year and show how this change has arisen:

Ginger Ltd Balance Sheets as at

	£ 1 Jan.	£ 31 Dec.		£ 1 Jan.	£ 31 Dec.
Share capital	60 000	65 000	Freehold land and		
			buildings	22 000	25 000
General reserve	4 000	5 000			
			Plant and machinery	38 000	40 000
Profit and loss					
balance	9 000	11 000			
Long-term loan	–	50 000			
				60 000	65 000
Current liabilities:			Current assets:		
Creditors	12 000	14 000	Stocks	17 000	70 000
Bills payable	11 000	12 000	Debtors	7 000	10 000
Proposed final			Cash	18 000	20 000
dividend	6 000	8 000			
	£102 000	£165 000		£102 000	£165 000

2. Clutterbuck is considering commencing a business on 1 January 1979, with a capital sum of £5000. He has made an estimate over the ensuing six months, as follows:

   (a) Sales. January, £6000; February, £8000; March, £10 000; April to July inclusive, £12 000 per month. Debtors are expected to settle their accounts at the end of the month following that of the sale; e.g. goods sold in February are paid for in March. The gross profit on sales is 25 per cent throughout.
   (b) Purchases. A stock is retained to cover the succeeding months' sales. All suppliers are paid at the end of the month following that of purchase.
   (c) Wages and salaries. These are estimated to be: January, £350; February, £450; thereafter £500 per month.
   (d) Expenses. General expenses of £350 per month are paid in the month in which they are incurred. Rent of £500 per annum is payable quarterly in advance, the first payment being on 1 January. Rates of £160 are to be paid on 1 April 1979.
   (e) Fittings and plant to be purchased in January, £3000; motor van to be purchased in February, £1500.

   Prepare a cash budget showing the estimated cash position at the end of each of the six months to June 1979.

3. Jumbo intends to commence business as a wholesaler on 1 July, with £5000 in cash which he will pay into a business bank account. It is anticipated that his sales for July will be £4000 and will increase at the rate of £2000 per month until October, when they will be £12 000 because of a sales promotion drive. In November and December the sales will be £10 000 in each month. It is anticipated that the gross profit percentage earned in each month will be 40 per cent, with the exception of October, when it will be 30 per cent, due to a reduction of prices during the promotion drive. In anticipation of high sales early next year it is intended to hold £1000 worth of stock (at cost) at the end of July and increase the stock levels by £500 per month throughout the first six months. All sales are on credit terms and the average period of credit allowed to debtors will be two months (except for the sale to Hardup Ltd, referred to below).

Creditors for the goods purchased for resale will allow one month's credit only. All sales will originate through the salesman employed by the company, who will receive a commission of 2 per cent of the sales value. This will be paid to him in the month after which the sales are effected.

The business will lease premises at a rental of £1200 per annum payable quarterly, the first payment falling due on 20 July. Wages and salaries will be £500 per month and other overheads will be £300 per month for the first three months and £400 per month for the ensuing three months. These expenses will be paid in the month to which they relate. On 1 September Jumbo will purchase a piece of equipment for £600 and pay for this on 30 November. On 1 October he will purchase and pay for a car worth £2400.

Included in the sales figure for July is an amount of £400 to Hardup Ltd. It is intended to grant Hardup Ltd extended credit, and it is confidently predicted that they will settle the amount due in March next year.

Depreciation is to be provided pro rata to time at the rate of 10 per cent per annum on cost for the equipment and 25 per cent per annum on the cost of the motor vehicle.

(a) Prepare a cash budget for each of the first six months of trading showing the anticipated bank balance at the end of each month.
(b) Prepare a forecast trading and profit and loss account for the six months ending 31 December.
(c) Discuss the differences between a cash budget and a profit and loss account.

4. During the Christmas holiday you went on a skiing holiday in the north of Scotland, and stayed with a relative who has developed a farm on ranching principles. One day he confided in you that he was rather worried that he might be in temporary financial difficulty during the early part of the year, and you agreed to put your business knowledge at his disposal in order that he might negotiate an overdraft with his bank in Fort William.

Prepare a cash budget for the months of January to April (inclusive) from the information given below:

(a) Balance at bank was expected to be £2000 on 1 January.
(b) Incomings: sales of cattle. There is a contract with an exporter for the supply of forty head of cattle each month for which forward prices have been negotiated and agreed: September to February inclusive, £115 per head; March to August inclusive, £100 per head. The money is paid over in the second month after the date of sale.

Surplus cattle, together with any suitable steers, are sent to the auctions, at which prices are expected to be: steers, £50 per head; beef cattle, £125 per head. The money for these is received immediately. The numbers of these expected to be available for auction are:

	Jan.	Feb.	Mar.	Apr.
Steers	12	20	20	26
Beef cattle	8	16	16	20

(c) Other income:

(i) There is a variation clause in the contract with the cattle exporters by which additional lump sum payments are made when weighted-average export prices exceed a certain figure. Taking price trends into account, the amounts likely to be received are: interim distribution, February, £700; final distribution, April, £2100.

(ii) He is due to receive a subsidy of £1000 from the Highlands Agricultural Development Board in March.

(d) Outgoings: labour. The salaries of the ranch manager and foreman together amount to £800 per month plus a bonus of 5 per cent of the combined sales value of the steers and beef cattle auctioned that month.

In addition to the nine permanently employed 'hands' hired at £150 per month each, a certain amount of part-time casual labour is employed at an average wage of £100 per month each. Numbers of casual hands expected to be hired are: January, fifteen; February, twelve; March, twelve; April, nine.

(e) Other costs:

(i) Fodder etc. During the spring and summer the cattle can obtain sufficient food by free ranging. This is gradually supplemented in early autumn and superseded in winter by bought-in fodder.

The cost of this and of vitamin concentrates, veterinary vaccines etc. is likely to be: December, £900; January, £900; February, £900; March, £500; and April, £300. These sums are paid to the suppliers one month after the items have been acquired.

(ii) The cost of grazing rights (£300) is paid to local landowners in advance in the month of February.

(iii) Payments for the use of rights of way are made to neighbouring landowners half-yearly in advance at the rate of £200 per annum. The first payment is made in January.

(iv) All other costs (paid currently) for vehicle running expenses, repairs, electricity etc. are expected to amount to £400 per month.

(f) Capital expenditure. It is proposed to acquire another truck in March at a cost of £6000 on hire purchase. The terms are 20 per cent deposit in March and 32 equal monthly instalments from April onwards.

In February the final instalment of £6000 is due for the supply and erection of some outbuildings.

(g) Personal drawings. To meet living expenses etc. he intends to withdraw £1000 per month.

(h) Taxation. An instalment of £5000 tax on business profits is to be paid in January.

22 | The Valuation of a Business

A business is valued when it is sold, when there is a change of partners, or when the proprietor dies and the value is computed to be added to his estate for the purposes of capital transfer tax. In the case of a limited company there may be a need to value the company in order to put a price on individual shares when a takeover or merger is proposed. Several methods are employed to find the value of shares in a business. A share in a public company will have a market value, since it is quoted on a stock exchange, but if a steady demand is experienced as an investor who intends to make a takeover bid seeks to build up a significant share stake in the business, the price will rise. The extent to which the investor will continue to buy as prices rise will be determined by the valuation he puts on the company. In the case of a private limited company there will be no such market value, and an offer will be made direct to an existing shareholder or his agent. The terms of such an offer will be in line with the valuation put on the business.

Accountants use several methods to value a business, but it must be emphasized that the value reached by their computation may bear little relation to the final price arrived at through bargaining, since various factors will influence the negotiations. Such factors are concerned with business strategy and include the re-employment of assets, the establishment of a monopoly or a foothold in a market, diversification, and integration. These factors may cause the business to be worth more than the accountant's valuation of it to a particular buyer who wants it very much.

From the accountant's viewpoint, when shares are purchased the buyer gains two things. First, as a shareholder he has a right to share in the assets of the business if and when the business is wound up, and second, he has a right to a share of the profits. Thus shares can be valued on the basis of the underlying assets which they represent, or on the basis of the income which they provide. When a small holding of shares is to be valued (this is termed a minority interest, since it does not give voting control of the company) recognition must be made of the fact that the buyer cannot dictate decisions at a general meeting of the company, and has little influence over board policy. Therefore such a holding is best valued on the basis of the income it yields. Such a valuation is made by comparing the yield on the share with the yield which can be earned on similar shares bearing an equivalent risk. Dividend is declared as a percentage of the face value of a share, e.g. a 20 per cent dividend on a £1 share provides a dividend of 20p. for every share held; but yield is expressed by computing the percentage of the dividend paid over the current market price of the share, e.g. if a £1 share has been purchased for £2, a 20 per cent dividend thereon, 20 pence per share, will yield 10 per cent. This method of valuation can be expressed in formula terms as the yield over the expected yield times the face value.

264

$$\frac{\text{Yield}}{\text{Expected yield}} \times \text{Face value} = \frac{20\%}{10\%} \times £1 = £2, \text{ or } \frac{8\%}{10\%} \times £1 = 80\text{p}.$$

Preference shares and securities, such as debentures or loan stock, which have a fixed rate of return can also be valued by means of this formula. The fixed return is set against the expected return or market rate of interest, as the case may be, and then applied to the face value. The value thus produced is what a prudent investor would expect to pay for the income involved at current market rates.

$$\frac{\text{Debenture coupon rate}}{\text{Market rate of interest}} \times \text{Face value} = \text{Price},$$

$$\frac{10\%}{15\%} \times £100 = £66 \ (15\% \text{ of } £66 = £10).$$

The £10 interest gives the investor the market rate of 15 per cent if he pays £66 for the right to receive that interest.

RISK

The most significant factor in the above formula is the expected yield from the shares. This figure can be derived from the expectations of investors revealed by the Stock Exchange, but these expectations themselves are an amalgam of a number of factors which determine whether or not an investment is a risky one.

The nature of the business itself will help to determine the risk, since in general the luxury trades are considered more risky than trades providing necessities, and the home market is considered less risky than the export market. Any factor which promotes the likelihood of fluctuation in the market, or of obsolescence, will increase the risk of an investment. The past record of a business, its earnings, and the dividends it has paid out will show the pay-out or plough-back policy of the directors. This financial policy can be compared with that of similar firms, and the result of this comparison will have an effect on risk. The trend of profits in a business will show whether there is growth or recession, and whether future earnings are likely to be sufficient to maintain the required rate of dividend. The ratio of net profit to capital employed can also be used in this context to show the return earned by a business on its capital to compensate for the risk taken in investing the capital in that way. Another factor influencing risk is gearing. A highly geared position is considered more risky than a low-geared position, since a large volume of prior right capital must be serviced before the highly geared ordinary shares can receive a return. The nature of the assets in a firm also contributes to the riskiness of an investment. A large proportion of fixed, as opposed to current assets means that the capital has been sunk into the business and it may be difficult to disinvest it. Current assets are relatively easy to turn back into cash. The degree of specificity of the fixed assets of a business will help to determine their marketability and also their ability to act as security for loan capital. Risk is also affected by the amount of goodwill shown on the balance sheet. It is necessary to investigate the factors which support the existence of the goodwill to determine whether they are easily transferable to a new management, whether they have been calculated properly, and whether the amount of goodwill is excessive when compared with the tangible assets and current earnings. The demand for the product, the share of the market, the level of competition, and the supply of raw materials and labour are other factors which can affect the risk of a business, and accordingly the return required from it. When a bid is made by one company for the shares of another, a number of factors concerning the economic logic of the merger and the advantages of the economies of large scale (vertical or horizontal integration) will influence the price that the buyer is willing to pay. Risk is also determined by 'cover'. This word is used to express the safety margin of the investor in two distinct ways. First, the excess of net assets less long-term liabilities over the ordinary share capital of the business will show up the extent of the reserves and the asset base on which the value of the shares rests. Second, the relationship of profits available to the amount of the expected dividend will show whether profits are sufficient to meet the required level of dividend and comment on the risk of non-payment of a dividend.

A CONTROLLING INTEREST

The valuation of a controlling interest in a company is undertaken by a somewhat different method. The controlling shareholder will be able to outvote others at general meetings of the company, and is thus in a position to determine its policy. When such an investor buys a controlling interest, he will buy the assets and what they earn, and accordingly the value of his shares could be computed on the basis of the underlying assets, and on their capacity to earn profit. The assets, however, must be realistically revalued so that their true current worth is known. The term used in this case is net tangible assets, being the value of all the things which the company possesses less the liabilities which it owes. Once this amount has been computed it can be divided by the number of shares in issue, so that the asset value per share is found. To this amount must be added the value of the goodwill, which is expressed as the value placed by an investor on the extra profits which the business is likely to make. Goodwill is sometimes defined as the capital value of future superprofits based on past superprofits. It is the amount which a prudent investor would pay for the fact that the business can earn more in profit than would be expected from that class of business taking that type of risk with its capital employed.

First, the amount of capital employed is computed, and the appropriate risk factor is applied to that amount to show what profits should be made by this business if a fair return to compensate for the risk taken is to be achieved. This is termed the expected profit.

Second, the past adjusted weighted average profit is computed. Profits for a number of past years are included, so that no single or abnormal year can affect the value of the goodwill, and these profits are adjusted to remove influences which will not apply after the business has changed hands. If an owner/manager pays himself £15 000 a year for doing a job which a hired manager would do for £10 000 a year, then £5000 must be added back to profits to show the level they are likely to achieve under new management. Past profits for a number of years are used to give a fair spread of the normal ups and downs of business, but these profits must be weighted to give greater significance to the profits of the most recent years, since they are more likely to reflect future conditions and should therefore have a greater significance when the average profits are calculated. During a period of inflation past profits may not reflect future earnings, and for this reason there is now a tendency to adjust them. It must, however, be recognized that the basis for such an adjustment will be an estimate, and difficult to substantiate.

Next the expected profit is subtracted from the past adjusted weighted average profit to determine whether excess or superprofits have been earned. The capital value of superprofits to be earned in the future is computed by multiplying superprofits by an agreed number of years' purchase thereof or by finding their capital value at an agreed rate. This is goodwill.

Example

The ABC Company Ltd has a balance sheet as follows:

	£	£
Share capital 100 000 ordinary shares of £1 each		100 000
Reserves		75 000
		175 000
Debentures (10 per cent)		60 000
Net capital employed		£235 000
Represented by:		
Fixed assets (net of depreciation):		
Buildings		120 000
Plant		40 000
Vehicles		15 000
		175 000
Current assets:		
Stock	40 000	
Debtors	20 000	
Cash	10 000	
	70 000	
Current liabilities: creditors	10 000	60 000
Net worth		£235 000

Suppose the buildings are revalued at £150 000, stock is written down to £30 000, and vehicles are considered to be worth only £5000. The net capital employed figure would then be £245 000 less £60 000 for debentures, equalling £185 000 as net tangible assets. This figure is divided by 100 000 ordinary shares to give an asset value of £1.85 per share, showing what the shares are worth in terms of assets, and representing a floor below which negotiations to purchase the shares will not allow the price to fall.

	£
Buildings	+ 30 000
Stock	− 10 000
Vehicles	− 10 000
Net	+ 10 000
Equity interest	+ 175 000
Net tangible assets	185 000

But what of the profits of the business? Suppose they have been: this year, £50 000; last year, £45 000; and the year before last, £40 000. The major shareholder pays himself a salary of £15 000 but could be replaced by a manager for a salary of £7000, thus profits for all years will have to be adjusted by adding £8000. If it is discovered that an extraordinary transaction last year which brought in a profit of £3000 is not likely to be repeated in the future, a further adjustment is needed so that past profits reflect future conditions.

The past adjusted weighted profits will be: this year, £58 000; last year, £50 000; and the year before last, £48 000. These profit figures need to be weighted for averaging purposes to allow the results of the most recent years to have a major influence on the past average profit figure.

	£	Weights	Product
This year	58 000	3	174 000
Last year	50 000	2	100 000
Year before last	48 000	1	48 000
		6	322 000

£322 000 ÷ 6 = £53 666 = PAWAP (past adjusted weighted average profits).

If a return of 20 per cent is considered sufficient to compensate for the risk involved, then a profit of 20 per cent on net tangible assets of £185 000 will be required, i.e. £37 000, so superprofits of £16 666 in excess of this figure can be expected in the future. The amount of the goodwill is the value to an investor of these superprofits. It can be computed as so many years' purchase of the superprofits, say three, so that goodwill is worth £49 998, and the company is then worth net tangible assets plus goodwill, an amount of 185 000 + 49 998 = £234 998, say £235 000.

	£
Profit required, 20 per cent of £185 000	37 000
Past adjusted weighted average profits	53 666
Superprofits	£16 666
Goodwill at three years' purchase of superprofits	49 998
Net tangible assets	185 000
Value of business (£2.35 per share)	£234 998

The goodwill multiplier is either agreed by the buyer and the seller or is a rate normally used in the particular trade or industry.

Alternatively, the superprofits can be capitalized at an appropriate rate. Since they represent a non-tangible and thus risky asset, this rate can be expected to be above the normal expected return. Suppose 30 per cent is considered appropriate. The superprofits would then be worth $£16\,666 \times \dfrac{100}{30}$, i.e. £55 553, and this amount of goodwill could be added to the net tangible assets to compute the valuation of the business at £240 553.

Capital Value of Superprofits

	£
$£16\,666 \times \dfrac{100}{30}$	55 553
Net tangible assets	185 000
Value of business (£2.40 per share)	£240 553

Three years' purchase of superprofits is equal to a capitalization rate of 33 per cent.

Yet another method can be used to value the shares by capitalizing the profits on the basis of the required yield. With past adjusted weighted profits of £53 666 and a required rate of return of 20 per cent, this would value the entire business at $£53\,666 \times \dfrac{100}{20}$, say £270 000. If the value of net tangible assets at £185 000 is subtracted from this figure, the difference of £85 000 would be goodwill.

Capital Value of Expected Profits

	£
$£53\,666 \times \dfrac{100}{20}$ (£2.70 per share)	270 000
Net tangible assets	185 000
Goodwill	£85 000

Thus we have seen three methods for the valuation of shares which have computed three different values for goodwill. This example illustrates the idea that share valuation methods are far from precise, and also shows the significance of the calculation of such estimates as the required rate of return etc.

The price/earnings ratio is another multiplier which can be used as a share valuation tool. This ratio sets earnings net of tax per share (EPS) against the current market price of the share, and is expressed as a number. It can be seen as the number of years which the investor must wait to recoup his invested sum out of earnings, whether they are distributed as a dividend or not. In a public company a net profit of £50 000 this year would give earnings of £25 000 after corporation tax at 50 per cent. Thus, with 100 000 ordinary shares, EPS would be 25 pence per share. If the market price of the shares was £2, the price/earnings ratio would be eight. This ratio reflects the market price of the share, which is the product of investors' expectations. Where growth and a capital profit are expected investors will bid up the share price and thus increase the price/earnings multiple. Companies of a similar size and prospects within the same industry can be expected to have a similar price/earnings ratio, so this figure can be used as a basis for valuing a private company of the same type. The appropriate price/earnings number, decreased slightly to take into account the extra risk concerned with the lack of marketability of a private company, is multiplied by the EPS, and a value is found. For example, suppose a price/earnings number of twelve is normal for companies like ABC Ltd quoted on the Stock Exchange, then deduct two, since ABC Ltd is a private company, and multiply the EPS of £25 000 by ten, to value the company at £250 000.

Note that the term 'net worth' on the balance sheet has little to do with the value of the share as computed by any of the methods shown above.

GOODWILL

This phenomenon is an important factor in the valuation of a business, but there has been considerable discussion about the precise meaning of the term and reasons for the existence of goodwill. The legal profession and accountants see goodwill in somewhat different terms, as the following two quotations from past judgements will show. First, Judge Warrington in Hill v. Fearis, 1905 (1CH466) defined goodwill as 'the advantage, whatever it may be, which a person gets by continuing to carry on, and being entitled to represent to the outside world that he is carrying on, a business which has been carried on for some time previously'. This legal definition seems to suggest that the goodwill of the business is derived from the fact that it is a going concern with an established clientele and reputation. In another case, that of CIR v. Muller, 1901 (AC217) Lord MacNaughton remarked that goodwill was 'a thing very easy to describe, very difficult to define. The benefit and advantage of a good name, reputation and connection of a business. The attractive force that brings in custom. The one thing which distinguishes an old established business from a new business at its first start. Goodwill is composed of a variety of elements. It differs in its composition in different trades, and in different businesses in the same trade. One element may preponderate here and another there.'

In this case an attempt has been made to explain some of the reasons why goodwill exists, and the elements in a business which improve its profitability, such as reputation and trade connection, which attract custom and increase turnover. The accountant also sees goodwill as a force which attracts custom, and from this derives the need to value it, since as custom and turnover are improved so profit will increase. To an accountant goodwill is that element arising from the connection and reputation which enables a business to earn larger profits than would otherwise be expected, and it is at this point that the idea of superprofits and their connection with goodwill emerges. The ability of a business to be more than normally profitable can be determined by a number of factors:

1. The business's reputation for the quality of its products, the service that it gives, and the fair trading of its managers or proprietors. While a good reputation will attract customers, the possession of a well-known trade name built up through advertising campaigns will persuade customers to ask for a specific product by name, and thus increase turnover and profit.

2. Location. If a company possesses business premises in a favourable place, e.g. a shop in a prime high street site or a factory well positioned for communication, then it can expect to derive advantages from its location. These advantages can be turned into superprofits, and thus contribute towards the goodwill of the business.

3. 'Knowhow' and experience. A company which has carried on business in a certain trade for a number of years builds up a body of knowledge of the best methods to employ in its chosen trade, so that it knows how best to tackle awkward projects and overcome difficult problems. This type of experience avoids mistakes, which can increase costs and reduce profits. The very fact that a company is a going concern means that it has an established body of customers who are used to trading with it, and who may return with repeat orders. A new entrant to a certain trade must not only build up its clientele but also learn by its own mistakes while it is establishing itself in the trade.

4. The possession of favourable contracts. A lease on good premises brings its own advantages of site, but a long-term contract to supply to a reputable customer, or a licence to manufacture or a dealership from a well-known company, will reduce the riskiness of the business and profits will thus be assured.

5. A team of keen and experienced executives and a body of contented and efficient employees will also contribute towards superprofits. Good relations with union representatives can reduce the disruption of business through strikes, and improve profitability.

Some of the above factors which contribute to the existence of goodwill are derived from the circumstances of the firm, while others are the product of the character of the managers or proprietors. Some of these elements of goodwill can be transferred easily and quickly to a new proprietor or management at the time of takeover, so the continued existence of goodwill will depend on them rather than on the actions of the proprietor who built up the business. If goodwill is derived from short-term factors this will be taken into account when the number of years' purchase of the superprofits is negotiated.

Example

Jon is the proprietor of an established business which has a good reputation for service and good labour relations. Raw materials for the business are bought from a trade supplier owned by Jon's father-in-law. Jon wishes to sell his business and emigrate with his capital to Canada. He has prepared a forecast of profits he expects the business to achieve over the next five years from the net tangible assets of £50 000.

	1981	1982	1983	1984	1985
Net profit	£11 000	£12 000	£14 000	£16 000	£17 000
Return on capital	22%	24%	28%	32%	34%

Jon is a shrewd business-man, and has recently employed a specialist to revalue his assets, which are well maintained and in a good condition. The figure of £50 000 quoted above is a good indication of their net realizable value.

Jos has just graduated from a business school and wishes to start up a business of his own. He has no business connections, but intends to combine youthful enthusiasm with his patrimony of £50 000. His projections of profit for the next five years are as follows:

	1981	1982	1983	1984	1985
Net profit	£3000	£5000	£7500	£10 000	£15 000
Return on capital	6%	10%	15%	20%	30%

Jon meets Jos and the conversation rapidly turns to the valuation of businesses. Jon points out that he will expect more than the net tangible asset value of £50 000 for his business.

As adviser to Jos what value would you put on Jon's business, and what arguments would you suggest that Jos uses to reduce the price which Jon might ask?

The answer to this problem can be in only the vaguest of terms, since much necessary information has been omitted. Briefly, however, Jon's position is that he is in an established business with a trade connection already built up, that his reputation is good, and this enhances his business connection, that his business has good labour relations and no disruptions through strikes, that there is experience and knowhow in the business, and that he benefits from certain family connections when buying his raw materials. All these factors contribute to Jon's profit, but it is difficult to quantify that contribution with any accuracy. It is equally certain that without these advantages the business would not be as successful as it is at present. Since the plant is well maintained and recently valued, an amount of £50 000 can be assumed for the net tangible assets of the business.

The profit forecasts of Jon and Jos are not really comparable, since the figures of Jos reflect the fact that he must learn his business in the early years. Jos has a faster rate of growth than Jon. Can he nearly catch up after five years of trading? Is the 50 per cent increase in profit for 1985 a feasible forecast?

The net asset value of £50 000 provides a good starting point for the valuation of Jon's business. Jon will want to value goodwill by computing the worth of his superprofits. If we assume a 20 per cent return on net tangible assets the required profits from Jon's business are 20 per cent of £50 000, or £10 000. Thus superprofits to be made by Jon in years 1981 to 1985 are £1000, £2000, £4000, £6000 and £7000 respectively. The factors which underpin the goodwill are largely connected with the personality of the proprietor, and do not seem to be permanent. Therefore it could be argued that goodwill should be valued as three years' purchase of the weighted average superprofits computed from the forecast figures for the next three years. Note that when weights are allocated to years the greatest weight is given to the most recent year.

	£	Weights	Multiple
1979	1000	3	3 000
1980	2000	2	4 000
1981	4000	1	4 000
		6	11 000

11 000 ÷ 6	= £1833 superprofits
Three years of purchase	= £5499 goodwill
Value of business	= £55 500

The arguments which Jos can use to reduce the value which Jon sets on his business will revolve around the valuation of goodwill, which in this business appears to be closely linked to the personality of the retiring proprietor. Jos will argue that many of the advantages from which Jon derives his superprofits may not be transferred when the business is sold. For example, Jon's personal reputation and his purchasing advantages with a relation will certainly not enhance the business when it is owned by Jos. What is more, Jos will have to work very hard to maintain some of the other advantages, such as the trade connection and good labour relations. The experience and knowhow on which future superprofits depend may also leave with Jon, unless key employees of the business have agreed to remain under Jos's management and continue to contribute their experience and knowhow in the future. Jos may argue that much of the superprofitability depends on his ability to continue to operate the business as well as Jon, and that it is unfair to ask him to pay Jon for profits he has to earn by his own efforts. Jon, of course, will answer that he has built up the firm, that the potential is there, and that he cannot be expected to give this away for nothing.

Jos may challenge Jon's figures in an attempt to reduce the value of the goodwill. If it is a risky business a return of 25 or even 30 per cent on capital employed might be expected to compensate for the risk, with a corresponding reduction of the amount of superprofits. Jos might also argue that three years' purchase of the superprofits is too long a period for the calculation, since the goodwill transfers much sooner to the new manager and must be maintained by him. An alternative computation of the value of the firm, computed on the basis of the 30 per cent expected return, would show no superprofits until 1984, and goodwill computed at 1½ years' purchase of the superprofits would further reduce the value of the goodwill. Jon may counter this argument by pointing out that a 30 per cent return is too much to expect, since Jos's own profit forecast does not reach 25 per cent even after a five-year period of experience.

As an accountant giving advice to Jos, you might comment that this is the wrong business for him to buy, and that he should try to find another. He cannot afford to pay more than £50 000 for a business without recourse to borrowing, and the cost of the interest on borrowed funds would reduce the profitability of the business. The profit forecasts of Jon and Jos are very different, and suggest that Jos is willing to accept a low return in the early years while he builds up his experience, while Jon, on the other hand, is trying to sell an established business at as high a price as possible. Jos must decide whether he wishes to leap-frog the next few years of low profits, whether he can afford to buy his way into this profitable business, and whether he should take the risk of borrowing and investing in an established business which he may not be able to operate successfully. It would be wise to point out to Jos that if he fails the goodwill of the business for which he has paid will rapidly evaporate, but he will still have to meet his creditors' demands for interest and repayment of principal, and that his own funds will be fully committed.

Example

The next person Jos meets in business is **Mr Kester**, who tells him that he is the proprietor of a profitable little business engaged in the manufacture of caravans, and that he is willing to sell his business if the price is right. **Mr Kester** shows Jos the accounts of the business for the year ending 30 June last, as set out below.

Kester's Caravans, Trading and Profit and Loss Account for Year Ended 30 June 19..

	£	£
Sales (100 caravans)		160 000
Cost of sales:		
Materials	80 000	
Labour	32 000	
	112 000	
		48 000
Expenses:		
Overheads	22 000	
Office salaries	4 000	
Directors' remuneration	8 000	
		34 000
Net profit		14 000
Losses brought forward from previous years		10 000
Profit carried forward		£4 000

Balance Sheet as at 30 June 19..

	£	£	£
Share capital: 4000 ordinary shares of £1			
each, fully paid			4 000
Undistributed profits			4 000
			£8 000
Represented by:			
Fixed assets:			
Plant			8 000
Vehicles			1 000
			9 000
Current assets:			
Stock·		11 000	
Debtors and bank		8 000	
		19 000	
Current liabilities:			
Creditors	16 000		
Directors' loans	4 000	20 000	(1000)
			£8000

Mr Kester offers Jos the entire share capital of the business at the net asset value as at 30 June last, subject only to the addition of goodwill valued at two times the projected earnings before tax for the next year and the revaluation of plant and machinery at £5000. He tells Jos that the following information is relevant in the computation of projected earnings for next year.

1. There are firm orders for 125 vans in the forthcoming year at last year's prices.
2. The cost of production per van should remain stable next year, except for the cost of labour, which will increase until it is 25 per cent of the selling price of each van.
3. The overheads will increase by £4000 and office salaries by 10 per cent.
4. A fair management remuneration for the work undertaken by the directors is £5000 per annum.

Jos notes all this information and when he sees you next asks you to compute the price at which the shares are being offered to him, and asks your advice on the basis of the information he has been given. When you answer Jos you should also suggest some other important pieces of information that he should know before he decides whether to buy the business.

The net tangible assets of the business, according to the balance sheet, are £8000, but after adjusting for the revaluation of plant this amount drops to £5000. Net profit in the forthcoming year is computed as follows:

	£	£
Sales (125 vans)		200 000
Cost of sales:		
Materials	100 000	
Labour	50 000	150 000
Gross profit		50 000
Expenses:		
Overheads	26 000	
Office salaries	4 400	
Management remuneration	5 000	35 400
Net profit		£14 600

If the net profit is £14 600 then goodwill at twice the projected earnings will equal £29 200, to which is added the net tangible assets (£5000) to give a total value of £34 200, or £8.55 per share.

As an accountant you should give Jos four major pieces of advice concerning this firm. First, superprofits, not total profits, are normally used in the computation of goodwill. It is fair to say, however, that with net tangible assets at so small an amount the expected return thereon, even at 50 per cent, would not be very significant. The second point follows from this revelation, since it concerns the fact that the purchase price covers very few tangible assets, and seems to be comprised almost completely of goodwill. Such a small asset base, especially when combined with the fact that losses have been made in the recent past, increases the risk of the venture. The third point concerns the working capital, in that the current liabilities exceed current assets and the company is technically insolvent. The ratio of quick assets to current liabilities underlines this perilous position. Fourth, the return on capital is projected at £14 600 profit on £32 400 invested, a rate of 43 per cent. Jos must determine whether this rate of return is sufficient for the risk of taking on this company, especially as losses have been made in the recent past.

The additional information which Jos might need to check Kester's accounting statement and price can be divided into two groups. First, the figures in the balance sheet and profit and loss account have to be clarified, and second, questions about business policy and future prospects have to be answered.

On the balance sheet it would be necessary to verify the values claimed for the assets which are entered at book value, and which may thus be worth more or less than that amount. The age and working condition of the plant and vehicles should be ascertained and an analysis made of the stocks. It should be noted that one figure in the balance sheet represents debtors and bank, and this figure should be analysed so that the true liquidity or cash position of the firm is revealed. Kester should be asked how he proposes to meet the current liabilities of creditors and directors' loans, since there seems to be little cash in the company to meet these claims. A suspicious accountant might enquire whether the directors' loans under current liabilities have any prior right to repayment, or whether they represent the directors' remuneration for the year in the trading account, which has not yet been paid. Only a company in a very poor liquidity position cannot afford to pay its directors. Further inquiries generated by the balance sheet would concern the availability of short- or long-term funds needed to finance the business in the near future, and whether or not any contingent liabilities existed.

Where the profit and loss account is concerned, an analysis of the past losses should be made in order to ascertain whether they are likely to recur in the future. The reason for the increase of fixed overheads in the estimates for the coming year should also be investigated, as should the firmness of the orders underlying the projected sales figures.

Other general information which is needed in order to form an opinion of the 'worthwhileness' of the company concerns prospects for increased sales in future years and the prices at which such sales will be made. The projected sales are based on firm orders, but these may be cancelled if the customers do not wish to trade with the new management, a factor which will reduce the value of the goodwill in the coming year. Enquiries about the possibility of an increase in prices, and about the relationship of the customers to Mr Kester should also be made. Future market prospects and the likely competition must be taken into account when assessing the viability of operating this firm under new management. Information about the availability of raw materials in the future, the connections of the retiring directors with suppliers, and the attitudes of key employees to the prospect of working under new management are all important factors in this decision.

Example

W. Rambler and Co. Ltd (founded in 1920) is engaged in fellmongery and hide and skin merchanting. It is based in Bermondsey (south-east London) and operates in hide and skin markets in Devon and Cornwall.

The summarized profit and loss accounts and balance sheet are set out below. No accounts have been drawn up in respect of any period subsequent to 30 September 19-8, and no dividends paid.

Profit and Loss Accounts, Years ended 30 September

	19–6	19–7	19–8
	£	£	£
Sales	982 373	989 660	865 550
Cost of sales	(894 933)	(920 798)	(763 464)
	87 440	68 862	102 086
Investment income (note 1)	20 483	14 832	23 800
Profit before taxation	107 923	83 694	125 886
Taxation	(40 338)	(43 573)	(66 754)
Profit attributable to shareholders	67 585	40 121	59 132
Dividends	12 120	12 120	20 200
Retained profit	£55 465	£28 001	£38 932

Balance Sheet at 30 September 19–8

	£	£	£
	Cost	Depreciation	
Fixed assets:			
Land and buildings, freehold	98 265	–	98 265
(Note 2). long leasehold	13 365	2 258	11 107
Plant, equipment and vehicles	68 512	52 898	15 614
	180 142	55 156	124 986
Investments (note 1)			279 611
Current assets:			
Stock and work in progress	43 300		
Debtors	62 613		
Bank and cash	69 602		
		175 515	
Less current liabilities:			
Creditors	20 915		
Taxation	93 069		
Proposed dividends	20 200		
		134 184	
Net current assets			41 331
			£445 928
Representing:			
Share capital: ordinary shares of £1		10 100	
Reserves		435 828	£445 928

Notes:

1. **Investments:**

   (a) At 30 September 19.8 investments comprised:

	£
Quoted investments (market value £71 001)	82 750
Corporation loans	190 000
Loans to employees	6 861
	£279 611

   (b) The market value of the quoted investments as at 1 June 19.9 was £89 750.
   (c) The investment income includes the related tax credit.

2. Land and buildings. The land and buildings have been valued on a going concern basis at 31 May 19-9 by Messrs Hope, Eternal and Co., Chartered Surveyors, as follows:

	$£$	
Freehold	90 000	
Long leasehold	28 500	$£118\,500$

Amalgamated Leather Holdings Ltd has liquid funds available for investment and is contemplating purchasing for cash as at 1 June 19-9 all the shares in Ramblers from Mr W. Rambler, who is retiring because of old age and poor health. The executive directors of Ramblers (the managing director and the fellmongery director) will continue to be associated with the business in their present capacities. The acquisition of Ramblers will increase the supply of raw materials to Amalgamated's tanneries.

(a) Assuming that the normal return on capital is 20 per cent (before tax) for the leather industry, and using weighted average profits, calculate the price you would expect Amalgamated to pay as at 1 June 19-9 for all the shares in Ramblers:

    (i) on an asset basis, valuing goodwill as two years' purchase of superprofits;

    (ii) on an earnings basis (for the trading profit/assets) plus investments.

(b) List six items (other than the information used in (a)) which might be taken into account in determining the actual price Amalgamated would be willing to pay for Ramblers. (The effect of capital gains tax can be ignored.)

The first step toward a solution is to calculate the weighted average trading profits. Investment income can be ignored here, since the investments will be valued separately according to the information in note (1).

$$\frac{£87\,440 + 2(£68\,862) + 3(£102\,086)}{6} = £88\,570$$

Note that the greatest weighting has been accorded to the profits of the most recent years. No adjustment has been made to the figures so they must be considered to adequately reflect future trading conditions.

Next the trading assets should be valued according to their current, rather than their book value.

	$£$	$£$
Trading assets:		
Land and buildings	118 500	
Plant etc.	15 614	
Net current assets	41 331	175 445
Investments at market value		
($£89\,750 + £190\,000 + £6861$)		286 611
(Check: $£445\,928 + £7000$ investment surplus $+ £9128$		
property surplus)		462 056
Post balance sheet profit		
8 months net profit (1 October 19-8 to 1 June 19-9)		
$\dfrac{8}{12} \times \dfrac{£67\,585 + 2(£40\,121) + 3(£59\,132)}{6} = \dfrac{8}{12} \times £54\,204 =$		36 136
Total assets (excluding goodwill)		498 192

The balance sheet is the basis of this valuation, but the assets shown therein will have increased by the valuation date by the amount of profit made net of tax since 30 September 19-8.

	£	£
Total assets excluding goodwill		498 192
Superprofit calculation:		
Assets £175 445 × 20 per cent	35 089	
Actual profit (WA)	88 570	
Superprofit	£53 481	
Goodwill:		
2 × £53 481		106 962
Value on assets basis plus goodwill		£605 154

Part (ii) of (a) is calculated as follows:

	£	
Profit: £88 570 × $\dfrac{100}{20}$	442 850	= Capital value of trading assets
Investments as above	286 611	
Value on earnings basis	£729 461	

Other items which might be considered when the company is valued would include matters which affected the future return of the business, and adjustments which might affect the present position. The valuation above is based on past profits, but estimates of future profits, perhaps even weighted in favour of the most recent year, might be used. If Mr Rambler has drawn a salary in excess of the market rate for the work he has performed, the amount of this excess must be added back to past profits so that they are adjusted to reflect the future after Mr Rambler has retired. The general economic prospects for the industry as a whole will affect the confidence of the purchasers, while the particular situation of Rambler Ltd (e.g. whether it is a forced sale, or whether a rival bidder is likely to make a counter offer) will also influence the price. If Rambler Ltd fits neatly into the operations of Amalgamated Leather Holdings (e.g. if Amalgamated Leather Holdings do not have a subsidiary in Devon or Cornwall and wish to expand in that area) this will improve the value of Rambler Ltd in the view of the management of Amalgamated.

The valuation above has been made on the basis of the book value of the plant, although a current value would be more helpful. The profits for the eight months since the last accounting date have been estimated, although actual figures may be available for use instead. If the goodwill is likely to evaporate when Mr Rambler leaves the business, because it is caused by factors related to his management, then the two-year purchase period for superprofits in the goodwill computation might be reduced.

The Accounting Treatment of Goodwill

In the past there has been little conformity in the way goodwill is dealt with in the accounts. Some companies show it as a balance sheet item and leave it at the same amount year after year, while others write it off against reserves, or to the profit and loss account.

There is no set rule about the rate at which such a write-off occurs. Another alternative is to ignore goodwill altogether in the accounts.

In a recent survey of published accounts the ICEAW found that out of 300 major companies surveyed, 95 included goodwill as a separate balance sheet item, 42 deducted it from the reserves, and 93 wrote it off as it arose. The remainder ignored goodwill in their accounts.

Some accountants differentiate between acquisition goodwill and classical goodwill. Acquisition goodwill arises when a company buys the assets of another business at more than the book value of the assets. The difference between the consideration (price paid) and the book value of assets purchased is goodwill. Some authorities suggest that, rather than this figure being retained in the balance sheet for an indefinite period, it should be written off over the period of its life, or some shorter period. Unfortunately the protagonists of this view cannot find a serviceable method of computing the expected life, if any, of goodwill.

Under the EEC Fourth Directive on accounts, goodwill is not to remain indefinitely as an intangible asset in the balance sheet. Companies will have to write off goodwill over a maximum five-year period, with provision for the period to be lengthened if it can be established that the useful economic life of the asset is longer than five years.

TUTORIAL DISCUSSION TOPICS

22.1. What factors influence the risk attached to an investment in a company?

22.2. Why should a controlling interest in a public company be valued differently from a minority interest in a private company?

22.3. Why is it necessary to adjust past profits when using them to compute a value for a business?

22.4. Reconcile the legal view of goodwill with that of the accountant.

22.5. Outline the factors which support the existence of goodwill in a company, and show how they can be related to the number of years' purchase of goodwill when a business is valued.

SEMINAR EXERCISES 13

1. (a) From the information which appears below calculate the value of each ordinary share on an assets basis, on a possible 'break-up' basis, and on a yield basis.

EWJ Co. Ltd, Balance Sheet as at 31 December

	£			£
Issued share capital:				
30 000 ordinary shares of £1				
each, fully paid	30 000	Goodwill		6 500
5 per cent debentures	15 000	Fixed assets		
		(net)		35 000
General reserve	6 000	Current assets:		
Profit and loss account	1 500	Stock	7 500	
Sundry creditors	13 500	Debtors	12 500	
		Cash	4 500	24 500
	£66 000			£66 000

Notes:

1. Goodwill is to be revalued to a figure which represents 10 per cent of proprietors' capital employed at 31 December.
2. Stock is found to be understated by 3 per cent.
3. The average annual profit over the past five years has been £4500.
4. The normal return for this period of activity may be taken as 10 per cent.

(b) If you were an investor, what other things would you look for in assessing a company's potential?

2. (a) 'Surely the balance sheet provides all the information required to value a business. After all, it usually shows an item labelled 'shareholders' funds'.' Comment.
   (b) The following is the balance sheet of Boozles, a wholesale wine merchanting business, at 31 March Year 5.

	£	£
Liabilities:		
Owners' capital		60 000
Creditors		10 000
		70 000
Assets (at written-down value):		
Land and buildings		20 000
Fixtures and fittings		10 000
		30 000
Current assets:		
Stock	30 000	
Debtors	7 000	
Cash	3 000	40 000
		70 000

You ascertain the following information:

(i) The land and buildings are currently valued at £50 000.
(ii) Included in the debtors is a balance of £1000 which may prove irrecoverable.
(iii) Businesses of this type usually provide a return of 25 per cent on the gross assets employed.
(iv) The profits over the past five years (before charging any remuneration for the owner) were as follows:

Year ended 31 March	Year 1	Year 2	Year 3	Year 4	Year 5
	£	£	£	£	£
Profits	25 000	30 000	35 000	40 000	40 000

It is anticipated that growth of profit in the future is extremely unlikely.

Suggest three alternative methods of valuation for the business, stating clearly any assumptions you make.

3. Ever since Mr Carrott died his wife has retained the family business, which has been run completely by Mr Parsnip. Mr Parsnip is now due to retire. Mrs Carrott is therefore considering selling the business. For every £1000 that she receives from the sale of the business she can buy a pension of £218 per annum, ceasing on her death.

   The following figures include the relevant extracts from the profit and loss account for the year to 31 December.

	£
Wages of department heads:	
Mr Parsnip	7 000
Mr Turnip	7 000
Mr Swede	7 000
Wages of other staff	49 000
Directors' emoluments:	
Mr Parsnip	5 000
Mrs Carrott	7 500
Transport	16 000
Interest	4 000
Heat and light	7 000
Bad debts	3 120
Loss on sale of car	2 500
Net profit	30 000

Balance sheet for the last three years:

	Year Before Last	Last Year	This Year
	£	£	£
Share capital	20 000	20 000	40 000
Reserves	50 000	65 000	70 000
Loans	–	–	20 000
Current liabilities	32 000	40 000	30 000
	£102 000	£125 000	£160 000
Fixed assets cost	60 000	60 000	120 000
Less depreciation	30 000	40 000	60 000
	30 000	20 000	60 000
Current assets:			
Stock	40 000	40 000	40 000
Debtors	20 000	30 000	25 000
Cash	12 000	35 000	35 000
	£102 000	£125 000	£160 000

Mr Ward is interested in buying the business and holds the following assets:

	Capital	Income per annum
	£	£
Building society	10 000	900
Quoted shares	10 000	400
Shares in private company	10 000	300

(a) Calculate the superprofit for the current year, indicating any assumptions you would wish to confirm.

(b) What is the purchase price of the business? (The basis of calculation of goodwill is to be the next two years' projected superprofits with the last three years assumed to indicate a constant trend in profit. This year's depreciation is to be reduced from 20 per cent to 15 per cent (there were no disposals).)

4. There has been a recent decline in the market for decorative watergarden plants, and Mr C. Weed is considering the sale of his business, Waterweeds Ltd, in which he owns all the shares, to Underwater Plants Ltd.

The most recent balance sheet and profits for the last five years are as follows:

Balance Sheet of Waterweeds Ltd as at 31 December 15

Share capital and reserves:	£	Fixed assets:	£	£
Ordinary share capital		Freehold land and		
of £1 each	30 000	buildings		20 000
General reserve	10 000	Plant and		
	40 000	equipment		10 000
Less deficit on profit and loss				
account	(20 000)			
	20 000			
Current liabilities:		Current assets:		
Creditors	30 000	Stock	30 000	
Bank overdraft	30 000	Debtors	20 000	50 000
	£80 000			£80 000

The stock is revalued at £20 000 and the land and buildings are considered to be undervalued by £10 000. All other assets represent market value.

Profits for the last five years are: year 11, £10 000 loss; year 12, £5000 loss; year 13, £5000 profit; year 14, £10 000 profit; year 15, £15 000 profit.

Profit and loss accounts have been prepared on a uniform basis and Mr Weed has charged only a nominal management fee for his services, taking out profits by way of dividends. A fair return for this kind of business is 20 per cent. Losses made in the past are not likely to recur.

(a) Compute a value for each ordinary share in Waterweeds Ltd.

(b) Discuss briefly those factors which cause goodwill to arise in a business.

5. Almond Ltd is an old family company in the south west of England. The company, which manufactures gliders, has an enviable reputation for good workmanship, prompt delivery and low prices. Purchases of raw materials are made from another

business, also owned by Mr Almond, which is not for sale. Mr Almond offers all of the issued share capital in the glider manufacturing business to Mr Cherry at the net asset value on 31 December plus the adjusted profits of the last three accounting years.

Any adjustments to profit are to be ignored for the purpose of calculating the net asset value.

For the purpose of the selling negotiations Almond produces the following information:

Balance Sheet Extract as at 31 December

	£	£	£
Issued share capital:			
20 000 ordinary shares of £1 each			20 000
Reserves:			
General reserve		10 000	
Profit and loss account:			
Profit for year	100 000		
Less losses brought forward	60 000		
		40 000	
			50 000
Long-term loan			60 000
			130 000
Current liabilities:			
Trade creditors	10 000		
Director's salary	60 000		
			70 000
			£200 000

A Statement of Past Profitability for the Three Years Ended 31 December

Year Before Last	Last Year	This Year
£60 000	£90 000	£100 000

The following information is also relevant:

(a) A reasonable management remuneration is estimated to be £40 000 per annum, not £60 000 per annum as deducted by Almond.

(b) Depreciation has been understated in each year by: £10 000 the year before last; £15 000 last year; and £20 000 this year.

Calculate the offer price and advise Mr Cherry.

Interpretation of
Financial Statements

23 | The Interpretation of Accounts

The means by which an accountant is able to understand a set of accounts and reveal their meaning to a non-accountant are among the most advanced techniques he can use. A blend of skill and experience is required to explain the relative importance of the figures and the relationship between one figure and another. A good accountant can translate what the statements show to be happening to a company, and can comment on the significance of the figures for the efficient operation of the business. This is not always a matter of hindsight, since comment on future planned positions is also helpful.

The accountant must bear in mind the recipient of his interpretation when drawing out the meaning of a set of accounts, as what is significant to one user may be less so to another. He may be commenting to management on the performance of various divisions in a group of companies, or, as an extension of the annual accounts, providing helpful statistics for the shareholders, or demonstrating the optimal use of the capacity available to the management. The accountant may also be called on to comment on the business to potential investors, such as a city institution or the client of a stockbroker, or to his own managers when they are considering a takeover bid. The profit record, dividend cover and growth potential will be important to an investor, whereas the asset base and profit/earnings ratio will usually be of greater interest in a takeover bid. When interpreting a set of accounts for a creditor or potential creditor, the accountant will accentuate the company's ability to repay a loan on the due date, to meet the interest required, or to provide security to cover the loan.

THE BASIC QUESTIONS

There is a set of basic questions to which the interpreter will seek answers. The answer to each question will lead to further questions, so that gradually a picture of what is happening in the company will emerge. The first question usually concerns profitability. It is not enough to discover whether a profit or a loss is being made, since a measure of the adequacy of profit is needed. The return on capital employed should show whether profits are sufficient to warrant the amount of funds invested in a business, the risk taken by investing those funds, and whether a better return for the same class of risk could be earned by an alternative employment of the funds. This approach leads on to questions to determine whether the assets are employed in the right way or in the best combination, and whether the company is on the threshold of a profit breakthrough after some lean years when reorganization has taken place.

The second question investigates solvency, or the ability of the firm to pay its way. Some argue that this should be the first question asked, as sometimes a profitable business is brought to a halt through insufficient liquid funds. The interpretation of the solvency position revolves around the availability of cash to repay creditors and the adequacy of working capital resources to finance the level of activity required by management. The liquidity of the current assets, the rate of expansion of stocks and debtors to an 'overtrading' position, and the ability of the business to borrow are all significant in this part of the pattern.

The third major question concerns ownership of the business. One individual or group may control a firm through significant shareholdings, and thus may be in a position to influence management policy. The voting rights of various classes of capital are important in this case. Rights to dividend and repayment of capital if the business is wound up are important matters to a potential shareholder. Often the ownership of shares is obscured through the use of nominee holdings. Ownership, however, has a deeper significance, since it can be used to comment on the relative importance of the various groups who have supplied the funds utilized to finance the business. In this sense all those who have provided funds for use in the business, shareholders, long-term lenders and current liabilities, are seen as owners of the assets which their finance has helped to buy, especially since, if the firm ceased trading, they would expect to be repaid out of the proceeds of those assets. If, for example, the trade creditors become a significant provider of finance, they may begin to have more power over the destiny of the firm than its legal owners, the shareholders. When assets are charged as security for loans the actions of the management may be inhibited, since they cannot dispose of certain assets without permission of the lender.

The fourth major question deals with financial strength. A weak company is one which has used up all its credit facilities and thus can borrow no more or one which is overdependent on sources of finance outside the business. If a company has unused overdraft facilities or uncharged assets which can act as security it can use this extra finance to extricate itself from financial difficulties or mount an expansion scheme. A different view of financial strength measures the amount of assets which the company controls year by year, so that growth in the assets, financed by increasing reserves from profits retained in the business, is seen as a healthy sign.

A fifth avenue of approach is to investigate trends. If the accounting statements for several years are expressed in columnar form and placed side by side, changes in the relative importance of certain items can be identified. For example, when all costs are expressed as a percentage of sales, the fact that one cost is becoming a larger proportion of the total as year succeeds year can be seen; or when all sources of finance are expressed as a percentage of total capital employed, the changing relative importance of the various classes of capital providers can be noted. When variations from a settled pattern are observed an attempt should be made to discover the cause. If, for example, the proportion of debtors or stocks to total assets has increased, further investigation to establish the reason for such a change should be initiated. It is also possible to extrapolate the figures to forecast what is likely to happen if the present rate of change is maintained.

The last basic question concerns cover, to reveal the adequacy of the margin of profits over a required rate of dividend, or of the value of a secured asset over the principal of the loan. Further questions concerning gearing are raised from this point to find the effect of a fluctuation in profit on the ability of the company to pay a dividend or to meet its liability for loan interest.

Once the answers to these six basic questions and their associated queries have been found, the accountant knows a great deal about the position of a business. Three techniques are used to answer these questions and to help form an opinion of a set of accounts. They are ratio analysis, funds flow statements, and balance sheet criticism. These techniques are not used in isolation, but together, each providing evidence to support the conclusions drawn from another.

RATIO ANALYSIS

A ratio shows the relationship of one figure to another and can be used in accounting to demonstrate the interplay between balance sheet items, or between features of the profit and loss account and the balance sheet. Ratios are useful in that they summarize a position and simplify an explanation of a complicated statement by its expression in one figure. However, a major disadvantage of their use is that they sometimes over-simplify a situation, and thus without a proper understanding of the definition of the constituent parts false conclusions may be drawn; e.g. the definition of net profit (before or after tax), or of capital employed, can seriously affect the return on capital employed. Accountants often use ratios to focus attention on important items in accounting statements or to illustrate points made in reports, but these techniques must be treated with caution. Ratios should be used as a guide, not as a basis for definitive conclusions. Too much reliance should not be placed on the impression gained from one ratio alone. The findings should be checked against other ratios, and perhaps against a movement of funds statement, until gradually a clearer picture emerges. Sometimes compensating changes in the constituent parts of a ratio can obscure the extent of the change that has taken place; e.g. although profit and capital employed may double, this important change does not show up in the ratio of net profit to capital employed. A change in both constituent parts at the same time will alter the ratios, but can cause confusion when the reason for the change is investigated.

Another use for ratios is as comparators. Absolute figures in an accounting statement are made more meaningful when they are put into perspective by comparison. Although the profit made by a company is always interesting, its significance is properly demonstrated only when it is measured against the capital employed in making that profit. An increase in profit may be considered as a good result until the extent of the extra capital employed to earn it is shown. The comparison of ratios of one company with those of another, or with the average ratios of a group of similar companies, is helpful, and comparison of the ratios of the same company at different time periods will reveal important changes from the established pattern for the company, which should prompt an investigation. Some companies treat ratios as guidelines or targets to be reached during the planning and budgeting operation. Because ratios reflect a relationship they can transcend national barriers. The ROCE, compiled from figures expressed in pounds, dollars or yen, enables international comparison to take place.

Ratios can be expressed as percentages, e.g. the rate of gross profit to sales, say 25 per cent; or as a relationship, e.g. current assets to current liabilities, say 1.7:1; or as one figure times another, e.g. the turnover of capital employed is, say, 2.4 times in a year; or in terms of time, e.g. debtors to credit sales may reveal an average credit period of sixty days.

RETURN ON CAPITAL EMPLOYED (ROCE)

One approach to ratio analysis is to compute the ratios in figure 10 and use their interaction to interpret the position of the company.

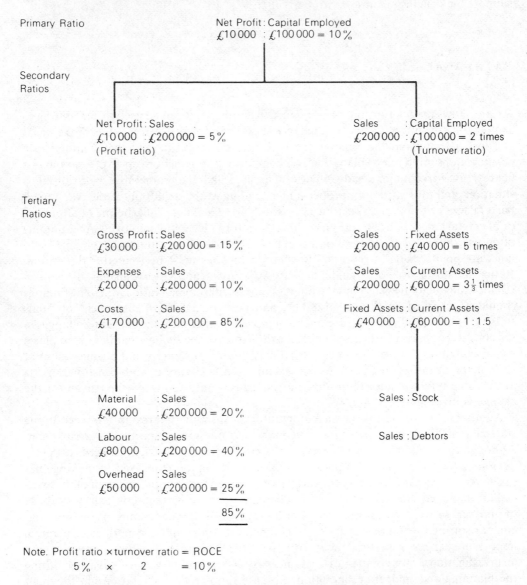

Primary Ratio

Net Profit : Capital Employed
£10 000 : £100 000 = 10%

Secondary Ratios

Net Profit : Sales
£10 000 : £200 000 = 5%
(Profit ratio)

Sales   : Capital Employed
£200 000 : £100 000 = 2 times
(Turnover ratio)

Tertiary Ratios

Gross Profit : Sales
£30 000   : £200 000 = 15%

Sales   : Fixed Assets
£200 000 : £40 000 = 5 times

Expenses   : Sales
£20 000   : £200 000 = 10%

Sales   : Current Assets
£200 000 : £60 000 = 3⅓ times

Costs   : Sales
£170 000 : £200 000 = 85%

Fixed Assets : Current Assets
£40 000   : £60 000 = 1 : 1.5

Material   : Sales
£40 000   : £200 000 = 20%

Sales : Stock

Labour   : Sales
£80 000   : £200 000 = 40%

Sales : Debtors

Overhead   : Sales
£50 000   : £200 000 = 25%

85%

Note. Profit ratio × turnover ratio = ROCE
        5%   ×   2   = 10%

Figure 10. Ratio Diagram.

The first ratio is the ratio of net profit to capital employed. It is known as the primary ratio, since it reveals the return on capital employed and comments on the efficiency of management in employing the funds placed at their disposal by shareholders and lenders. This ratio is often expressed as a percentage and can be used to compare performance with other companies in the same industry, or other industries, or other economies, or at other time periods. The return on capital employed is seen by the investor as the return he receives for placing his funds at risk, and is compared with the return available for alternative investments in the same risk category.

The definition of capital employed remains the subject of discussion among accountants. The ratio of net profit to shareholders' funds (share capital and reserves) expresses the return on the capital contributed by the legal owners of the business. This figure is a valuable guide to the profitability of the shareholders' investment, but, since it uses a limited definition of capital employed, cannot comment well on managerial efficiency. The net capital employed, defined as fixed assets plus working capital, is often used for ROCE in published accounts. It provides an acceptable figure, but of course does not set profit against all the capital employed, since current liabilities, an important source of capital employed, are ignored. It is argued that current liabilities provide finance for only a few weeks or months and should therefore be ignored, but when one current liability is repaid, usually another takes its place, so the total funds employed do not fluctuate very much. It seems wrong to calculate the ROCE after excluding bank overdraft and taxation awaiting payment.

Some authorities prefer to set net profit against gross capital employed (fixed and current assets) to show what the management have really produced from all the assets at their disposal. This definition is incomplete if it uses historic. figures derived from a balance sheet. Perhaps a fairer view of managerial efficiency is found by setting net profit against the current value of all the assets, but this of course presupposes that the current value can be determined easily. Where net profit is set against the net capital employed, which includes long-term liabilities, there is a case for adding back loan interest to the net profit figure so that a true return on the capital employed is shown. If this argument is carried to its logical conclusion, overdraft interest should be added back to profit if the gross capital definition is favoured.

There is some difference of opinion among accountants about whether net profit before or after tax should be used for this ratio. Some argue that managerial efficiency should be measured before tax is deducted, while others hold the view that a good management should minimize the tax burden, and that profit after tax shows what is available for dividend or reinvestment in the company.

A good or bad return on capital employed can be explained by two basic reasons. Either the profit on the activity is not large enough, or the capital employed is not worked hard enough. Further investigation of these reasons can be achieved by the use of secondary ratios. Net profit to sales shows the profitability of sales made, and can be expressed as a percentage or as so many pence of profit for every pound of sales. This ratio can be further analysed by the tertiary ratios. If net profit to sales is not satisfactory the cause may be either in the pricing policy of the firm, if the mark-up is insufficient, or in the cost structure, if expenses and costs are too high. The difference between the percentage of net profit and gross profit to sales is the percentage of expenses to sales. When the gross profit margin is adequate, the reason for an unsatisfactory profit to sales ratio should lie in the cost structure, which can be further analysed by computing the percentage of various costs to sales, and revealing the changing position of the various cost headings.

Alternatively, if net profit to sales shows an adequate return, the reason for low profitability could be that not enough sales are being made. In other words, the productive capacity or assets of the firm are not working hard enough. The ratio of sales to capital employed (the turnover ratio) shows how many pounds of sales are earned by each pound of capital employed, or how many times the capital is turned over, the idea being that every time a firm turns over its capital it makes the profit margin. When the ratio of net profit to sales is multiplied by the turnover ratio, the result is equal to the primary ratio. If the turnover ratio is inadequate further analysis to pinpoint that part of the asset structure where underutilized capacity exists will investigate the ratios of sales to fixed assets, and sales to current assets (or sales to working capital if the net capital employed definition is used in the primary ratio). The ratio of fixed assets to current assets will show whether the business has the right combination in its asset structure or whether there is a preponderance of current or fixed assets. Sales can then be set against the individual assets to reveal over-investment in any one classification. The ratio of stock to sales in this context shows how many pounds of sales are earned for each pound of stock held. In other circumstances stocks would not be set against sales since they are at cost while sales include the profit margin.

Although ROCE is useful for making comparisons over time and between firms in different industries or different economies, it is not without its disadvantages as a measure of managerial efficiency. It is misleading if all capital employed is not included, and if profits are computed at current prices while the capital employed is stated at book value based on historic cost. Even when ROCE is computed a further appraisal must be made to establish the risk taken with the investment to measure whether the ROCE is adequate. The impact of factors outside the control of management must be defined before ROCE can be used to comment on managerial performance. Capital investment is a long-term operation, with projects which may have lives of ten years or more, and perhaps with the return not flowing in evenly over the years of this life. ROCE shows only the result of one year's transactions.

Efficiency is a loose term and means different things to different people, e.g. the engineer, the cost accountant and the economist. To the engineer it might be the input/output ratio of a machine, to the cost accountant the difference between standard and actual cost, and to the economist the achievement of maximum output from a given input (productivity). Profit is the return that a management has made on the capital employed in the business and it is right that their efficiency should be judged on the basis of this return. The risk incurred in the business must be taken into account, by computing a risk factor and applying it to the capital employed, to show how much profit should be made by a particular business. The success of the return on capital employed as a measure of business efficiency also depends upon the objectives of the firm. Not all firms seek to maximize their profits: their objective may be a satisfactory return on capital or the provision of a good service.

Comparison between the operating units within a large organization may help the departmental management by showing how each department compares with others and by pinpointing areas in which improvement can take place. Such comparison may also help the central department in the firm, which is concerned with providing management advisory services to the constituent units. Intra-firm comparison on the basis of return on capital employed will help central management to judge whether the performance of operating units is satisfactory and will show where improvements can be made and central funds allocated. There are, however, certain points which must be discussed, such as what is meant by efficiency, how it is to be measured, what the causes of differences in efficiency are, and how much similarity is necessary before useful comparisons can be made.

The return on capital employed as a measure for comparison compares operating profit to capital employed and acts as a common denominator between firms when comparing the efficiency of managements in using available resources. Other comparison measures which might be used are as follows:

(a) the rate of growth of assets (depends on policy, not efficiency);
(b) profit alone (this has limited benefit unless related to capital employed);
(c) value added per employee;

(d) output per man- or machine-hour;

(e) sales per employee or per £ of payroll.

The last three measures may all show a favourable position while the firm itself is inefficient in other ways. As tests they are not valid, since they do not show an overall view of the business. Return on capital employed is important because it shows whether adequate use is being made of the funds in the business, irrespective of the source of the capital. It must be established whether the funds have earned the return that should have been made from them. Any discussion of business efficiency and the return on capital employed must take into account the fact that good management ensures continuity and expansion, and will not squeeze out extra profits in the short term, which will harm the long-term position of the business. Development periods for large-scale capital projects, when a low return is to be expected, must also be taken into account.

Further action which can be instigated after the return on capital is computed is to investigate whether profits are adequate and/or whether there is room for improvement. Profit is the motivating force in industry, and it must continue to be made at the correct rate if capital is to continue to be attracted into the business.

The Limitations of Return on Capital Employed

1. Definitions of capital employed vary, and confusion may arise when return on capital is discussed unless terms are rationalized.
2. The return on capital is a misleading guide to efficiency unless assets are valued at current prices. Profits are counted in terms of current prices, so it will be misleading if they are compared with capital computed on a historic basis.
3. Comparison of efficiency between firms by means of return on capital employed will be difficult if they are not truly comparable businesses; e.g. one business may lease its plant, another may have new plant, while another may work with old-fashioned plant. Any device to reduce these differences to a common figure will introduce an element of unreality into the comparison.
4. The return on capital employed does not take risk into account. Thus a business may appear to be making a high return, but the fact that a high return is necessary to compensate for risk taken is not taken into account.
5. Capital investment is a long-term phenomenon and often a low return is experienced in the early years of a long-term project. It is therefore necessary that the return on the project over its full life, not just part of its life (say, a year), is used if a true conclusion about its profitability is to be reached. A business is a going concern, while accounting periods tend to be closed systems measuring the return on capital during only part of a full cycle. Difficulty is experienced in deciding what horizon is to be used in measuring efficiency. Some firms will accept low profits at present for larger returns in the future, while others will prefer high profits now and smaller returns later.

Example

The following skeleton final accounts relate to firms X and Y. Using ratio analysis compare the financial situations of the two companies from the information available.

Profit and Loss Account

	X £	Y £
Sales	220 000	240 000
Less cost of sales	176 000	168 000
Gross profit	44 000	72 000
Less expenses	28 600	55 200
Net profit	£15 400	£16 800

Balance Sheet

	£	£	£	£
Share capital and reserves		40 000		110 000
Long-term liabilities		10 000		10 000
Net capital employed		£50 000		£120 000
Fixed assets		20 000		100 000
Current assets:				
Stock	40 000		16 000	
Debtors	12 000		40 000	
Cash	4 000		4 000	
	56 000		60 000	
Less current liabilities:				
Trade creditors	26 000		40 000	
Working capital		30 000		20 000
Net assets		£50 000		£120 000

Note: 50 per cent of sales are on credit terms. All purchases are on credit terms. Opening stocks are: X, £50 000; Y, £10 000. (Using cost of sales and closing stock you can compute purchases.)

	X	Y
The primary ratio, profitability:		
Net profit to capital employed	15 400:50 000	16 800:120 000
Company X is the more profitable	30.8%	14%
If the gross capital had been		
used in this ratio	15 400:76 000	16 800:160 000
	20.2%	10.5%

This underlines the importance of the definition of the ratio being used. Strictly speaking, the interest on long-term capital should have been added back to net profit.

	X	Y
The secondary ratios:		
Net profit to sales	15 400:220 000	16 800:240 000
	7%	7%
Sales to capital employed	220 000:50 000	240 000:120 000
Turnover ratio	4.4 times	2 times
	4.4 ×7 = 30.8%	2 ×7 = 14%

Both companies earn the same return on their sales, but X makes its capital work harder and is thus more profitable. Further investigation of the asset structure reveals:

	X	Y
Sales to fixed assets	220 000:20 000	240 000:100 000
	11 times	2.4 times
Sales to working capital	220 000:30 000	240 000:20 000
	7.3 times	12 times
Fixed assets to working capital	20 000:30 000	100 000:20 000
	1:1.5	5:1

X is more efficient in the use of fixed assets, while Y makes working capital work harder. The larger proportion of fixed assets to working capital in Y perhaps shows underutilized capacity. Further ratio analysis of the asset structure shows:

	X	Y
Sales to stock	220 000:40 000	240 000:16 000
	5.5 times	15 times
Sales to debtors	220 000:12 000	240 000:40 000
	18.3 times	6 times

In Y the stocks work three times as hard as in X, whereas the debtors of X support three times as much sales as those of Y. Both companies have the same profit ratio, but what happens with further investigation?

	X	Y
Gross profit to sales	44 000:220 000	72 000:240 000
	20%	30%
Expenses to sales	28 600:220 000	55 200:240 000
	13%	23%

Company Y has a real advantage over X, either on mark-up or on cost of goods sold, but this is nullified by the impact of higher expenses. Perhaps the higher expenses of Y reflect the impact of extra depreciation and maintenance on the extra fixed assets which it possesses.

THE ALTERNATIVE APPROACH TO RATIO ANALYSIS

This approach investigates one aspect of the firm's affairs at a time. Ratios can be used in groups to comment on solvency, earnings, stocks, capital, sales etc.

Solvency

Two main ratios are used to originate comment on this important aspect of business affairs, and other ratios can be used to substantiate the situation. The first ratio is the working capital ratio, or current ratio, which sets current assets against current liabilities. It expresses the surplus of current assets over current liabilities, or the amount of the firm's own funds used to finance short-term assets. It is also used by short-term creditors to assess the risk of lending to the firm, since a surplus of current assets over current liabilities means that there are sufficient current assets as a fund from which to repay trade creditors and others. When current liabilities exceed current assets (negative working capital) it appears that short-term funds have been recruited to finance long-term assets – a danger sign. Bracketed with the current ratio is the quick asset or 'acid test' ratio, which sets against current liabilities those current assets which can be quickly turned into cash (debtors, investments and cash). This ratio is a useful indicator of whether the firm can meet current liabilities with liquid funds, and a 1:1 relationship is considered prudent if a firm is to be able to pay its way. However, it must be made clear that this ratio is somewhat bogus, since the so-called quick assets often cannot be turned into cash in a short time, and in any case many of the current liabilities do not fall due immediately and may be payable in three or four months' time.

In the example the current and quick asset ratios are computed as follows. Note the impact of stock on the liquidity of X.

	X	Y
Current ratio	56:26	60:40
	= 2.2:1	= 1.5:1
Quick asset ratio	16:26	44:40
	= 0.6:1	= 1.1:1

Clearly the solvency position is affected by debtors, creditors and stocks. The ratio of debtors to credit sales comments on the average length of time that debtors take to pay their bills, and the ratio of trade creditors to purchases reveals the average credit period taken by the company. Both these ratios can be computed in terms of time, as follows:

	X	Y
Debtors to credit sales	$\dfrac{12\,000}{110\,000} \times \dfrac{365}{1} = 40$ days	$\dfrac{40\,000}{120\,000} \times \dfrac{365}{1} = 122$ days
Trade creditors to purchases	$\dfrac{26\,000}{166\,000} \times \dfrac{365}{1} = 57$ days	$\dfrac{40\,000}{174\,000} \times \dfrac{365}{1} = 84$ days

Furthermore, the ratio of debtors to creditors highlights the amount of trade credit received and given by the firm.

	X	Y
Debtors to creditors	12 000 : 26 000 1 : 2.16	40 000 : 40 000 = 1 : 1

Company Y is in balance, while Company X is seen to use more credit than it gives, which reflects the position as shown by the quick asset ratio.

The ratio of bad debts to credit sales will show up reckless selling if the volume of bad debts has reached an unacceptable level.

Stocks

The purpose of stock ratios is to comment on the adequacy of stock levels in the light of the reason for holding the stock concerned. These ratios can be computed for different kinds of stock, usually in terms of time and on the basis of the average stock held for the year, i.e. opening plus closing stock divided by two. Alternatively, the ratios can be expressed as a single figure representing the number of times the stock is turned over during the year.

$$\text{Average material stock to Cost of material used} = \frac{(\text{Opening Stock} + \text{Closing Stock} \div 2)}{\text{Material Usage}} \times \frac{365}{1} \text{ days} = - \text{days}$$

If the lead time between ordering raw materials and their delivery is short, then some very convincing reasons will be required to support a high level of investment in stock.

$$\frac{\text{Average work in progress stock}}{\text{Cost of production for a year}} \times \frac{365}{1} \text{ days} = - \text{ days}$$

The above ratio comments on the time spent by semi-finished goods on their way through the factory, and can suggest reasons for production holdups when compared with the estimated time to complete the production cycle. Caution is needed when conclusions are considered, since the stock involved will be incomplete in terms of cost whereas cost of production is at full cost.

$$\frac{\text{Average finished goods stock}}{\text{Cost of sales for a year}} \times \frac{365}{1} \text{ days} = - \text{ days}$$

In circumstances where production and sales are not well co-ordinated, the above ratio helps to reveal the length of time that completed goods wait in the stores before being sold.

Capital

The main ratios used to explore this aspect of a firm's activity are as follows:

1. Capital employed to total indebtedness. This is the ownership ratio, which highlights the proportions of the assets financed by the legal owners and by lenders. Over-dependence on finance from outside the firm is a sign of weakness, although in circumstances of inflation it can bring benefits. The ratio can take two forms:

    total assets to long-term liabilities and current liabilities; and
    share capital plus reserves to long-term liabilities and current liabilities.

2. The gearing ratio, which can be computed by a number of alternative formulae, points out the importance of fixed return capital in the capital structure. In a highly geared company the proportion of fixed return capital is high, so when profits exceed the amount required to service the fixed return capital the ordinary shareholders will benefit. An upward fluctuation of profits in these circumstances will lead to a more than proportionate increase in the return to the ordinary shareholders. The usual formula is:

    ordinary shares to preference shares and long-term liabilities.

3. Another capital ratio comments on the disposition of the assets financed by the capital employed. The ratio of fixed assets to capital employed, or of fixed assets to current assets, will highlight the proportions in which management have divided their investment of the funds at their disposal in a long- or short-term form.

    Some accountants hold the view that it is prudent to ensure that the fixed assets are covered by the ownership interest in the business, i.e. share capital and reserves, but others, with an eye to the advantage of raising the gearing and post-inflation repayment of long-term loans, are more flexible in their attitude.

Earnings

The managers, shareholders and potential investors all have an interest in these ratios.

1. Net profit after preference dividend and tax to equity interest (ordinary shares plus reserves).

   The return earned on the shareholders' investment in the company must be sufficient to warrant the risk they are taking in entrusting their funds to the management. The funds involved consist in this case of the original investment in shares and profits retained since the company began trading. The return on ownership capital invested shows whether the company is organized in such a way as to maximize the shareholders' proportion of the profit, whether or not it is paid to them as a dividend.

2. The 'pay out' ratio sets profit available for dividend against dividend paid, to explore the dividend policy of the board and at the same time to comment on the ability and/or determination of the company to expand by ploughing back profits. Further analysis using the ratio of profit available for dividend to dividend required or paid shows the dividend cover position. If profits are sufficient to cover the dividend at a certain rate then there is greater security or certainty that the dividend required by a potential investor will be paid. For example, 100 000 ordinary shares of £1 each are in issue. A dividend of 20 pence in the pound is required to meet the investors' calculation of the risk involved, so £20 000 is needed to pay a dividend. If the profit is £40 000 then the required dividend is 'twice covered', and there is an ample margin for profit retention. The amount of profit to be retained in the business is often a very finely balanced decision. If too much profit is retained the dividends will be restricted and demand for the shares will be reduced. If too little is 'ploughed back' then, although dividends are high in the short term, development and replacement of capital equipment is cut back so that obsolescence follows and in time earning capacity is reduced.

3. Yield. This ratio sets dividend paid per share against the current market price of the share and shows what return an investor can expect to receive from funds laid out in the purchase of a share. It suffers from the weakness that the dividend paid is only part of the earnings attributable to the shareholder. Another ratio, the P/E (price to earnings) ratio, is often used as a remedy. The earnings per share (EPS) are set against market price to show the shareholder what return he is getting on the current value of his share, either as dividend or in the form of profits retained and invested on his behalf by the directors. The EPS are calculated by dividing the net profit after tax and preference dividend by the average number of ordinary shares in issue during the year.

   According to Standard Accounting Practice 3, the EPS should be shown as a note on the face of the published profit and loss account. This standard applies to all quoted companies other than banks and discount companies, and is so arranged that a potential investor can compute a P/E ratio for the company to compare it with those of similar companies, or with its own figure for a previous year. The basis of the calculation of EPS must also be shown as a note to the published accounts. Difficulties arise in the calculation where the number of shares at issue is unclear. If the company has issued convertible loan stock, the owners of such stock could exchange their holdings for ordinary shares, and if these extra potential shares are in the EPS calculation they will dilute the EPS figure. SSAP 3 states that diluted EPS must be shown as well as the basic EPS where equity shares which do not rank for dividend in the period under review are at issue, or where conversion rights exist, or where options have been granted to persons who can exercise them to subscribe for shares.

THE GROSS PROFIT RATIO

This ratio is considered to be so important to accountants that it merits separate discussion. It is computed by setting the gross profit against sales, and is expressed as a percentage. Clearly it can be used as a control device, since it brings together all the elements of the trading account. The gross profit is computed by adding opening stock to purchases and subtracting closing stock to show the cost of goods sold. This figure is then subtracted from sales to give gross profit. The mark-up or profit percentage added to cost when selling price is determined should be reflected by the gross profit percentage, and if there is a difference the accountant knows that some figure in the trading account contains an error.

Many factors can contribute to such a difference. Suppose, for example, that the closing stock figure is wrong. This will have an effect on the cost of goods sold and thus on gross profit. An error in the closing stock can be caused by miscounting the number of items in stock, by extending them at the wrong cost on the stock sheet, or by miscalculating when the amounts are multiplied and added up on the stock sheet. Alternatively, the sales figure may be wrong, perhaps because some sales have not been recorded by mistake, or on purpose if the cash received has been stolen. If stock has been stolen by customers or staff, the cost of the goods sold will increase and the gross profit percentage will not agree with the mark-up. Sometimes the cut-off point is the cause of an error. At the end of an accounting period stock is taken by a physical count, and the books should be closed at this point. If, however, purchases are entered after the cut-off point they will not be in stock, and the cost of goods sold will be distorted.

TUTORIAL DISCUSSION TOPICS

23.1. 'Solvency is more important than profitability in business.' Discuss.

23.2. 'Overdependence on finance from outside the company is a sign of weakness.' Do you agree?

23.3. Discuss the advantages and disadvantages of ratio analysis as a tool of interpretation.

23.4. Explain the interaction of ratios in the diagram approach to ratio analysis.

23.5. Why is the gross profit ratio considered to be so important? What factors can cause this ratio to be different from the mark up on goods sold by a company?

SEMINAR EXERCISES 14

1. Puzzle Ltd is a small manufacturing company with premises in the East Midlands. The
   balance sheet of the company is shown below, together with other significant figures
   extracted from the accounts.

Puzzle Ltd, Balance Sheet as at 31 March

	£	£	£
Capital:			
Ordinary shares of £1 each,			
authorized and issued			240 000
Reserves			480 000
			720 000
Long-term liabilities:			
10 per cent loan stock			800 000
Current liabilities:			
Creditors		200 000	
Tax		60 000	
Overdraft		300 000	560 000
			£2 080 000
Represented By			
Fixed assets:			
Buildings	400 000		400 000
Plant	800 000	424 000	376 000
Vehicles	30 000	6 000	24 000
	1 230 000	430 000	800 000
Current assets:			
Stock		480 000	
Debtors		720 000	
Investments		80 000	1 280 000
			£2 080 000

Sales: £1 600 000   Gross profit: £320 000   Net profit: £160 000

Using simple ratio analysis, comment on the performance of this company for the year
to 31 March.

2. Ours Ltd and Theirs Ltd are two companies of similar size in the same industry. They
   have drawn up their accounts on a common basis so that they can exchange certain
   accounting information for their mutual benefit. As accountant to Theirs Ltd you
   have recently received the following information from Ours Ltd:

Current ratio	2.4:1
Stock turnover	5.4 times
Debtors' collection period	32 days
Gross profit	38 per cent
Return on total investment	15.6 per cent

The most recent accounts of Theirs Ltd are as follows:

Income Statement

	£
Opening stock	28 000
Add purchases	384 000
	412 000
Less closing stock	32 000
Cost of sales	380 000
Add overhead expenses	92 000
Add net profit	8 000
Sales	£480 000

Balance Sheet

	£
Share capital	80 000
Add retained profits	40 000
	120 000
10 per cent debentures	20 000
Net capital employed	£140 000

Represented by

	£	£
Fixed assets		88 000
Current assets:		
Stock	32 000	
Debtors	72 000	
Cash	16 000	
	120 000	
Less creditors	68 000	
Working capital		52 000
Net assets		£140 000

(a) Calculate the relevant ratios for Theirs Ltd.

(b) Suggest reasons for the differences between the two companies revealed by your analysis.

3. The managing director of Roper Ltd, a company in the boot and shoe industry, has just received a statistical bulletin showing the performance of the industry as a whole for the year ended 30 June. He would like to assess the results of the company for the same period, using these statistics for comparison purposes.

The accounts of Roper Ltd for the year ended 30 June this year are given below.

Balance Sheet

Liabilities	£	Assets	£
General reserve	13 000	Trade debtors	75 000
Ordinary share capital	50 000	Equipment at cost	26 000
Trade creditors	47 500	Long-term investment in	
Taxation (payable		associated company	2 500
1 January next year	7 000	Goodwill	20 000
Long-term loan	30 000	Cash at bank	11 000
Provision for depreciation		Freehold property at cost	21 000
on equipment	13 000	Stock	55 000
Profit and loss account	42 000		
Taxation (payable			
1 January year after next	8 000		
	£210 500		£210 500

Profit and Loss Account

	£		£
Balance of undistributed			
profit at 30 June this year	42 000	Sales	652 000
Loan interest (10 per cent)	3 000	Balance of undistributed	
General expenses	49 000	profit at 1 July last year	39 400
Depreciation of equipment	2 500	Dividend on shares in	
Cost of goods sold	584 500	associated company	100
Dividend on share capital	2 500		
Corporation tax	8 000		
	£691 500		£691 500

The following ratios were extracted for the industry:

Return on gross capital employed	10 per cent
Stock turnover	15 times
Current ratio	1.8:1
Gross profit on sales	20 per cent
Debt ratio	33 per cent

(a) Redraft the accounts in a form suitable for presentation to management.

(b) Calculate the above ratios for Roper Ltd.

(c) Compare the two sets of ratios and advise the managing director.

4. David and Charles each carry on business as whosesalers of the same product. Their respective accounts for the year to 31 January are as follows:

Trading and Profit and Loss Accounts

	David		Charles	
	£	£	£	£
Sales		144 000		140 000
Cost of sales:				
Opening stock	28 000		3 200	
Purchases	124 000		121 600	
	152 000		124 800	
Closing stock	32 000		4 800	
		120 000		120 000
Gross profit		24 000		20 000
Selling expenses	7 200		2 800	
Administration expenses	8 160		9 500	
		15 360		12 300
Net profit		£8 640		£7 700

Balance Sheets at 31 January

	David	Charles
	£	£
Freehold property	20 000	14 000
Fixtures, fittings and equipment	21 750	13 840
Motor vehicles	12 000	6 000
	53 750	33 840
Stock	32 000	4 800
Debtors	28 800	11 200
Bank	8 950	11 360
	£123 500	£61 200
Capital	108 000	30 800
Creditors	15 500	30 400
	£123 500	£61 200

Notes:

(i) All fixed assets are at written-down value.

(ii) You may assume that stocks increased over the year at an even rate.

(iii) All sales are on credit.

(iv) The amounts of creditors and debtors have not changed significantly over the year.

Compare the profitability and financial position of the two businesses by:

(a) calculating at least eight suitable ratios for each business;

(b) commenting on the significance of the results of your calculations.

5. Jean Sellar runs a dress shop and her husband acts as a book-keeper. Recently the couple have been worried in case their accounts are not accurate, and they ask you to check the figures. From a preliminary survey of the books you compute a trading account for the last two years ended 31 December.

	Year 1		Year 2	
	£	£	£	£
Sales		571 660		686 480
Opening stock	52 900		62 720	
Add purchases	390 948		502 868	
	443 848		565 588	
Less closing stock	62 720		50 860	
		381 128		514 728
Gross profit		£190 532		£171 752

You meet Jean Sellar and her husband to discuss the figures, and their explanation of the reduction in gross profit is that from January Year 2 their suppliers had increased their prices to them by 15 per cent while they had been able to increase their selling price by only 10 per cent.

(a) Verify Jean Sellar's explanation for the fall in gross profit.
(b) Suggest six other reasons which might account for the reduction in gross profit.
(c) Comment briefly to Jean Sellar on her stock level.

24 | Funds Flow Analysis

The balance sheet shows the sources from which funds have been recruited to finance the business and, on the assets side, the ways in which those funds have been applied. Unfortunately, a balance sheet is produced only at stated intervals to show the position at a specific time. A very useful interpretative tool which the accountant can produce to help the users of accounting information is a statement which analyses the changes that have taken place between two balance sheet dates so far as sources and uses of funds are concerned. Such a statement will show changes in the capital structure and asset structure of a business during the period and will, together with the income statement, explain the events which have led up to the most recent position statement. It is important to note that the position of a business is affected by income (sales less expenses) as well as by the flow of funds both in and out, and it must be recognized that a company can make losses in the short run and survive if it remains solvent, whereas profitable operations can be brought to a halt by a lack of liquid funds to pay wages and creditors in the immediate future.

WHAT ARE FUNDS?

As one might expect, there is much confusion over the use of the term 'funds'. Some accountants believe that all sources of finance, or means by which a business can gain control over or use of assets, should count as funds employed in the business. Others, however, think that funds should be associated with liquidity, and prefer to define them either as cash resources or as working capital, since the constituent parts will be turned into cash or settled in cash in the near future. Stocks which may be held for longer than the accounting year are sometimes excluded, so the definition of funds is limited to 'monetary items' in the working-capital cycle. This idea restricts the usefulness of the statement to be produced.

Funds introduced into a business, whether or not in the form of cash, enable the firm to use those funds to acquire assets. Share capital raised and long-term loans will flow in as cash, whereas trade credit will be shown by an increase in stocks not yet paid for. Amounts owed to the Inland Revenue for taxation can be used in the business until the due date for payment. A fixed asset sold will provide cash to be used to acquire other assets, fixed or current, or to discharge a liability. In this case a change in the asset structure has liquified funds for use elsewhere in the business. No new funds have been introduced unless the asset was sold at a profit, but the use to which existing funds are put has been changed. When shares are issued in exchange for an asset acquired by the firm no cash has changed hands, but the capital structure and asset structure of the company have both altered. Funds in the form of purchasing power have been created by the company, which has exchanged a liability (its shares) for an asset. The outflow of cash has been avoided by the use of an alternative method of payment or source of finance to support the transaction.

Sources and Uses of Funds

The sources and uses of funds can be set out as follows.

Sources:

(a) funds generated by trading operations; cash received from sales net of cash paid out for expenses (the term cash flow is sometimes given to this amount);
(b) funds injected into the business on a long-term basis; issues of shares plus any premium received on issue; debentures and other long-term loans;
(c) funds released from long-term applications for use elsewhere in the business; sales of fixed assets such as land, buildings, plant and vehicles; loans to subsidiary companies repaid by them;
(d) funds used in the business on a short-term basis; trade creditors; bank loans and overdrafts; amounts payable to the Inland Revenue; bills of exchange payable.

Uses:

(a) funds lost in trading operations, i.e. when the payment of expenses exceeds receipts from sales;
(b) funds used to acquire permanent assets such as land, buildings, plant, vehicles, fixtures and fittings and long-term investments;
(c) funds paid away outside the business to repay debentures and loan stock, or to redeem share capital;
(d) funds invested outside the business in loans made to subsidiary companies;
(e) funds used to acquire assets of a short-term nature, stocks of material, work in progress and finished goods; trade credit allowed to debtors who have not yet paid for goods sold to them; short-term investments as a temporary repository of idle funds; bills of exchange receivable.

If sources exceed uses there will be a balance of cash representing funds provided but not yet put to use in the business.

The 'capital employed' in figure 11 acts as a reservoir into which funds flow from four major streams. The funds are then tapped off as a result of managerial decisions to irrigate the five fields shown, and any funds remaining in the reservoir will be represented by the bank balance. If, however, uses exceed sources, the reservoir will run dry and, unless extra short-term credit can be arranged at short notice, some of the uses will not receive all the funds they need and the business will suffer as a result. Funds, like water, can run in different directions, so funds from any source can be used to finance any use, although it is imprudent to use short-term funds to acquire fixed assets, unless long-term funds will be raised to cover the position quickly. Circumstances such as these would be highlighted in a funds flow statement.

Sources

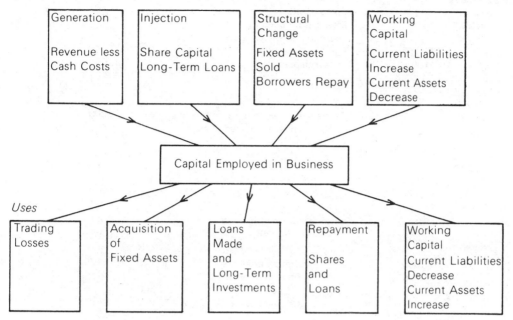

Figure 11. Funds Flow Diagram.

FUNDS FLOW STATEMENT

This statement has several alternative names. Some accountants refer to it as a movement of funds statement, while to others it is a source and application of funds statement. When projected forward from a recent balance sheet to a budgeted position it is sometimes called a long-term cash budget. There are, of course, alternative forms of statement which express the flow of funds. The statement is computed by finding the differences between the opening and closing balance sheets and arranging them in groups as illustrated in figure 11. For example, if the stock figure in the earlier balance sheet is deducted from stock in the later balance sheet, the extent of investment or disinvestment in stocks can be ascertained. The basic rule is that if an asset has increased during a period that is an application of funds, whereas if an asset is reduced this is counted as a source, since funds have been withdrawn from that asset for use in some other way. If a liability has increased more funds have been loaned to the business and this is a source, but if a liability is reduced, funds have been applied to repay the liability.

The statement shows more than just the extra funds used during the year: it is extended to show changes in the way in which the funds are used.

Example

The balance sheet of Simpleton Ltd is set out below. Compute a funds flow statement.

Last Year £	£		This Year £	£	This Year £
		Fixed assets			
150 000		Freehold property at cost			190 000
6 000		Leasehold property at cost			–
	176 000	Plant and machinery at cost		217 000	
	74 000	Less depreciation		95 000	
102 000					122 000
258 000					312 000
16 000		Investment in associated company at cost		16 000	
		Add loan to associated company		6 400	
					22 400
274 000					334 400
		Current assets			
	45 000	Stocks		52 000	
	61 000	Debtors		66 000	
	19 800	Cash at bank and in hand		8 400	
	125 800			126 400	
		Less current liabilities			
	83 000	Sundry creditors	80 000		
	10 000	Proposed dividend (gross)	12 500		
	15 000	Corporation tax	17 900		
	108 000			110 400	
17 800		*Working capital*			16 000
291 800					350 400
200		*Preliminary expenses*			–
292 000					350 400
60 000		Less *deferred liabilities*			50 000
		4 per cent debentures			
£232 000					£300 400
		Represented by:			
		Capital			
190 000		Ordinary shares			240 000
		Capital reserves			
–		Share premium account		10 000	
–		Profit on sale of leaseholds		2 500	
–		Profit on redemption of debentures		400	12 900
		Revenue reserves			
31 000		General		36 000	
11 000		Unappropriated		11 500	47 500
£232 000					£300 400

A comparison of the two balance sheets will show how the following figures are derived.

Simpleton Ltd, Funds Flow Statement

	£	£
Sources		
Cash flow (NP + DEP)	26 700	
Sale of leasehold (book value + profit on sale)	8 500	
Shares issued + premium	60 000	
Dividend payable	12 500	
Taxation owed	17 900	125 600
Uses		
Purchase of freehold property	40 000	
Purchase of plant	41 000	
Loan to associate company	6 400	
Stocks purchased	7 000	
Debtors increased	5 000	
Creditors repaid	3 000	
Debentures repaid, cash amount	9 600	
Tax paid	15 000	
Dividend paid	10 000	137 000
Reduction in cash resources £(19 800–8400)		£11 400

The cash flow figure is found by adding non-cash costs to net profit. The non-cash costs are depreciation (£21 000) and preliminary expenses written off (£200). Net profit after tax and dividend must equal the amount by which reserves and unappropriated profits have increased, i.e. £5500. Therefore the net trading profit was £35 900, leaving £5100 after deducting the appropriations of tax and dividend of £17 900 and £12 500 made this year.

	£	£
General reserve (36 000 – 31 000)		5 000
Unappropriated profit (11 500 – 11 000)		500
Unappropriated profit after tax and dividend		5 500
Appropriated to meet taxation	17 900	
Appropriated to pay dividend	12 500	
		30 400
Net trading profit		£35 900
Net profit after tax and dividend (ploughed back)		5 500
Depreciation for the year		21 000
Other non-cash cost		200
Cash flow		£26 700

The funds flow statement for Simpleton Ltd can be restated in a more informative way as follows:

	£	£	£
Opening cash			19 800
Cash flow:			
Trading profit		35 900	
+ Depreciation		21 000	
+ Other non-cash cost		200	
		57 100	
− Tax	17 900		
− Dividend	12 500	30 400	26 700
Long-term sources:			
Shares issued		60 000	
Leasehold property sold		8 500	68 500
			115 000
Long-term application:			
Purchase of freehold property		40 000	
Purchase of plant		41 000	
Loan to associate		6 400	
Debenture repaid		9 600	97 000
		Surplus	18 000

Working capital:	Source	Application	
Stock		7 000	
Debtors		5 000	
Creditors		3 000	
Dividend	2 500		
Tax	2 900		
	5 400	15 000	Net application 9 600
Closing cash			£8 400

This form of statement tells a story. It shows the liquid resources available at the beginning of the year, then the funds generated by the business for retention and then the funds injected from outside or made available by the sale of fixed assets. Not only can these sources be compared *inter se* but their total can be set against the long-term application of funds. The resulting surplus or deficit shows to what extent long-term applications are funded by long-term sources, and whether working capital has been reduced to finance long-term applications.

The statement provides a useful analysis of how funds have been used during the period, and shows the relative importance of the various sources of funds. A separate section to analyse changes in working capital reveals the funds used or provided by increases and decreases in current assets and current liabilities.

Computational Difficulties

Cash flow is the difference between cash flowing in from sales and cash flowing out to pay costs and expenses. It is not the same as net profit, since some costs used in the profit computation do not flow out in cash during the period, e.g. depreciation and preliminary expenses written off. It follows that cash flow can be computed by adding back the non-cash costs to the net profit figure. Any cash costs not paid out by the end of the period yet charged against profit will be picked up in the statement as accruals, which increase the creditors figure. Suppose an electricity bill is unpaid at the year end, yet it has been set against profit, thus reducing cash flow. The bill will also increase the creditors figure, so it will show up on the statement as a short-term source in the working capital section.

The fact that depreciation is added back to compute cash flow sometimes leads people to believe in error that it is a source of finance. In fact it is the surplus of inflow over outflow of cash that is the source, and depreciation is a means of computing that figure. Even so, it is true to say that depreciation is a sum set aside out of profit to replace funds originally invested in the firm which have been used up during the period. Depreciation reduces profit so that less is available for dividend and capital depletion is avoided. Following this line of reasoning, cash flow appears to be an amalgam of funds generated by the business to be reinvested therein and amounts set aside to replace funds used up during the period.

Recognition must be given to the fact that not all of the profit element in cash flow will be retained in the business, since part of it will flow out eventually as tax or dividend. Therefore the tax and dividend appropriated out of profit must be subtracted from it in the cash flow computation, thus leaving the problem of how to deal with tax and dividend paid in cash during the period. This point can be accounted for in the working capital section of the statement by showing the difference between opening tax and dividend and closing tax and dividend as a source or application of funds. Some accountants would, however, criticize this form of statement as not showing the amount which has flowed out during the period as dividend and taxation. These amounts are itemized in the form of statement suggested in SSAP 10.

Sometimes balance sheets are available, but there is no income statement from which to take details of profit and depreciation. An accountant has to write up the appropriation account, which he can deduce from the two balance sheets, so the balancing figure in the recreated appropriation account is the trading profit.

Dr.	Appropriation Account		Cr.
	£		£
Transfer to general reserve		Unappropriated profit b/d	
Set aside for taxation		Profit on sales of fixed assets	
Set aside for dividend		Trading profit as the balancing figure	
Loss on sales of fixed assets			
Unappropriated profit c/f			

It is also possible to work back to the depreciation charge for the year by contrasting the opening and closing positions and taking out the cost and cumulative depreciation of assets sold during the period.

The sale of fixed assets at more or less than book value presents a computational difficulty. Some accountants prefer to show the profit element in the transaction as part of cash flow and the book value as a long-term source of funds. However, this method has been criticized as showing a confused picture of what has happened, and it is argued that the full cash sum released by the sale should be shown as a long-term source, and the cash flow figure restricted to include only the trading profit.

Example

The balance sheet of Bradmore Bakeries Ltd for the last two years is set out below:

As at 31 December	Last Year £	This Year £
Capital authorized:		
Ordinary shares of £1 each	600 000	700 000
10 per cent redeemable preference shares	40 000	40 000
	£640 000	£740 000
Capital issued:		
Ordinary shares of £1 each, fully paid	410 000	460 000
10 per cent redeemable preference shares	22 000	–
Reserves:		
Capital redemption reserve fund	–	22 000
Share premium account	–	5 000
General reserve	60 000	85 000
Unappropriated profits c/f	5 425	11 196
Long-term liabilities:		
8 per cent debentures (redeemable this year and next year)	108 000	38 000
Unsecured loan from associated company	–	35 000
Net capital employed	£605 425	£656 196

Represented by:

	Last Year Cost £	Last Year Depreciation £	Last Year Net £	This Year Cost £	This Year Depreciation £	This Year Net £
Fixed assets:						
Freehold land and buildings	265 000	–	265 000	215 000	–	215 000
Plant and machinery	250 000	120 000	130 000	320 000	125 000	195 000
Vehicles	50 000	20 000	30 000	40 000	20 000	20 000
	£565 000	£140 000	£425 000	£575 000	£145 000	£430 000
Trade investments						70 000
Current assets:						
Stock	79 896			95 300		
Debtors	60 104			86 210		
Investments	97 100			66 000		
Cash	39 646			–		
		276 746			247 510	
Less current liabilities:						
Trade creditors	74 321			62 503		
Current taxation	12 000			14 000		
Dividend payable	10 000			12 000		
Overdraft	–			2 811		
		96 321			91 314	
Working capital			180 425			156 196
			£605 425			£656 196

Investigation into the balance sheet figures produces the following significant information:

1. A freehold building was sold during the year for £75 000.
2. Plant which originally cost £30 000 was sold during the year for its written-down value of £5000 and replaced by new machinery which cost £100 000.
3. Some old vehicles which originally cost £10 000 were sold during the year for £750, at a book loss of £1250.
4. Current taxation in the balance sheet represents tax on the profits for that year.

(a) Compute a movement of funds statement for the company, from the data given above.
(b) Prepare a memorandum for submission to the managing director, commenting briefly on the information revealed by the statement.

Some authorities suggest that the latest balance sheet figures should be deducted from those on the earlier balance sheet to reveal the movements which have taken place. It must be stressed, however, that this is only a working document and is not a management statement and, as we shall see, it is inadequate to provide all the details needed. Note that authorized capital is of no significance to a funds flow statement unless it is issued.

	Sources £	Applications £
Ordinary shares	50 000	
10 per cent redeemable preference shares		22 000
CRRF	22 000	
Share premium	5 000	
General reserve	25 000	
Unappropriated profits	5 771	
8 per cent debentures		70 000
Loan from associate	35 000	
Land and buildings	50 000	
Plant		70 000
Plant depreciation	5 000	
Vehicles	10 000	
Vehicle depreciation	–	–
Trade investments		70 000
Stock		15 404
Debtors		26 106
Investments	31 100	
Cash	39 646	
Creditors		11 818
Tax	2 000	
Dividend	2 000	
Overdraft	2 811	
	£285 328	£285 328

Next the trading profit must be computed. An income statement is not provided, but one can work back to the appropriation account from the balance sheet. The trading profit is the balancing figure.

Dr.		Profit and Loss Appropriation Account		Cr.
	£			£
Appropriated to CRRF	22 000	Opening balance b/d		5 425
Appropriated to general reserve	25 000	Profit on sale of building		25 000
Appropriated to taxation	14 000	Trading profit		55 021
Appropriated to dividend	12 000	(balancing figure)		
Loss on sale of vehicle	1 250			
Closing balance c/f	11 196			
	£85 446			£85 446

The trading profit should be used to compute the cash flow, but to include the profit on buildings and loss on vehicles in this figure would obscure the amount of funds generated by the business. It is preferable to show the full amount of funds released by the sale of the property as a long-term source, rather than to split the amount between book value as a source and the capital profit as funds generated. The choice of this method is reinforced by a consideration of the sale of vehicles at a loss, since it is better to show £750 cash received as a source than to enter the book value of £2000 as a source and then reduce cash flow by the book loss of £1250. Depreciation can be calculated as follows:

Plant £(000s)	*Cost*	*Depreciation*	*Net*	
Opening balances	250	120	130	
Less Sale at written-down value	30	25	5	
Remainder	220	95	125	
Purchases	100			
Balancing figure = depreciation		30*	70	
Closing balances	320	125	195	

Vehicles £(000s)	*Cost*	*Depreciation*	*Net*	
Opening balances	50	20	30	
Sold during year	10	8	2	(written-down value)
	40	12	28	
Balancing figure = depreciation	–	8*	8	
Closing balances	40	20	20	

*Depreciation on plant and vehicles for the year is £38 000

Funds Flow Statement, Year Ending 31 December

	£	£	£
Opening cash			39 646
Cash flow:			
Trading profit		55 021	
Add depreciation		38 000	
		93 021	
Less appropriated for tax	14 000		
Less appropriated for dividend	12 000		
		26 000	
		67 021	
Long-term sources:			
Share capital and premium	55 000		
Loan from associated company	35 000		
Sale of fixed assets:			
Freehold	75 000		
Plant	5 000		
Vehicles	750		
		170 750	
		237 771	
Long-term applications:			
Preference shares redeemed	22 000		
Debenture repaid	70 000		
Plant purchased	100 000		
Trade investment	70 000		
		262 000	
Deficit of long-term application over long-term source			24 229
Cash resources available for working capital			15 417

	£ Source	£ Application	
Working capital changes:			
Creditors		11 818	
Tax	2 000		
Dividend	2 000		
Overdraft	2 811		
Stock		15 404	
Debtors		26 106	
Investment	31 100		
	£37 911	£53 328	
			£15 417
Closing cash			Nil

Some points which should be included in the explanatory memo to the managing director are as follows:

1. No certain conclusions can be drawn from such sketchy evidence, but the figures in the statement can lead an accountant to form an opinion which can be confirmed by further questioning.
2. The liquidity position of the company has been drastically reduced. Nearly £40 000 of the firm's assets stood idle as a cash balance at the beginning of the year, but these have now been utilized in the business, and overdraft of nearly £3000 has also been drawn on. Short-term investments have been liquified in the sum of £30 000 and these funds have been employed.

3. Funds generated and funds injected are insufficient to finance the long-term application, so £24 000 of cash resources have been used to fill the gap.
4. The purchase of plant and an increase in stocks and debtors suggest an expansion. It is odd that buildings and vehicles have been sold at such a time.
5. The expansion has been financed by several sources: fresh share capital, loan from an associate company, the sale of a freehold and the liquidation of some short-term investments.
6. The expansion has taken place at a time when long-term funds (debentures and preference shares) have been repaid. It is financially imprudent to repay long-term funds when they are needed to finance the expansion scheme, unless the debentures are nearing their redemption date. If this is so, a further £38 000 will flow out in the near future.
7. Why have trade creditors been reduced during the expansion period, when stocks and presumably purchases have increased?
8. The gearing ratio has changed. Fixed return capital has been repaid and fresh ordinary shares have been raised. The loan from an associate is probably at a fixed rate of interest and thus it also will affect the gearing.
9. What has to be paid out in the immediate future? Dividend, taxation and debenture repayment amount to more than £60 000. In the absence of cash resources to meet these payments the remaining short-term investments may have to be sold. Will there be a capital gains tax liability?
10. Further expansion will probably be financed by creditors and the bank. In the absence of an injection of more long-term funds the point at which overtrading commences may have been reached.

Funds Flow Statement: Some Conclusions

The funds flow statement provides a link between the opening balance sheet, the income statement and the closing balance sheet. If this link is to be effective the information must be conveyed in a form that is easily assimilated by the non-technical reader. Statement of Standard Accounting Practice 10 reminds us in its explanatory notes that the funds flow statement is not a substitute for the accounts, but that it contains figures which cover the same transactions except that the information has been selected, reclassified and summarized.

Funds flow analysis reveals the financial changes in a firm during an accounting period. The statement seeks to show the funds generated by the company's own efforts, the funds injected from outside the business, and the changes in asset structure which have made funds available for use elsewhere in the business, e.g. when a fixed asset is sold to help pay for other fixed assets or to ease a liquidity problem, or when current assets are squeezed to provide funds for fixed assets. It also shows how funds have been applied by the management to command more assets, to lend to others, or to repay amounts lent to the business. The analysis is extended to an examination of short- and long-term fluctuations to reveal whether long-term sources are sufficient to cover long-term applications of funds or whether short-term funds are used to finance the purchase of fixed assets – borrowing short to tie up long.

Most fund flow statements begin and end with opening and closing cash or working capital, so that any change in the liquidity position of the company is brought into focus. Therefore they can often be used to explain the situation when, although profits have increased, liquid funds are scarce in a business, by showing how available cash resources have been withdrawn or are tied up in assets. The statement can be projected forward from the present position to a budgeted balance sheet. This long-term cash budget is a useful aid to financial planning in a firm.

SSAP 10 is an advisory standard, rather than a mandatory one. The standard lays down that all financial statements for companies with a turnover in excess of £25 000 per annum should have a movement of funds statement appended thereto and that such a statement should be covered by the normal audit of the accounts. The standard requires that the statement should show comparable figures for a previous year, and stipulates that certain features, e.g. the profit or loss for the period with adjustments for non-cash items, should be revealed. Other amounts which should be shown on a funds flow statement according to SSAP 10 are: dividends paid; acquisitions and disposals of fixed and non-current assets; funds raised by increasing share capital, and long-term loans and funds used to repay capital and loans; any increase or decrease in working capital to show movements of individual current assets or liabilities and changes in liquid funds.

Unfortunately the standard does not define funds. It does, however, give several examples of funds statements in an appendix, in which taxation paid in the period, as well as dividend paid, is shown. Such treatment of current liabilities seems to work against the stated need to show changes in working capital, and also fails to treat all current liabilities consistently. The standard does, however, permit accountants to use a form of statement other than its own example, so it is hoped that the profession will find a working solution to these difficulties, in its usual pragmatic way.

International Accounting Standard No. 7 uses the term 'statements of changes in financial position' for funds flow statements, and specifies that such statements should be an integral part of the financial statements of a business. It states that funds provided from or used in the operations of an enterprise should be shown separately from unusual items which are not part of the ordinary activities of the enterprise, so that funds generated by the business can be identified. As an alternative to adding back depreciation etc. to net profit, the standard suggests that costs and expenses should be deducted from revenues which provide funds, to compute a figure for funds from operations. Other sources and uses of funds are to be shown separately, but the list includes dividends paid during the period. The term 'funds' for the purpose of this statement refers to cash, cash equivalents and working capital.

BALANCE SHEET APPRAISAL

To an experienced accountant each item on the balance sheet of a company has a certain significance which leads him to make further enquiries. These questions are largely a matter of trying to discover the reality of the situation and to ascertain that all is as it should be. The following are some enquiries an accountant might make to discover the significance of various items in the balance sheet.

First, capital. An accountant would ask himself whether the issued capital had been called up and, if not, what calls were outstanding. A prospective purchaser of partly called shares should be warned that he will be liable if the remaining calls are made. To a lender the uncalled capital represents a form of security, since if the company is wound up such capital can be called up by the liquidator to meet amounts owed to creditors. The relative voting rights of different classes of share capital are of interest to a prospective purchaser. The existence of convertible loan stock can change the voting pattern of a company in the future. If there are any arrears of preference dividend they may need to be made good before a dividend on ordinary shares is paid.

Second, the reserves. It is important to discover whether they are available for dividend or are of a capital nature. Reserves created by the issue of shares at a premium reflect the confidence of investors, and reserves built up from the revaluation of fixed assets give an indication of the accuracy of the figure for those assets shown elsewhere in the balance sheet. Capital reserves can be used to pay up shares for a bonus or scrip issue, and their existence makes the tactic a possibility, if not a probability. The size of revenue reserves shows the financial strength of a company, but the rate at which they are increasing reflects the ploughback/pay-out policy of the directors and the ability of the company to grow by retaining its profits. A potential lender to the company may suggest that revenue reserves are capitalized before he lends, since this tactic will prevent the payment of a dividend from such reserves, using the funds that the lender has injected.

Long-term loans are significant for the gearing of the company. Where debentures are concerned, an accountant automatically asks himself whether they are secured, whether the security is adequate, when the redemption date is, how they are going to be redeemed (sinking fund?) and how the rate of interest on them compares with the current market rate for such securities. Redemption in the near future can mean an outflow of cash unless a sinking fund has been established or the firm intends to reborrow on the market, where higher interest rates on the replaced funds could mean an increase in costs. A sinking fund implies that funds are set aside annually and invested to produce, with compound interest, a capital sum equal to the amount required on the debenture redemption date.

The significance of adequate working capital has already been dealt with. The existence of liquid funds in the balance sheet can suggest either an undynamic management which is unable to put all the company's assets to work, or that management are liquifying their assets with some strategic move in view. A company with unutilized cash resources will be a takeover prospect, since profitability can be improved by employing all the assets in the business, and the share price is likely to be depressed by the impact of low profits or dividends. The trade creditors deserve analysis to discover, if possible, whether any of them are secured and so are first to be repaid if the company is liquidated, to the detriment of the claims of other creditors. The existence of a few large creditors who can join together to form a pressure group on the management is important, but if trade creditors are a large disparate group of individuals to whom only small amounts are owed, such co-ordination and pressure are less likely to occur. The size of the overdraft, together with amounts owing to other creditors, highlights any overdependence on financial sources other than the owners, and the extent of unused overdraft facilities shows the freedom of action remaining to management. The amount owed to the Inland Revenue is always of interest to an accountant. He must find out when it will need to be paid and what its constituent parts are. The amount may be an amalgam of corporation tax, VAT, schedule E deductions etc., each with a different payment date. The impact of corporation tax on the cash flow may be reduced if ACT can be set off against it. If a dividend payable is shown among the current liabilities, an accountant will ask himself how its payment will affect the cash reserves available, and he will look for the amount of ACT to be paid consequent upon that dividend.

With regard to the fixed assets, an accountant will ask how far the balance sheet figures reflect their market value, and whether the depreciation written off in the past has been sufficient to charge the profit computation with a true amount for the fall in the value of the asset. The impact of inflation on fixed assets, especially property, can be hidden if those assets are shown at historic cost, or were last revalued some years ago. Shareholders could be misled as to the true value of their assets, and may accept a takeover bid for their shares at a low price. If fixed assets are undervalued the depreciation charge will be insufficient and profits will be overstated, and where goodwill has been computed on the basis of these past profits it will also be overstated.

The precise description of fixed assets will interest the accountant, e.g. to separate such items as freehold and leasehold property. In cases where a company occupies premises held on lease the accountant will consider the terms of the lease, such as when the next rent review is, what its impact on the costs of the company will be, and how long the lease has to run. The adequacy of fixed assets in relation to the business of the company is important. The historic cost of the plant will not be a good guide to its value in a period of inflation, but if the plant is well written down this implies that it is nearing the end of its working life, is likely to be expensive in terms of repair bills, and perhaps will have to be replaced in the near future. If plant resources are small relative to the turnover, it could mean that machinery is leased rather than owned, in which case the terms of the lease should be investigated. If the depreciation rates have not been computed properly the plant may be insufficiently written down, which gives a misleading view of its age and efficiency. An accountant will always ask what method is used to depreciate machinery, and satisfy himself that the estimated life or rate built into the computation is realistic in current circumstances. Fixed assets may also be set against current assets to ensure the optimum combination to maximize profits. Too much investment in fixed assets can lead to machinery standing idle, while too little in current assets can result in stock shortages and an inadequate credit line to support the efforts of the sales force.

The current assets raise a separate set of questions in the mind of the accountant. Apart from the adequacy of stock levels and the cost of funds tied up in stock, the accountant also considers the efficiency with which the stock has been counted at the year end, and the basis used to value stocks once they are entered on the stock sheets. Any mistake in counting, calculation or valuation will not only invalidate the balance sheet figure but will also distort the profit measurement. The computation of the amount for stock of work in progress is also interesting, since some overhead expenses may be allocated to stocks and carried forward in the stock figures from one accounting period to another, with a consequent effect on profit. The item debtors is significant when compared with credit sales, and the adequacy of the provision for doubtful debts, which also has an impact on profit, must be borne in mind. Further investigation using an 'ageing debtors list' may show up some important discrepancies.

Intangible assets shown in a balance sheet will always raise questions about their valuation, and whether their existence as assets can be substantiated. Goodwill is an example of an asset which must be treated with caution. It will not be realized until the company is wound up, yet its existence depends on the superprofits made by the company. The accountant considers whether the present and future profitability is sufficient to support the goodwill figure, especially after consideration of the riskiness of the company and the capital employed that is tied up there.

It is not unknown for the balance on the profit and loss account to be found among the assets on the balance sheet. A debit balance on the profit and loss account means that past losses have been made, and this is certainly not an asset of the business. The accountant is alerted by these past losses and asks whether they are likely to continue, what has been done to bring the company into a profit situation, and whether the past losses must be made good before a dividend is paid.

The notes to the accounts showing an analysis of balance sheet figures and an explanation of accounting policies are very helpful in providing some answers to these questions. It must be realized, however, that the balance sheet shows the position at a specific point in time, and it may be out of date and not at all representative of the current situation. Some significant items appear in the notes rather than on the face of the balance sheet, e.g. information concerning contingent liabilities and future capital commitments.

Example

This is an example of an interpretation which actually took place. The figures are real but the name fictitious.

Harry Gaff has some criticisms of the accounting profession. His main complaint is that over the last two accounting years (to 30 June Year 10 and Year 11) his profits, and consequently his tax burden, have risen dramatically. He suspects that the accountants measuring that profit have made some error and that the profits are overstated, but he is being asked to pay out money to the Inland Revenue on the basis of these profits. He has contacted the accountants concerned but, since he and his partner, Mrs Roggles, have only a small business (a jeweller's shop), the accountants seem disinclined to make the investigations which Harry considers his situation warrants.

(a) Review the accounts for Year 10 and Year 11, suggesting reasons for the apparent increase in profits.

(b) Compute a movement of funds statement from the accounts and comment on the information revealed by your statement.

Note: These are laid out exactly in the form used by the practising accountants who produced them.

Harry A. Gaff Esq. and Mrs Grace Roggles, trading as

Year 10

		Capital accounts: Harry A. Gaff:			
18 475		Balance 1 July, Year 10		18 819.17	
2 817		Share of net profit for year to date		8 717.43	
21 292				27 536.60	
		Less:			
418		Income tax	790.76		
2 055	18 819	Drawings for year to date	11 523.93	12 314.69	15 221.91
		Mrs Grace Roggles:			
Dr. 12		Balance 1 July, Year 10		131.69	
704		Share of net profit for year to date		2 179.36	
692				2 311.05	
		Less:			
–		Income tax	159.26		
560	132	Drawings for year to date	573.56	732.82	1 578.23
	18 951				16 800.14
	9 000	Unsecured loans (interest free)			12 000.00
					28 800.14
	13 918	Mortgage, Goulston Banking Corporation Current liabilities:			
	4 182	Creditors and provisions		5 620.96	
	–	Lloyds Bank Limited		8 545.01	14 165.97
	£46 051				£42 966.11

H. A. Gaff, Balance Sheet as at 30 June, Year 11

Year 10

			Cost	Depreciation	
		Fixed assets:			
31 101		Freehold property	31 101.42	–	31 101.42
5 000		Goodwill	5 000.00	–	5 000.00
		Furniture, fittings and			
787		equipment	1 083.30	187.30	896.00
1 049		Motor vehicle	1 151.01	288.01	863.00
37 937			38 335.73	475.31	37 860.42
		Current assets:			
		Stock in trade as valued by			
3871		the partners		4 950.32	
130		Debtors and prepayments		155.37	
3843		Balance at bank		–	
270	8 114	Cash in hand		–	5 105.69
£46 051					£42 966.11

Trading Account for the Year

Year 10				
£	£		£	£
4 806		To opening stock	3 870.65	
26 604		To purchases	26 180.81	
31 410			30 051.46	
3 871	27 539	Less closing stock	4 950.32	25 101.14
		Less gross profit carried to profit and		
	11 385	loss account		16 559.40
	£38 924			£41 660.54

Profit and Loss Account for the

3050		To wages	2489.90	
278		To rates and water	315.20	
362		To insurance	320.60	
151		To lighting and heating	155.35	
104		To telephone	118.98	
152		To postage	127.61	
67		To printing and stationery	72.32	
2		To advertising	14.25	
185		To bank charges and cheque books	281.63	
73		To accountancy	126.00	
252	4 676	To general expenses	129.55	4 151.39
	237	To travelling and motor expenses		263.94
	314	To repairs and renewals		89.75
	126	To loss on sale of motor vehicle		39.00
		To depreciation:		
87		Furniture, fittings and equipment	99.95	
350	437	Motor vehicle	288.01	387.96
	2 074	To mortgage interest		730.57
	7 864			5 662.61
	3 521	To net profit for year to date carried down		10 896.79
	£11 385			£16 559.40

To balance carried to capital accounts and divided thus:

	2817	H. A. Gaff 80 per cent		8 717.43
	704	Mrs G. Roggles 20 per cent		2 179.36
	£3521			£10 896.79

Ended 30 June, Year 11

    Year 10

       £   £

38 924   By sales and valuation fees   41 660.54

£38 924   £41 660.54

Year Ended 30 June, Year 11

11 385   By gross profit brought from trading account   16 559.40

£11 385   £16 559.40

3521   By net profit brought down   10 896.79

£3521   £10.896.79

Draft Report, Harry Gaff and Mrs Grace Roggles

It is apparent from the accounts that in Year 11 the firm made a much higher profit than in Year 10. The difference in net profit amounts to £7375. A number of factors can contribute to this phenomenon, but there are three basic reasons which explain the situation.

First, an increase in sales. Turnover has risen by £2736, which at a gross profit percentage of 39.7 per cent has added approximately £1090 to the gross profit.

Second, sales made at a higher profit margin. The ratio of gross profit to sales has risen from 29.2 per cent in Year 10 to 39.7 per cent in Year 11. This suggests either that the firm has increased its profit margins (mark up) or that it has changed the lines it sells in the shop to a type of merchandise on which the profit margin is greater. The proprietors must look back on what happened during Year 11 to see if either of these alternatives occurred. A third reason for the change in the profit margin could be an inaccuracy in the stock figures used in the profit calculation. The stock figures at 30 June each year were as follows: Year 9, £4806; Year 10, £3871; and Year 11, £4950. It is apparent that the stock figure for 30 June Year 10 is out of line with the others by about £1000. If the stock figure carried forward from Year 10 to Year 11 was about £1000 too low, this would have the effect of inflating the profits for Year 11 and reducing the profits for Year 10 by this amount, and could account for £2000 of the difference in profits between the two years. The stock figures can be further investigated by reviewing the ratio of closing stock to cost of goods sold each year. This ratio has risen from Year 10 to Year 11 and thus supports the premise that the stock figure at 30 June, Year 10 was incorrect. I note that the accountant who draws up the accounts of the firm is particular to state that the valuation of stock in trade is made by the proprietors, and I venture to suggest that either the stocks were not counted properly on 30 June Year 10 or they were not valued properly once they had been counted.

The third reason for the increased profits concerns a reduction in costs in Year 11 from their Year 10 level. The significant figures on the analysis sheet attached are reductions in wages, mortgage interest (caused by a repayment of principal during the year), and repairs and renewals (which seemed abnormally high in Year 10).

The movement of funds statement (attached) sheds further light on changes in the financial structure of the business during Year 11. The first significant feature is the change in the solvency position, from a bank account in excess of £4000 to an overdraft of more than £8500. The working capital ratio of current assets to current liabilities highlights this change: working capital ratio Year 10, 1.9:1; working capital ratio Year 11, 0.3:1. The short-term financial situation has certainly deteriorated, since at the end of Year 11 current liabilities exceeded current assets, so that short-term credit was being used to finance long-term fixed assets. Although the mortgage loan has been repaid during the year, extra trade credit, overdraft and cash resources have been used to finance the repayment. Another serious point is that Harry Gaff's drawings and tax thereon for the year are in excess of his share of the net profit made. The proprietors have in fact disinvested their own funds by £2150 (1763 + 388) while borrowing from creditors and the bank. However, interest-free loans have increased by £3000, and these are probably lent to the firm by the proprietors.

Harry Gaff. Movement of Funds Statement

	£	£	£
1. Cash at 30 June, Year 10			4113
2. Cash flow:			
Net profit for year		10896	
Add depreciation		388	
		11284	
Less drawings	12097		
Less taxation	950		
		13047	
			(1763)
3. Long-term sources:			
Interest-free loans			3000
			5350
4. Long-term application:			
Furniture and fittings purchased		209	
Net expenditure on new car		102	
Mortgage repaid		13918	
			14229
			(8879)

5. Change in the form of working capital:

	Source	Application
Stock		1079
Debtors		25
Creditors	1439	
Overdraft	8545	
	9984	1104

6. Cash at 30 June, Year 11	Net source	8880
(Difference of 1 due to rounding.)		Nil

Harry Gaff, Analysis of Accounts

	Year 10		Year 11		Difference
	£		£		£
Sales	38924		41660		+2736
Gross profit	11385		16559		+5174
Percentage	29.2%		39.7%		
Wages	3050		2490		−560
Repairs	314		90		−224
Mortgage interest	2074		730		−1344
Net profit	3521		10896		+7375
Closing stock	3871		4950		
Ratio of cost to goods sold	1:7		1:5		
Return on proprietors' capital employed	$\frac{3521}{27951} \times \frac{100}{1}$		$\frac{10897}{28800} \times \frac{100}{1}$		
	12.5%		37%		
Net profit to sales	9%		26%		
Capital employed to sales (turnover ratio)	$\frac{38924}{27951}$		$\frac{41660}{28800}$		
	1.4 times		1.5 times		

TUTORIAL DISCUSSION TOPIC

A company is currently in negotiation with the branch officials of the trade union to which most of its employees belong. As accountant to the company you have been asked by the managing director to comment on the financial arguments used in a wage claim put forward by local union negotiators. Make a brief comment on each of the following arguments.

1. It is a well known fact that accountants can manipulate profit and thus it is likely that the figure of £200 000 in the accounts is an understatement of the true position. The accounting policy adopted towards the valuation of stocks of work in progress alone is capable of transferring overhead expenses from one year to another.
2. The profit of £200 000, when set against net capital employed as recorded in the balance sheet, shows a return on investment of 28 per cent. This high profit rate puts the ability of the company to pay higher wages in perspective.
3. Although the accounts for the year show a profit of £200 000 it is noted that during the year £240 000 has been transferred to an associated company and £260 000 has been repaid to debenture holders. This tranfer of cash and loan repayment is an attempt to conceal the true profit figure and if it was written back the company's real ability to meet the claim for higher wages would be revealed.
4. In relation to the profit shown in the accounts for the year there are large reserves of undistributed profits built up in past years. It is unfair that past surpluses should be set aside for the shareholders and kept in reserve accounts beyond the reach of employees with wage claims.
5. The dividend rate on the shares of the company has risen over the past ten years from 15 per cent to 25 per cent. The financial press shows the average yield on ordinary shares as about 6 per cent. The distribution to shareholders is therefore excessive and some of this money should be channelled to employees.
6. Profits are retained in the business as a device to avoid the payment of tax on them by shareholders.

The solution to this problem is in the appendix.

SEMINAR EXERCISES 15

1. The following represent (in abbreviated form) the balance sheets of Jingles Ltd on 31 December this year and last year.

	Last Year £000s	This Year £000s
Ordinary share capital	100	120
Share premium account	4	8
Reserves	56	82
	160	210
10 per cent debentures	50	40
Long-term capital employed	210	250

	Last Year				This Year	
	£	£	£	£	£	£
Fixed assets:						
Land and buildings at cost		90				95
Plant and machinery at cost	60				70	
Accumulated depreciation	15	45			20	50
Motor vehicles at cost	25				30	
Accumulated depreciation	10	15			13	17
		150				162
Trade investment at cost		40				40
Current assets:						
Stock	80			50		
Debtors	60			65		
Cash in hand	–			10		
	140			125		
Less current liabilities:						
Creditors	60			50		
Tax payable	20			15		
Dividends payable	10			12		
Bank overdraft	30	120	20	–	77	48
			210			250

For simplicity advance corporation tax on the dividends payable has been ignored. No sales of fixed assets took place during the year and no interim dividends were paid.

Prepare a source and application of funds statement for the year ended 31 December this year.

2. Mr James commenced business on his own account on 1 May two years ago, with £180 000 in cash. A balance sheet for his business as at 30 April this year is set out below. Mr James is satisfied with the profits he has made during the year, but he does not understand why he owes money to the bank. He approaches his accountant with this problem, complaining that the business always seems to be short of cash. 'Surely', he says, 'if my business is doing so well I should have more to show for it in the bank.'

James & Co, Balance Sheet as at 30 April This Year

Last Year					
£		£	£		£
180 000	Capital				200 000
120 000	Net profit		160 000		
(40 000)	Less Taxation	60 000			
(60 000)	Drawings	60 000	120 000		40 000
200 000					240 000
–	Long-term loan				200 000
£200 000					£440 000

James & Co, Balance Sheet as at 30 April This Year (continued)

£		£	£	£
	Represented by:			
	Fixed assets			
72 000	Buildings at cost			72 000
100 000	Plant at cost		340 000	
(20 000)	Less depreciation		88 000	252 000
152 000				324 000
	Current assets:			
100 000	Stock		364 000	
100 000	Debtors		300 000	
8 000	Cash		–	
			664 000	
	Current liabilities:			
(120 000)	Creditors	272 000		
(40 000)	Taxation	100 000		
	Overdraft	176 000	(548 000)	
	Working capital			116 000
£200 000				£440 000

Draw up a movement of funds statement for each of the last two years to explain Mr James's problem and comment briefly on the information revealed by your statements.

3. Summarized figures from the accounts of Flowcom Ltd for the last two years are as follows:

Profit and Loss Account for Year Ended 30 November

	Last Year	This Year		Last Year	This Year
	£	£		£	£
Proposed dividend	40 000	50 000	Balance b/f	10 000	19 000
General reserve	30 750	4 270	Net profit	79 750	52 410
Balance c/f	19 000	17 140			
	£89 750	£71 410		£89 750	£71 410

Balance Sheets as at 30 November

		Last Year		This Year
	£	£	£	£
Share capital		400 000		432 000
General reserve		80 000		84 270
Profit and loss account		19 000		17 140
Equity interest		499 000		533 410
Loan mortgage				98 000
Net capital employed		£499 000		£631 410

Balance Sheets as at 30 November (continued)

Represented by:	£	£	£	£
Fixed assets at cost		736 200		951 000
Less depreciation		380 200		472 000
		356 000		479 000
Trade investments		13 000		17 610
Current assets:				
Stock	107 240		135 630	
Debtors	118 430		116 220	
Cash	56 590		59 770	
	282 260		311 620	
Less current liabilities:				
Creditors	(112 260)		(126 820)	
Proposed dividend	(40 000)		(50 000)	
Working capital		130 000		134 800
Net assets		£499 000		£631 410

(a) Compute a funds flow statement for Flowcom for the year ended 30 November this year.

(b) Comment briefly on the figures revealed by the statement.

Note: Taxation is to be ignored.

4. Holland Swede is a Lincolnshire tenant farmer. One of Mr Swede's main crops is potatoes, and due to the drought last summer the sale price of potatoes has been very high. Largely because of this Mr Swede made a profit (before taxation) of £75 300 in the year ended 31 March this year, compared to £9500 in the previous year. Because of this abnormal profit Mr Swede decided to give £5000 to his daughter Lindsey and

H. Swede Esq., Balance Sheet at 31 March This Year

Last Year £		£	£	£
	Fixed assets (Note 1):			
–	Dutch barn		29 400	
18 200	Farm implements etc.		25 500	54 900
6 000	Trade investment:			10 000
	(Shares in Dumpling and Swede (Grain Dryers) Ltd)			
24 200				64 900
	Current assets:			
21 700	Valuation (Note 2), stocks	32 100		
3 500	Debtors and prepayments	8 500		
–	Bank balance	12 700	53 300	
	Less current liabilities:			
(2 800)	Creditors	4 300		
(6 700)	Bank overdraft	–	4 300	49 000
£39 900				£113 900
	Representing			
–	Loan: Fenland Farmers Friendly Loan Corporation Ltd			15 000
39 900	H. Swede capital account (Note 3)			98 900
£39 900				£113 900

£10 000 to his son Kesteven, who works on the farm. In April last year Mr Swede received a legacy of £10 000 from the estate of his aunt, Mrs Norfolk Dumpling; this he immediately utilized by having a new Dutch barn built at a total cost of £30 000. To finance most of the remainder of the cost he borrowed £15 000 from the Fenland Farmers Friendly Loan Corporation Ltd (repayable over twenty years). Ignore capital transfer tax. The balance sheet of Mr Swede is shown above.

Produce a source and application of funds statement, showing the net increase or decrease of working capital, for Mr Swede covering the year ended 31 March. The statement should include all the information that you consider Mr Swede (a farmer with only an elementary knowledge of book-keeping) would find helpful.

Notes:
1. Fixed assets.

	£ Farm implements etc.	£ Dutch barn
Book value at 31 March last year	18 200	–
Net additions in year	13 700	30 000
	31 900	30 000
Depreciation for year	6 400	600
Book value at 31 March this year	£25 500	29 400

2. Valuation. The valuation covers growing crops, live and dead stock, unexhausted manurial values and other 'tenant rights'.
3. Capital account.

Last Year £		£	This Year £
35 600	Balance at 31 March last year	39 900	
9 500	Profit for year (before taxation)	72 300	
–	Legacy: Mrs N. Dumpling	10 000	122 200
–	Gifts to Lindsey and Kesteven	15 000	
	Taxation paid (1 July last year) 2200		
(3 400)	(1 January this year) 2900	5 100	
(1 800)	Other cash drawings	3 200	23 300
£39 900	Balance at 31 March this year		£98 900

5. Forest Ltd is a manufacturer of sportswear with a factory by the River Trent. During the year ended 31 March the company issued £25 000 of shares at par to provide funds to redeem £15 000 of the debenture stock and provide additional working capital. The debentures were redeemed at par and fixed assets (Note 1) were sold at their net book amount. The balance sheet and profit and loss account of Forest Ltd are shown below.

(a) Produce a source and application of funds statement, showing the net increase or decrease in working capital for Forest Ltd for the year ended 31 March.
(b) Discuss five points which you consider to be the main purposes of a source and application of funds statement.

Forest Ltd, Balance Sheet at 31 March This Year

Previous Year £		£	£	£
150 000	Ordinary shares of £1 each			175 000
56 112	Reserves			92 458
206 112				267 458
75 000	10 per cent debenture stock 1991/96			60 000
£281 112				£327 458
	Represented by:			
203 009	Fixed assets (Note 1)			224 117
9 114	Deferred assets, ACT recoverable			9 741
	Current assets:			
110 011	Stock		147 438	
185 783	Debtors		257 610	
			405 048	
	Less current liabilities:			
(122 439)	Creditors	182 873		
(44 720)	Bank overdraft	50 259		
(42 720)	Taxation (Note 2)	59 407		
(16 926)	Dividends	18 909		
			311 448	
	Net current assets			93 600
£281 112				£327 458

Notes:
1. Fixed assets.

	Freehold Land and Buildings £	Plant and Machinery £	Total £
Cost:			
At 1 April last year	120 745	201 514	322 259
Additions	6 660	39 352	46 012
Disposals	–	(7 469)	(7 469)
At 31 March this year	127 405	233 397	360 802
Depreciation:			
At 1 April last year	–	119 250	119 250
Charge for the year	–	21 515	21 515
On disposals	–	(4 080)	(4 080)
At 31 March this year	–	136 685	136 685
Net book amount at 31 March this year	127 405	96 712	224 117

2. Taxation. The taxation creditor at the year end comprises:

	This Year £	Last Year £
Corporation tax on profits for the year at 52 per cent	58 780	41 887
Less ACT on dividends paid in the year	(9 114)	(8 281)
	49 666	33 606
Add ACT on proposed dividends	9 741	9 114
	£59 407	£42 720

3. Forest Ltd, profit and loss account for the year ended 31 March.

Last Year £		£	£
790 754	Turnover		996 455
80 855	Trading profit		114 035
	After charging:		
	Depreciation	21 515	
	Debenture interest	6 750	
	Bank overdraft interest	6 958	
	Corporation tax on profits for the		
41 887	year at 52 per cent		58 780
38 968	Profit after tax		55 255
(16 926)	Dividend, proposed		(18 909)
22 042	Retained profit for the year		36 346
34 070	Reserves at 1 April last year		56 112
£ 56 112	Reserves at 31 March this year		£ 92 458

Solutions

SEMINAR EXERCISES 1

2. Grange's capital comprises all the assets he has injected into the business, whether in cash or kind.

Opening Journal Entry

	£ Dr.	£ Cr.
Warehouse	24 000	
Fixtures and fittings	17 000	
Car	2 800	
Van	900	
Bank	8 500	
Capital account		53 200
Being assets injected into the business as capital		
Stock	1 446	
Collie and Co.		471
Lot and Mee		360
Edmunds Ltd		615
Being goods bought for stock on credit terms		

If an account is opened for each of these amounts the nucleus of a set of accounts is formed. The next task is to enter the transactions in the daybook and write up cash and bank accounts. A separate book could be used for returns, but in this case they are merged with purchases in the daybook.

Purchases Daybook

			£
1 September	Apple Ltd	Typewriters	360
5 September	J. Lewin	Goods	171
7 September	J. Lewin	Returns	(20)
9 September	Edmunds Ltd	Goods	280
			£791

Debit purchases	£451
Debit fixtures	£360·
Credit returns	£20

Purchases are credited to the suppliers' personal accounts.

Sales Daybook

			£
2 September	T. Veron	Goods	627
2 September	K. Jones	Goods	460
6 September	T. Veron	Returns	(127)
7 September	H. Same Ltd	Goods	430
10 September	H. Same Ltd	Goods	165
			£1555

Credit sales	£1682
Debit returns	£127

Sales are debited to the customers' personal accounts.

Petty Cash

	£		£
1 September, bank	250	4 September, wages	83
		8 September, wages	76
		8 September, office expenses	18
		10 September, drawings	5
		11 September, bank	18
		11 September, balance	50
	£250		£250
12 September, balance	50		

Bank Account

	£		£
1 September, journal	8500	1 September, stationery	174
3 September, sales	165	1 September, petty cash	250
8 September, sales	431	2 September, packing	61
9 September, Veron	475	2 September, cleaning	16
11 September, petty cash	18	5 September, Collie and Co.	300
		5 September, Edmunds Ltd	600
		7 September, rates	181
		9 September, insurance	160
		10 September, Lot and Mee	200
		11 September, carriage	29
		11 September, telephone	23
		11 September, balance	7595
	£9589		£9589
12 September, balance	7595		

Discount Allowed

9 September, Veron	25

Discount Received

5 September, Edmunds Ltd	15

Next post the opening journal entries, the total and individual items from the daybooks, and items from bank and petty cash. Remember that bank and petty cash are daybooks as well as ledger accounts. Note that trade discount is deducted from the price but cash discount is the subject of a separate account.

The vehicle transaction on 7 September should go through the journal, but it has been posted direct to the vehicles account.

Warehouse

	£		
1 September, journal	24 000		

Fixtures and Fittings

	£		
1 September, journal	17 000		
11 September, purchases daybook	360		
	17 360		

Capital Account

			£
		1 September, journal	53 200

Stock

	£		
1 September, journal	1446		

Purchases

	£		
11 September, purchases daybook	451		

Returns Outwards

			£
		11 September, purchases daybook	20

Vehicles

	£		£
1 September, car	2800	7 September, van to car sales	900
1 September, van	900	11 September, balance	5600
7 September, van from car sales	2800		
	6500		6500
12 September, balance	5600		

Collie and Co.

	£		£
5 September, bank	300	1 September, journal	471
11 September, balance	171		
	471		471
		12 September, balance	171

Lot and Mee

	£		£
10 September, bank	200	1 September, journal	360
11 September, balance	160		
	360		360
		1 September, balance	160

Sales

		£
	3 September, bank	165
	8 September, bank	431
	11 September, sales daybook	1682
		2278

Returns Inwards

	£
11 September, sales daybook	127

Car Sales Ltd

	£		£
7 September, vehicles	900	7 September, vehicles	2800
11 September, balance	1900		
	2800		2800
		12 September, balance	1900

Stationery

	£
1 September, bank	174

Packing

	£
2 September, bank	61

Office Expenses

	£
2 September, bank, cleaning	16
8 September, cash, miscellaneous	18
	34

Rates

	£
7 September, bank	181

Edmunds Ltd

	£		£
5 September, bank	600	1 September, journal	615
5 September, discount	15	9 September, purchases daybook	280
11 September, balance	280		
	895		895
		12 September, balance	280

Apple Ltd

	£
1 September, purchases daybook	360

J. Lewin

	£		£
7 September, purchases daybook	20	5 September, purchases daybook	171
11 September, balance	151		
	171		171
		12 September, balance	151

T. Veron

	£		£
2 September, sales daybook	627	6 September, sales daybook	127
		9 September, bank	475
		9 September, discount allowed	25
	627		627

K. Jones

	£
2 September, sales daybook	460

H. Same

	£
7 September, sales daybook	430
10 September, sales daybook	165
	595

	Insurance			Wages	
	£			£	
9 September, bank	160		4 September, cash	83	
			8 September, cash	76	
	Carriage			159	
	£				
11 September, bank	29				

	Telephone			Drawings	
	£			£	
11 September, bank	23		10 September, cash	5	

All daybook items are now posted. If every debit has a credit a trial balance extracted at this stage will balance, but first accounts should be closed off and balances brought down. You should check the entries for all items in the exercise.

Trial Balance of Brian Grange as at 11 September

	£ Debits	£ Credits
Warehouse	24 000	
Fixtures and fittings	17 360	
Vehicles	5 600	
Capital		53 200
Stock at start	1 446	
Purchases	451	
Returns outwards		20
Sales		2 278
Returns inwards	127	
Creditors:		
Car Sales Ltd		1 900
Collie and Co.		171
Lot and Mee		160
Edmunds Ltd		280
Apple Ltd		360
J. Lewin		151
Discount allowed	25	
Debtors:		
K. Jones	460	
H. Same	595	
Discount received		15
Wages	159	
Drawings	5	
Stationery	174	
Packing	61	
Office expenses	34	
Rates	181	
Insurance	160	
Carriage	29	
Telephone	23	
Petty cash	50	
Bank	7 595	
	£58 535	£58 535

SEMINAR EXERCISES 2

1.   *Position Statement Company A as at 31 December*

		£
Capital:		
Share capital		50 000
Reserves*		58 972
Ownership interest		108 972
Long-term liabilities, loan		20 000
Capital employed		£128 972

Represented by	£ Cost	£ Depreciation	£ Net
Fixed assets:			
Land and building	95 000	10 000	85 000
Plant	25 000	6 000	19 000
Vehicles	8 000	–	8 000
	£128 000	£16 000	112 000
Investments, shares in Company X			7 000
Current assets:			
Stock		29 941	
Debtors		19 487	
Nottingham bonds		8 000	
Payments in advance		904	
Bank		8 186	
Cash		1 270	
		67 788	
Less current liabilities:			
Creditors	43 614		
Wages payable	1 202		
Taxation owed	13 000	57 816	
Working capital			9 972
Net assets			£128 972

* The balancing figure is that for reserves, since assets less liabilities equals capital, and the share capital is £50 000.

2. (a) Increase capital, liability; increase cash, asset.
   (b) Cash reduced, current liability; 'wages payable' disappears.
   (c) Increase stock, an asset; reduce cash, an asset.
   (d) Increase stock, an asset; increase creditors, a liability.
   (e) Reduce freehold land and buildings, an asset; increase cash, an asset.
   (f) Reduce cash, an asset; reduce creditors, a liability.
   (g) Increase cash, an asset, but the asset 'Nottingham Bonds' disappears.
   (h) Reduce cash, an asset; reduce taxation owed, a liability.

3. (a) Note how the accountant seeks the figures he requires.

Balance Sheet for Company B as at. . . .

	£
Capital:	
Share capital, 100 000 ordinary shares of £1 each	100 000
Reserves*	118 000
Ownership interest	218 000
Long-term liability:	
Mortgage loan (secured on land and buildings)	70 000
Net capital employed	£288 000

	£	£	£
Represented by:			
Fixed assets:			
Land and building (at valuation)			156 000
Plant and vehicles (at valuation)			64 000
			220 000
Investments			18 000
Current assets:			
Stock		74 000	
Debtors		52 000	
Bank		36 000	
Cash		8 000	
		170 000	
Less current liabilities:			
Creditors	80 000		
Inland Revenue	40 000		
		120 000	
Working capital			50 000
Net assets			£288 000

Notes:
(i) No date for the balance sheet is given in the question.
(ii) The fixed assets are shown as 'at valuation' not 'cost less depreciation'.
(iii) The loan is not set off against land and buildings but a note in brackets shows that it is secured.
(iv) Investments are between fixed and current assets since it is not known whether they are to be held for a long or a short period.

(b) The figure for reserves marked* is a balancing figure. It is needed to ensure that the capital employed equals the net assets. The accounting equation assets − liabilities = capital is needed to find the ownership interest and reserves are that part of ownership interest which is unknown.

4. Note that this balance sheet is drawn up in traditional rather than vertical form.

Balance Sheet of Mr See as at 31 January 19 . .

	£		£	£
Capital introduced		Fixed assets:		
£(5894 + 2150)	8 044	Premises		13 000
Less withdrawn	285	Fittings		2 714
	7 759	Vehicle		2 150
				17 864
Long-term loan	13 000	Investment		500
Current liabilities		Current assets:		
Creditors £(714 + 1831)	2 545	Stock	2761	
	£23 304	Bank	2179	4 940
				£23 304

Note that capital consists of assets introduced as well as money, and that the purchase of the freezer is outside the scope of the business entity and is treated as a withdrawal of capital.

5. (a) (i) Current asset; (ii) fixed asset, plant; (iii) fixed asset, plant; (iv) not an asset since it is not owned by the business; (v) a cost, not an asset, and should be set against revenue to find the profit figure; wages paid in advance are an asset; (vi) fixed asset; (vii) current asset, stock, but it must be decided whether it is material enough to warrant the expense of counting it for balance sheet purposes; (viii) outside business entity activities, treat as a drawing; (ix) current liability, repayable within twelve months; (x) current asset, debtor; (xi) current asset, payment in advance but only for the proportion not used up at balance sheet date; the amount used up is a cost; (xii) current asset, stock, but it must be decided whether it is material enough to be included; (xiii) current asset; (xiv) long-term liability.
   (b) Air compressor, if bought for resale.
   (c) Capital, reserves and other liabilities.

SEMINAR EXERCISES 3

			£
1. (a)	(i) £2430 in closing balance sheet as stock		35 282
	(ii) £360 is stock and £3840 is a creditor		3 480
	(iii)		800
	(iv)		-
	(v)		230
	(vi) £180 is a payment in advance		180
	(vii)		1 790
	(viii) Depreciation (a non-cash cost)		1 000
	(ix) Accrued expense, creditor in balance sheet		380
			43 142
(b) Net profit			1 858
Sales			£45 000

(c)

Opening Balance Sheet

	£		£
Capital *	6413	Equipment	4000
Creditors	937	Stock	800
		Debtors	2100
		Cash	450
	£7350		£7350

*Balancing figure A − L = C.

(d)

Cash Book

	£		£
Balance at beginning	450	Payments:	
Receipts:		Goods, £(37 712 + 937)	38 649
Sales	45 000	Wages	230
Debtors	2 100	Insurance	360
		Expenses	1 790
		Balance at end	6 521
	£47 550		£47 550

(e)

Closing Balance Sheet

	£		£
Opening capital	6 413	Equipment (net of depreciation)	3 000
Add profit	1 858	Stock, £(2430 + 360)	2 790
		Debtors	Nil
	8 271	Payment in advance	180
Trade creditors	3 840	Cash	6 521
Accrued expense	380		
	£12 491		£12 491

(f) (i) No capital has been introduced or withdrawn.
    (ii) The opening debtors have all paid.
    (iii) The business is a going concern, so it is correct to depreciate the equipment.
    (iv) Stock will be sold at least for its cost so that no element of loss is ignored in its valuation.

2. The profit made is computed as the difference between the opening and closing capital of John Ash, if this difference is adjusted for capital amounts injected into or drawn from the business. Opening capital, £23 510; closing capital, £24 777; difference, £1267. This represents profit retained, so if 52 × £20 is withdrawn, profit is £2307. It is assumed that the shop premises have not fallen in value during the year.

	£	£
3. (a) Opening cash (£20 000 – £10 000)		30 000
Add sales		10 800
Less payments:		
Rent	500	
Expenses	980	
Insurance	1 200	
Suppliers	7000	
		(9 680)
Closing cash		£31 120

	£	£
(b) Sales		53 000
Cost of sales (£47 000 – £15 000)		32 000
Gross profit		21 000
Less expenses:		
Electricity	50	
Insurance	100	
Rent	250	
Expenses	980	
		1 380
Net profit		£19 620

Can you now compute a balance sheet as at 31 January? It should balance at net assets of £49 620.

4. (a) Opening capital:	£	Closing capital:	£
Stock	1200	Stock	1360
Bank	400	Bank	880
Debtors	1120	Debtors	3040
Barrow	800	Barrow	800
	3520		6080

∴. Net profit should be £2560

Cash balance:	£	
Opening	400	
Cash sales	2520	
Debtors	480	£(1120 + 2400 – 3040)
	3400	
Less paid out	2300	
Closing balance should be	1100	
Closing balance is	880	
Difference	£220	Assume drawings

This means the profit before drawings was £2780. You can check this figure by subtracting cost of sales from sales. In the closing balance sheet capital would be the opening figure plus profit less drawings, and would equal assets of £6080.

(b) Assumptions made, apart from the drawings, include:
  (i) no wear and tear to barrow;
  (ii) no doubtful debts;
  (iii) all stocks are likely to be sold for at least their cost.

5.

Dr		Rent, Rates and Insurance Account		Cr.
	£			£
1 July balance, insurance (PIA)	600	1 July balance, rates (accrued)		200
1 July balance, rent (PIA)	400	30 June profit and loss, insurance		1200
10 July paid, rates	400	30 June profit and loss, rent		1600
30 September paid, rent	400			
30 September paid, rates	500			
31 December paid, rent	400	30 June profit and loss, rates		950
1 January paid, insurance	1200	30 June balance c/f, rent		400
31 March paid, rent	400	30 June balance c/f, insurance		600
30 June paid, rent	400			
30 June balance c/f, rates accrued	250			
	£4950			£4950
1 July balance, rent	400	1 July balance, rates		250
1 July balance, insurance	600			

If you cannot make this answer agree write out separate accounts for the three constituent parts.

SEMINAR EXERCISES 4

1. (b) $\dfrac{\text{Cost} - \text{Scrap}}{\text{Life}}$ $\dfrac{330\,000 - 10\,000}{8} = £\,40\,000$ $\dfrac{200\,000}{5} = £\,40\,000$

Dr.		Plant Account		Cr.
	£			£
Year 2 purchased	330 000	Year 7 disposal account		330 000
Year 5 purchased	200 000	Year 7 balance		200 000
	£530 000			£530 000
Year 7 balance	£200 000			

Dr.		Disposal Account		Cr.
	£			£
Plant account	330 000	Depreciation account		240 000
Profit and loss account	16 000	Cash		106 000
	£346 000			£346 000

Dr.		Depreciation Account		Cr.
	£			£
Year 7 disposal		Year 2 profit and		
account	240 000	loss account		40 000
Year 7 balance	80 000	Year 3 profit and		
		loss account		40 000
		Year 4 profit and		
		loss account		40 000
		Year 5 profit and		
		loss account		40 000
		Year 6 profit and		
		loss account		80 000
		Year 7 profit and		
		loss account		80 000
	£320 000			£320 000
		Year 7 balance		80 000

Note. A profit on disposal is credited to the profit and loss account. Depreciation has been charged in the year of disposal.

Balance Sheet Entry

	£	£	£
Fixed assets	*Cost*	*Depreciation*	*Net*
Plant	200 000	80 000	160 000

(c) Will this plant be used in Years 8, 9 and 10? This is unlikely if the process for which it was purchased is obsolete, so the plant should be written down to an estimate of its current market value. Life and current value are required.

2. Reducing balance methods ensure a high depreciation charge in the early years of machine life and a smaller charge in the later years. This is said to reflect the earning capacity of the asset and to counteract the effect of increasing maintenance costs experienced in later life.

Straight line depreciation: $\dfrac{32\,000 - 1000}{12} = £\,2583$ per annum.

Assume a 15 per cent reducing balance. Wrong estimation of rate to use may give a false answer as in this case, since the asset is not written off at the end of its life.

Year	Reducing Balance	Maintenance	Total	Total with Straight Line
	31 000			
1	4650	200	4850	2783
	26 350			
2	3952	400	4352	2983
	22 398			
3	3360	600	3960	3183
	19 038			

Year	Reducing Balance	Maintenance	Total	Total with Straight Line
4	2856	800	3656	3383
	16 182			
5	2427	1000	3427	3583
	13 755			
6	2063	1200	3263	3783
	11 692			
7	1754	1400	3154	3983
	9938			
8	1491	1600	3091	4183
	8447			
9	1267	1800	3067	4383
	7180			
10	1077	2000	3077	4583
	6103			
11	915	2200	3115	4783
	5188			
12	778	2400	3178	4983
WDV	4410			

Note the difference in the total charge for the two methods in Year 1 and Year 12 and the different shape of the depreciation 'profile' you would show if the two total columns were graphed.

3. (a) This problem deals with the classic dilemma of depreciation, i.e. should the charge spread the cost evenly over the life of the asset, or should it attempt to charge more in the early years, or should it depreciate according to use?
The straight line, reducing balance and production hour methods should be discussed. A variation of the production hour method based on miles run is recommended, so that use is a prime factor in the depreciation charge. However, this method ignores depreciation in years when little or no use is made of the asset.

$$\frac{\text{Cost} - \text{Scrap}}{\text{Miles in Life}} = \frac{86\,000 - 1000}{100\,000} = 85 \text{ pence per mile.}$$

(b) Assume miles run were as follows: last year, 35 000; this year, 21 000; next year, 4000. Depreciation charges: last year, £29 750; this year, £17 850; next year £3400. This method avoids difficulties which present themselves when an asset is bought part-way through the year. Some businesses depreciate pro rata to time.

Balance Sheet as at 30 September Next Year

Fixed assets	£ Cost	£ Depreciation	£ Net
Vehicles	86 000	51 000	35 000

SEMINAR EXERCISES 5

1. (a)

	£	£
Opening balance of debtors		61 803
Add sales		538 112
		599 915
Less Discount allowed	4 762	
Cash received	519 267	
Returns inwards	26 916	
Cheque written back	1 015	
Bad debts written off	4 328	556 288
Closing balance of debtors		£43 627

Note. This reconciliation could be expressed in the form of a debtors ledger control account (see Chapter 9).

(b) Dr.   Bad and Doubtful Debts Account   Cr.

	£		£
Bad debts written off	4328	Provision for doubtful debts b/d	4300
Provision c/f	4362	Charge to profit and loss account	4390
	£8690		£8690
		Provision b/d	4362

(c) Current assets:

	£	£
Debtors	43 627	
Less provision	4 362	39 265

2. (a)

FIFO

Purchases		Cost of Sales	£	Stock	£
January	1000 ×5				
	600 ×8				
				1000 ×5 ⎫	
				600 ×8 ⎭	
				100 ×5 ⎫	
		900 ×5	4 500	600 ×8 ⎭	
February	600 ×9				
	400 ×10				
				100 ×5 ⎫	
				600 ×8 ⎪	
				600 ×9 ⎬	
				400 ×10 ⎭	
		⎧ 100 ×5	500		
	1100	⎨ 600 ×8	4 800		
		⎩ 400 ×9	3 600	200 ×9 ⎫	
				400 ×10 ⎭	
March	1200 ×11			200 ×9 ⎫	
				400 ×10 ⎬	
				1200 ×11 ⎭	
	600	⎧ 200 ×9	1 800		
		⎩ 400 ×10	4 000	1200 ×11	£13 200
		Cost of sales	19 200	Balance	
		Sales	26 300	sheet	
		Net profit	£7 100	figure	

LIFO

Purchases		Cost of Sales		£	Stock	£
January	1000 ×5				1000 ×5 ⎫	
	600 ×8				600 ×8 ⎭	
		900	600 ×8	4 800		
			300 ×5	1 500	700 ×5	
February	600 ×9				700 ×5 ⎫	
	400 ×10				600 ×9 ⎬	
					400 ×10 ⎭	
		1100	400 ×10	4 000		
			600 ×9	5 400		
			100 ×5	500	600 ×5	
March	1200 ×11				600 ×5 ⎫	
					1200 ×11 ⎭	
			600 ×11	6 600		
					600 ×5 ⎫	
					600 ×11 ⎭	£9 600
			Cost of sales	22 800		Balance
			Sales	26 300		sheet
			Net profit	£3 500		figure

Weighted Average

Purchases			Cost of Sales	£	Stock	£
January	1000 ×5	= 5000				
	600 ×8	= 4800				
	1600	9800				
	9800/1600	= 6.125			1600 ×6.125	= 9800
			900 ×6.125	5 512.5	700 ×6.125	= 4287
February	600 ×9	= 5 400				
	400 ×10	= 4 000				
	700 ×6.125	= 4 287				
	1700	13 687				
	13 687/1 700	= 8.05			1700 ×8.05	= 13 687
			1100 ×8.05	8 855	600 ×8.05	= 4830
March	1200 ×11	= 13 200				
	600 ×8.05	= 4 830				
	1800	18 030			1800 ×10.01	= 18 030
	18 030/1800	= 10.01	600 ×10.01	6 006	1200 ×10.01	= £12 012
			Cost of sales	20 373.5		Balance
			Sales	26 300		sheet
			Net profit	£ 5 926.5		figure

3. Purchases: 10 Bens @ £30 =   300
                20 Bens @ £31 =   620
                20 Bens @ £32 =   640
                20 Bens @ £33 =   660
                20 Bens @ £34 =   680
                20 Bens @ £35 =   700
                                £3600

	FIFO		LIFO
Purchases	3600		3600
Less closing stock			
$(20 \times 35) + (10 \times 34)$	1040	$(10 \times 30) + (20 \times 31)$	920
Cost of sales	£2560		£2680

The change from FIFO to LIFO increases the cost of sales, thus reducing profit by £120.

SEMINAR EXERCISES 6

1. Workings:

Rates		*Insurance*		*Heat and Light*	
Trial balance	2600	Trial balance	1460	Trial balance	3574
Paid in advance		Paid in advance		Accrued, balance	140 +
$(\frac{1}{4} \times 2040)$, balance	$510 -$	$(\frac{1}{2} \times 642)$ balance		sheet	
sheet		sheet		$321 -$	5⌐3714
	5⌐2090		5⌐1139	Administration $\frac{1}{5}$	743 −
Administration $\frac{1}{5}$	412 −	Administration $\frac{1}{5}$	228 −	Factory $\frac{4}{5}$	2971
Factory $\frac{4}{5}$	1678	Factory $\frac{4}{5}$	911		

Repairs		*Power*		*Telephone*	
Trial balance	1580	Trial balance	8600	Trial balance	662
Office	83 −	Accrued, balance	430 +	Accrued, balance	31 +
		sheet		sheet	
Works	1497	Works	9030	Administration	693

Depreciation				*Doubtful Debts*	
Buildings	25 000	Plant	54 000	Debtors	19 600
5 per cent for		10 per cent for		5 per cent for	
year	1 250	year	5 400	year	980
To date	8 000	To date	22 000	Provision now	750
				Increase, profit	
Balance sheet	9 250	Balance sheet	27 400	and loss account	230

John Doe, Manufacturing, Trading and Profit and Loss Account for the Year Ended 31 December

	£	£	£
Sales			140 500
Material, opening stock		7 800	
Add purchases		34 630	
		42 430	
Less closing stock		8 240	
		34 190	
Labour		39 720	
Prime cost		73 910	
Factory overheads:			
Repairs and renewals	1 497		
Rates	1 678		
Insurance	911		
Heat and light	2 971		
Power	9 030		
Supervisory wages	8 656		
Depreciation			
Buildings	1 250		
Plant	5 400	31 393	
Factory cost:		105 303	
Finished goods stock adjustment			
Add opening stock	21 600		
Less closing stock	23 420	(1 820)	
Cost of sales			103 483
Gross profit			37 017
Miscellaneous income, investment and loan interest			2 380
			39 397
Administration expenses:			
Rates	412		
Insurance	228		
Heat and light	743		
Repairs	83		
Telephone	693		
Office expenses	2 140		
Office salaries	5 460	9 759	
Selling and distribution			
Expenses	10 400		
Provision for doubtful debts	230	10 630	20 389
Net profit			19 008
Drawings			7 650
Unappropriated profit c/f			£11 358

John Doe, Balance Sheet as at 31 December

	£	£	£
Capital			68 400
Unappropriated profit c/f			11 358
			£79 758

	£	£	£
Represented by:			
Fixed assets:	Cost	Depreciation	Net
Land	8 500	–	8 500
Buildings	25 000	9 250	15 750
Plant	54 000	27 400	26 600
	87 500	36 650	50 850
Investments at cost			8 000
Current assets:			
Stock			
Materials		8 240	
Finished goods		23 420	
Debtors	19 600		
Less provision	980	18 620	
Loans		5 000	
Payments in advance		831	
		56 111	
Current liabilities:			
Creditors	27 970		
Accruals	601		
Overdraft	6 632	35 203	
Working capital			20 908
			£79 758

2.

*Paul Over, Manufacturing, Trading and Profit and Loss Account
for the Year Ended 30 April*

	£	£
Raw materials:		
Opening stock	24 200	
Plus purchases	125 600	
	149 800	
Less closing stock	28 000	121 800
Factory wages		48 800
Prime cost		170 600
Factory overheads:		
Manager's salary	4 500	
Depreciation:		
Buildings	960	
Plant	1 860	
Power	2 298	
Maintenance	615	
Proportion of expenses	9 640	19 873
Factory cost		190 473
Factory profit loading, 20 per cent		38 094
Transferred to sales department		£228 567

Trading Account	£	£
Sales		255 000
Opening stock of finished goods	7 800	
Transferred from factory	228 567	
	236 367	
Less closing stock	8 400	
Cost of goods sold		227 967
Gross profit		27 033
Selling expenses:		
Manager's salary	4200	
Wages and salaries	7100	
Depreciation, cars	2475	
Proportion of expenses	2410	
Motor expenses	1206	
Doubtful debts	453	17 844
Net profit on sales		£9189

	Factory	Sales Department	Total
	£	£	£
Profit	38 094	9189	47 283
Bonus($\frac{1}{9}$)	4 233	1021	5 254
			42 029
Add discount			600
Less stock provision,			
£1 300 − (1/6 ×£8400)			(100)
Net profit			£42 529

(b)   *Paul Over, Balance Sheet as at 30 April*

	£	£	£
Capital			95 000
Add profit		42 529	
Less drawings		6 600	35 929
			£130 929

Represented by:

	Cost	Depreciation	Net
Fixed assets:			
Factory	75 000	8 780	66 220
Plant	18 600	8 760	9 840
Vehicles	9 900	8 125	1 775
	103 500	25 665	77 835
Current assets:			
Stock			
Material		28 000	
Finished goods	8400		
Less provision	1 400	7 000	
Debtors, £(14 200 −298)	13 902		
Less provision	1 275	12 627	
Prepayments		600	
Bank		26 211	
		74 438	

	£	£	£
Less current liabilities:			
Creditors	15 600		
Bonus	5 254		
Accruals	490	21 344	
Working capital			53 094
			130 929

Note that the profit element in stock transferred from the factory but not yet sold cannot be included as a profit since it is not yet realized.

(c) High costs increase the factory profit loading on which the manager's commission is computed. This is not conducive to economy.

3. *Andy Pinder, Manufacturing, Trading and Profit and Loss Account for the Year Ended 31 May*

	£	£	£
Sales, net of returns (£416 per note (e) +£263)			123 109
Opening stock		17 456	
Add purchases (net of returns)		52 362	
		69 818	
Less closing stock		18 760	
		51 058	
Labour		17 020	
Prime cost		68 078	
Factory overheads:			
Power	4511		
Plant			
Depreciation	1500		
Maintenance	3114		
Factory			
Rates and insurance	994		
Light and heat	3129		
Sundry expenses	600		
Salaries	2200	16 048	
Factory cost		84 126	
Work in progress stock adjustment			
Add opening stock	15 900		
Less closing stock	14 900	1 000	
Cost of production		85 126	
Finished goods stock adjustment			
Add opening stock	18 700		
Less closing stock, £(19 100 + 338)	19 438	(738)	
Cost of goods sold			84 388
Gross profit			38 721
Add discounts received			1 830
			40 551
Administration expenses:			
Rates and insurance		331	
Light and heat		1 043	
Sundry expenses		200	
Salaries		13 000	
Depreciation of fixtures		196	
		14 770	

	£	£	£
Selling expenses:			
Advertising	1400		
Transport	1670		
Vehicle depreciation	276		
Bad debts	181		
Doubtful debts	1376	4903	
Financial expenses:			
Loan interest	3000		
Bank charges	415	3415	23 088
Net profit			£17 463

Andy Pinder, Balance Sheet as at 31 May

	£	£	£
Capital			57 112
Add profit			17 463
			74 575
Less drawings			4 220
			70 355
Long-term loan			30 000
Net capital employed			£100 355

Represented by:	Cost	Depreciation	Net
Fixed assets:			
Land and buildings	25 000	–	25 000
Plant and machinery	20 000	11 500	8 500
Vehicles	2 604	1 776	828
Fixtures and fittings	3 438	1 666	1 772
	51 042	14 942	36 100
Current assets:			
Stock			
Materials		18 760	
Work in progress		14 900	
Finished goods		19 438	
Debtors	17 316		
Less provision	1 732	15 584	
Prepayments		107	
Cash		4 384	
		73 173	
Current liabilities:			
Creditors	5866		
Accruals	52		
Loan interest	3000	8 918	
Working capital			64 255
Net assets			£100 355

SEMINAR EXERCISES 7

1.   *Mr Feckless, Statement to Compute the Stock as at 30 November*

	£	£
Sales, September, October, November		85 627
Less goods despatched in August		7 346
		78 281
Add goods despatched but not yet invoiced		7 912
		86 193
Less mark-up of 25 per cent		21 548
Cost of sales		£64 645
Opening stock per accounts		53 278
Less error of transposition	(1 800)	
Add pricing error	6 120	
Less casting error	(81)	4 239
		57 517
Add purchases during the quarter	64 539	
Less received in August	2 643	
	61 896	
Add received but not yet entered	3 129	
	65 025	
Less returns	958	64 067
		121 584
Less cost of sales net of returns, £[64 645 − (796 × 75 %)]		64 048
		57 536
Less scrapped		725
Stock as at 30 November		£56 811

2.   *Reconcile Ltd, Cash Book Adjustment*

		Receipts £	Payments £
Balance c/d		1888	
Standing charges:			
Loan interest			1200
HP			732
Dividend received		1248	
Opening balance c/d in error		9	
Cheque returned written back			167
Cheque drawn entered at a higher figure		27	
Cheque drawn entered as receipt			341
Bank charges			213
Receipts side undercast		400	
Balance c/f	£919	£3572	£2653

Note. Item (b) is to be ignored.

Reconciliation to Bank Statement

	£
Balance per cash book	919
Add receipts not yet credited	780
Less cheques not yet presented	(830)
Balance per bank statement	£869

Balance per question £757 and bank cheque debited in error £112 = £869.

3. Dr.   Naunton Knitwear, Suspense Account   Cr.

	£		£
Opening balance	1227	Debtor balance omitted	57
Sales omitted	83	Cash book undercast	400
		Credit note posted to wrong side	542
		Cash posted to Mr Exe written back	311
	£1310		£1310

(b) A capital revenue adjustment will not affect the trial balance.

(f) This item has not yet been entered in the books so cannot affect the balance.

Effects of errors:

(a) Debtors increase in balance sheet.

(b) Capitalize £1138, assets increase, expenses decrease, so profits increase. Remember to depreciate the new asset.

(c) Cash increased in balance sheet.

(d) Sales increase, profit increases.

(e) Creditors reduced in balance sheet.

(f) Cost increases, profit decreases.

(g) Cash increases in balance sheet. Provision against this debt can now be removed. Affects profit and balance sheet.

4.   *Harold Darby*

	£	£
To plant	2930	
By labour cost		2930
Being capitalization of labour cost of constructing the foundation of a new machine		
To profit and loss	293	
By depreciation		293
Being depreciation on newly capitalized foundation		
Loan interest	1200	
Creditors		1200
Being loan interest for the half year, due but unpaid		
Sales (2400 + 25 per cent)	3000	
Debtors		3000
Being goods on sale or return written back		
Drawings	179	
Repairs		179
Being repairs to Mr Darby's flat charged to drawings		
Vehicle disposal account	406	
Depreciation on vehicles	1194	
Vehicle account		1600
Being transfer of balances to disposal account		
Cash	406	
Vehicle disposal account		406
Being sale of vehicle at written-down value		
Profit and loss account	400	
Provision for doubtful debts		400
Being provision for a bad debt		

Profit and Loss Reconciliation

		Increase £	Decrease £
(Assume 10 per cent depreciation)	Adjustment 1	2930	293
	2		1 200
	3		3 000
	4	179	
(No effect, sold at written-down value)	5	–	–
	6		400
		3109	4 893
			3 109
	Net decrease		1 784
	Profit per		
	accounts		12 500
	True profit		£10 716

5.   *D. Lerr, Trading and Profit and Loss Account for the Year to 31 December*

	£	£
Sales, £(11 600 + 3000 + 1000)		15 600
Purchases	14 800	
Less closing stock	3 500	11 300
Gross profit		4 300
Provision for doubtful debts (10 per cent of £1000 o/s)	100	
Rent	700	
Petrol and diesel	800	
Expenses	500	
Interest (accrued)	200	
Lorry depreciation (£1680 ÷ 6)	280	2 580
Net profit		£1 720

Balance Sheet as at 31 December

	£
Capital at 1 January	10 000
Add net profit	1 720
Less drawings, £(2080 + 1200)	(3 280)
	8 440
Loan	2 000
Capital employed	£10 440

Represented by:	£	£	£
Fixed assets:			
Lorry at cost			1 680
Less depreciation			280
			1 400
Less loan outstanding			1 280
			120
Current assets:			
Stock, £(3000 + 100 + 400)		3 500	
Debtors less provision		900	
Prepayment		100	
Bank		9 800	
Cash		620	
		14 920	

	£	£	£
Less current liabilities:			
Creditors, £(4000 + 400)	4400		
Accruals	200	4 600	
Working capital			10 320
Net assets			£10 440

6.   *John Grey. Journal*

Profit and loss account	8000	
Stock account		8000
Being stock written down to net realizable value set against profit		
Profit and loss account	12 000	
Sundry debtors, Mr Black		12 000
Being bad debt written off against profit		
Provision for doubtful debts	1890	
Profit and loss account		1890
Being adjustment of provision to 10 per cent of debtors		
Machinery account	10 000	
Trade creditors, Mr White		10 000
Being purchase of machinery on credit terms		
Profit and loss account	1000	
Provision for depreciation		1000
Being depreciation on new asset, 10 per cent straight line assumed		
Drawings account	1032	
Profit and loss account		1032
Being goods withdrawn by proprietor charged to him and cost of sales reduced as appropriate		
Profit and loss account	3300	
Sundry creditors, Mr Green		3300
Being loan interest accrued charged against profits		
Profit and loss account	1260	
Cash book		1260
Being interest and bank charges set against profit		
Vehicles account		2400
Depreciation account	2000	
Cash book	400	
Being sale of vehicle at book value, cash recorded and vehicle written off		

The balance sheet balances after adjustment at £244 660. Fixed assets £189 018, current assets £97 518, current liabilities £41 876.

SEMINAR EXERCISES 8

1. *Check and Mate, Trading, Profit and Loss Appropriation Account for the Year Ended 31 December*

	£	£
Sales		24 800
Opening stock	3 000	
Plus purchases	16 450	
Plus carriage inwards	400	
	19 850	
Less closing stock	3 225	16 625
Gross profit		8 175
Expenses:		
Wages	2 150	
Salaries	820	
Rates	325	
Depreciation:		
Plant	300	
Vehicles	800	
Provision for doubtful debts	55	
Interest	300	4 750
Net profit for appropriation		3 425
Interest on capital:		
Check	250	
Mate	100	
Salary, Check	575	
Share of profits:		
Check	1 250	
Mate	1 250	(3 425)

Dr.			Current Account			Cr.
	Check	Mate		Check	Mate	
	£	£		£	£	
Balance b/d	550	350	Interest on capital	250	100	
Contra per guarantee	50		Salary	575	–	
Balance c/f	1475	1050	Share of profit	1250	1250	
			Contra per guarantee	–	50	
	£2075	£1400		£2075	£1400	

Check and Mate, Balance Sheet as at 31 December

	£	£	£
Capital:			
Check			5 000
Mate			2 000
			7 000
Current account:			
Check		1475	
Mate		1050	2 525
Owners' equity			9 525
Long-term loan			5 000
Net capital employed			£14 525

	£	£	£
Represented by:			
	Cost	*Depreciation*	
Fixed assets:			
Buildings	8 000	–	8 000
Plant	6 000	2 300	3 700
Vehicles	3 200	1 600	1 600
	17 200	3 900	13 300
Current assets:			
Stock		3 225	
Debtors	13 100		
Less provision	655	12 445	
Bank		1 200	
		16 870	
Less current liabilities:			
Creditors	15 345		
Interest	300	15 645	
Working capital			1 225
Net assets			£14 525

2. *Utopia Road Nurseries, Trading and Profit and Loss Account for the Year Ended 31 March*

	£	£
Sales, £ (101 349 + 25 644 + 18 – 3000 – 773 + 352 + 870)		124 460
Opening stock	7 935	
Plus purchases, £ (81 035 + 2900 – 2820 + 3250)	84 365	
	92 300	
Less closing stock	9 080	83 220
Gross profit		41 240
Expenses:		
Wages	16 080	
Repairs	670	
Insurance	835	
Sundries	2 982	
Electricity, £ (1300 + 1660 – 180 + 300)	3 080	
Tractor expenses	877	
Tractor depreciation	450	
Rates	2 400	
Notional rent, Hope	1 500	
Depreciation, greenhouse	1 200	30 074
Net profit for appropriation		11 166
Salary, Crosby	2 500	
Interest on capital:		
Hope	1 000	
Crosby	500	
Share of profits:		
Hope	4 300	
Crosby	2 866	(11 166)

Utopia Road Nurseries, Balance Sheet as at 31 March

	£	£
Capital:		
Hope		10 000
Crosby		5 000
		15 000
Current account:		
Hope. £ (1000 + 4300 − 6000 − 350 + 1500)	450	
Crosby, £ (2500 + 500 + 2866 − 5500 − 520)	(154)	296
		£15 296

Represented by:	£	£	£
Fixed assets:	*Cost*	*Depreciation*	
Greenhouse	12 000	6 400	5 600
Tractor	1 800	1 050	750
	13 800	7 450	6 350

Current assets:		
Stock	9 080	
Debtors	352	
Bank	2 954	
Cash	110	
	12 496	
Less current liabilities, £ (3250 + 300)	3 550	
Working capital		8 946
Net assets		£15 296

3. *Leek and Bean, Manufacturing, Trading and Profit and Loss Account for the Year Ended 30 June*

	£	£
Raw materials consumed:		
Stocks at start		4 028
Purchases		28 650
		32 678
Less stocks at end		3 180
		29 498
Productive wages		15 300
		44 798
Add work in progress at start		3 400
		48 198
Less work in progress at end		5 050
Prime cost of goods produced		43 148
Works expenses:		
Factory expenses	14 160	
Depreciation of plant	2 575	16 735
Works cost of goods produced		59 883
Factory profit		8 517
Value of goods transferred to warehouse		68 400
Stock of finished goods at start		48 000
		116 400
Stock of finished goods at end		40 500

	£	£
Cost of goods sold		75 900
Sales		111 020
Gross profit		35 120
General expenses:		
Warehouse wages	6 030	
Warehouse expenses	11 100	
Depreciation of vans	1 610	
Depreciation of car	800	
Provision for doubtful debts	200	19 740
Net profit on trading		15 380
Add profit earned by factory		8 517
Net profit for the year		£23 897

Appropriation	Leek	Bean	£
	£	£	
Factory profit	6 388	2 129	
Selling profit	3 845	11 535	
	10 233	13 664	
Adjustment (see below)	75	(75)	
	10 308	13 589	23 897
Interest on drawings	(600)	(500)	
Interest on capital	2 400	2 450	
	1 800	1 950	
Adjustment	75	(75)	
	£1 875	£1 875	

Leek and Bean, Balance Sheet as at 30 June

	£ Cost	£ Depreciation	£
Fixed assets:			
Freehold factory	42 150	–	42 150
Plant	25 750	8 625	17 125
Vans	8 050	5 060	2 990
Car	4 000	800	3 200
	79 950	14 485	65 465
Current assets:			
Stocks and work in progress		48 730	
Debtors	18 000		
Less provision for doubtful debts	1 800	16 200	
		64 930	
Less current liabilities:			
Sundry creditors	9 450		
Bank overdraft	7 048	16 498	48 432
			£113 897

	£	£	£
Represented by:			
Capital accounts:			
	Leek	*Bean*	
Balance 1 July	48 000	49 000	
Add profit for the year	10 308	13 589	
Capital introduced	4 000	–	
	62 308	62 589	
Less drawings	6 000	5 000	
	56 308	57 589	£113 897

Leek and Bean, Workings

Lawnmowers

	£
Stock of completed items at start	1 200
Produced (to warehouse 1520 ×£45 = £68 400)	1 520
	2 720
Less sold	1 820
Stock at end	900
Stock to be valued at £45	£40 500

Overheads

	Trial Balance	Creditors	Profit and Loss Account	Total Manufacturing Account
	£	£	£	£
Factory overheads	12 070	2090		14 160
Warehouse overheads	10 020	1080	11 100	
Factory wages	15 020	280		15 300
		3450		
Creditors from trial balance		6000		
Creditors for balance sheet		£9450		

Depreciation

	Cost		Depreciation for Year	Depreciation at Start	Balance Sheet
	£		£	£	£
Plant	25 750	10%	2575	6050	8625
Vans	8 050	20%	1610	3450	5060
Car	4 000	20%	800	–	800

Provision for Doubtful Debts

Debtors	£18 000	10% required	1800
b/f			1600
Charge to profit and loss account			£200

4.

Dr.   Capital Accounts   Cr.

	Henrietta £	Maud £	Nellie £	Emma £		Henrietta £	Maud £	Nellie £	Emma £
Cash	18 000				Balances b/d	10 000	8 000	2 000	
Balances c/f		13 300	5 700		Salary	–	1 000	–	
					Interest	1 000	800	200	
					Share of				
					profit	3 500	1 750	1 750	
					Revaluation	500	250	250	
					Goodwill	3 000	1 500	1 500	
	£18 000	13 300	5 700			£18 000	13 300	5 700	
Goodwill		2 000	2 000	2 000	Balances b/d		13 300	5 700	
Balances c/f		11 300	3 700	5 000	Cash				5 000
					Car				2 000
		£13 300	5 700	7 000			£13 300	5 700	7 000

Balance Sheet as at 1 January

	£			£	£
Capital accounts:			Fixed assets:		
Maud	11 300		Freehold property		25 000
Nellie	3 700		Vehicle		2 000
Emma	5 000		Fixtures and fittings		2 000
	20 000				29 000
Creditors	2 500		Current assets:		
			Stock	3000	
Bank overdrawn	10 500		Debtors	1000	4 000
	£33 000				
					£33 000

5. (a)

Dr.   Red, Green and Blue, Capital Accounts   Cr.

	Red £	Green £	Blue £		Red £	Green £	Blue £
Goodwill							
written back	4 500	–	4 500	Balances b/d	13 000	5 000	7 000
Loss on							
revaluation	600	600	600	Goodwill	3 000	3 000	3 000
Cash	–	4000	–				
Loan	–	3400	–				
Balances c/f	10 900	–	4 900				
	£16 000	8000	10 000		£16 000	8000	10 000

Balance Sheet after Retirement of Green

	£	Fixed assets:		£	£
Capitals:		Freehold			2 500
Red	10 900	Plant			3 000
Blue	4 900				5 500
	15 800				
Loan account, Green	3 400	Current assets:			
Current liabilities, creditors	5 000	Stock		7300	
		Debtors		6900	
		Cash		4500	18 700
	£24 200				£24 200

SEMINAR EXERCISES 10

1.   *Sandal Ltd, Profit and Loss Account for the Year Ended 31 December*

	£	£
Turnover		606 740
Net profit before tax		45 042
After charging:		
Depreciation	7 049	
Audit fee	1 050	
Directors' emoluments	21 808	
Interest on loan		
(repayable after more than five years)	800	
After crediting investment income:		
Quoted	1 170	
Unquoted	800	
UK corporation tax based on profit for the year (45 per cent)		13 104
		31 938
Appropriations, dividends:		
$7\frac{1}{2}$ per cent preference paid	7 500	
Ordinary 10 per cent proposed	10 000	
		17 500
Retained earnings		14 438
Unappropriated profits b/d		52 335
Unappropriated profits c/f		£66 773

Balance Sheet as at 31 December

	£ Authorized	£ Issued
Share capital:		
$7\frac{1}{2}$ per cent preference shares of £1 each	150 000	100 000
Ordinary shares of 50 pence each	150 000	100 000
	£300 000	200 000

	£	£
Reserves:		
Share premium	20 000	
General reserve	30 000	
Undistributed profit	66 773	116 773
		316 773
Long-term liabilities, 8 per cent debentures (1990–2001)		10 000
Net capital employed		£326 773

Represented by:	Cost	Depreciation	Net
Fixed assets:			
Land	85 000	–	85 000
Vehicles	25 600	12 800	12 800
Furniture	10 400	4 840	5 560
	£121 000	£17 640	103 360
Investments:			
Quoted, market value £17 582		10 000	
Unquoted, directors' value £12 500		5 000	15 000
			118 360
Deferred asset, ACT recoverable			9 423
			127 783
Current assets:			
Stock at cost		105 246	
Debtors, less provision		162 104	
Bank		59 149	
Cash		1 763	
		328 262	
Less current liabilities:			
Creditors	80 605		
Proposed dividend	10 000		
ACT	9 423		
Current tax	16 140	116 168	
Working capital		212 094	
Less future tax, payable 1 January.		13 104	198 990
			£326 773

Notes:

(a) Directors:
   Chairman, £2500;
   Highest paid director, £9000;
   One other director in band £7501–£10 000.
(b) Capital expenditure, £20 000 on freehold land and buildings.
(c) No depreciation on freehold land and buildings.
(d) Capital gains tax of £9000 payable if investments are realized at directors' valuation.

2.

Milton Ltd, Workings

	£	£
Profit adjustment		
Sales		843 800
Less:		
Cost of sales	505 810	
Administrative expenses	200 250	
Directors' remuneration	30 650	
Debenture interest	1 500	
		738 210
		105 590
Less Adjustments:		
Debenture interest	1 500	
Directors' bonus	1 500	
Directors' fees	2 500	
Depreciation, land and buildings	2 260	
Depreciation, plant and machinery	32 550	
Depreciation, motor vehicles	9 640	
Bad debt	4 367	
Stock provision	6 960	
Audit fee	1 380	62 657
Profit before tax		£42 933

Milton Ltd, Balance Sheet as at 31 March

	Authorized	Issued and Fully Paid
	£	£
Capital:		
Ordinary shares of £1 each	150 000	132 000
Reserves, profit and loss account		181 258
		313 258
9.9 per cent (+ tax credit) preference shares of £1 each, authorized, issued and fully paid		20 000
		333 258
7½ per cent debentures (1996–2001)		40 000
		£373 258

	£	£	£
Represented by:			
Fixed assets (Note (b))			213 110
Deferred asset, ACT recoverable			8 330
Current assets:			
Stock		167 040	
Debtors		180 823	
Cash		192	
		348 055	
Less current liabilities:			
Creditors	122 920		
Bank overdraft	28 154		
Taxation	28 993		
Dividends	16 170		
		196 237	
			151 818
Net current assets			£373 258

Milton Ltd, Profit and Loss Account for the Year Ended 31 March

	£	£	£
Turnover			843 800
Net profit for the year before tax			42 933
Arrived at after charging:			
Directors' salaries	32 000		
Directors' fees	2 500		
		34 500	
Audit fee		1 380	
Interest on debentures		3 000	
Overdraft interest		2 079	
Depreciation		44 450	
Hire of plant		1 500	
Corporation tax based on profits for the year			
at 52 per cent			21 173
Net profit after taxation			21 760
Dividends:			
Preference			
4.95 per cent paid		990	
4.95 per cent proposed		990	
		1 980	
Ordinary, 11.5 pence proposed		15 180	
			17 160
Retained profit for the year			4 600
Reserves at 1 April			176 658
Reserves at 31 March			£181 258

Notes:

(a) Directors' remuneration:
    The chairman received £7300.
    The highest paid director received £8000.
    Other directors receiving £5001–£7500, three.

(b)

Fixed Assets

	Freehold Land and Buildings £	Plant and Machinery £	Motor Vehicles £	Total £
Cost:				
At 1 April	105 000	325 500	39 200	469 700
Additions	8 000		9 000	17 000
At 31 March	113 000	325 500	48 200	486 700
Depreciation:				
At 1 April	11 320	197 060	20 760	229 140
Charge for the year	2 260	32 550	9 640	44 450
At 31 March	13 580	229 610	30 400	273 590
Net book value:				
At 31 March 1978	99 420	95 890	17 800	213 110

(c) Taxation. The taxation creditor at 31 March comprises:

	£
Tax charge on profits for the year	21 173
Less ACT on dividends paid in year	(510)
	20 663
Add ACT on proposed dividends	8 330
	28 993

3.   *Sampler Ltd, Profit and Loss Account for the Year Ended 30 June*

	£	£
Turnover for the year to 30 June		1 560 000
Net profit before tax		71 980
After charging:		
Bank interest	1 460	
Loan interest repayable in more than five years' time	12 000	
Directors' emoluments	27 300	
Depreciation	33 200	
Audit fee	950	
And crediting income from investments:		
Quoted	2 500	
Unquoted	3 500	
Less corporation tax based on profits for the year provided at 50 per cent		27 000
Net profit after tax		44 980
Add unappropriated profits b/d	24 755	
Less underprovision for corporation tax in a previous year	8 104	16 651
		61 631
Less:		
Dividends paid, 7 per cent preference	3 500	
Dividends proposed		
10 per cent ordinary	20 000	
7 per cent preference	3 500	27 000
Undistributed profits c/f		£34 631

Notes:

(a) Contingent tax liability to tax of £9000 if investments are sold at current value shown.
(b) Capital expenditure contracted for £38 740.
(c) Additions to plant and machinery, £16 000.
(d) Directors' emoluments:
   Chairman, £7500;
   Highest paid, £10 500;
   Number in band £7501 – £10 000, one.
(e) No depreciation on freehold land and buildings.

(f) Stock at cost, £80 000, and at net realizable value, £24 000. Total at lower of cost or net realizable value, £104 000.

(g) ACT $= \frac{35}{65} + £27\,000 = £14\,538$. Assume ACT on preference interim not yet paid.

Sampler Ltd, Balance Sheet as at 30 June

	Authorized £	Issued £
Share capital:		
7 per cent preference shares of £1 each, fully paid	100 000	100 000
Ordinary shares of £1 each, 50 pence paid	400 000	200 000
	500 000	300 000
Reserves:		
Share premium account		25 000
Undistributed profit c/f		34 631
Long-term loans:		
8 per cent loan stock (1985–94)		150 000
		£509 631

Represented by:

	Cost £	Depreciation £	Net £
Fixed assets:			
Freehold land and buildings	223 000	–	223 000
Plant and machinery	146 000	103 200	42 800
	369 000	103 200	265 800
Investments:			
Quoted, market value £27 000		16 500	
Unquoted, directors' valuation £48 000		27 000	43 500
Deferred asset ACT recoverable			14 538
Current assets:			
Stock at lower of cost or net			
realizable value (see note (f))		104 000	
Work in progress, prime cost and overheads		150 000	
Debtors		97 655	
		351 655	
Less current liabilities:			
Bank overdraft, secured	44 160		
Creditors	28 560		
Current tax	28 104		
ACT	14 538		
Proposed dividend	23 500	138 862	
		212 793	
Less corporation tax payable 1 January 19.		27 000	185 793
			£509 631

Compilation of the Net Profit before Taxation

		£	£
Sales			945 300
Less:			
Cost of sales	Given	595 299	
Administrative expenses	in trial	256 432	
Directors' remuneration	balance	30 500	
Audit fee		1 000	
Debenture interest		2 500	885 731
			59 569

	£	£	£
Adjustments			
Debenture interest ($\frac{1}{2}$ year)		2 500	
Depreciation:			
Plant and machinery	4500		
Motor vehicles	2500	7 000	
Bad debt provision increase,			
£(9453–7500)		1 953	
Directors' fees		4 000	15 453
			£44 116

Note:

Fixed Assets	*Freehold Land*	*Plant and Machinery*	*Motor Vehicles*
	£	£	£
Cost b/f	200 000	35 000	18 000
Additions during year	–	10 000	–
	200 000	45 000	18 000
Depreciation b/f	–	20 000	8 000
Depreciation during the year	–	4 500	2 500
	–	24 500	10 500
Written-down value as per balance sheet	200 000	20 500	7 500

Golf Ltd, Profit and Loss Account for the Year Ended 31 December

Turnover			£945 300
	£	£	£
Net profit for the year before tax			44 116
Arrived at after charging:			
Directors' salaries	30 500		
Directors' fees	4 000	34 500	
Audit fee		1 000	
Interest on debentures		5 000	
Overcast interest		1748	
Depreciation		7 000	
Corporation tax based on the profit of the year at 52 per cent			20 000
Net profit after taxation			24 116
Dividends:			
Preference:			
$3\frac{1}{4}$ per cent paid	650		
$3\frac{1}{4}$ per cent proposed	650	1 300	
Ordinary, 13 per cent proposed		13 000	14 300
Net profits after dividends			9 816
Transfer to general reserve		(5 000)	
Add net profit brought forward from last year		21 701	16 701
Net profit carried forward to next year			£26 517

Notes:

(a) The chairman received £9000.
   The highest paid director received £11 000.
   Other directors receiving £5001 – £7500, two.
(b) No depreciation on freehold land and buildings.

Golf Ltd, Balance Sheet as at 31 December

	£	£	£
Fixed assets (see Note (b)):			
Freehold land and buildings			200 000
Plant and machinery			20 500
Motor vehicles			7 500
			228 000
Trade investment at cost (directors'			
valuation £5000)			24 000
Current assets:			
Stocks and work in progress		94 176	
ACT recoverable		7 350	
Debtors		146 991	
		248 517	
Less current liabilities:			
Creditors	130 174		
ACT payable	7 350		
Dividends payable	13 650		
Corporation tax payable on			
30 September	19 650		
Bank overdraft	118 176	289 000	40 483
Net assets			£211 517

Financed by:	*Authorized*	*Issued Fully Paid*
	£	£
Share capital:		
Ordinary shares of 50 pence	£200 000	100 000
Reserves:		
Profit and loss account	26 517	
General	15 000	41 517
		141 517
Preference share capital:		
6$\frac{1}{2}$ per cent preference shares of £1 authorized and		
fully paid		20 000
10 per cent debentures (1990–93)		50 000
Net capital employed		£211 517

SEMINAR EXERCISES 12

1.

Current assets:	£	1 January £	£	31 December £	Change £
Stock		17 000		70 000	+ 53 000
Debtors		7 000		10 000	+ 3 000
Cash		18 000		20 000	+ 2 000
		42 000		100 000	

	£	£	£	£	£
Current liabilities:					
Creditors	12 000		14 000		+ 2 000
Bills payable	11 000		12 000		+ 1 000
Dividends proposed	6 000		8 000		+ 2 000
		29 000		34 000	
Working capital		£13 000		£66 000	

The major factor in the change in working capital is the increase in stocks. Small increases in debtors and cash are balanced by increases in current liabilities. The stock increase appears to have been financed in part by a long-term loan.

2.

Clutterbuck, Cash Budget

	Jan.	Feb.	March	Apr.	May	June
	£	£	£	£	£	£
Receipts	Nil	6 000	8000	10 000	12 000	12 000
Payments:						
Purchases	–	10 500	7500	9 000	9 000	9 000
Wages	350	450	500	500	500	500
Expenses	350	350	350	350	350	350
Rent	500	–	–	500	–	–
Rates	–	–	–	160	–	–
Assets	3000	1 500	–	–	–	–
Total	4200	12 800	8350	10 510	9 850	9 850
Surplus/deficit	(4200)	(6 800)	(350)	(510)	2 150	2 150
Opening balance	5000	800	(6000)	(6 350)	(6 860)	(4 710)
Closing balance	800	(6 000)	(6350)	(6 860)	(4 710)	(2 560)

3.

Jumbo Ltd, Cash Budget for the First Six Months

	July	Aug.	Sept.	Oct.	Nov.	Dec.
Receipts:						
Opening balance	5000	3900	(380)	(1800)	(4860)	(7 500)
Sales	–	–	3600	6000	8000	12 000
	5000	3900	3220	4200	3140	4 500
Payments:						
Purchases		3400	4100	5300	8900	6 500
Commission		80	120	160	240	200
Rent	300			300		
Wages and salaries	500	500	500	500	500	500
Other overheads	300	300	300	400	400	400
Motor car				2400		
Plant					600	
Closing balance	3900	(380)	(1800)	(4860)	(7500)	(3 100)
	5000	3900	3220	4200	3140	4 500

Anticipated Profit and Loss Account for the First Six Months

	July	Aug	Sept.	Oct.	Nov.	Dec.	Total
Sales	4000	6000	8000	12 000	10 000	10 000	50 000
Cost of sales	2400	3600	4800	8 400	6 000	6 000	31 200
Gross profit	1600	2400	3200	3 600	4 000	4 000	18 800

Expenses:		
Commission at 2 per cent		1000
Rent		600
Wages and salaries		3000
Other overheads		2100
Depreciation:		
Plant	20	
Motor vehicle	150	170	6 870
Net profit		£11 930

4.   *Ranch William, Cash Budget January to April*

	Jan.	Feb.	March	Apr.
	£	£	£	£
Budgeted opening balance b/f	2000	(2930)	(6730)	(5130)
Add budgeted receipts:				
Sales of cattle (no. × £115/£100)	4600	4600	4600	4600
Auctions:				
Steers (no. × £50)	600	1000	1000	1300
Beef cattle (no. × £125)	1000	2000	2000	2500
Supplementary payments:				
Interim		700		
Final				2100
Development Board subsidy			1000	
Total receipts	6200	8300	8600	10500
Sub-total	8200	5370	1870	5370
Less budgeted payments:				
Salaries:				
Basic	800	800	800	800
Bonus (5 per cent of auction sales)	80	150	150	190
Wages, hired hands:				
Regular	1 350	1 350	1350	1350
Casual	1 500	1 200	1200	900
Fodder	900	900	900	500
Grazing rights		300		
Rights of way	100			
Other costs	400	400	400	400
Capital expenditure:				
Buildings		6 000		
Truck:				
Deposit			1200	
Instalment				150
Personal drawings	1 000	1 000	1000	1000
Tax	5 000			
Total payments	11 130	12 100	7000	5290
Budgeted closing balance c/f	(2 930)	(6 730)	(5130)	80

SEMINAR EXERCISES 13

1. *Assets Basis*

	£
Gross assets	66 000
Less debentures and creditors	28 500
Equity interest	37 500 = Book value

| Adjust goodwill (£6500–10 per cent of £37 500) | − 2750 | |
| Adjust stock | + 225 | (2 525) |

£34 975, or £1.17 per share

Break-up Basis. This means that assets are sold piecemeal, so goodwill is ignored. Therefore £34 975 − £3750 = £31 225 or £1.04 per share.

Yield Basis. What are the profits worth at a market capitalization rate?

$$4500 \times \frac{100}{10} = £45\,000 \text{ or } £1.50 \text{ per share.}$$

	£
It is interesting to note that the yield basis gives	45 000
Less net tangible assets	31 225
Goodwill	13 775

Therefore why has the company written down goodwill in the assets basis computation?

2. (b) *Assets Basis*

	£
Net book value	60 000
Write up land and buildings	30 000
Provide for doubtful debts	(1 000)
Value of business	£89 000

Assumptions:

(i) The assets will realize their book values. Property has been revalued and doubtful debts provided for, but will fixtures and stock sell for the book amounts?

(ii) The business is worth only the market value of its constituent assets. There is no goodwill.

Yield Basis

Average profits for last three years, £115 000 ÷ 3	£38 333
Net tangible assets of £89 000 should earn 25 per cent	£22 250
Superprofits	£16 083
Net tangible assets	89 000
Three years' purchase of superprofits = goodwill	48 249
Value of business	£137 249

Assumptions:

(i) Past average profits represent future. Should they have been weighted to be more representative of recent years?

(ii) Is a three-year purchase of superprofits suitable in the circumstances? This means that intangible assets are given a capitalization rate of 33 per cent.

(iii) Is it fair to apply the 25 per cent rate for all companies to this particular company?

Capitalization Basis. Average annual profit × capitalization rate =

$$£38\,333 \times \frac{100}{25} = £153\,332$$

= value of business. Assumptions (i) and (iii) above apply to this method.

3. (a) The major assumption which must be made to compute superprofit is the capitalization rate or rate of return which can be earned in a similar business. The return on an annuity is not helpful, since it includes an element of capital repayment and depends on life expectancy rather than business risk. The building society return of 9 per cent is post tax and when grossed up might give a pre-tax return of 14 per cent, but this too is a relatively risk-free investment. The income from quoted and unquoted companies is not a satisfactory guide, since it is post-tax and is computed on profits distributed as dividend, not on all of the profit made. The investor may accept a small return in order to achieve capital growth. The return is also typical of small holdings of shares and thus cannot be used to value a company as a whole. A required return of 20 per cent should be assumed in a small private company, since this reflects the interest rate paid by the company on its loan.

   Other considerations are whether Mr Parsnip can be replaced at the same salary (£12 000 per annum), whether the loss on the car is an extraordinary item, whether the bad debts are normal, and whether the profit figures are normal and reflect future performance.

	£	
Net profit	30 000	
Add back:		
Mrs Carrott's fees	7 500	
Loss on car	2 500	
Expected future profit	£40 000	
Capital employed, net tangible assets, £110 000		
Expected return, £110 000 × 20 per cent	£22 000	Expected return
	£40 000	Adjusted future profit
	£18 000	Superprofit

(b) Depreciation has increased by £20 000 this year. This must be the charge for the year, and would put back £5000 into profit if the rate is reduced from 20 per cent to 15 per cent ($\frac{1}{4}$). Superprofit would then be £23 000 and at three years' purchase, goodwill would be worth £46 000. Net tangible assets and goodwill combined make the company worth £156 000.

4. (a) The net tangible assets of this company are nil after revaluation of property and stock. Any value of the business depends on the fact that the shareholders own the assets and combine them in such a way as to show a profit. In this case all profits are superprofits so far as the shareholders are concerned, since their investment has been lost by past trading losses and the revaluation.

   Since the losses are not likely to be repeated, it seems fair to take a weighted average profit of the last three years as a goodwill foundation.

$$
\begin{array}{lrl}
\text{Year 13} & 5000 \times 1 = & 5\,000 \\
\text{Year 14} & 10\,000 \times 2 = & 20\,000 \\
\text{Year 15} & 15\,000 \times 3 = & 45\,000 \\
\hline
& 6 & 70\,000 \\
\hline
\end{array}
\qquad \frac{70\,000}{6} = \underline{\underline{£11\,666}}
$$

Average profit times the capitalization rate is $£\,11\,666 \times \dfrac{100}{20} = \underline{£\,58\,330}$

This is what an investor expecting a 20 per cent return would pay for the right to receive these profits. Each ordinary share is worth £1.94.

5. (a)

	Year Before Last	Last Year	This Year	£
Net tangible assets				70 000
Profits				
	£	£	£	
Profits	60 000	90 000	100 000	
Adjust. Mr Almond	(20 000)	(20 000)	(20 000)	
Adjust. depreciation	(10 000)	(15 000)	(20 000)	
	30 000	55 000	60 000	145 000
			Offer price	£215 000
Weight	1	2	3	
Profit	30 000	110 000	180 000	

$$\frac{320\,000}{6} = £53\,333 \text{ as PAWA}$$

(b) (i) $\dfrac{53\,333}{215\,000} = 25$ per cent. Almond is valuing his business at a high-risk capitalization rate.

(ii) Superprofits, not profits, should be used to value the firm.

(iii) Tangible assets comprise only one third of the price.

(iv) The advantage of material from associate company will be lost.

(v) Enquire about past losses: How? When? Will they be repeated?

SEMINAR EXERCISES 14

1. Net profit to capital employed = 160:2080 = 7.7 per cent. Disappointing return. Investigate whether the profitability of operations or the underuse of capacity is the cause.

   Net profit to sales = 160:1600 = 10 per cent. Sales to capital employed = 1600:2080 = 0.77 times. The profit margin on sales is fairly good, but could be improved. Resources do not appear to be working hard enough, since every £1 of assets earns only 77 pence of sales in the year. 0.77 × 10 per cent = 7.7 per cent.

   Sales to fixed assets = 1600:800 = 2 times. Sales to current assets = 1600:1280 = 1.25 times. Fixed assets to current assets = 800:1280 = 1:1.6. Current assets earn less per £1 than fixed assets, yet current assets have more weight in the asset structure. This may reflect the nature of the business, or could be evidence of over-investment in current assets.

$$\text{Debtor period} = \frac{720}{1600} \times \frac{365}{1} = 164 \text{ days} = \text{five months} +. \quad \text{Stock turnover} = \frac{480}{1280}$$

$$\times \frac{365}{1} = 137 \text{ days} = \text{four months} +. \text{ Five months' credit to customers seems excessive.}$$

   Credit control could reduce the investment here, so long as it did not harm sales effort. Perhaps stock control could reduce the four-month period which, on average, stocks wait in stores before being used.

   Gross profit to sales = 320:1600 = 20 per cent. Expenses to sales = 160:1600 = 10 per cent. Half of the gross profit margin is used up by the expenses.

2. It must be stressed that apparent reasons for differences are derived from speculation, and therefore should not be treated as definite conclusions, but should be investigated further.

   Current ratio = 120:68 = 1.77:1 (Ours 2.4:1). Theirs has less current asset cover for its current liabilities. Therefore it may be more dependent on short-term credit than Ours.

$$\text{Stock turnover} = \frac{\text{Average Stock}}{\text{Cost of Sale}} = \frac{30}{380} = 12.7 \text{ times (Ours 5.4 times). Stocks are}$$

   turned over faster at Theirs, so the capital employed in stocks works harder. This may mean that they have good stock control or that they prefer to take the risks inherent in low stocks. If they are dependent on creditors for finance they would tend to reduce stocks to minimize borrowings.

$$\text{Debtor collection} = \frac{72}{380} \times \frac{365}{1} = 69 \text{ days (Ours 32 days). Theirs give more trade}$$

   credit to their customers, perhaps to support sales effort, perhaps through inefficient credit control.

$$\text{Gross profit} = \frac{100}{480} \times \frac{100}{1} = 21 \text{ per cent (Ours 38 per cent). Ours is more profitable}$$

   than Theirs, perhaps because of a different pricing policy or a lower cost of sales resulting from better buying (see stock turnover above).

$$\text{Return on total investment} = \frac{8}{208} \times \frac{100}{1} = 3.8 \text{ per cent or } \frac{8}{140} \times \frac{100}{1} = 5.7 \text{ per cent}$$

   (Ours 15.6 per cent). Theirs is less profitable than Ours. This reflects the difference in gross profit rate, or more interest to pay (current ratio).

3. (a)   *Roper Ltd, Trading and Profit and Loss Account to 30 June*

	£	£
Sales		652 000
Less cost of sales		584 500
Gross profit		67 500
Add investment income		100
		67 600
Less expenses:		
Loan interest	3 000	
General	49 000	
Depreciation	2 500	54 500
Net profit		13 100
Less appropriations:		
Taxation	8 000	
Dividend	2 500	10 500
Unappropriated profit for the year		2 600
Unappropriated profit b/d		39 400
Unappropriated profit c/f		£ 42 000

Balance Sheet as at 30 June

	£	£	£
Share capital			50 000
General reserve			13 000
Unappropriated profit			42 000
Equity interest			105 000
Long-term loan			30 000
Net capital employed			£135 000

Represented by:

	Cost	Depreciation	
Intangible asset, goodwill			20 000
Fixed assets:			
Freehold property	21 000	—	21 000
Equipment	26 000	13 000	13 000
Investment			2 500
			56 500
Current assets:			
Stock		55 000	
Debtors		75 000	
Cash		11 000	
		141 000	
Current liabilities:			
Creditors	47 500		
Taxation	15 000		
		62 500	
Working capital			78 500
Net assets			£135 000

(b), (c) $\text{ROCE} = \dfrac{13\,100}{197\,500} \times \dfrac{100}{1} = 6.6$ per cent (industry 10 per cent). Less profitable than average for industry. Investigate profitability and underuse of capacity.

$$\text{Stock turnover} = \dfrac{584.5}{55} = 10.6 \text{ times (industry 15 times). This suggests that}$$

stocks are not working hard enough. Other companies manage with less stock per £1 of sales. Stock control.

Current ratio $= 141{:}62.5 = 2.3{:}1$ (industry 1.8:1). Less dependent on outside finance to fund current assets. Perhaps does not take as much trade credit as it could.

$$\text{Gross profit} = \dfrac{67.5}{652} \times \dfrac{100}{1} = 10.4 \text{ per cent (industry 20 per cent). Less}$$

profitable per £1 of sales made than average for industry. Investigate pricing policy of buying department to isolate mark-up or cost of sales as the reason.

$$\text{Debt ratio} = \dfrac{75}{652} \times \dfrac{100}{1} = 11.5 \text{ per cent or 1.38 months (industry 33 per}$$

cent or 4 months). The company is giving less credit than average to customers. This reflects efficient collection policy, but is the sales effort being supported by a good credit line? More credit may mean more sales and a faster stock turnover at higher prices.

	David	Charles
4. (a) ROCE	7 per cent	12.6 per cent
Net profit to sales	6 per cent	5.5 per cent
Sales to capital employed	1.16 times	2.29 times
Gross profit	16.7 per cent	14.3 per cent
Expenses to sales	10.7 per cent	8.8 per cent
Fixed assets to sales	2.68 times	4.14 times
Current assets to sales	2.06 times	5.12 times
Fixed assets to current assets	1:1.3	1:0.8
Stock turnover	4 times	30 times
Debtors	10 weeks	4 weeks
Current ratio	4.5:1	0.9:1

(b) Charles has a better return on capital than David, not because his business is more profitable, but because he works his capital harder. He has a lower gross profit margin, but his expenses ratio is lower too, so this compensates for much of the difference. Charles earns more sales per pound on both fixed and current assets, but this difference is most marked for current assets. The two firms have different asset structures. Charles uses less current assets and this is reflected in his much better stock turnover and debtor performance and in the current ratio. The profitable operations of Charles may be halted, since he has negative working capital.

5. (a)

	Year 1	Year 2
Gross profit rate	$\dfrac{190\,532}{571\,660} \times \dfrac{100}{1} = 33.3$ per cent	$\dfrac{171\,752}{686\,480} \times \dfrac{100}{1} = 25$ per cent

Gross profit has fallen from one third to one quarter. A gross profit of 33 per cent last year means a mark-up on cost of 50 per cent. Thus goods costing £100 would be sold for £150. If Jean's explanation is correct, this year the same goods would cost £115 (£100 + 15 per cent) and sell for £165 (£150 + 10 per cent) to show a profit of £50. Gross profit rate would be $\dfrac{50}{165} \times \dfrac{100}{1} = 30$ per cent. Thus Jean's explanation accounts for only part ($\frac{3}{8}$) of the fall in gross profit.

(b) Other reasons:

   (i) Stock errors in opening or closing stocks, e.g. items omitted or costs or extensions wrong.
   (ii) Cash from sales stolen, not banked. False sales figure.
   (iii) Goods stolen by customers or staff.
   (iv) Cash or goods withdrawn by Jean Sellar: not in books.
   (v) Wrong 'cut-off point'. Goods in purchases but not in stock.
   (vi) Gross profit is an average. Change mixture of sales to less profitable lines.

(c) *Stock Turnover*   *Year 1*   *Year 2*

$\dfrac{\text{Average Stock}}{\text{Cost of Sales}} \times \dfrac{52}{1}$ $\dfrac{57\,810}{381\,128} \times \dfrac{52}{1} = 7.9$ weeks $\dfrac{56\,790}{514\,728} \times \dfrac{52}{1} = 5.7$ weeks

SEMINAR EXERCISES 15

1.   *Jingles Ltd, Funds Flow Statement for the Year to 31 December (£000s)*

	£	£	£
Cash flow:			
Profit retained		26	
Depreciation, £(5 + 3)		8	34
Long-term source, ordinary shares + premium			24
			58
Long-term application:			
Debentures repaid		10	
Assets purchased:			
Land		5	
Plant		10	
Vehicles		5	30
			28

Working capital:	*Source*	*Application*	
Stock	30		
Debtors		5	
Creditor		10	
Tax		5	
Dividend	2	–	
	32	20	12 Net source

Change in liquid resources (−10 to 30)   £40

Note. A slightly different form of statement is used in this example from that shown in the chapter.

2.

Mr James, Funds Flow Statement for Two Years to 30 April (£000s)

	Last Year				This Year		
	£	£	£		£	£	£
Cash flow:							
Net profit		20				40	
Depreciation		20	40			68	108
Long-term source							
loan			–				200
			40				308
Long-term application:							
Buildings		72				–	
Plant		100	172			240	240
			(132)				68

Working capital:	Source	Application			Source	Application	
Stock		100				264	
Debtors		100				200	
Creditors	120				152		
Tax	40				60		
	160	200	(40)		212	464	(252)

Financed by a reduction in cash resources			
(180 − 8)	£172	(+8 to − 176)	£184

Comments:
(a) Year 1. The position is much as expected in the first year of business. The opening capital has been invested in buildings, plant, stock and debtors with some help from creditors and retained profits.
(b) Year 2. A further increase in plant and notable expansion in stock and debtors. Altogether £700 000 has been invested, financed by a loan, £200 000; overdraft, £176 000; current liabilities, £212 000; and cash flow £108 000. This rapid expansion has relied for finance on sources outside the business. The cash flow has not been enough to keep pace with the growth, and has in any case been reduced by drawings of £120 000 in two years.

3. (a)

Flowcom Ltd, Funds Flow Statement for the Year Ended 30 November

	£	£	£
Cash flow:			
Net profit		52 410	
Depreciation		91 800	
		144 210	
Less dividend		50 000	94 210
Long-term sources:			
Share capital		32 000	
Loan		98 000	130 000
			224 210

	£	£	£
Long-term applications:			
Fixed assets		214 800	
Investments		4 610	219 410
			4 800

Working capital:	*Source*	*Application*	
Stock		28 390	
Debtors	2 210		
Creditors	14 560		
Dividend	10 000		
	26 770	28 390	(1 620)

Resulting in an increase in liquid funds (£59 770 − £56 590)   £3 180

(b) Funds generated by the business cannot keep pace with the funds applied, and need a large injection of loan and fresh share capital to help fund the extra plant laid down in the year. The extra loan capital will change the gearing ratio. Current asset expansion has been financed mainly by extra current liabilities. It seems odd that plant and stock should expand and debtors should be decreased at the same time.

4.   *H. Swede Esq., Funds Flow Statement for the Year to 31 March*

	£	£	£
Cash flow:			
Net profit		72 300	–
Depreciation		7 000	
		79 300	
Less:			
Cash withdrawn	3 200		
Gifts made	15 000		
Tax paid	5 100	23 300	56 000
Long-term sources:			
Capital introduced legally		10 000	
Loan from Fenland Farmers		15 000	25 000
			81 000
Long-term applications:			
Dutch barn		30 000	
New implements		13 700	
Investments		4 000	47 700
Surplus			£33 300

Working capital movements:	*Source*	*Application*	
Stock		10 400	
Debtors		5 000	
Creditors	1 500		
Cash, £(6700 + 12 700)		19 400	
	1 500	34 800	
Net application to working capital			£33 300

These figures can be reconciled:	
Opening working capital	15 700
Closing working capital	49 000
Increase	£33 300

Mr Swede should be told of the improvement in his liquid position resulting from a profitable year with a large proportion of the profits retained in the business. He must be warned, however, that his profits will attract tax, resulting in a cash outflow next year.

5. (a)   *Forest Ltd, Funds Flow Statement for the Year Ended 31 March*

	£	£
Sources of funds:		
Profit before tax and dividend		114 035
Depreciation		21 515
Total generated from operations		135 550
Funds from other sources:		
issue of shares	25 000	
disposal of fixed assets	3 389	28 389
		163 939
Application of funds:		
Dividends paid	16 926	
Tax paid	42 720	
Additions to buildings	6 660	
Additions to plant	39 352	
Debentures redeemed	15 000	120 658
		£43 281
Increase/decrease in working capital:		
Increase in stocks	37 427	
Increase in debtors	71 827	
Increase in creditors	(60 434)	
	48 820	
Movement of liquid funds:		
Increase in bank overdraft	(5 539)	£43 281

Note. This form of statement is more in line with the example in SSAP 10 than previous examples given. Although it shows the amounts paid out in tax and dividend, it does not show the funds generated to be retained in the business or the extra credit from tax and dividend owed at the year end. ACT owed and recoverable cancel each other out.

SOLUTION TO TUTORIAL DISCUSSION TOPIC, CHAPTER 24

1. The profit figure for a period can show different results if computed using different accounting policies. Such policies, however, must be used consistently and if a new policy is adopted the impact of the change on the profit figure should be shown by way of a note to the accounts. It is true that a proportion of overhead expenses charged against work in progress can be carried forward to another year and set off against revenue in that year when the goods are finished and sold. This practice seems fair, especially when it is applied consistently year after year.

2. The return on capital employed may be artificially high. Net capital employed ignores current liabilities, which contain such sources of capital as bank overdraft, taxation and trade credit. Fixed assets, especially property, shown in the balance sheet at historic cost may be undervalued in a period of inflation. Depreciation based on historic cost may be insufficient for the same reason, so profits may be overstated.

3. The transfer of cash and loan repayment have no effect on the current profit position. Even if the transactions could be reversed (and the loan repayment cannot) this would affect liquidity, not profitability. If cash is available this does not necessarily mean that it is part of a profit surplus. It may represent part of the capital of the business held in liquid form, and to pay increased wages from such funds would deplete the capital of the business and reduce its ability to employ its labour force. The repayment of debentures will reduce future interest charges, and thus increase the profitability of the company.

4. Undistributed profits represent profits made in the past which could have been distributed in full to shareholders when they were made. It was decided instead to plough these profits back into the company, to enable it to expand and thus maintain the employment it provides in the area. These reserves are part of the shareholders' investment in the business and, although it is not illegal to use them to meet wage claims if the shareholders agree, it is imprudent, since increased costs are borne by running down the capital employed. Reserves may not be in the form of cash.

5. The dividend rate is quoted on the face or nominal value of the shares. Yield is the dividend per share expressed as a percentage of the current price and represents the true return on the investors' income. Shareholders bear the risk of the business, allow their capital to be tied up, and also pay income tax on dividends received, thus their return at 6 per cent is not excessive.

6. Profits retained are re-invested in the business to expand or maintain its productive capacity and to avoid recourse to the capital market. Thus these retained profits help the company to improve employment opportunities for its labour force. Tax must be paid on such profits when and if they are eventually distributed, and they have already suffered corporation tax.

Index